HYBRID SOVEREIGNTY IN WORLD POLITICS

The idea of 'hybrid sovereignty' describes overlapping relations between public and private actors in important areas of global power, such as contractors fighting international wars, corporations regulating global markets, or governments collaborating with nongovernmental entities to influence foreign elections. This innovative study shows that these connections—sometimes hidden and often poorly understood—underpin the global order, in which power flows without regard to public and private boundaries. Drawing on extensive original archival research, Swati Srivastava reveals the little-known stories of how this hybrid power operated at some of the most important turning points in world history: spreading the British empire, founding the United States, establishing free trade, realizing transnational human rights, and conducting twenty-first century wars. In order to sustain meaningful dialogues about the future of global power and political authority, it is crucial that we begin to understand how hybrid sovereignty emerged and continues to shape international relations.

Swati Srivastava is Assistant Professor of Political Science at Purdue University. Her research has received awards from the National Endowment for the Humanities, Andrew Mellon Foundation, American Council of Learned Societies, and International Studies Association. She is the founder of the Big Tech and Political Responsibility research lab at Purdue.

T0371246

Hybrid Sovereignty in World Politics

Editors

Evelyn Goh
Christian Reus-Smit
Nicholas J. Wheeler

Editorial Board

Cambridge Studies in International Relations is a joint initiative of Cambridge University Press and the British International Studies Association (BISA). The series aims to publish the best new scholarship in international studies, irrespective of subject matter, methodological approach or theoretical perspective. The series seeks to bring the latest theoretical work in International Relations to bear on the most important problems and issues in global politics.

Series list continues after index

Hybrid Sovereignty in World Politics

SWATI SRIVASTAVA

Purdue University

CAMBRIDGE
UNIVERSITY PRESS

Shaftesbury Road, Cambridge CB2 8EA, United Kingdom

One Liberty Plaza, 20th Floor, New York, NY 10006, USA

477 Williamstown Road, Port Melbourne, VIC 3207, Australia

314–321, 3rd Floor, Plot 3, Splendor Forum, Jasola District Centre, New Delhi – 110025, India

103 Penang Road, #05–06/07, Visioncrest Commercial, Singapore 238467

Cambridge University Press is part of Cambridge University Press & Assessment, a department of the University of Cambridge.

We share the University's mission to contribute to society through the pursuit of education, learning and research at the highest international levels of excellence.

www.cambridge.org
Information on this title: www.cambridge.org/9781009204477

DOI: 10.1017/9781009204453

First published 2022
First paperback edition 2024

A catalogue record for this publication is available from the British Library

ISBN   978-1-009-20450-7   Hardback
ISBN   978-1-009-20447-7   Paperback

Cambridge University Press & Assessment has no responsibility for the persistence or accuracy of URLs for external or third-party internet websites referred to in this publication and does not guarantee that any content on such websites is, or will remain, accurate or appropriate.

For my parents,
Namita and Chandra Shekhar Srivastava

Contents

Figures

Tables

Acknowledgments

Reading the right book at the right time is life-steering. The three books that steered me toward this project are not obviously connected. David Foster Wallace's *Infinite Jest* stirred me to write about complex relations; Zadie Smith's *White Teeth* confirmed that I had valuable things to say; Alex Wendt's *Social Theory of International Politics* made me feel less alone. This book would not have been possible without them.

The steering continued past these origins. Ian Hurd trusted me to pursue a project of immense ambition. He alternately let me run wild and queried my wildness, always at the necessary times. His imprints of *how* to think about politics are on every page of this book without any imposition of *what* to think. With Mary Dietz, I ruminated on conceptualizing the problems of sovereign power and how they escape easy resolutions. Jim Mahoney guided in organizing case materials and proved a model for mapping the metaphorical larger forest from the details of specific trees. Bruce Carruthers encouraged exploration in various archives and offered support in corralling the different stories into coherent narratives.

Deborah Avant, Sammy Barkin, Virginia Haufler, Ian Hurd, Stephen Krasner, and Hendrik Spruyt participated energetically in a book workshop held at Purdue University in summer 2019. I especially thank Steve for his generous reading of the argument, Hendrik for his detailed constructive comments, Debbi and Sammy for thoughtful marginalia, and Ian and Virginia for helping place the workshop feedback in context. I also thank Ann Clark for providing written comments. Lejla Dervisevic and Lauren Muscott were excellent graduate participants and rapporteurs. I am grateful to Eric Waltenburg, interim department head, and Purdue's College of Liberal Arts for funding the workshop.

Others too assisted in this journey. From courses and conversations at Northwestern, Ana Arjona, Wendy Espeland, Beth Hurd, Steve Nelson, Will Reno, Andrew Roberts, Hendrik Spruyt, and Jessica Winegar shared insights on tackling the intricacies of political distinctions. The International Studies Association (ISA)-Northeast crew of Sammy Barkin, Harry Gould, Patrick

Thaddeus Jackson, Dan Levine, Dan Nexon, Laura Sjoberg, and Brent Steele provided fierce mentorship. Siba Grovogui, Michelle Jurkovic, Jennifer Mitzen, and Jelena Subotic read the entire manuscript and pushed for necessary revisions at the 2018 ISA-Northeast Scholars' Circle. I also thank Andrew Ross for inviting me as the Circle's honoree. Bentley Allan, Cecelia Lynch, and Joshua Shifrinson offered fantastic advice on the book submission process. Patrick Jackson's feedback on Chapter 2 came at the right moment. Special thanks to Arjun Chowdhury for helping with the revisions. Gary Herrigel, Anne Holthoefer, and Michael Reese were the original shepherds of these ideas in a master's thesis at the University of Chicago. My high school English teacher and debate coach, Yen-Yen Chiu, was the first to encourage me to analyze arguments and write them. Mr. Ireland's drama class introduced me to the poem I use as an epigraph in the Introduction.

Humboldt State University was a great short-lived intellectual home as a new faculty member embarking on manuscript revisions. Purdue University continues to be so. I thank my department colleagues for their encouragement, advice, and Wine Wednesdays. I have benefited immensely from my mentorship committee: Ann Clark, Rosie Clawson, and Keith Shimko. Cherie Maestas has been a generous department head. A shout-out to the junior faculty: Tara Grillos, Kyle Haynes, Molly Scudder, Logan Strother, Joan Timoneda, Giancarlo Visconti, Zach Warner, and Melissa Will. I also thank my graduate students for their engagement with the manuscript in seminars.

My peers were equally inspiring. Early drafts benefited from the feedback of participants of the Northwestern International Relations Working Group. Mariana Borges, Giuseppe Cumella, Gina Giliberti, and Sidra Hamidi were relentless in their friendship. Bantering with Josh Freedman led to many new ideas in these pages. In Erin Lockwood I found a similar drive and interpretive focus to study practical international politics and corporate power. Mara Suttmann-Lea offered equal parts respite and motivation in our weekly writing group meetings in the final two graduate school years. Sofia Fenner, Spencer Headworth, and Aditi Shirodkar traded notes from the field. From ISA-Northeast again, Yoni Abrahamson, deRaismes Combes, and Simon Pratt were excellent conspirators in forming a supportive and enduring coalition.

Many others played a crucial role. The Andrew Mellon Foundation and the American Council of Learned Societies financially supported writing and research, as did Northwestern's Buffett Institute for Global Studies, the Graduate School, and the Political Science Department. Over the years, many archivists at national libraries and organizations gave their time to locate, hold, and scan materials. I especially thank Stéphanie Torkomyan. I received generous feedback at the London School of Economics, University of Notre Dame, University of Chicago, Boston University, University of Warwick, and University of Cambridge. Coffee shops and musicians helped fuel the writing. The Coffee Studio in Chicago is a jewel.

At Cambridge University Press, I thank John Haslam for ably shepherding the project during a pandemic. I also express gratitude to two anonymous reviewers for their generous and constructive feedback. Joining the Cambridge Studies in International Relations series is a dream come true.

Portions of the book have appeared in previous publications, including "Corporate Responsibility," *Oxford Research Encyclopaedia of International Studies* (2020); "How to Hold Unjust Structures Responsible in International Relations," with Lauren Muscott, *International Studies Quarterly* (2021); "Navigating NGO–Government Relations in Human Rights: New Archival Evidence from Amnesty International, 1961–1986," *International Studies Quarterly* (2022); and "Corporate Sovereign Awakening and the Making of Modern State Sovereignty: New Archival Evidence from the English East India Company," *International Organization* (2022).

Outside academia, friends and family were gracious enough to pretend to care about unclear typologies. Claire Mueller, Marina Kato, Christina Lee, Amber North, Shibani Rajadhyksha, Austin Rubino, Ashley Russell, Vanessa Soma, and Soren Sudhof stepped in and out of ongoing conversations over the years, picking up where we left off. My grandfathers, Sirish Chandra Mathur and J. P. Srivastava, eagerly followed my progress. Aunts, uncles, and cousins in New Delhi, Mumbai, Sydney, and San Diego offered encouragement along the way. Vera and Anil Kripalani, in particular, helped arrange and accommodate my family's initial move to the United States. Susan and Bruce McElhattan engaged good-naturedly with my research (even sitting through a practice job talk!) and provided nourishing food, drink, and company at every available opportunity from Pittsburgh to Puerto Vallarta. John McElhattan and Matt Elwell helped tremendously with the fun factor. Amand Srivastava shared my love of research, albeit not of a political kind, and his generous and gregarious spirit always uplifted me at the right moments. Welcoming Divya Mathur to the family was a joyful distraction from revisions.

My parents, Namita and Chandra Shekhar Srivastava, have started over many lives to give me one worth living. They have changed and left jobs, foregone educational opportunities, moved across four continents, separated from their loved ones, all to provide a stable home and create a wider universe of options for my brother and me. As an international civil servant, my father can relate to the many lived experiences in these pages and feel the politics of hybridity more intuitively than I ever could. My research is driven in part to explain his reality and the many like him. My mother is the source of all my confidence. Her warmth, compassion, humor, and resilience are contagious, even though she remains unmatched. My parents audaciously believed in and fought for my future. I dedicate this book to them.

Finally, David McElhattan is the concentrated form of all my inspirations and loves. He helps me untangle Latourian diagrams, gin cocktails, late '60s rock,

David Lynch, The Bachelor franchise, and many other mysteries of life. His observations and unparalleled articulations of social problems have sharpened mine. His support, in work and play, was uncompromising and indispensable. I thank him most of all for steering me through my daily routines of writing about the world and navigating it.

Introduction

The sea is the land's edge also, the granite
Into which it reaches, the beaches where it tosses
Its hints of earlier and other creation
                                    T.S. Eliot, *The Dry Salvages*

American forces killed seventeen Iraqi civilians in Nisour Square, Baghdad, on
September 16, 2007. The Americans did not wear military uniforms nor did they
adhere to US military protocol. Instead, they worked for Blackwater, a US firm that
held the largest State Department contract for diplomatic security in Iraq.[1]
Blackwater was part of a growing contractor force. More contractors than US troops
were used in the last two major American wars.[2] In particular, military and security
contractors like Blackwater carried weapons and engaged in combat, often making
them indistinguishable from the military.

For many, the important question is whether Blackwater is public or private. The
answer matters for accountability in law and responsibility in politics. Consider
another incident in 2006. On Christmas Eve, a drunken Blackwater contractor fatally
shot a guard of the Iraqi vice president. The contractor was fired, fined $2,000, and
sent back to the United States without facing any charges. An American legislator
noted the problem succinctly: "If this had happened in the United States, the
contractor would have been arrested and a criminal investigation launched. If
a drunken U.S. soldier had killed an Iraqi guard, the soldier would have faced
a court martial."[3] Holding Blackwater contractors legally responsible for the Nisour
Square shootings in the United States has proven complicated, with mistrials, appeals,
retrials, and pardons stretching a definite resolution across three presidential

---

[1] Blackwater has undergone many name changes and now goes by Academi. In 2014, Academi merged
    with Triple Canopy under Constellis Holdings. I refer to the company as Blackwater since this is its
    most easily recognizable form in public discourse.
[2] By 2007, 190,000 contractors and 160,000 soldiers were in Iraq. By 2009, 104,000 contractors and 64,000
    American troops were in Afghanistan (Congressional Research Service 2017: 4). These numbers are
    hard to pin down, which I discuss in Chapter 4.
[3] House of Representatives 2007a: 3.

administrations. Politically, Blackwater colors how Iraqis see the war, as journalist Ghaith Abdul-Ahad lays out:

> The word Blackwater is synonymous with the worst of the American occupation of Iraq. There is not a single Iraqi that I know who you would just mention the word Blackwater to who would not say corruption, violence, and I'm not talking only about the Nisour Square kind of massacre, but I'm talking about the whole ten years of the existence of [its] mercenaries. And I think part of the failure of the American project in Iraq was due to the using of contractors.[4]

Not all contractors in Iraq were armed and not all security contractors were like Blackwater. But Blackwater provided high-profile flash points, like the Nisour Square massacre, which channeled Iraqi frustration with the larger war efforts. Contractors were necessary for America's war, but perceptions of contractor impunity also undermined American success.

Blackwater's Nisour Square killings represent a microcosm of what this book is about: hybrid public/private entanglements in global sovereign politics and their multifaceted consequences for International Relations (IR). In one of the Nisour Square trials, an Iraqi witness made a startling observation: "Blackwater had power like Saddam Hussein. The power comes from the United States."[5] Sovereign power like Saddam Hussein's allows governments to access protections of sovereignty, a uniquely powerful ideational resource in world politics. Indeed, sovereignty has a "primal status as a term that underpins and gives permanence to flitting everyday politics."[6] Sovereignty defines the bounds of international legality and ethics. Killing is not prohibited for sovereign states. It is legal if you are a sovereign state claiming self-defense. It is ethical if you are a sovereign state intervening on humanitarian grounds. However, as much as leaders may want material indicators of sovereignty, there are no sovereignty bank balances. Instead, sovereignty relies on making successful claims, which in turn draws from theories of power and authority.

Following Max Weber, we often think of sovereign power as "nothing more than the name of an established apparatus of government."[7] Sovereign power is what a state *does*. But it is not settled that we know what a state does or should do. In the United States, liberals and conservatives disagree about the size and scope of the state, for instance whether the state should include a social safety net. In Japan, there is disagreement about whether the state should provide for its own self-defense. Indeed, as political philosopher Quentin Skinner observes, "there has never been

---

[4] Hasan 2019.
[5] Apuzzo 2015.
[6] Agnew 2009: 1.
[7] Skinner 2010: 26.

any agreed upon concept to which the word *state* has answered."[8] American Pragmatist John Dewey also diagnoses:

> The moment we utter the words "The State" a score of intellectual ghosts rise to obscure our vision. Without our intention and without our notice, the notion of "The State" draws us imperceptibly into a consideration of the logical relationship of various ideas to one another, and away from facts of human activity. It is better, if possible, to start from the latter and see if we are not led thereby into an idea of something which will turn out to implicate the marks and signs which characterize political behavior.[9]

But the marks of core sovereign functions have changed over time. As the Monty Python recount of their Roman oppressor: "All right, but apart from the sanitation, the medicine, education, wine, public order, irrigation, roads, a fresh water system, and public health, what have the Romans ever done for us?"[10] Public goods like sanitation, education, infrastructure, and public health are increasingly viewed as core pillars of modern sovereign power. But this was not always so. For Thomas Hobbes, trash collection did not feature in the "marks of a sovereign." Even today, the specifics of sovereign obligation for public goods are not fixed. The Scandinavian model of public goods is different than the American and Chinese ones.

Security contractors like Blackwater further complicate clean definitions of sovereign boundaries. French theorist Bruno Latour asks whether when we see a police car go by, we exclaim: "There goes the state!"?[11] Seems plausible. But do we make the same exclamation when it is the private security car of state leaders? This book wrestles with the somewhat bounded forms of sovereign power – police cars – with its many expressions – not *just* police cars. In other words, there are no universal necessary or sufficient conditions of sovereign power. Yet, something resembling sovereign authority exists with profound consequences for global violence, markets, and rights.

One explanation for this puzzle is that while what counts as sovereign varies, there remain dominant narratives of who counts as sovereign. For instance, the origins and meanings of racial categories are contested, but racialized effects nonetheless constitute dominant patterns of stratification.[12] Similarly, capitalism is constantly changing on the surface while also operating as "a more stable deep structure of schemas."[13] In social science, race and capitalism are examples of *structures* defined as unobservable "constraining conditions"[14] that also "produce social capacities."[15] Ideational structures constrain and enable social capacities through the power of

[8] Skinner 2010: 27.
[9] Dewey 1927: 8–9.
[10] Monty Python's *Life of Brian*.
[11] Latour 2007.
[12] Srivastava 2020a.
[13] Sewell 1992: 25.
[14] Waltz 1979: 73.
[15] Barnett and Duvall 2005: 53.

enduring ideas. Adopting this understanding, I argue that while the meaning of sovereignty is socially contingent and thus not fixed, sovereignty as an ideational structure nonetheless generates deep and powerfully patterned effects in international politics.

A FOUNDATIONAL MYTH

Sovereignty's ideational structure is visible in a foundational myth of IR, which presumes that international politics is played by discrete nation-states who possess sovereign independence from each other and private forces.[16] Hans Morgenthau's succinct book title exemplifies the claim that IR is about *Politics Among Nations*. The foundational myth advances that governments are the exclusive holders of sovereign authority following the successful monopoly over the use of violence and recognized international legal authority.[17] As a result, sovereign states "are the dominant form of subjectivity in contemporary world politics."[18] The field's conception of sovereign authority draws from Western political theory, which has "designated the state as the quintessentially public actor, leading to one characterization of the public/private distinction as political/nonpolitical."[19] The myth thus promotes that only public actors may be sovereign and that private actors are nonsovereign.

Scholars of diverse theoretical commitments rely on the myth. Kenneth Waltz justifies: "Just as economists define markets in terms of firms, so I define international-political structures in terms of states."[20] Prominent liberals and some constructivists have many problems with realists, but the reification of sovereign authority as exclusively public is not one of them. Alexander Wendt echoes that "states still are at the center of the international system, and as such it makes no more sense to criticize a theory of international politics as 'state-centric' than it does to criticize a theory of forests for being 'tree-centric.'"[21] Neoliberal institutionalists criticize state-centrism but also treat nonstate actors as intervening variables in interstate relationships.[22] Early global governance scholarship on private actors highlighted their epistemic, market, and moral authority instead of *political* or *sovereign* authority.[23]

Following the myth, we may interpret Blackwater as a case of private power eroding sovereignty since "states have primary responsibility for and monopoly over legitimate security services."[24] We may inquire whether Blackwater's private power *matters* for state behavior or whether the rise of American

[16] Morgenthau 1966; Waltz 1979.
[17] Weber 2004 [1919]: 32; Hinsley 1986.
[18] Wendt 1999: 9.
[19] Lu 2006: 19–20.
[20] Waltz 1979: 94.
[21] Wendt 1999: 9.
[22] Milner and Moravcsik 2009: 5.
[23] Cutler, Haufler, and Porter 1999; Josselin and Wallace 2001; Hall and Biersteker 2002.
[24] Avant 2005: 69.

security contractors mean the United States is in decline. We may also view security contractors as unique to the current moment to assert that "not since the eighteenth century has there been such reliance on private soldiers to accomplish tasks directly affecting the tactical and strategic success of military engagement."[25] The literature on security contractors is vast and has made important contributions to international politics, as I discuss in Chapter 4.[26] But it does not appropriately situate Blackwater's story in sovereign politics. As the Iraqi witness observed, Blackwater's power comes from the United States. We may invert the statement to mean that American sovereign power comes from Blackwater (and others like it). Contractors allow the United States to do more outside the official scope conditions of war. Moreover, security contractors did not suddenly reappear on the world stage, even though their use has expanded in the American context. Nor is Blackwater unique.

This book shows that Blackwater's story recurs in other public/private hybrid relations that help accomplish global sovereign power in managing empires, regulating markets, and protecting rights. A century ago, a historian referred to the British Empire's charter companies as "little '*imperia* in *imperio*,' little states within a state, which the orthodox political scientists so abhor, but which persist, nevertheless."[27] While the discipline has evolved over the past 100 years, this insight still holds today. However, rather than viewing entities like charter companies and others as states within a state, I argue that public/private hybridity makes sovereign power possible in the first place. Moreover, such hybridity creates new legitimation challenges for sovereign authority. The adjudication of these trade-offs allows a rare look at the socially contingent yet structurally patterned dynamics of sovereignty.

Understanding the competing dynamics of sovereignty in IR requires innovating beyond the foundational myth. Challengers have identified three shortcomings in the myth.[28] First, it relies on public and private as mutually exclusive poles. Second, it places private outside the state and outside politics. Third, it assumes sovereign power as a finished project expressed in "the state." I build on this work to probe whether sovereign power has always spilled beyond public and private boundaries out of which we fashion coherent forms like states. If so, what other forms of sovereign power exist? How do we accommodate them in theories of sovereignty? What are their implications for sovereign governance?

[25] Singer 2001: 187.
[26] Brooks 2000; Singer 2003; Avant 2005; Leander 2005; Kinsey 2006; Krahmann 2010; Abrahamsen and Williams 2011; Dickinson 2011; McFate 2014; Dunigan and Petersohn 2015; Fitzsimmons 2015; Eckert 2016; Mahoney 2017.
[27] Adams 1922: 155.
[28] Mitchell 1991; Hardt and Negri 2000; Haufler 2001; Grovogui 2002; Avant, Finnemore, and Sell 2010; Owens 2010; Best and Gheciu 2014; Green 2014; Hurt and Lipshutz 2016.

THE ARGUMENT

This book responds to these questions through a fresh approach to sovereignty in world politics that centers on hybridity. Hybridity is the condition of being multiple things at once, like in the epigraph how "the sea is the land's edge also." The edge is perhaps sharpest when standing on a beach that is both land and sea simultaneously. From here, we cannot definitively characterize the beach as land or sea alone; it is inescapably both. In our enjoyment of the beach, we experience the pluralism afforded by the vantage point of hybridity. But hybridity is also destabilizing as the waves continuously shift the ground beneath our feet. In cultural studies, where hybridity was first conceptualized outside the natural sciences, "the hybrid is a usefully slippery category, purposefully contested and deployed to claim change."[29] I build from this understanding of the term and embrace the elasticity of hybridity as a conceptual lens that allows us to see how multiple simultaneous meanings are constantly in negotiation and contestation.

The conceptual lens of hybridity helps advance two related arguments about sovereignty. In the first argument, I introduce a hybridized framework that accounts for how sovereignty is at the same time perceived as indivisible public authority and also experienced through divisible public/private competence. I call these two kinds *Idealized Sovereignty* and *Lived Sovereignty*, discussed in this chapter, and in greater length in Chapter 1. In the second argument, the book uses the lens of hybridity to focus on the management of public/private relations within *Lived Sovereignty*. I show that not all public/private hybridity is the same, which is the subject of Chapter 2. Thus, I deploy hybridity in two ways: (1) Sovereignty is both *Idealized* and *Lived* at once; and (2) public/private hybridity takes multiple forms within *Lived Sovereignty*.

In this book's first contribution, I double down on the importance of sovereignty for IR while updating its conceptual repertoire for more wide-ranging studies of world politics. The effort begins with distilling debates surrounding sovereignty to two stylized modes of *Idealized* and *Lived Sovereignty*. *Idealized Sovereignty* is the classic conception of indivisible, public, supreme sovereign authority promoted from Jean Bodin to Donald Trump. Representing traditional approaches, Morgenthau endorses indivisibility in *Idealized Sovereignty*: "Two or more entities – persons, groups of persons, or agencies – cannot be sovereign within the same time and space."[30] Jens Bartelson notes that sovereignty "cannot be divided without ceasing to be sovereignty proper, and precisely this quality of being indivisible distinguishes sovereign authority from other forms of political power."[31] Moreover, sovereignty also applies to the international realm where "the state is sovereign in that it must answer to no higher authority in the international sphere."[32] While many

---

[29] Hutnyk 2005: 80.
[30] Morgenthau 1948: 360.
[31] Bartelson 2011: 85.
[32] Gilpin 1981: 17.

IR scholars have complicated *Idealized Sovereignty*, its core doctrine of indivisibility maintains a strong pull for political operatives. More broadly, while the meaning of sovereignty is socially constructed, *Idealized Sovereignty* as an organizing principle remains "the primary identity value of the international life world."[33]

In contrast, *Lived Sovereignty* is the divisible performance of sovereign competence through public/private hybridity where entities are both private and public at once. *Lived Sovereignty* builds on political and social theorists for whom sovereign power has always been a bargain between various actors. Harold Laski remarks: "Everywhere we find groups within the state, a part of it. . . . Whether we will or no, we are bundles of hyphens."[34] *Lived Sovereignty* allows us to see how Blackwater makes American sovereign power possible by assisting in organizing violence abroad. Such participation fundamentally alters the demarcation of contractors as "private." Feminist perspectives in international law have long complicated the production of public and private as it relates to sovereign power.[35] Patricia Owens also suggests paying attention to what is *"made* public" and *"made* private."[36] When operating within the foundational myth, one may ask "what we learn by acknowledging that not all interesting actors within the international system are fully sovereign."[37] *Lived Sovereignty* shifts the emphasis to inquire instead what we learn by acknowledging that *all* interesting actors within the international system reflect public/private hybridity.

The lens of hybridity brings together the two modes of sovereignty to show that divisible public/private relations underlie sovereign power in *Lived Sovereignty*, while simultaneously the contours of who counts as sovereign authority are informed by *Idealized Sovereignty*. Crucially, both *Idealized* and *Lived* forms coproduce sovereignty in world politics. The analytical payoff is a realignment of the traditional axis of sovereignty debates away from inquiring whether sovereignty is declining or resurging.[38] Most conventional scholarship "is obscured by public definitions of authority that render privatized authority relations analytical and theoretical impossibilities."[39] Introducing hybridity into sovereign politics unsettles this occlusion. In the real politics of world affairs, there is no autonomous public or private; all we have is their mingling to various degrees and levels of success. The "illusion of free markets" extends to the illusion of autonomous sovereigns.[40] Hybridity thus is not incidental or detrimental to sovereignty, but *integral* to it.

[33] Reus-Smit 1999: 29.
[34] Laski 1916a: 425, quoted in Stern 2011: 9.
[35] Romany 1993; Walker 1994; Charlesworth 1995; Landes 1998; Prokhovnik 1998; Cohen and O'Byrne 2013.
[36] Owens 2010: 32; emphasis original.
[37] Lake 2003: 307.
[38] Sassen 1996, 1998; Strange 1996; Gill 1998; Arrighi 1999; Falk 1999; Hardt and Negri 2000; Jayasuriya 2001; Spruyt 2002; Slaughter 2004; Cohen 2006; Goldsmith and Wu 2006; Jackson 2007.
[39] Cutler 2003: 35.
[40] Harcourt 2011.

Hybridizing *Idealized* and *Lived Sovereignty* responds to Morgenthau's call that "the denunciation of sovereignty occurs much more frequently than does a serious endeavor to comprehend its nature and the function it performs for the modern state system."[41]

But where there is hybridity, there is also contestation. Divisible sovereign competence in *Lived Sovereignty* must be accommodated within indivisible sovereign authority in *Idealized Sovereignty*. For instance, by using Blackwater, the US bureaucracy is forced to continually rearticulate its core sovereign missions, or "inherently governmental functions," when determining how to deal with public/private hybridity in warfare. Thus, following Dewey, a marker of *Idealized Sovereignty* is determining *what* counts as public and private in the bundles of hyphens that make up *Lived Sovereignty*. Moreover, new dilemmas emerge in public/private hybridity where entities perform sovereign functions without corresponding governing responsibilities. Since *Idealized Sovereignty* assumes indivisible public authority, it fails to provide sound criteria for holding responsible divisible public/private relations in *Lived Sovereignty*. Blackwater's security contract, a feature of *Lived Sovereignty* in American wars, resulted in legal and political accountability gaps from governance structures operating in *Idealized Sovereignty*. We are unable to address these governance challenges until coming to terms with hybridity and its consequences for sovereignty.

This book's second contribution is to highlight different types of public/private hybridity in *Lived Sovereignty* and their unique legitimation challenges for *Idealized Sovereignty*. I develop three ideal-types based on the relative formalization and publicization of public/private hybridity.

Contractual hybridity features more formalized and publicized hybrid performances of sovereign functions through contracts. For instance, prison and school contractors provide policing and education in the United States and elsewhere. *Contractual hybridity* faces challenges of distributed accountability because public/ private hybrid configurations evade defined obligations in law and politics. As such, contractors do not typically face the same financial disclosure or conflict of interest rules as traditional government employees.

Institutional hybridity features less formalized and publicized hybrid performances of sovereign functions embedded in institutional networks. For instance, lobbyists and corporate lawyers embed themselves in global trade institutions for informal access to negotiating technocratic deals. *Institutional hybridity* faces challenges of exclusivity because public/private hybrid configurations are implicated in elite networks that exclude nonmembers. Consider that corporations can take governments to arbitration in commercial courts based on privileges granted by the bilateral investment network, whereas consumers cannot.

---

[41]   Morgenthau 1966: 299.

Shadow hybridity features the least formalized and publicized hybrid perform-ances of sovereign functions exchanged in the shadows. For instance, credit rating agencies rely on confidential information and access to continually monitor sover-eign bonds undergirding a government's creditworthiness. *Shadow hybridity* faces challenges of undermined trust because public/private hybrid configurations rely on behind-the-scenes deals with unlikely partners. For example, the agencies may soften a downgrade to maintain governmental access, thereby jeopardizing societal trust in their independence.

Finally, in the book's third contribution, the empirical subject matter traverses the traditional IR subfields to show public/private hybridity in practice across four diverse global organizations: The English East India Company, Blackwater, the International Chamber of Commerce, and Amnesty International. The English East India Company was created by royal charter in 1600 for trade to "the Indies" and was the primary conduit of the British Empire in India until 1858. Blackwater was founded in 1997 as a weapons training facility and became infamous during the 2003 War in Iraq as the State Department's largest security contractor. The International Chamber of Commerce, founded in 1919, is a world federation for free trade composed of more than 8,000 corporations and chambers of commerce in 130 countries. Amnesty International, formed in 1961, is the world's leading human rights international nongovernmental organization with over seven million mem-bers. These cases are typically conceived as private authority challenging *Idealized Sovereignty*, but I reclassify them as representative of public/private hybridity in *Lived Sovereignty*. I elaborate on the empirical strategy in Chapter 2, but I selected the "most important" cases for each ideal-type of hybridity in the domains of violence, markets, and rights, where I argue sovereign competence especially mat-ters. This is central to my Weberian-inspired interpretivist methodology that looks for usefulness of ideal-types in as many diverse contexts as the discipline allows.

The research draws on extensive multisited original archival material collected from the United Kingdom, France, the Netherlands, and the United States, includ-ing minutes from 23,552 organizational meetings covering 193 years, and news data covering 70 years. The data collection deliberately sought traces of sovereign power outside the standard governmental archives to instead focus on how sovereign politics emerges in seemingly nongovernmental records. I often rely on previously restricted data that have not been presented before. The analysis uncovers a range of experiences in the making of global sovereign power, including secret company committees negotiating imperial wars, contractors conducting foreign policy, lobby-ists killing international organizations, and NGOs collaborating with governments under their scrutiny to protect individual dignity.

The empirics ultimately show that IR is unable to fully comprehend empire, war, capitalism, human rights, or great power status without examining public/private hybridity. I developed the ideal-types inductively through analyzing the English East India Company from 1678 to 1780. During this time, the Company cycled between *contractual*, *institutional*, and *shadow hybridity*. In *Lived Sovereignty*, the Company's hybridity constituted Britain's sovereign power by reversing global capital flows from the East to the West and set the course for empire and capitalism. The Company's hybridity also helps see the tensions generated from the hybridized framework of *Idealized* and *Lived Sovereignty*. In *Lived Sovereignty*, the Company developed an increasingly more self-possessed understanding of its sovereign authority, which conflicted with emerging discourses of British *Idealized Sovereignty* and led to reining in the Company at the close of the eighteenth century. The more contemporary cases help reveal the payoffs and pitfalls of each ideal-type for sovereign governance. Blackwater highlights that *contractual hybridity* sustained the United States' war efforts, but also exposed distributed accountability in governing war contracting. The International Chamber of Commerce shows that *institutional hybridity* shaped rulemaking for global capital, but also created exclusionary networks, generating unequal outcomes for governance. Amnesty International demonstrates that *shadow hybridity* built a global polity for human rights, but also engendered mistrust by working with those under its watch. Finally, the book underscores that public/private hybridity operates across multiple levels within (Blackwater), between (International Chamber of Commerce), and above states (Amnesty International).

PLAN OF THE BOOK

The rest of the pages proceed as follows. The theoretical heart of the book is in two chapters. Chapter 1 hybridizes seemingly irreconcilable approaches in *Idealized* and *Lived Sovereignty* on the question of sovereign indivisibility. I draw from early modern political philosophy and international theory, taking a brief detour into the founding of the United States to show how the debate about indivisibility played out in practice. Then, I use hybridity to reorient the major IR debates on sovereignty. Chapter 2 builds on the hybridized framework to introduce the analytical core of the book in the ideal-types of public/private hybridity. I also engage with Weber by first outlining the process of ideal-typification and then extracting an interpretivist methodology that sets up the research design for the cases.

The empirical investigations form the bulk of the book. Chapter 3 analyzes the English East India Company from 1678 to 1780 to show *contractual hybridity* in formalized charter negotiations, *institutional hybridity* in more use of political networks, and *shadow hybridity* in secret deals. I also use legal cases and correspondence to highlight the transformation in the Company's self-understanding of sovereign authority from a privilege to a right. Chapter 4 explores *contractual hybridity* in Blackwater organizing international violence. I present the history of contracting and situate Blackwater's role in conducting American wars. I follow the policy repercussions from the governance challenge of distributed accountability related to Blackwater's problematic practices, such as the bureaucratic redefinitions of "inherently governmental functions." In Chapter 5, I analyze *institutional hybridity* in the International Chamber of Commerce (ICC)'s wide-ranging global regulatory functions on trade and investment through issue-definition and agenda-setting as the institutional "voice of global business." The chapter also evaluates the governance challenge of the ICC's exclusionary "self-regulatory" rulemaking apparatus, especially international commercial arbitration. Chapter 6 examines *shadow hybridity* in Amnesty International's first twenty-five years (1961–86) as it organized a global polity to translate human rights ideals into a reality and became a household name. I use Amnesty's experience to highlight the governance challenge of undermined trust as the organization simultaneously relied on projecting moral purity by claiming independence from governments while developing extensive governmental backchannels and side bargains for access and reform.

Chapter 7 concludes by reconsidering power in world politics given a turn to hybrid sovereignty. It sketches a structural approach to responsibility to deal with any sovereign abuses in public/private hybridity by arguing for the adoption of a "hybrid subjectivity."

To sum, this book argues that the global sovereign order is constructed from relations of hybridity where power flows without regard to public and private boundaries. I clarify the stakes of these hybrid configurations in a new theoretical framework on sovereignty and provide analytically useful ways to differentiate hybrid types. Hybridity implicates sovereignty and responsibility in ways IR has yet to fully consider. If we are to sustain meaningful dialogues about the future of sovereign governance and authority, it is crucial that we begin to reflect on *Hybrid Sovereignty in World Politics*.

1

Hybrid Sovereignty in International Theory

Sovereignty is fundamental, but it is also contingent.[1]

There is a contradiction at the heart of sovereignty. It is fundamental yet contingent; universal yet socially constructed. Practices of sovereignty have evolved to accommodate divisibility in sovereign functions. Yet, representations of sovereignty have remained static in assuming indivisible sovereign authority. This chapter forwards a new framework that hybridizes opposing positions across international theory, arguing that understanding sovereignty's contradiction is vital to its future and the future of IR.

As perhaps the key concept in international politics, sovereignty invokes equal parts apathy and contention. It is simultaneously "revered and reviled."[2] Most IR scholars do not define sovereignty, preferring instead to get on with studying all the phenomena that sovereignty makes possible. However, for theorists of sovereignty, it remains a highly contested and ambiguous "sponge-concept."[3] Resultantly, sovereignty has many paradoxes. It stands for both absolute authority and freedom from absolute authority. Sovereign inequality makes hierarchy possible within a state and anarchy endurable among states.[4] Sovereignty may inhere in a single person (e.g. Kim Jong Un), a group of persons (e.g. British Parliament), a dynasty (e.g. Bashir al Asad), a religious lineage (e.g. House of Saud), a founding document (e.g. US Constitution), nations within a state (e.g. Native American tribes), or a nation consisting of a state (e.g. Denmark). Popular sovereignty may be expressed through a social contract, general will, social compact, or institutional design.[5] The people may participate directly (e.g. referendums), indirectly (e.g. electoral college), or not at all (e.g. North Korea). They may have only one shot to negotiate the terms of a sovereign contract or infinite shots.[6] Sovereignty may be indivisible and held

---

[1] Patrick 2017.
[2] Aradau 2018.
[3] Bartelson 1995: 237; Connolly 2005: 141; Kalmo and Skinner 2010: 1.
[4] Brown 2010: 53.
[5] Locke 1988 [1689]; Hegel 1991 [1820]; Hobbes 1996 [1651]; Rousseau 1997 [1762].
[6] Hobbes 1996 [1651]; Rousseau 1997 [1762].

absolutely by one supreme ruler or may be divided among many ruling institutions.[7] Sovereignty is constant and also changing.[8]

Nowhere is the paradox of sovereignty more evident than in its treatment by two formative thinkers in international politics. Stephen Krasner acknowledges that the 1648 Peace of Westphalia is a flawed origin story of sovereign statehood that in fact rolled back sovereign autonomy compared to the 1555 Peace of Augsburg, but he also creates a typology where "Westphalian sovereignty" is of paramount importance.[9] Alexander Wendt argues that sovereignty should not be thought of as an attribute like a person's height but also defines sovereignty as an "inherent attribute of states, like being six-feet tall."[10] Krasner has spent a lot of time thinking about sovereignty. Wendt is aware of the particularities of drawing up social facts. Neither are casual observers nor callous writers of international politics. Rather, their inconsistencies are symptomatic of wrestling with sovereignty as "one of the most difficult problems of modern political science."[11]

Indeed, scholars have outlined, contended, realized, rethought, reconsidered, relocated, historicized, contemporized, fragmented, and deconstructed sovereignty.[12] The various analyses of sovereignty "disagree about almost everything – what sovereignty is and where it resides, how it relates to law, whether it is divisible, how its subjects and objects are constituted, and whether it is being transformed in late modernity."[13] Researchers variously posit that one cannot meaningfully speak of sovereignty before the sixteenth or the nineteenth century.[14] Some propose abandoning sovereignty in "the most urgent task for political theory."[15] But defenders of sovereignty retort that it "cannot simply be wished away."[16] Indeed, "those who would banish sovereignty as an outworn fiction are really only trying to shirk the whole problem of politics."[17] Thus, as a recent review on sovereignty surmised: "Far from watching sovereignty disappear as a useless trope, the discipline finds itself grappling with ever more nuanced and contradictory treatments and appraisals of sovereignty's continued conceptual import."[18]

This chapter refocuses the many disagreements about sovereignty to a contradiction expressed in two modes of analysis: *Idealized Sovereignty* and

---

[7] Bodin 1992 [1576]; Madison, Hamilton, and Jay 2003 [1788].
[8] Waltz 1979; Bartelson 1995.
[9] Krasner 1993, 1999.
[10] Wendt and Friedheim 1996: 246; Wendt 1999: 280.
[11] Korff 1923: 404.
[12] Morgenthau 1948; Thomson 1989; Walker and Mendlovitz 1990; Onuf 1991; Inayatullah and Blaney 1995; Osiander 2001; Lake 2003; Slaughter 2004; Bartelson 2006; Walker 2006; Kalmo and Skinner 2010; Glanville 2013b.
[13] Wendt and Duvall 2008: 607.
[14] Costa Lopez et al. 2018.
[15] Kalmo and Skinner 2010: 1; Cocks 2014; Herzog 2020.
[16] Bartelson 2011: 86.
[17] Collingwood 1989: 106. On this point, see also: Bickerton, Cunliffe, and Gourevitch 2007.
[18] Shinko 2017.

Lived Sovereignty. Sovereignty is idealized as foundational, universal, and solid in regards to who possesses sovereign authority (something singular and cohesive called "the state"),[19] but sovereignty is also lived as contingent, socially constructed, and changing in regards to who discharges sovereign power (a whole variety of hybridized state, substate, suprastate, and nonstate entities).[20] The two modes offer different answers to the question: Is sovereignty divisible? *Idealized Sovereignty* answers "no." *Lived Sovereignty* answers "yes." The remarkability of sovereignty is that it accommodates both modalities. Jens Bartelson observes that

> the relocations of sovereignty from God to kings, from kings to particular peoples, and then from these peoples to humanity as a whole have been made possible by the underlying assumption that the nature of political authority remains essentially the same irrespective of its source and locus, and this precisely by virtue of its inherent indivisibility.[21]

Thus, while sovereignty encompasses much more than indivisibility, I foreground indivisibility as the core feature at stake in developing theories of sovereignty given public/private hybridity in international politics, discussed more in the next chapter.

This chapter advances IR theory in three ways. First, it introduces the dual modalities of *Idealized* and *Lived Sovereignty* to organize diverse approaches to sovereignty. Moreover, it argues that the dual modality is key to sovereignty's survival. David Lake remarks, "although sovereignty may be a social construct that changes over time, it is still perceived as a system-wide attribute inhering in all state members identically."[22] For Lake, this is a fault in constructivist theorizing. But the kaleidoscopic quality of sovereignty is actually necessary for its longevity. *Idealized Sovereignty* creates a conceptual anchor across time, while *Lived Sovereignty* changes what the concept means. Indeed, sovereignty as both stable maxim and unstable practice is "not a *confusion* in the idea of sovereignty – a misunderstanding to be eliminated by a sharper definition of the term. It is rather, the *zone of instability* that sovereignty inhabits."[23]

Second, the chapter reframes the terms of debate among leading scholars of sovereignty. The contradiction at the heart of sovereignty is ultimately a conflation

---

[19]   On sovereignty as indivisible, see: Morgenthau 1948; Waltz 1979; Hinsley 1986; Bodin 1992 [1576]; Hobbes 1996 [1651]; Philpott 1995; Jackson 1999; Krasner 1999; Wendt 1999.
       On the universal foundationalism of sovereignty, see Collingwood 1989; Krasner 1995; Wendt 1999; Lake 2003; Bickerton, Cunliffe, and Gourevitch 2007; Chowdhury and Duvall 2014.

[20]   On sovereignty as divisible, see Ruggie 1993; Murphy 1996; Agnew 2005; Slaughter 2005; Doty 2007; Duffield 2007; Cooley and Spruyt 2009; Avant, Finnemore, and Sell 2010; Best and Gheciu 2014; Phillips and Sharman 2015; 2020.
       On the social construction of sovereignty, see Cox 1986; Kratochwil 1986; Kratochwil and Ruggie 1986; Walker 1990; Weber 1995; Biersteker and Weber 1996; Doty 1996; Wendt and Friedheim 1996; Ruggie 1998; Blaney and Inayatullah 2000; Reus-Smit 2001; Phillips 2007; Glanville 2013a; Patrick 2018.

[21]   Bartelson 2011: 93.

[22]   Lake 2003: 308.

[23]   Connolly 2005: 141, some emphases removed.

between power and authority. Sovereignty may be "the possession by an actor or set of actors of exclusive authority over some domain of competence."[24] Here, sovereign power is the management of some "domain of competence," whereas sovereign authority is the exclusive claim to sovereign competence vis-à-vis others. For instance, while Robinson Crusoe may have sovereign control over the functioning of his island and thus exhibited sovereign competence, "it would be meaningless to say that [he] had sovereignty over his island. Sovereignty is about the *social terms* of individuality, not individuality per se."[25] In other words, sovereign power is about what one does (achieving sovereign competence), but sovereign authority is about securing legitimation (claiming the rights to sovereign competence). There is no theoretical justification to assume one necessarily flows to the other. For some, "sovereign status implies at least some minimal degree of concentrated power."[26] However, I argue that sovereign power exercised in and obtained through *Lived Sovereignty* is necessary but insufficient to meet the social terms of sovereign status set in *Idealized Sovereignty*. Thus, hybridizing *Idealized* and *Lived Sovereignty* highlights the challenge of translating power into authority and repositions opposing conceptions of sovereignty in IR as making different wagers about the feasibility of this translation.

Third, the chapter proposes a different future for sovereignty. An increased diffusion of supra/nonstate sovereign competence has no obvious correspondence with an increased diversity in sovereign authority. In fact, it could lead to the opposite. While this might recall post-Cold War debates on whether state sovereignty is retreating[27] or resurging,[28] my contribution here is different in argument and implication. I do not seek to explain supra/nonstate influence on state power (operationalized as change in behavior or identity) but to argue that sovereign power is experienced in more diverse ways than sovereign authority allows. Converting sovereign power into authority relies on the social terms of legitimation or the ideas accepted as appropriate markers of sovereign status, which have come to include norms of nonintervention and policy independence.[29] I focus on the relatively less examined doctrine of indivisibility in *Idealized Sovereignty*, where indivisible claims to sovereign authority are exclusively recognized in "the state." Yet, indivisibility does not capture *Lived Sovereignty*'s divisible performances of sovereign competence in state/nonstate relations. As such, the two modalities of sovereignty escape easy resolution, coexisting as dueling forces in international politics until a new ideational structure emerges that accommodates more divisible and nonstate terms of legitimating sovereign power *as* authority.

[24] Wendt and Friedheim 1996: 247.
[25] Wendt and Friedheim 1996: 247, emphasis added.
[26] Fowler and Bunck 1995: 16.
[27] Sassen 1996; 1998; Strange 1996; Gill 1998; Arrighi 1999; Falk 1999; Slaughter 2004.
[28] Spruyt 2002; Cohen 2006; Goldsmith and Wu 2006; Jackson 2007.
[29] Krasner 1999; Lake 2003; Finnemore 2004; Barkin 2021.

In the rest of the chapter, I first trace *Idealized Sovereignty*'s indivisibility doctrine in early modern thought along with its durability in IR. I discuss how the ideational structure of *Idealized Sovereignty* appeared as both opportunity and constraint in the founding of the United States to highlight the stakes of contesting the indivisibility doctrine. Next, I turn to the divisible practices of sovereignty and recent IR scholarship on *Lived Sovereignty*. I keep this section relatively brief as the next chapter examines the varieties of hybrid relations within *Lived Sovereignty* in more detail. Finally, I present a hybridized framework where both *Idealized* and *Lived Sovereignty* serve as clashing focal points to recast the future of sovereignty.

IDEALIZED SOVEREIGNTY

In sketching the contours of *Idealized Sovereignty*, I follow Jens Bartelson's advice that "we should avoid the direct question of what sovereignty is, and instead ask how it has been spoken of and known throughout a period of time."[30] Early modern thinkers proposed legitimating secular sovereigns as representing indivisible, supreme, political authority. These ideas percolated to European and American polities from the sixteenth to the eighteenth centuries and acquired resonance as an ideational structure by the nineteenth century. By the twentieth century, the founders of modern international relations reified *Idealized Sovereignty* in order to carve out space for the discipline, a process that continues today.

Conceptualizing Idealized Sovereignty *in Early Modern Thought*

Early modern thinkers articulated absolutist indivisible sovereign authority for a gradually emergent "commonwealth" or "state." French theorist Jean Bodin wrote in 1576 that "sovereignty is the absolute and perpetual power of a commonwealth."[31] Bodin argues that "persons who are sovereign must not be subject in any way to the commands of someone else."[32] For Bodin, the sovereign, made after god's image, is infinite. Thus, "the prerogatives of sovereignty have to be of such a sort that they apply only to a sovereign prince. If, on the contrary, they can be shared with subjects, one cannot say that they are marks of sovereignty. ... By logical necessity two infinities cannot exist."[33] Theorists have since come to interpret this as "a theory of ruler sovereignty," where "the high powers of government could not be shared by separate agents or distributed among them, but all had to be entirely concentrated in a single individual or group."[34] Bodin's conception of indivisible

---

[30] Bartelson 1995: 4.
[31] Bodin 1992 [1576]: 1.
[32] Bodin 1992 [1576]: 11.
[33] Bodin 1992 [1576]: 49–50.
[34] Franklin in Bodin 1992 [1576]: xiii.

sovereignty meant a division of sovereign powers, like in the United States, cannot "even be imagined" and would result in anarchy "worse than the cruelest tyranny."[35] For Bodin, public authority rests in the sovereign (as monarch), requiring that "each individual and entire people as a body must swear to keep the laws and take an oath of loyalty to the sovereign."[36] Quentin Skinner traces Bodin's absolutist theory of the state to the divine right of Kings, which was challenged by populists who advocated sovereignty should "be possessed by the union of the people themselves."[37]

Thomas Hobbes was equally displeased with the populist notion of the people "united" in a body and the absolutist notion of the people passively obedient to a sovereign head. Instead, Hobbes argued that "when a multitude of men do agree and covenant, every one with every one" to authorize a sovereign "to be their representative," they are transformed from a passive people to a body politic. However, "if sovereigns are representatives, what is the name of the person whom they represent?" For Hobbes, the "multitude so united in one person is called a commonwealth, in Latin *Civitas*" or the state.[38] Hobbes went even further than Bodin to secure stable legitimation for secular political power and move away from the "divine right of kings."[39] For Hobbes, sovereigns "represent the state" in a "fictional" theory of the state enduring beyond sovereigns.[40] Hobbes theorized that "only through such sovereign representation could a public interest be distinguished from a shifting and unstable collation of private interests and their domination over (or conflict with) the interest of others. Here, *the public only becomes a public through its representation*."[41] Hobbesian sovereignty, in turn, argues this representation is "indivisible, unlimited and illimitable."[42] Hugo Grotius, the Dutch legal theorist, too conceived of "'sovereignty as a unity, in itself indivisible'. In this view, a state is either sovereign – or it is not a state."[43]

I want to pause here to recognize the blurred lines between theories of the state and sovereignty. Scholars have recognized that "it is almost impossible to discuss sovereignty without referencing the state."[44] We know that the "concepts are so intimately related that the ambiguity affecting one of them necessarily spills over to the other."[45] While my focus in this chapter is making sense of various theories of sovereignty, the implication is to also make sense of the state since "sovereignty and the state are mutually constitutive."[46] However, I rhetorically use "sovereign power"

---

[35] Bodin 1992 [1576]: 92, 103.
[36] Bodin 1992 [1576]: 25.
[37] Skinner 2010: 30.
[38] Hobbes 1996 [1651]: 109.
[39] Kantorowicz 1957.
[40] Skinner 2010: 37, emphasis added.
[41] Abrahamsen and Williams 2014: 246.
[42] Hobbes 1996 [1651]: 81.
[43] Keene 2002: 44.
[44] Shinko 2017.
[45] Kalmo and Skinner 2010: 12.
[46] Jackson 1999: 454.

and "sovereign authority" rather than "state power" and "state authority" because I conceptualize sovereign as broader than state. Thus, I intend to analytically show "nonstate" forms of sovereign power while also acknowledging that only something cohering as "the state" is assigned sovereign authority and thus obligations for sovereign responsibility.

From its very creation, the doctrine of indivisibility faced challenges. The early modern theories of sovereignty found different expressions in European state-formation projects. During this period, England was "not so much a clear hierarchy as an interlocking matrix of commonwealths, churches, associations, communities, officeholders, agencies, and families."[47] In the mid-sixteenth century, the struggle between the papacy and monarchy was confronted by declaring England "an 'empire', whose King possessed full and plenary jurisdiction in all causes, both secular and spiritual ... [and] that the King, and not the Pope, was the supreme head of the English Church."[48] Then, monarchical sovereignty came under pressure from parliamentary sovereignty. Starting in the 1640s, "the King increasingly came to be identified as an estate or constituent of the society along with the Commons and Peers, at last making it possible to conceive of the King in Parliament, or a mixed government, actually sharing an indivisible sovereignty."[49] The basis for this was laid a century earlier with the 1553 case of *Wimbish* v. *Taillebois*, "when the King's High Court of Parliament was gradually becoming the representative body of the nation," marking an important "point in the transition of Parliament from a judicial to a legislative body."[50] Yet, questions remained: "Parliament was the King in Parliament, but was its authority that of the King alone, which he chose to exercise only in Parliament, or that of a composite institution, the 'King-in-Parliament'?"[51] By 1688, the system was formalized with legislative and war-making functions accorded to Parliament such that "no judicial court could decide that an act of Parliament was contrary to any superior rule of binding power."[52]

Even as legal doctrine emerged to sort out the locus of sovereignty, the question was not so easily resolved. Parliamentary sovereignty was built on "the notion that the entire society was represented in Parliament."[53] However, the "representational basis was always in danger of being forgotten and falling away, leaving the sovereign authority simply as the stark power to command."[54] While continental theorists like Rousseau proposed versions of popular sovereignty, English legal scholars contended that "in the day-to-day workings of the state it was impossible for the people

[47] Stern 2011: 9.
[48] Goldsworthy 1999: 52.
[49] Wood 1998 [1969]: 347.
[50] Wood 1998 [1969]: 346–347.
[51] Goldsworthy 1999: 53.
[52] Adams 1922: 123.
[53] Wood 1998 [1969]: 347.
[54] Wood 1998 [1969]: 348.

themselves to exert sovereign power, for the essence of sovereignty was the making of law: the sovereignty had to be concretely legal, not simply theoretically political."[55] For these theorists, sovereignty was a question about obedience, following John Austin's definition of a sovereign as "a determinate person who, without a habit of obedience to another, receives habitual obedience from the bulk of a given society."[56] English scholars resisted popular sovereignty by separating the exercise of sovereign authority from the possession of it: "the king, peers and commons did not possess sovereignty but merely exercised it; sovereignty was possessed by the State."[57] England's juridical move of tying the state to sovereignty resembled France's solution of locating sovereignty in the nation. Both the Declaration of the Rights of Man and Citizen and the 1791 French Constitution "took the ground of national sovereignty and made king, legislature and judiciary a part of the nation."[58] Even in American divided government, as discussed in the next section, the doctrine of indivisible sovereignty was accommodated in "the people" as otherwise the nascent state "would be like a monster with more than one head, continually at war with itself."[59] This doctrine, known as *imperium* in *imperio* ("empire within an empire"), made repeated appearances in Revolutionary America.

Early modern thinkers used indivisibility to resolve the challenge of "transfer[ring] elements of transcendent authority to the temporal realm without appealing to a divine will or to a cosmic order within which human communities were embedded."[60] Sovereignty had to maintain a sufficiently indivisible order for its unifying function independent of previous forms of authority. Philosophers and legal theorists in the seventeenth and eighteenth centuries tied sovereignty to a unified entity like an abstract person, the state, the nation, or the people. Tracing this early intellectual history reveals that "whether thought to be upheld by an individual or a collective, or embodied in the state as a whole, sovereignty entails self-presence and self-sufficiency; that which is sovereign is immediately given to itself, conscious of itself and thus acting for itself."[61] Political theorist Wendy Brown observes how in *Idealized Sovereignty*, "the state can be divided, disunified, subordinated, even captured, and still survive. Not so political sovereignty, which, is finished as soon as it is broken apart."[62] Bartelson connects the two together: "the indivisibility of sovereignty is thus a necessary condition of the unity of the state."[63] To show the practical import of these abstract ideas, I next discuss how the early modern positions on sovereignty ricocheted across the grand experiment of founding America. The

[55] Wood 1998 [1969]: 346.
[56] Willis 1929: 440.
[57] Willis 1929: 440–441.
[58] Willis 1929: 439.
[59] Wood 1998 [1969]: 346.
[60] Bartelson 2011: 87.
[61] Bartelson 1995: 28.
[62] Brown 2010: 70, emphasis removed.
[63] Bartelson 2011: 85.

American debates on how to situate a divisible government within the indivisibility doctrine offer one of the earliest examples of the emergence of *Idealized Sovereignty* as an ideational structure.

Experimenting with Idealized Sovereignty *in the Founding of America*

George Washington, the first American president, derided "the monster of sovereignty."[64] John Adams, the second president, referred to sovereignty as "the greatest Question ever yet agitated."[65] It never received a coherent answer. Historian Gordon Wood argues that theories of "sovereignty pervaded the arguments of the whole Revolutionary generation from the moment in the 1760s when it was first raised through the adoption of the federal Constitution in 1787."[66] Examining the founding of America reveals how accommodating *Idealized Sovereignty's* indivisibility doctrine within a divisible federal arrangement was central to the US Constitution.

Sovereignty in the founding of the United States featured three key moments of transformation. First, the colonies asserted independence against the British Parliament and king. Second, the newly formed confederation of states resisted a strong central government. Third, the states adopted a stronger federal structure in the US Constitution. In each of these three moments, some of the same actors took opposing positions on how to think about sovereignty. Revolutionaries arguing for indivisibility became Federalists promoting divisibility. However, even though the forms of government changed, the Americans derived the social terms of legitimating sovereign authority from European doctrines of indivisibility.

In the first moment of transformation in the revolutionary era, American colonists developed claims based on the indivisibility doctrine against the British. Sir William Blackstone's landmark *Commentaries on the Laws of England*, published in 1765, argued that there must be in every state "a supreme, irresistible, absolute, uncontrolled authority, in which the *jura summi imperii*, or the rights of sovereignty, reside."[67] John Adams echoed Blackstone in his diary that "in all civil states it is necessary, there should some where be lodged a supreme power over the whole."[68] In 1768, Benjamin Franklin wrote that "no middle doctrine can be well maintained ... [Either] Parliament has a right to make *all laws* for us, or it has a power to make *no laws* for us."[69] In the *Massachusetts Gazette*, Tory Daniel Leonard argued for staying with the Crown, declaring that "two supreme or independent authorities cannot exist in the same state," since "it would be what is called

64   Adams 1922: i.
65   John Adams, March 4, 1773, Butterfield 1961, Vol. 2: 77.
66   Wood 1998 [1969]: 345. The following section is indebted to Wood's history of the founding of America. I thank Logan Strother for introducing me to this literature.
67   Blackstone 1765, Vol. 1: 49; Adams 1922.
68   John Adams, March 4, 1773, Butterfield 1961, Vol. 2: 77.
69   Benjamin Franklin, March 13, 1768, Smyth 1905, Vol. 5: 115.

imperium in *imperio*, the height of political absurdity . . . . If then we are a part of the British empire, we must be subject to the supreme power of the state which is vested in the estates of parliament."[70] Adams responded by agreeing with Leonard on the indivisibility principle but asserted its implications meant "that our provincial legislatures are the only supreme authorities in our colonies."[71] Alexander Hamilton amplified in a pamphlet: "A supreme authority, in the Parliament, to make any special laws for this province, consistent with the internal legislature here claimed is impossible; and cannot be supposed, without falling into that solecism, in politics, of *imperium in imperio*."[72]

Importantly, the Americans did not dispute the idea of parliamentary sovereignty, just its location in Britain as opposed to the colonies. Samuel Adams, cousin of John Adams, argued that "the legislative of any commonwealth must be the supreme power."[73] But to the British, "unable to conceive of the empire as anything but a single community with a final undivided authority located somewhere, all such distinctions were absurd and ultimately would lead to the dissolution of the union between England and America."[74] Exposing the weakness of the representational link to sovereignty that the British Parliament had advanced in the "King in Parliament" system a century earlier, the British now "put less and less emphasis on American representation in Parliament, virtual or otherwise, and instead stressed the logic of sovereignty itself."[75] In 1774, when the First Continental Congress met in Philadelphia, Thomas Jefferson circulated an essay listing grievances, arguing that "we do not point out to his majesty the injustice of these acts," but instead that "the British parliament has no right to exercise authority over us."[76] In 1775, British writer Samuel Johnson retorted:

> In sovereignty there are no gradations. There may be limited Royalty . . . but there can be no limited Government. There must, in every society, be some power or other from which there is no appeal; which admits no restrictions; which pervades the whole mass of the community; regulates and adjusts all subordination; enacts laws or repeals them; erects or annuls judicatures; extends or contracts privileges; exempts itself from question or control; and bounded only by physical necessity.[77]

Johnson referred to sovereign indivisibility as "the primary and essential condition of all political society."[78] The Americans agreed. In the 1776 Declaration of Independence, the Americans "found the doctrine of sovereignty unassailable and

---

[70] Leonard 1775.
[71] Adams 1775.
[72] Alexander Hamilton, "The Farmer Refuted etc.," February 23, 1775, Syrett and Cooke 1961 Vol. 1: 82.
[73] Adams 1771.
[74] Wood 1998 [1969]: 349.
[75] Wood 1998 [1969]: 348.
[76] Thomas Jefferson, "A Summary View of the Rights of British America," 1774.
[77] Samuel Johnson, "Taxation no Tyranny," 1775.
[78] Samuel Johnson, "Taxation no Tyranny," 1775.

made it in fact a major weapon in their argument."[79] For Wood, sovereignty "was the single most important abstraction of politics in the entire Revolutionary era. Every new institution and new idea sooner or later had to be reconciled with this power-fully persuasive assumption that there could be but one final, indivisible, and incontestable supreme authority in every state to which all other authorities must be ultimately subordinate."[80] However, the same weapon created a problem in the success of a young United States.

In the second moment of transformation, the same arguments for indivisible sovereignty that the revolutionaries lobbed against England were now turned onto the Americans themselves by the newly independent states in the Articles of Confederation. The Albany Plan, a pre-independence movement under Benjamin Franklin, organized two branches of government in a "Grand Council" and a British "president General." The Grand Council had the ability to tax and conduct rela-tions with Native Americans. But the Albany Plan failed, in part because the colonies did not want to share sovereignty with a central institution. Franklin again took charge in drafting the "Articles of Confederation and Perpetual Union" in 1775. The Articles created a "sovereign, national government, and, as such, limited the rights of the states to conduct their own diplomacy and foreign policy."[81] But unlike the Albany Plan, the 1781 Articles of Confederation did not give the central government the right to tax, which could aid in raising a military to keep British forces at bay. Samuel Adams told the Carlisle Commission in 1778 "that in every kingdom, state, or empire there must be, from the necessity of the thing, one supreme legislative power, with authority to bind every man in all cases the proper object of human laws."[82] The Articles instead "provided for a one-house legislature, a weak executive, no national power of taxation, a lack of standard currency, and voting by state."[83]

The American confederacy also privileged popular sovereignty in the states. This soon created problems as state legislatures "were becoming simply the instruments and victims of parties and private combinations, puppets in the hands of narrow-minded, designing men."[84] The states rushed to condemn the excesses of popular sovereignty where "binding instructions from local districts fomented by 'a directing club or committee' would prove to be 'a dangerous Jesuitical *imperium in imperio*' and make the legislature 'as a body contemptible.'"[85] In Massachusetts, a rebellion led by Daniel Shays in 1786 against excessive state taxation on indebted

---

[79]   Wood 1998 [1969]: 353.
[80]   Wood 1998 [1969]: 345.
[81]   Department of State. 2021. "Articles of Confederation, 1777–1781."
[82]   Adams 1778.
[83]   Library of Congress. 2021. "Creating the United States."
[84]   Wood 1998 [1969]: 369.
[85]   Wood 1998 [1969]: 373.

farmers and laborers threatened the stability of the confederation. Benjamin Rush, one of the signers of the Declaration of Independence, summed up in 1787:

> The people of America have mistaken the meaning of the word sovereignty: hence each state pretends to be *sovereign*. In Europe, it is applied only to those states which possess the power of making war and peace—of forming treaties, and the like. As this power belongs only to congress, they are the only *sovereign* power in the united states.[86]

As states faced challenges to their sovereign authority, a new constitution with a stronger central government became necessary.

Thus, in the third moment of transformation, the Americans attempted a new constitution that accommodated a divisible federalist government structure within the strictures of indivisibility. Before the 1787 Constitutional Convention in Philadelphia, James Madison argued that "a sovereignty over sovereigns, a government over governments, a legislation for communities, as contradistinguished from individuals," was "subversive of the order and ends of civil polity."[87] But then Madison "had become a thorough nationalist, intent on subordinating the states as far as possible to the sovereignty of the central government."[88] Madison along with George Washington drafted the Virginia Plan, which created a bicameral national legislature with a veto over state laws along with proportional representation. A New Jersey Plan, which called for a unicameral legislature with equal votes of states, also had support. Eventually, the delegates compromised on equal representation in the Senate and proportional representation in the House. All the while, the Americans did not have any precedent for dividing sovereignty between a strong federal government and the states. While the British "King in Parliament" system effectively divided sovereign authority between the monarch and Parliament, the Americans did not have a monarch or the fiction of the Crown at their disposal. Instead, theirs was the first experiment in nonelitist sovereign authority enshrined in a constitution.

Meanwhile, the Antifederalists adopted the same language the Federalists had used as Revolutionaries by rejecting divisible sovereignty. William Grayson from Virginia protested: "I never heard of two supreme co-ordinate powers in one and the same country before. I cannot conceive how it can happen. It surpasses everything that I have read of concerning other governments, or that I can conceive by the utmost exertions of my faculties."[89] George Mason agreed: "These two concurrent powers cannot exist long together. The one will destroy the other."[90] Madison countered that the Constitution was "not completely consolidated, nor is it entirely federal," but rather "of a mixed nature," made up "of many coequal sovereignties."[91] Antifederalists remained unpersuaded. According to Wood's interpretation of the

---

[86] Benjamin Rush, "Address to the People of the United States," January 1787.
[87] James Madison, *Federalist Papers* No. 20, December 11, 1787.
[88] Wood 1998 [1969]: 472–473.
[89] William Grayson, Elliot 1836–1859, Vol 3: 281.
[90] George Mason, Virginia Ratifying Convention, June 4, 1788.
[91] James Madison, Virginia Ratifying Convention, June 5, 1788; June 14, 1788.

debates, sovereignty was "the most powerful obstacle to the acceptance of the new Constitution the opponents could have erected."[92] Ultimately, the prevailing argument belonged to James Wilson, who asked in the Pennsylvania Ratifying Convention: "For whom do we make a Constitution? Is it for men, or is it for imaginary beings called states?"[93] Wilson argued: "In all governments, whatever is their form, however they may be constituted, there must be a power established from which there is no appeal, and which is therefore called absolute, supreme, and uncontrollable. The only question is: where is that power lodged?"[94] Wilson referred to Blackstone's *Commentaries* and rejected the source as the state legislature, federal government, and even the constitution itself. Instead, Wilson claimed that sovereignty "remains and flourishes with the people . . . as the fountain of government."[95] Wilson's formulation became the Federalist position: "state legislatures could therefore never lose their sovereignty under the new Constitution, as the Antifederalists claimed, because they never possessed it."[96] The move was similar to the French solution of locating indivisible sovereignty in a unified "nation," happening around the same time.

Revolutionaries, Colonists, Founding Fathers, Confederates, Federalists, and Antifederalists, all treated *Idealized Sovereignty*'s indivisibility doctrine as an opportunity and a constraint in their struggle for a new America. In other words, they regarded *Idealized Sovereignty* as an ideational structure. Of course, the question of how to accommodate divided American sovereign authority within *Idealized Sovereignty* was not finally settled by the new constitution. Notably, the Civil War was fought over states' authority to preserve slavery. The US Supreme Court in the following centuries generated a "process of de-sovereignizing the states" by striking down sovereign mandates, for instance of requiring exclusive English-language instruction in schools, regulating the size of loaves of bread, or school segregation.[97] "States' rights" remains an important rallying cry in American debates ranging from election management to abortion to gun control. Indeed, "there is little consensus in the United States about what sovereignty actually entails."[98] However, we can still appreciate that the indivisibility doctrine was central to American political development.

The early modern European and American political experiences show that even though the indivisibility doctrine was violated almost as soon as it was proposed, indivisibility nonetheless created a baseline around which arguments about sovereignty came to be socially adjudicated. The discussion thus far underscores that *Idealized Sovereignty* assumes indispensability because "it draws together a cluster of

---

[92]   Wood 1998 [1969]: 529.
[93]   Adams 1922: 151.
[94]   James Wilson, Pennsylvania Ratifying Convention, November 24, 1787.
[95]   James Wilson, Pennsylvania Ratifying Convention, November 24, 1787.
[96]   Wood 1998 [1969]: 531.
[97]   Willis 1929: 467–473; Aleinikoff 2002.
[98]   Patrick 2018: 8.

values including order, terms of membership, status, legal equality, coexistence, pluralism, and respect, and there is no other 'world-wide political institution that can perform that service for humankind.'"[99] It is in this sense that I refer to *Idealized Sovereignty* as an ideational structure that emerged from early modern political theorists and solidified in the ensuing state-making projects. I now turn to how *Idealized Sovereignty* also serves as a potent structural resource in modern IR.

Idealized Sovereignty *in IR*

Foundational scholars draw on early modern thought in constructing sovereignty as an organizing principle for IR. Hans Morgenthau argues, "the conception of a divisible sovereignty is contrary to logic and politically unfeasible."[100] He promotes "the sovereign" as "a centralized power which exercised its law making and law enforcing authority within a certain territory."[101] F. H. Hinsley settles on the classic definition of sovereignty as "the idea that there is a final and absolute political authority in the political community . . . *and no final and absolute authority existed elsewhere.*"[102] IR approaches to *Idealized Sovereignty* as a state attribute promote sovereign authority as indivisible, public, and territorial-based.[103] As such, "a polity cannot be a little bit sovereign."[104] Even critics of absolutist sovereignty admit that "if sovereignty is divided, it loses its distinguishing trait."[105]

Idealized Sovereignty also appears in IR as an international institution, where members grant each other "immunity from external interference"[106] with "the exclusive authority to intervene coercively in activities within [one's] territory."[107] Therefore, "when states recognize each other's sovereignty as a right then we can speak of sovereignty not only as a property of individual states, but as an institution shared by many states"[108] that in fact constitutes them *as* states.[109] In a "sovereignty cartel,"[110] sovereignty's institutional status is "alive and well among both the more powerful and less powerful states."[111] Therefore, "so long as many in the society of states view sovereignty as contributing to world stability, security, and peace, the concept will remain a sturdy foundation for the superstructure of international politics."[112]

[99] Shinko 2017.
[100] Morgenthau 1948: 364.
[101] Morgenthau 1948: 341.
[102] Hinsley 1986: 26, emphasis original.
[103] Jackson 1999: 439–440.
[104] Lake 2003: 306.
[105] de Witte 2006: 518.
[106] Thomson 1995: 219.
[107] Philpott 2001: 18.
[108] Wendt 1999: 280.
[109] Onuf 1991: 430–431.
[110] Barkin 2021.
[111] Lyons and Mastanduno 1995: 265.
[112] Fowler and Bunck 1995: 164.

As an ideational structure, *Idealized Sovereignty* "empowers states vis-à-vis people" and nonstate actors.[113] The purpose of *Idealized Sovereignty* is "to express and realize the principles that make a state a particular state."[114] Thus, "sovereignty is articulated and legitimized within a given knowledge, and by which a given knowledge is articulated and legitimized through a given concept of sovereignty."[115] Sovereignty is also the rare concept actively used outside the academy. *Idealized Sovereignty* is deployed by those who produce and consume sovereign myths, such as leaders, "citizens, non-citizens, theorists, and diplomats."[116] We conjure *Idealized Sovereignty* in abstract symbols, ideologies, promises, visions, five-year plans, party platforms, pro-sovereignty caucuses, policy justifications, and media discourses. Through *Idealized Sovereignty*, we collectively imagine the sovereign state into existence.

Scholars have also complicated sovereignty as multifaceted within *Idealized Sovereignty*. E. H. Carr warned that "sovereignty is likely to become in the future even more blurred and indistinct than it is at present."[117] Robert Jackson captures the malleability of *Idealized Sovereignty* as "Lego: it is a relatively simple idea but you can build almost anything with it, large or small, as long as you follow the rules."[118] More generally, studies have remarked on departures from de jure or legal sovereignty in de facto or effective sovereignty.[119] In this vein, Krasner outlines four different types:

> *Domestic sovereignty*, referring to the organization of public authority within a state and to the level of effective control exercised by those holding authority; *interdependence sovereignty*, referring to the ability of public authorities to control transborder movements; *international legal sovereignty*, referring to the mutual recognition of states or other entities; and *Westphalian sovereignty*, referring to the exclusion of external actors from domestic authority configurations.[120]

John Agnew also introduces different sovereignty regimes based on a consolidated or open view of territoriality and a stronger or weaker central state authority.[121] For David Lake, "domestic hierarchy and international anarchy are flip sides of the same coin" in a continuum on variations of domestic sovereignty from alliance to empire.[122] These various taxonomies innovate by relaxing standard assumptions of strict territoriality, external autonomy, and separating control from recognition. But they also leave unquestioned the indivisibility doctrine in *Idealized Sovereignty*.

[113]   Thomson 1994: 5.
[114]   Inayatullah and Blaney 1995: 13.
[115]   Bartelson 1995: 7.
[116]   Biersteker and Weber 1996: 18.
[117]   Carr 1981 [1939]: 230.
[118]   Jackson 1999: 431.
[119]   Murphy 1996.
[120]   Krasner 1999: 9; emphasis added.
[121]   Agnew 2005: 445.
[122]   Lake 2003: 305.

Representations of sovereign indivisibility in *Idealized Sovereignty* are sticky despite divisible arrangements of sovereign governance. For Luke Glanville, this is "the product of a tendency of scholars to write the present into the past and to either misunderstand or simply ignore sovereignty's rich history."[123] But as Bartelson notes, "while theories of popular sovereignty later shifted the locus of sovereignty from kings to people, they did so without questioning the indivisibility of sovereignty."[124] Janice Thomson too observes, "state control has waxed and waned enormously over time, regions, and issue-areas while the state's claim to ultimate political authority has persisted for more than three centuries."[125] The Hobbesian "genesis of the people as a public required a corresponding recognition by the public authority – the sovereign state – that its end must be to represent the public as the constituent power of the people."[126] *Idealized Sovereignty* may be a "political delusion,"[127] but it has endured to become a "potent political weapon."[128]

Indeed, *Idealized Sovereignty* maintains a powerful hold on popular imaginations by promoting sovereignty as zero-sum.[129] Leaders go to war for *Idealized Sovereignty*. People demand to leave political unions for *Idealized Sovereignty*. Secessionist movements couch their claims in *Idealized Sovereignty* despite economic repercussions of sovereign statehood, as seen recently in Quebec, Catalonia, and Puerto Rico.[130] Donald Trump's 2016 campaign promise to "defend America's sovereignty and always put America first" profited from *Idealized Sovereignty*.[131] Trump mentioned sovereignty twenty-one times in his first address to the United Nations (UN) General Assembly in 2017. By contrast, Barack Obama's first UN speech in 2009 mentioned sovereignty just once. The Trump administration used sovereignty to justify putting migrant children in cages across its Southern border, withdrawing from the Paris Accord on Climate Change, and criticizing the North American Treaty Alliance (NATO).[132] Meanwhile, Britain's 2016 vote to leave the European Union presented the referendum as "about the supremacy of Parliament."[133] Anticipating these undertones, a British judge articulated in 1990: "Our sovereignty has been taken away by the European Court of Justice. ... Our courts must no longer enforce our national laws. They must enforce Community law."[134] The day of the Brexit referendum, a survey of 12,369 voters showed that the number one motivation for 49 percent of Leave voters was that "decisions about the UK should

[123] Glanville 2013b: 14.
[124] Bartelson 2011: 92.
[125] Thomson 1995: 214.
[126] Abrahamsen and Williams 2014: 246.
[127] Cocks 2014.
[128] Morgenthau 1948: 341.
[129] Heller 2019.
[130] Fowler and Bunck 1995: 17.
[131] White House 2019.
[132] Patrick 2017.
[133] Pritchard 2016.
[134] Denning 1990: 48, as quoted in Ringeisen-Biardeaud 2017.

be taken in the UK."[135] Indeed, "for Brexiteers, sovereignty is something that a State has wholly or not at all, and which may thus not be shared or divided."[136]

Trump and Brexit are not instances where sovereignty, vanished in the post- Cold War era, returned with a vengeance.[137] Instead, *Idealized Sovereignty* remains a powerful ideational structure as it is both "historically generated and generative of particular understandings of what counts as community, authority, legitimacy, and agency."[138] Sovereign status, in turn, "creates the very possibility of a political subject, while discounting other subjects as nonpolitical."[139] If the aim is to reclaim "sovereignty to resist global power structures,"[140] then we must begin outside the modality of *Idealized Sovereignty*.

LIVED SOVEREIGNTY

Lived Sovereignty more closely reflects the actual experiences of producing sovereign power. Rather than idealizing sovereign authority as being exclusively represented in the indivisible "state" or "people," *Lived Sovereignty* constitutes the diverse practices of accomplishing sovereign competence in divisible arrangements.

Evolution in Sovereign Functions

Lived Sovereignty begins from the premise that sovereign functions are ever-changing. Sovereigns have been deemed responsible "for the protection of the safety and security of subjects, citizens, religious and national minorities, foreign nationals, and entire populations."[141] Aristotle points out "three parts of a state, one in deliberating and taking counsel; another in creating officers and establishing the duties of each; and the third in rendering justice."[142] Bodin identifies the necessary "marks" of a sovereign as: "who gives law to all his subjects, makes peace and declares war, provides all the officers and magistrates of the land, levies taxes and exempts whom he pleases, and pardons persons who deserve to die."[143] Bodin combines rule-making and enforcement with functions like taxation.[144] For Hobbes, sovereign power is to judge "peace and defence" and "opinions and doctrines"; make "rules of propriety and of good, evil, lawful, and unlawful"; decide "all controversies which may arise concerning law"; make "war and peace

---

[135]   Ringeisen-Biardeaud 2017.
[136]   Ringeisen-Biardeaud 2017.
[137]   Cha 2016.
[138]   Aradau 2018.
[139]   Aradau 2018; See also Edkins and Pin-Fat 1999.
[140]   Aradau 2018.
[141]   Glanville 2013b: 19.
[142]   As rendered in Bodin 1992 [1576]: 47.
[143]   Bodin 1992 [1576]: 48.
[144]   Franklin in Bodin 1992: xvii.

with other nations" and "levy money"; choose "all counsellors, ministers, magistrates, and officers; rewarding and punishing"; give "titles of honour"; "coin money, dispose of the estate and persons of infant heirs, and have preemption in markets."[145] Hobbes too distills three marks of sovereignty: controlling the military, raising money, and governing doctrines.[146]

Drawing from these theorists, we may argue that sovereign functions are those that organize violence, markets, and rights. However, even in these general realms, the specific nature of sovereign power is contested in two ways. First, sovereign functions change over time in content and salience. For instance, trash collection was not a sovereign function in the eighteenth or nineteenth century, but is widely seen as one today.[147] In modernity, "the state's increasing concern with productivity, health, sanitation, education, transportation, mineral resources, grain production, and investment was less an abandonment of the older objectives of statecraft than a broadening and deepening of what those objectives entailed in the modern world."[148] Taking care of wounded soldiers went from nonexistent before the nineteenth century to an integral part of international humanitarian law in the twentieth century. Managing the rights of foreigners have evolved from simple expulsions of merchants in war during the early modern period to complicated visa regimes today. Second, even widely accepted functions do not contain self-evident criteria for *how* sovereigns should organize violence, markets, or rights. For instance, sovereigns can organize economic relations along a spectrum of invisible to visible hand or provide different tiers of welfare benefits. Such variation in the conduct of sovereign politics is precisely what informs differences in regimes, political economies, and legal cultures. It is hard, then, to say anything universal about sovereign functions.

Yet, sovereign functions are treated as self-evident. Consider Jason Sharman's study of microstates like the Seychelles, which he considers "remarkably close to the sovereign ideal."[149] Microstates have rented or sold their sovereign prerogatives, including diplomatic recognition (e.g. Nauru negotiating with China on Taiwan), passports and formal citizenship (e.g. a St Kitts and Nevis passport is available to those investing $400,000 in real estate), tax havens and corporate citizenship, and artifacts like stamps and coins.[150] Deborah Avant also paraphrases Oliver Williamson's "sovereign transactions" to consist of "foreign affairs, the military, foreign intelligence, managing the money supply and, possibly, the judiciary."[151] If there was nothing distinctive about sovereign functions, however inconsistently

---

[145] Hobbes 1996 [1651]: 113–115.
[146] Hobbes 1996 [1651]: 115.
[147] I thank Sammy Barkin for this point.
[148] Scott 1998: 52.
[149] Sharman 2017: 569–570.
[150] Sharman 2017: 571–572.
[151] Avant 2005: 47.

agreed-upon, then microstates would have no market for their "sovereign" artifacts or services.

Ultimately, the evolution of sovereign functions "codifies a historically specific answer to historically specific questions about political community."[152] *Lived Sovereignty* emphasizes that *what* is sovereign cannot be easily settled. Per Richard Ashley, "the empirical contents [of sovereignty] are not fixed but evolve in a way reflecting the active practical consensus among coreflective statesmen who are ever struggling."[153] However, the struggle has meaning only if we assume that the imperative to demonstrate sovereign competence is a necessary feature of international politics. For the purposes of this book, I focus on sovereign competence in the domains of violence, markets, and rights, achieved through various public/private hybrid relations in *Lived Sovereignty*.

Conceptualizing Lived Sovereignty

In *Lived Sovereignty*, a "sovereign state" is inseparable from a "nonsovereign society." Timothy Mitchell characterizes a "state effect" where "the power to regulate and control is not simply a capacity stored within the state, from where it extends out into society. The apparent boundary of the state does not mark the limit of the processes of regulation. It is itself a product of those processes."[154] A "sovereign state" is the accomplishment of various sovereign functions, needing continual reproduction. In *Lived Sovereignty*, performances of sovereign competence are diffused over many agents, state and nonstate. As mentioned in the book's opening, US sovereign competence for war-making in Iraq and Afghanistan relied on contractors and troops. Georgio Agamben also argues that the sovereign decides the exception.[155] In *Lived Sovereignty*, the sovereign may decide the exception, but it is not guaranteed that *one* sovereign will make *one* exception. For instance, church agents exert sovereign exception when granting sanctuary to those facing deportation.[156] *Lived Sovereignty* involves multiple, often contradicting, exceptions emanating from a variety of sources rather than "a specific person or body of persons whose actions are equivalent to the actions of the state."[157]

Consider James Scott's *Seeing Like a State*, which has multiple meanings embedded in the title that connect to *Lived Sovereignty*.[158] First, Scott studies *how* a state sees, like its surveillance, as tied to capacities of state power. Second, *what* a state sees in its built environment is about projecting state power. Third, Scott tells us *why* a state sees in the kinds of subjects produced by state power. Scott emphasizes that

---

[152]   Walker 1990: 173.
[153]   Ashley 1984: 272, fn101.
[154]   Mitchell 1991: 90.
[155]   Agamben 1995.
[156]   Lippert 2004, as paraphrased in Aradau 2018.
[157]   Kalmo and Skinner 2010: 15.
[158]   Scott 1998.

seeing like a state means getting into the details of the how, what, and why of state vision. Extending this analysis, *Lived Sovereignty* asks: *Who* sees like a state? How does a divisible source of sovereign power affect the other dimensions?

While *Idealized Sovereignty* sustains the doctrine of indivisibility, *Lived Sovereignty* asks: "What if the absolute and indivisible political authority implicit in this story about state sovereignty and its presumed territorial basis is problematic to begin with?"[159] From this view, "it is no less a paradox that the standard conception proclaims sovereignty to be indivisible even as it divides sovereignty along internal and external dimensions."[160] *Idealized Sovereignty* attributes the social terms of the boundaries of sovereign authority as resting with "the state," which bestowed with indivisible qualities interacts with other sovereign states. When operating within the modality of *Idealized Sovereignty*, carrying out sovereign functions beyond the state would not register as recognizably sovereign at all. Instead, nonstate sovereign performances would bring "the end of sovereignty and the beginning of some fundamentally different post-sovereign arrangement of world politics."[161] But if we conceive of *Lived Sovereignty* as another coequal modality of sovereignty, then divisible sovereign relations are not playing a different game than *Idealized Sovereignty*. Instead, in *Lived Sovereignty*, sovereign competence is maintained by a rotating cast of public/private performers who together prop up a "sovereign state."

Michel Foucault refers to the coproduction of sovereign power as reflecting a government rationality or "governmentality."[162] For Foucault, "power is not founded on itself or generated by itself," meaning that power is not self-generating and must be accomplished.[163] Foucault urges a focus not on what power *is*, but on what power *does*.[164] A Foucauldian perspective in *Lived Sovereignty* means taking seriously multiple sites of sovereign power such that the category of "nonsovereign" loses analytical bearing. Instead of upholding artificial public/private dualities, Foucault urges the examination of how "private" excludes particular forms of sovereign power from being visible. Thus, those "who hold that the state is being marginalized by other kinds of agents ... overlook the way in which states are working *through* these other agents."[165]

By conceptualizing *Lived Sovereignty*, I nod to Mitchell, Foucault, and Scott. However, I do not promote any one theorist or theoretical framework in advancing *Lived Sovereignty*. Instead, I treat *Lived Sovereignty* as the diverse relations necessary for producing sovereign power that is remarked upon from a range of theoretical

---

[159] Agnew 2005: 440.
[160] Onuf 1991: 432.
[161] Jackson 1999: 434.
[162] Foucault 2007: 108.
[163] Foucault 2007: 2.
[164] Foucault 1980: 52.
[165] Neumann and Sending 2010: 1, emphasis added.

perspectives. I cohere these insights into a modality to better organize global sovereign politics.

Lived Sovereignty *in IR*

IR scholarship on social construction has been attuned to the dynamics of *Lived Sovereignty*. Glanville maintains, "the 'traditional' meaning of sovereignty is not as foundational and timeless as is commonly assumed."[166] Wendt argues that "the sovereign state is an ongoing accomplishment of practice, not a once-and-for-all creation of norms that somehow exist apart from practice."[167] Critical perspectives have long complicated sovereignty's intellectual trajectory.[168] Bartelson traces how "sovereignty and knowledge implicate each other logically and produce each other historically."[169] For Biersteker and Weber, "rather than proceeding from the assumption that all states are sovereign, [they] are interested in considering the variety of ways in which states are constantly negotiating their sovereignty."[170] Spruyt demonstrates that the sovereign state's win over other institutional forms was not inevitable.[171] Thomson shows how sovereign legitimation screened out nonstate actors from the international system.[172] Osiander questions if Westphalia really brought about sovereign equality.[173] Even Krasner, who is more comfortable with *Idealized Sovereignty*, does not assume sovereignty is perfectly applied: "There is no single definition of sovereignty because the meaning of the term depends on the theoretical context within which it is being used."[174] There is thus a robust tradition in IR of both reifying sovereignty as indivisible authority and also critically challenging this conception.

IR research has also empirically analyzed the diverse and divisible sovereign arrangements in *Lived Sovereignty*. Cooley and Spruyt examine contractual sovereign agreements and describe sovereignty as "a bundle of rights and obligations that are dynamically exchanged and transferred between states."[175] Phillips and Sharman study how heterogeneous actors in the Indian Ocean with differing statist, imperial, and corporate forms create a stable regional order.[176] In another study on company-states, such as the Dutch and English East India Companies, Phillips and Sharman assert that "the current international system may be exclusively composed of sovereign states, but that does not mean it was built by them."[177] Avant, Finnemore, and

---

[166]   Glanville 2013a: 79.
[167]   Wendt 1992: 413.
[168]   Weber 1995; Edkins and Pin-Fat 1999; Grovogui 2002; Teschke 2003; Walker 2004; Doty 2007.
[169]   Bartelson 1995: 5.
[170]   Biersteker and Weber 1996: 11.
[171]   Spruyt 1994.
[172]   Thomson 1994.
[173]   Osiander 2001.
[174]   Krasner 1995: 121.
[175]   Cooley and Spruyt 2009: 4.
[176]   Phillips and Sharman 2015: 8.
[177]   Phillips and Sharman 2020: 16.

Sell assemble a framework for diffuse global governors with varied authority without reducing the stakes to the sovereign state's survival.[178] Best and Gheciu consider the return of different practices to constitute "the public" in global governance.[179] Doty explores vigilantism at the US–Mexico border as sovereign actions.[180] Duffield regards developmental aid NGOs as "petty sovereigns."[181] (I deal with this literature in more detail in the next chapter where I focus more squarely on the forms of hybridity within *Lived Sovereignty*.)

Scholars have focused on the implications of sovereign power's diverse sources in *Lived Sovereignty*. Early inquiries centered on whether the state is disappearing or *Idealized Sovereignty* is declining, as summarized by this statement: "Over the past half-century, the monopoly of [Westphalian sovereignty] attributes by nation-states has been severely compromised by growing transnational flows, neoliberal rationality, international economic and governance institutions, and postnational and international assertions of law, rights, and authority."[182] A typical conclusion was that "although nonsovereign actors may seem to be crowding the stage, the sovereign states remain the chief protagonists in the international drama."[183] Yet, as UN Secretary-General Boutros Boutros-Ghali observed: "A major intellectual requirement of our time is to rethink the question of sovereignty – not to weaken its essence, which is crucial to international security and cooperation, but to recognize that it may take more than one form and perform more than one function."[184] In this vein, using a Foucauldian framework, Iver Neumann and Ole Jacob Sending study nongovernmental organizations and international organizations to argue that "transformations entailed by globalization do not result in states losing their power, but that the rationality of governing shifts–resulting, for example, in the emergence of a global-level governmental rationality that reconstitutes the meaning and significance of sovereignty."[185] For Neumann and Sending, "while sovereignty has been universalized as the central *form* of institutionalized political authority, it does not determine the *contents* of political rule at the national or global level."[186]

Finally, *Lived Sovereignty* is also reflected in IR's "practice turn."[187] From this perspective, "it does not make sense to say that an institution – such as international law or multilateralism or sovereignty – structures or secures a certain order. It is the continual use or performance of the material and symbolic resources that are recognized as being vested in these institutions that helps produce and reproduce

---

178 Avant, Finnemore, and Sell 2010.
179 Best and Gheciu 2014.
180 Doty 2007; Aradau 2018.
181 Duffield 2007, as paraphrased in Aradau 2018.
182 Brown 2010: 22.
183 Fowler and Bunck 1995: 20.
184 Fowler and Bunck 1995: 70.
185 Neumann and Sending 2010: 2.
186 Neumann and Sending 2010: 6, emphasis original.
187 Adler and Pouliot 2011.

certain orders."[188] Sending, Pouliot, and Neumann's edited volume on diplomatic practices shows that "sovereignty is produced and reproduced (and transformed) through changing diplomatic practices, whereby recognition as a competent participant (diplomat) hinges on deploying or enacting some strategies and roles that reproduce the state as a recognized sovereign."[189] In analyzing sovereignty as practice, one should "focus on the relations inside a given social configuration."[190] I adopt this methodology for showing *Lived Sovereignty* in the empirics, as I elaborate in the next chapter. But I also retain how sovereignty is represented in *Idealized Sovereignty* as an ideational structure in the hybridized framework introduced later in this chapter.

The actual experience of sovereignty relies on divisible public/private practices to construct a "sovereign state effect." Such a *Lived Sovereignty* perspective has gained ground in IR. But this literature has not theorized how divisible practices of sovereign power are perpetually in productive friction with representations of indivisible sovereign authority. In other words, how can IR theory make sense of both Blackwater and Brexit?

HYBRID SOVEREIGNTY

This chapter so far conceptualized *Idealized Sovereignty* as the stylized representations of indivisible sovereign authority and *Lived Sovereignty* as the divisible performances of sovereign competence. I now hybridize *Idealized* and *Lived Sovereignty* in a new framework.

Hybridity reflects being multiple things at once. Hybrid cars run on a combination of electricity and fuel. They are neither fully electric nor gas, but both are essential to their operations. Biology references hybrids in crossbreeding (liger as lion and tiger) or hybridity in maturation processes (caterpillar to butterfly). Hybrids proliferate the political world as well. In a "mixed market economy," states organize political economy as a combination of market control and deference to mobile capital.[191] "Competitive authoritarianism" describes regimes with competitive elections but without broad protection of civil liberties or a reasonably level-playing field.[192] Contemporary transitional justice features various hybrid tribunals and peace-building institutions.[193] In New Public Management, public service delivery may be carried out by firms, nonprofits, or government-created entities with a corporate status like Fannie Mae and Freddie Mac.[194] Similarly, one can explore "hybrid rule" where market forces

---

[188]   Sending, Pouliot, Neumann 2015: 7.
[189]   Sending, Pouliot, Neumann 2015: 17.
[190]   Sending, Pouliot, Neumann 2015: 10.
[191]   Hall and Soskice 2001.
[192]   Levitsky and Way 2010: 7.
[193]   Millar 2014.
[194]   Denis, Ferlie, and Van Gestel 2015.

engage in national security.[195] While hybrid phenomena are not hard to find, the conceptualization of hybridity itself is scarce.[196] In the aforementioned studies, political scientists variously describe new hybrids or revisit old amalgamations to then evaluate these forms against more traditional varieties. Thus, the standard approach is to present and analyze hybrids as mixtures. However, I am interested in the condition of *being* hybrid or hybridity itself.

Hybridity has been conceptualized most usefully in cultural and diasporic studies, but even there its definition is contested and "maddeningly elastic."[197] Still, I take my cues from hybridity in the cultural construction of postcolonial identity as a "difference 'within,' an 'in-between' reality."[198] In an in-between reality, subjects assume multiple identities and characteristics. Cultural pluralism offers resources beyond a single origin. Postcolonial identity draws from both the former colony and metropole at once. In this way, hybridity enables postcolonial subjects to choose from a menu of options. But hybridity also engenders a constant negotiation of being in-between and the contestation from not belonging to one or the other.

Food offers one example. Chicken tikka masala, a dish featuring Indian tandoori spices in a European-inspired creamy tomato sauce, is often considered the "national dish" of Britain. Yet, many Indians are puzzled by the fusion as well as the formulaic "tikka masala" moniker added to other dishes: paneer tikka masala, cauliflower tikka masala, and so on. Chicken tikka masala's hybridity has helped elevate its Western status by offering it more resources to draw from: the dish appears friendly to Western palates while still seeming "exotic" enough. Moreover, chicken tikka masala has been further hybridized with Western cuisine. One can now order chicken tikka masala pizzas, calzones, and tacos. But this hybridity is also contested by traditionalists who reject the appropriation, mocking the Western impulse to "tikka masala" everything.[199] Hybridity exceeds preestablished categories and hence invites disciplining. Perhaps over time India will come to embrace chicken tikka masala and reconfigure the categories. Or the dish itself might change when adopted by Indians, as some chefs acknowledge in the United Kingdom: "Chicken tikka masala does exist in India, but with a completely different recipe—with onion, tomatoes, ginger, garlic and coriander and hand pounded spices—unlike the tomato creamy version we serve."[200]

This book is not about food, but chicken tikka masala helps highlight the analytical potential of hybridity for politics. Paul Gilroy's sociological history, *The Black Atlantic*, captures "the inescapable hybridity and intermixture of ideas" in the transatlantic movements of people, ideas, and culture, where hybridity appears as "narratives of

[195] Hurt and Lipshutz 2016. There is also a global governance literature that engages with public/private hybridity, which I regard in more detail in the next chapter.
[196] Lottholz 2017.
[197] Kraidy 2005: 3.
[198] Bhabha 1994: 19; Canclini 1995.
[199] Ruane 2018.
[200] Digby 2021.

historical entanglement."[201] For Gilroy, hybridity exists both "uneasily" and "unashamedly" in the Black Atlantic.[202] I carry this cultural sensibility throughout the book when using hybridity as a conceptual lens to analyze how things come together by inhabiting multiple meanings at once. While cultural studies initially proposed hybridity as a "third space,"[203] recent applications treat hybridity not as "a third term that resolves the tension between two cultures, but rather holds the tension of the opposition and explores the spaces in-between fixed identities through their continuous reiterations."[204]

When such a conceptualization of hybridity is applied to sovereignty, it allows us to see how *Idealized* and *Lived Sovereignty* fit together. Each form is individually insufficient to meaningfully capture sovereignty, but when hybridized they become jointly necessary to generate sovereignty in world politics. Figure 1.1 presents this hybridized framework of sovereignty. Hybridity makes sense of the duality in the chapter's epigraph that "sovereignty is fundamental, but it is also contingent." Sovereignty's "association with absoluteness, inevitability and indispensability is what convinces its supporters that a world without it is untenable, while it gives its most radical critics pause and in frustration they call for its elimination, as if merely the word itself was the problem."[205] Sovereignty's interlocutors confront two related questions: How can something so fundamental to international relations be so contingent? And how can something so contingent on international relations be assumed as so fundamental? Hybridity enables an answer to these questions by introducing the two modalities of sovereignty as acting in concert. Sovereignty is

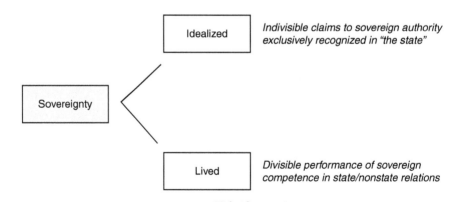

FIGURE 1.1 Hybrid sovereignty

[201] Gilroy 1993: xi, as cited in Kraidy 2005: 57–58.
[202] Gilroy 1993: 61, 99.
[203] Bhabha 1994.
[204] Lemay-Hebert and Freedman 2017: 5.
[205] Shinko 2017.

both idealized as indivisible and lived as divisible at once. The implication is that while IR should undoubtedly depart from ahistorical adoptions of "traditional Westphalian sovereignty,"[206] the field should not abandon *Idealized Sovereignty* as something fictitious to be replaced with only studying *Lived Sovereignty* as a more "real" version of sovereignty. Hybridity emphasizes that both forms are important and are simultaneously held in suspension vis-à-vis each other.

Consider there is a frontstage and a backstage to sovereignty.[207] *Idealized Sovereignty* is the frontstage projecting absolute indivisibility that is a useful political resource to draw an audience. *Lived Sovereignty* is the backstage keeping the show running with divisible sovereign practices. Even though the actual practices of sovereign competence use diverse agents and vary across national contexts in *Lived Sovereignty*, as a social claim to political authority, sovereignty is sustained as indivisible within the ideational structure of *Idealized Sovereignty*. Moreover, the hybridized framework encompasses both Brexit and Blackwater. Brexit might not make sense in *Lived Sovereignty*, but it does in *Idealized Sovereignty*. Blackwater might not fit in *Idealized Sovereignty*, but it does in *Lived Sovereignty*.

Since hybridity situates *Idealized* and *Lived Sovereignty* in suspended dialogue, changes in how sovereign power lives can lead to changes in how sovereign authority is idealized. The contingent expressions of sovereignty is a core contribution of the social construction approach in IR: "Throughout the course of history, the meaning of sovereignty has undergone important change and transformation – from the location of the source of its legitimacy (in God, in the monarch, or in a people) – to the scope of activities claimed under its protection."[208] This book exemplifies this perspective in the empirics, for instance by noting in Chapter 6 that Amnesty International's transnational advocacy as a feature of *Lived Sovereignty* expanded the sovereign compact in *Idealized Sovereignty* to include the realization of universal rights. Ideals certainly evolve by being exposed to diverse practices and "off performances." But the changes might not keep pace with each other. Even historically attuned scholars remark on an unchanging *Idealized Sovereignty*: "In the history of sovereignty one can skip three hundred years without omitting noteworthy change."[209] Another proposes that dominant understandings of sovereignty have historically fluctuated between a "systemic view" with "a commitment to the integrity of an existing territorial order" and an "anarchic view" that privileged "an exemption from any such commitment."[210] But even in this historization, the state as an indivisible unit is treated as the preferred holder of sovereignty.[211]

---

[206] Osiander 2001; Glanville 2013a, b.
[207] Goffman 1956.
[208] Biersteker and Weber 1996: 14.
[209] Philpott 1996: 43.
[210] Murphy 1996: 87.
[211] Murphy 1996: 88–89.

The changing or unchanging dynamics of sovereignty represent a major debate among IR scholars, especially Krasner and his critics. Glanville summarizes:

> The challenge for the student of sovereignty is not to determine a timeless definition of the meaning and rules of sovereignty but to explore the ways in which sovereignty has been socially constructed and reconstructed over time. Indeed, Krasner provides abundant empirical evidence for such an exploration, though he refuses to admit that his evidence points to anything other than hypocritical breaches of a static model that has never really existed.[212]

The social construction approach privileges tracing "processes through which entities such as the state are constituted and how constitutive norms such as sovereignty become established and evolve over time."[213] Krasner for his part imbues sovereignty with a "certain resilience and ability to tolerate alternatives," while allowing that sovereignty should not be viewed as an "organically related, inseparable set of rules."[214] But he is unwilling to make the jump from changes in practices of sovereign competence automatically resulting in the legitimation of sovereign authority beyond the state. The constructivists are correct that the social terms of *Idealized Sovereignty* are neither given nor timeless; they must be perpetually reproduced. But Krasner's position too has merit. It took two and a half centuries to collectively imagine beyond the sovereign as a literal embodiment of divine will to an assembly of sovereigns. It might take longer still to fully jettison the doctrine of indivisibility and its potency for a new divisible *Idealized Sovereignty*. Indeed, even scholars wishing to escape *Idealized Sovereignty* are still caught in its reification. As mentioned in the chapter's introduction, Lake critiques constructivists for still assuming sovereignty "to be an absolute condition."[215] But when developing a continuum of domestic sovereignty by weighing security, economy, and political relationships of one state to another, Lake qualifies: "One could also weight issue areas differently. Clearly, some issues are more central to the claim of sovereignty than others."[216] If IR stopped idealizing sovereignty tomorrow, it would not eliminate how sovereignty operates in the world as an ideational structure promoting the early modern doctrines of indivisibility. As the previous discussion on the founding of America demonstrated, the indivisibility doctrine in *Idealized Sovereignty* did not lose its value even in the throes of revolution and experimentation, despite being terribly inconvenient. Thus, "ignoring the significance of sovereignty assumes that ideas and beliefs are simply the outcome of circumstance, not also shapers of circumstance."[217] As such, while pursuing a social constructionist approach, I retain a focus on *Idealized Sovereignty* so as not to reject the power of ideas in international politics.

---

[212]   Glanville 2013b: 16.
[213]   Phillips 2007: 67.
[214]   Krasner 2001b: 248; Shinko 2017.
[215]   Lake 2003: 308–309.
[216]   Lake 2003: 312, fn6.
[217]   Murphy 1996: 87.

Rather than resolve the debate, hybrid sovereignty centers on the tensions between seemingly fixed doctrines of sovereign authority against changing practices of sovereign power. Where for Krasner this disconnect between ideas and actions means sovereignty is an "organized hypocrisy,"[218] the conceptual lens of hybridity leverages the disconnect to reveal what is at stake in sovereign politics. Not all political power constitutes authority, conceived socially as the "right to rule."[219] In hybridity, sovereign politics unfolds precisely in the suspension between reified sovereign authority and contingent sovereign power. Seen in this light, the "ambiguity of sovereignty has historical depth; it is not the result of conceptual confusion born out of a persistent misunderstanding of its 'true nature.'"[220] Hybridity turns our analysis to the contested dialogue between the ideational structure of sovereignty and its varied lived realities, pivoting to consider new challenges for managing sovereignty: Would the strain between *Idealized* and *Lived Sovereignty* result in a sovereign breakdown? In other words, would the front and backstage performances result in completely different shows? The rest of the book works through these implications of hybrid sovereignty.

CONCLUSION

This chapter theorized sovereignty as the interplay of two contrasting modalities. In *Idealized Sovereignty*, sovereign authority is represented exclusively in "the state" per the doctrine of indivisibility developed by early modern theorists and reified in conventional IR theory. In *Lived Sovereignty*, achieving sovereign competence involves divisible practices of state and nonstate actors in a variety of social relations. We would do a disservice to sovereignty's complexity if only one of the two modes persevered in analyses of sovereignty. Instead, the chapter intervened in major IR debates to argue that sovereignty should be hybridized. This overarching framework will guide the ideal-types of public/private hybridity in the next chapter and the empirical analyses in the remainder of the book where hybrid sovereignty is necessary to build a global empire (Chapter 3), go to war (Chapter 4), regulate global markets (Chapter 5), and protect rights (Chapter 6). The empirical chapters uncover varied public/private relations in *Lived Sovereignty*; however, the political stakes of these hybrid relations only come into focus when counterposed with *Idealized Sovereignty*. All along, this chapter reminds the reader that such coproduction of sovereign power does not transform into sovereign authority by *fiat*. Instead, there is a productive tension between *Idealized* and *Lived Sovereignty* that makes them hugely powerful shapers of international politics. Ultimately, hybrid sovereignty recognizes both lived sovereign competence and idealized representations of sovereign authority as critical to addressing sovereignty's many paradoxes.

---

[218] Krasner 1999.
[219] Raz 1990.
[220] Kalmo and Skinner 2010: 11.

2

Ideal-Types of Public/Private Hybridity

So which is the lie? Hard or soft? Silence or time?
The lie is that it's one or the other.
A still, floating bee is moving faster than it can think.
David Foster Wallace, *Brief Interviews with Hideous Men*

Sovereign power is constructed through public/private hybridity in *Lived Sovereignty*. We observe public/private hybridity in major stories of global politics. Americans elected Donald Trump, a "businessman president" for whom it was unclear where business ended and politics began. The 2014 Ukrainian crisis was instigated when security contractors working for Russia took over airports in Crimea. Brexit prompted a slew of lawyers, trade experts, lobbyists, and public relations firms to advise the British government in its negotiations with the European Union. WikiLeaks and Russian hackers collaborated to release emails of the Democratic National Committee to influence the 2016 American election. Facebook helps governments in Pakistan identify blasphemy, Norway police communities, Philippines troll activists, and Russia block pages supporting Putin's critics. When analyzing such public/private relations, the conceptual lens of hybridity reminds us that as things take on multiple meanings at once, "the lie is that it's one or the other."

Thus, hybridity unsettles the public/private "master distinction" in law and politics.[1] Public/private is a master distinction because it "allows us to distinguish between various social relations, such as society/individual, civil society/family, state/family, state/civil society, state/market, and we may add international society/domestic state, and international society/global civil society."[2] The book could just as easily be organized around state/market or domestic/international divides.[3] However, I agree with political theorists that public/private is at the center of legitimating political authority as the "first question of politics."[4] Constructing the

---

[1] Arendt 1958.
[2] Lu 2006: 15.
[3] On state/market, see Strange 1996; Cutler, Haufler, and Porter 1999; Cashore, Auld, and Newsom 2004. On domestic/international, see Waltz 1959; Lake 2003.
[4] Williams 2005: 4.

public/private distinction means creating political authority and allocating who counts as legitimate with what powers and obligations.[5] But public/private is also historically contingent. While we now conceive of levying taxes as a public function, "as late as the sixteenth century, English judges still analyzed taxation, not as an exaction by the state but as a private gift from the donor – the taxpayer. Parliament was thought to have simply arranged this consensual private transaction."[6] I argue throughout this book that changes in the historical contours of public/private are often inspired by wrestling with hybridity. In hybridity, public/private become indeterminately attached to each other, moving from a "grand dichotomy" to "a grand relationship."

Public/private hybridity is evident in recent appraisals of geopolitics. In 2017, the American National Security Advisor and the chair of the White House Economic Council together argued: "The world is not a global community, but an arena where nations, nongovernmental actors, and businesses engage and compete for advantage, to which the U.S. brings unmatched military, political, economic, cultural, and moral strength."[7] While the statement's purpose was to distance the Trump administration from liberal notions of "global community," the identification of actors other than governments as major players is a useful starting point for understanding public/private hybridity in *Lived Sovereignty*. Unlike the American position, I rebrand the arena as not just for competition but also for the coproduction of global sovereign power: National governments, nongovernmental actors, and businesses engage and compete *with each other to produce shared* military, political, economic, cultural, and moral strength in the world. Thus, configurations of public/private hybridity enable sovereign competence such as conducting wars or regulating markets.

Public/private hybridity plays a key role in understanding early modern Europe in standard histories. Polities used mercenaries and privateers to help control populations from rivals and secure revenue.[8] Long-distance traders were the first movers in creating new market alliances.[9] Janice Thomson observes that prior to the nineteenth century, it was "impossible to draw distinctions between the economic and political, the domestic and international, or the nonstate and state realms of authority when analyzing these practices. All lines were blurred."[10] Eventually, mercenaries and privateers complicated emerging international norms of neutrality, which created a demand for sovereigns to draw cleaner borders between "state" and "nonstate" violence. Per Thomson, mercenaries, pirates, and privateers did not label themselves as "private" actors, but were rather marked as such by governments

5   Haufler 2001.
6   Horwitz 1982: 1423–1424.
7   McMaster and Cohn 2017.
8   Tilly 1990: 30.
9   Spruyt 1994: 31.
10   Thomson 1994: 41.

to legitimate state sovereigns from nonstates "after some three hundred years of state-building."[11] Hendrik Spruyt summarizes the state-formation narrative when he argues that at the end of this process, "the state claims a domestic and external monopoly of force. As a consequence, nonstate actors are stripped of coercive means – mercenaries and privateers thus have disappeared."[12]

Yet, public/private hybridity also thrived in the modern state system. The British relied on "foreign" troops from its colonies in World Wars I and II. The development of American nuclear and weapon superiority was made possible by partnerships with science and industry. The post-World War II global economy reflected a "redistribution of responsibilities for the production of common goods among public and private actors, the emergence of new forms of private interest government (i.e., the private production of public goods), and new modes of cooperation between public and private actors (e.g., policy networks and public-private partnerships)."[13] The rest of this book gives numerous examples of public/private hybridity organizing empires, violence, markets, and rights from the seventeenth to the twenty-first centuries. In these instances, hybridity endows public/private entities with access to sovereign power in *Lived Sovereignty*; however, as discussed in the previous chapter, sovereign authority relies on legitimation available in ideational representations of *Idealized Sovereignty*. Exercising sovereign power without sovereign authority forms the major challenge of public/private hybridity.

The disappearance of public/private hybridity from the state-formation narrative is better seen as capturing dynamics of *Idealized Sovereignty*, which relies on distinguishing state from nonstate to assign roles and responsibilities. For instance, the construction of British colonial troops as "foreign" is a feature of imposing indivisible standards of *Idealized Sovereignty* onto hybrid relations in *Lived Sovereignty*. Scholars in international law have recently turned to investigate "the blurring line between what is public and what is private, the emergence of hybrid forms of governance, the proliferating relations between different actors which currently dominate the global legal landscape, and the crisis of legality enhanced by the growth of norm-making activities beyond the state."[14] The "crisis of legality" has meaning only if hybridity's transformation of public/private has serious consequences for how law and politics operate through the public/private distinction. Thus, on the one hand, hybridity overcomes the public/private distinction in *Lived Sovereignty*, while, on the other hand, hybridity provides the impetus for reifying the public/private distinction in *Idealized Sovereignty*. I argue that attempts to resolve this tension is a constitutive feature of sovereign politics, but it is understudied in global governance.

---

[11]   Thomson 1994: 11.
[12]   Spruyt 1994: 16.
[13]   Grande and Pauly 2005: 5.
[14]   Casini 2014: 412.

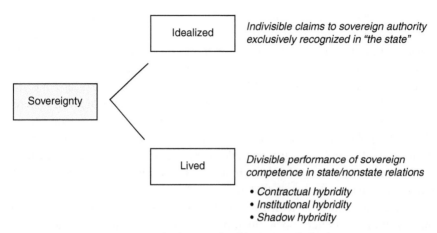

FIGURE 2.1 Ideal-types of public/private hybridity

Moreover, while public/private hybridity in sovereign politics is pervasive, its varieties have yet to be examined in IR. This chapter develops three ideal-types where public/private hybrid relations vary in how much they are formalized and publicized. *Contractual hybridity* features formal and publicized performances where sovereign power is negotiated in public/private contractual exchanges. *Institutional hybridity* features informal and partly publicized performances where sovereign power is negotiated through public/private institutional linkages. *Shadow hybridity* features nonformalized and nonpublicized performances where sovereign power is negotiated in public/private shadowy bargains. Figure 2.1 depicts how the ideal-types fit into the framework of hybrid sovereignty introduced in the previous chapter. Public/private hybridity in *Lived Sovereignty* also invites a serious reconsideration of the conventional legitimation of sovereign authority that takes its cue from *Idealized Sovereignty*. I thus examine both sovereign power payoffs and sovereign legitimation trade-offs in the different ideal-types.

The rest of the chapter first situates public/private hybridity in understanding complexity in global governance. Then, I sketch the key contours of Weberian ideal-typification analysis and present the three ideal-types of public/private hybridity. I end the chapter with the research design of the book, stating why I rely on particular data and cases for studying public/private hybridity in practice.

PUBLIC/PRIVATE HYBRIDITY IN GLOBAL GOVERNANCE

My thinking on public/private hybridity owes its intellectual lineage to scholars who study the influence of private power in global governance. Following Susan Strange's pioneering insight into the eclipsing power of corporations relative to states,[15] early work on transnational private authority recognized different arrangements of corporate governors ranging from firm-level partnerships to industry-wide cooperation.[16] Scholars have since examined market-based private regulation[17] in environmental governance,[18] financial accounting,[19] bond ratings,[20] and Internet commerce.[21] Moreover, the literature has introduced moral, expert, and illicit logics alongside the market,[22] thereby broadening the scope of investigation to include religious organizations,[23] INGOs,[24] policy networks,[25] and criminal enterprises.[26] For more specific measurement, some limit the operationalization of private authority as meaning to "make rules or set standards that others in world politics adopt."[27] In this frame, it is typical to assert that nonstate "campaigning is unlikely to bring positive results unless at least some state actors endorse the agenda of private organizations."[28] Others open up private authority to include structural and discursive power to account for more diffuse effects on governance.[29] Studies also theorize the underlying legitimation claims of delegated, institutional, and expert-based authority in global governance.[30]

In addition, recent research challenges the separation of public from private authority,[31] focusing instead on how interdependence produces global regulatory change[32] through concepts like "the Governance Triangle"[33] and "new interdependence."[34] These frames echo the idea of multistakeholderism as "two or more classes of actors engaged in a common governance enterprise concerning issues they regard as public in nature, and characterized by polyarchic authority relations constituted by procedural rules."[35] Growing scholarship on public–private partnerships[36] argues that such collaborations may mitigate public actors' perceived

[15] Strange 1996.
[16] Cutler, Haufler, and Porter 1999.
[17] Abbott et al. 2015.
[18] Bartley 2003; Cashore, Auld, and Newsom 2004; Green 2014.
[19] Büthe and Mattli 2011.
[20] Sinclair 2005.
[21] Sisley and Flyverbom 2008.
[22] Josselin and Wallace 2001; Hall and Biersteker 2002.
[23] Ryall 2001; Agensky 2019.
[24] Keck and Sikkink 1998; Clark 2001; Stroup and Wong 2017.
[25] Avant and Westerwinter 2016.
[26] Flanigan 2012; Varese 2018.
[27] Green 2014: 4; Büthe and Mattli 2011; Green and Auld 2017.
[28] Josselin and Wallace 2001: 257.
[29] Fuchs 2007; Mikler 2018.
[30] Avant, Finnemore, and Sell 2010.
[31] Graz and Nölke 2008.
[32] Mattli and Woods 2009.
[33] Abbott and Snidal 2009a: 48.
[34] Farrell and Newman 2014.
[35] Raymond and DeNardis 2015: 573.
[36] Börzel and Risse 2005; Tallberg et al. 2013; Andonova 2017.

inefficiency and lack of expertise along with private actors' perceived legitimacy deficits.[37]

From this diverse literature, I borrow the scope conditions of my research as formally organized transnational (ostensibly) nonstate actors. More broadly, I am also motivated by understanding the dynamics of how private authority emerges and interacts with the public. However, in conceptualizing public/private hybridity, I depart from this scholarship in three ways. First, I do not deploy apolitical logics, such as market, expert, or moral, but instead represent all instances of public/private hybridity as wrestling with sovereign politics and its contradictions. As such, my starting point is fundamentally different from global governance scholars who argue that private authority "is not properly understood as *political* authority or governance subject to the need for *political* legitimacy."[38]

Second, I downplay essentializing characteristics of public and private that must be overcome through collaboration. Instead, public/private hybridity inheres in entangled governance structures that refuse easy categorizations. Even cases of private authority seemingly untethered from public relations reveal hybrid linkages upon closer inspection. For instance, the Greenhouse Gas Protocol (GGP), created by two INGOs as the leading accounting standard for firm-level emissions, is understandably emblematic of "entrepreneurial" or self-generated private authority.[39] But the GGP's legitimacy was also undergirded by the US Environmental Protection Agency's funding and participation.[40]

Third, risking parsimony, I do not restrict public/private hybridity to only matter when influencing others to adopt privately made rules. Instead, I examine how public/private hybridity, in a variety of ways, makes it possible to run empires, fight wars, regulate markets, and guarantee rights. Twenty years ago, one of the earliest IR treatments on nonstate actors concluded that "a weakening state apparatus might encourage governments and transnational companies to hire mercenaries; but rather than revealing a terminal decline of the state, such practices should be seen as partnerships between public and private actors to shore up fragile state structures."[41] I extend this foresight to apply public/private hybridity not just to fragile or weak states, but also to a general condition of being sovereign in the first place.

In a different vein, global governance scholarship has also invoked hybridity implicitly and explicitly. Abrahamsen and Williams study global security assemblages that are "simultaneously public and private, global and local" and whose "power stems not primarily from the barrel of the gun but from embeddedness in contemporary structures of governance."[42] For Andonova, hybrid governance is

---

[37] Abbott and Snidal 2001: 363.
[38] Bernstein 2014: 122, emphasis original.
[39] Green 2014: 132.
[40] Green 2014: 141.
[41] Josselin and Wallace 2001: 259.
[42] Abrahamsen and Williams 2011: 3. "Assemblages" draws from a broader lineage in social theory. See Srivastava 2013 for an overview.

evident when public–private partnerships in international organizations "deliberately pool public and private authority" and represents a "different modality of governance innovation compared to private regulations made largely by nonstate actors."[43] Similarly, Best and Gheciu's edited volume criticizes the private authority literature for not being attuned to "what appear to be private actors (NGOs, civil society, firms) [as] increasingly engaged in public practices ... redefining those actors as public because of what they do, not where they are situated."[44] For Best and Gheciu, the public as practice helps see that "the relationship between 'public' and 'private' is to be sought less in the characteristics of specific actors or institutions than in the qualities of the interactions between them."[45] Avant and Haufler's chapter in the volume highlights "changes in who is part of the public, what part of managing violence counts as public, and what processes are deemed public" to "challenge the assumption that states alone provide security as a matter of common concern."[46] Separately, Leander makes sense of the US intelligence landscape as "a hybridity of the public and private, in the strong sense of the two categories being *joined* into a new kind of 'public' practice."[47] In international political economy, Graz conceptualizes "global hybrids" that "confer authority on non-state actors previously deprived of such attributes."[48] For Graz, "what is new with contemporary hybrids is not so much the extent and intensity of their influence as their new relationship with the polity. This relationship is neither clandestine, nor strictly confrontational, but complementary and subsidiary to state functions."[49] In international law, hybrids for Teubner are "not simply mixtures, but social arrangements in their own right."[50]

I build on this literature when conceptualizing public/private hybridity. Like Abrahamsen and Williams' focus on assemblages, I also study the phenomena that are public/private at once. With Best and Gheciu, I agree that public/private are constituted in relational interactions that change over time. I echo Graz's contextualization of hybridity complementing sovereign functions and Teubner's insight of hybridity as social arrangements rather than stand-alone entities. I find Leander's portrayal helpful when conceptualizing public/private hybridity as *"enmeshed: the actors, their activities, their purposes, and the applicable rules and regulations turn out to be public and private simultaneously."*[51] Leander also emphasizes that "observers and practitioners

[43] Andonova 2017: 9, fn13.
[44] Best and Gheciu 2014: 17.
[45] Best and Gheciu 2014: 11.
[46] Avant and Haufler 2014: 49–50.
[47] Leander 2014: 198.
[48] Graz 2006: 232.
[49] Graz 2006: 235.
[50] Teubner 2002: 331, as quoted in Leander 2014: 212.
[51] Leander 2014: 199, emphasis original.

fall back on the [public/private] divide and mobilize it for their own ends."[52] Yet, these characterizations underspecify the variations and dynamics of hybridity, which makes public/private relations seem like a "a slippery mass of intertwined ropes heaped in the dark, damp hold of a ship."[53] I advance the theoretical space by organizing the public/private entanglements into ideal-types with unique payoffs and trade-offs for sovereign politics, which I turn to later in this chapter.

For now, I want to discuss how I depart more seriously from how the literature conflates public functions, power, and authority.[54] From Best and Gheciu's framework it is clear that "non-state actors can come to be seen as agents who perform important public functions" separate from "purely private actors."[55] For them, performing public functions can be a source of authority, defined as the "ability to induce deference in others."[56] In this understanding, "generating deference (or gaining authority) confers power."[57] The relationship, in a simplified sense, is:

$$\text{public functions} \rightarrow \text{public authority} \rightarrow \text{power}$$

The argument rests on practices: "What counts as public depends more on what is *done* than on whether an individual or institution is associated formally with what we traditionally define as the public or private realm."[58] Bernstein's contribution in the Best and Gheciu volume argues that "global governance concerns efforts to create political authority beyond the state."[59] However, as the previous chapter highlighted, questions of *who* is an authority and *how* is power expressed are precisely in tension in *Idealized* and *Lived Sovereignty*. As such, analyzing nonstate practices of public power is insufficient to fully grasp what is at stake in sovereign politics. Perceptive scholars have recognized that nonstate authority is not "simply the emergence of significant transnational or sovereignty free actors in international politics, but private actors exercising power that is perceived as *legitimate*," which "accrues through a process that culminates in the governed deferring to the governors."[60] I expand this insight to argue further that these are not "private" actors, nor are they always perceived as "legitimate."

Thus, I conceptualize sovereign authority as a more specific type of "public" or "political" authority usually conceived in the literature. In public/private hybridity,

---

[52] Leander 2014: 210.
[53] Fowler and Bunck 1995: 19.
[54] I welcome Stroup and Wong (2017)'s intervention in clarifying that a very small number of international nongovernmental organizations (INGOs) actually have the ability to get deference from multiple audiences (a proxy for INGO authority), and these *leading INGOs* challenge the easy characterization of INGOs as automatically authoritative in the private authority literature.
[55] Best and Gheciu 2014: 18.
[56] Avant and Haufler 2014: 48.
[57] Avant and Haufler 2014: 48.
[58] Best and Gheciu 2014: 15.
[59] Bernstein 2014: 121.
[60] Kobrin 2009: 354; emphasis original; Green 2014: 34.

who counts as sovereign does not align with *what* counts as sovereign. Instead, the relationship looks more like this:

sovereign functions → sovereign power –? sovereign authority

All cases in this book depict the struggle it takes to make the jump from establishing sovereign competence to wielding sovereign authority. In fact, not only is the chasm between power and authority hard to bridge, public/private hybridity provides the impetus for breakdown by presenting legitimating crises for sovereign authority. Scholars have long argued that the "alliance between public and private agents, between governmental and corporate elites, is working a reconfiguration of authority relations. It is blurring the distinction between the public and private realms and enhancing the legitimacy of the latter as a source of authority."[61] Normative concerns follow, like the aforementioned "crisis of legality" in the hybridization of international law. If sovereign power is muddled, whom do we hold responsible for sovereign abuses? We demand that "hybridity can and should be unpacked in order to realize whether it is the result of pursuing the most powerful interest, instead of the very public interests that required the emergence of a global regime."[62] Public/private hybridity is thus both integral to sovereign power and a challenge to sovereign authority. These dynamics are reflected in a long-standing debate on whether the medieval Law Merchant existed.

Did the Medieval Law Merchant Exist?

The Law Merchant (*lex mercatoria*) refers to the medieval custom of merchants getting together in guilds and fairs to create rules for trade. Economic institutionalists argue that by the end of the eleventh century, "the Law Merchant came to govern most commercial transactions in Europe, providing a uniform set of standards across large numbers of locations."[63] The Law Merchant as a body of customary law refers to "the commercial law rules – contractual, customary, and statutory – that govern transactions among merchants. It includes the rules governing sale, credit, insurance, transportation, and, probably, partnership."[64] Within international law, the Law Merchant has special status because of its influence on the growth of international commerce, its ties to a long legal history, and its contentious debates about public and private authority:

> The modern *lex mercatoria* is unlike any other field of law. People never tire of asking whether it exists. Debates over its existence and over its nature hinge largely on its supposed autonomy and, in particular, on its purported independence of national law on the one hand and of international law on the other. It is consistently

---

[61] Cutler 1997: 279.
[62] Casini 2014: 403.
[63] Milgrom, North, and Weingast 1990: 5.
[64] Epstein 2004: 1.

presented as a third legal system, neither national nor international, whose claim to autonomy is anchored in historical precedent and founded on necessity.[65]

As already mentioned, there is an active debate in legal studies on the existence of the Law Merchant. The account in favor of existence claims the Law Merchant was coherent; it was accepted across Europe; it was spontaneously created by merchants; its custom set the stage for domestic law; and it was commercial law.[66] The challengers argue the opposite: "The law merchant was not a systematic law; it was not standardized across Europe; it was not synonymous with commercial law; it was not merely a creation of merchants without vital input from governments and princes."[67] At stake in these debates is what it means for sovereign competence through public/private hybridity to manifest as sovereign authority: Was the Law Merchant law? Did it develop independent of governments?

The first challenge to the Law Merchant's existence is whether it should be seen as law. Those who oppose its existence "adopt, often implicitly, some version of the Austinian theory that marks law as a general command of the sovereign. Those who support it tend to take a different view of law, which looks at it as a set of immanent principles that is so powerful that all sovereigns feel obliged to adopt it."[68] Sovereign command is important because law is not only the ability to make rules but also to enforce them. Law Merchant skeptics argue that enforcement capacity only resides in public state authority.[69] Therefore, "norms of *lex mercatoria* are law only insofar as they cease to be elements of *lex mercatoria* and become part of the law of the state."[70] However, "proponents point out that *lex mercatoria* is not only law in every relevant sense but is even superior to national laws because of its transnational character."[71]

The second challenge is about merchant autonomy from public authority. Medieval merchants were not synonymous with traders more generally since they "either did business outside the jurisdiction of their native law or did business with other merchants who lived under different laws."[72] Given the lack of recourse to local law, merchants may have developed their own legal regimes in order to conduct business securely.[73] However, "the entire framework within which commerce took place very early depended upon – and often was restrained by – government authority."[74] Examples of government intervention in merchant courts and supra-local legislation suggest that "medieval merchants did participate in the operation of courts that dealt with mercantile matters, but they rarely, if ever, did it totally independently of local political

---

[65] Fassberg 2004: 67.
[66] Berman 1983; Trakman 1983; Basile et al. 1998; Sachs 2006.
[67] Kadens 2004: 40–41.
[68] Epstein 2004: 3.
[69] Sutherland 1934; Baker 1979.
[70] Michaels 2005: 1232–1233.
[71] Michaels 2005: 1220.
[72] Kadens 2004: 46.
[73] But see Volckart and Mangels 1999.
[74] Kadens 2004: 48.

power."[75] It may also be incorrect to assume that "governments got involved only after the law merchant had become a customary legal system. Governments were intertwined with commerce from the beginning of the commercial revolution of the high Middle Ages. Consequently, when nations began to write codes in the seventeenth century, they were not innovating, they were merely expanding on earlier practices."[76]

These arguments about the existence of the Law Merchant underscore that sovereign competence does not automatically translate into sovereign authority. Sovereign authority is legitimated through discourses of indivisible *Idealized Sovereignty* subject to varied interpretations. However, *Lived Sovereignty* rarely lives up to these ideals of an independent private from public. Thus, public/private hybridity presents a dilemma where the performance of sovereign power involves interdependent relations, even though the representation of sovereign authority privileges absolute autonomy. Moreover, hybridity is key to the vitality of the Law Merchant as an object of inquiry precisely because "no one can be confident whether it had a separate and autonomous existence."[77] The debate over its hybrid existence is not meant to be resolved.

This section argued that hybridity complicates the public/private relationship, creating a disjuncture between how power and authority is allocated in international politics. While sovereign power is performed through public/private hybrid relations in *Lived Sovereignty*, sovereign authority relies on legitimating indivisibly public notions of the state in *Idealized Sovereignty*. Ultimately, public/private hybridity is a battleground for multifaceted contests between *Idealized* and *Lived Sovereignty*. However, we are unable to see the contests or their outcomes without distinguishing forms of hybridity. I next overview the methodology of ideal-types and later develop three ideal-types of public/private hybridity.

THE LOGIC OF IDEAL-TYPES

Ideal-types are often used in IR, but rarely discussed as a method.[78] This section presents some core aspects of ideal-typification drawn from Weber and his interpreters. I engage at some length with sociologists who have explicitly advanced typological methods because my aim is to highlight what is distinct about ideal-types when analyzing social phenomena. To some readers, ideal-types may appear overly simplified to capture the richness of public/private hybridity conceptualized so far. Thus, before I introduce the ideal-types, I thought it necessary to lay out why I see the ideal-typification method as suitable for my claims. I bring up Weber again in the research design section of the chapter to promote a specific amalgamation of interpretive and empirical social science.

---

[75] Donahue 2004: 36.
[76] Kadens 2004: 56.
[77] Epstein 2004: 4.
[78] But see Jackson 2017.

Social theorist John McKinney's articulation of the typological method remains a classic. For McKinney, a constructed type is "a purposive, planned selection, abstraction, combination, and (sometimes) accentuation of a set of criteria with empirical referents that serves as a basis for comparison of empirical cases."[79] Types are constructed by analysts to capture some phenomena in the world. Democracy is a constructed type. It is a planned abstraction that accentuates some features of a political regime. Importantly, a constructed type is a "pragmatic expedient."[80] Abstractions do not reflect every nuance of reality. Instead, a constructed type's "value as a component of knowledge is not to be measured by the accuracy of its correspondence to perceptual experience (although some degree of correspondence is essential), but *in terms of its capacity to explain*."[81] In other words, whether or not the pure type of democracy actually exists in reality is beside the point for the typological method. For some types, "nothing but exceptions to the constructed types exist."[82] The mismatch is precisely the point: "It is scientifically advantageous and necessary to utilize theoretical constructs which are only approximated in the empirical world."[83] It is advantageous for social science analysis because the function of typological method is not to most accurately approximate the world. Thick description would do just fine for that. Instead, constructed types generate theory *from* which we analyze the world.

An ideal-type is a subset of the constructed type. It is standard to quote Weber at length on the definition:

> An ideal-type is formed by the one-sided *accentuation* of one or more points of view and by the synthesis of a great many diffuse, discrete, more or less present and occasionally absent *concrete individual* phenomena, which are arranged according to those one-sidedly emphasized viewpoints into a unified *analytical construct* (*Gedankenbild*). In its conceptual purity, this mental construct cannot be found empirically anywhere in reality. It is a *utopia*. Historical research faces the task of determining in which individual case, the extent to which this ideal-construct approximates to or diverges from reality.[84]

Three points stand out. First, Weberian ideal-types are purposively one-sided; they forgo some ideas in favor of others. As social constructs, ideal-types are artificially heightened abstractions. The goal is not to qualify the one-sidedness by overcomplicating the ideal-type. Instead, powerfully simple ideal-types embrace the heightened quality of being "like deliberate caricatures or partial sketches."[85] Second,

---

[79] McKinney 1966: 3, emphasis removed.
[80] McKinney 1966: 12.
[81] McKinney 1966: 11, emphasis original.
[82] McKinney 1966: 12.
[83] McKinney 1966: 17.
[84] Weber 1949: 90, emphasis original. Translations of Weber are contested, especially from Talcott Parsons. I rely on Shils and Finch's translation from *The Free Press* edition (1949).
[85] Jackson 2017: 82.

ideal-types are the purest distillation of an abstraction. Weber is clear that they "cannot be found empirically anywhere in reality." They are utopias disguised as concepts. Scholars of democracy can relate well to this insight. Third, the goal of social science research is to treat the ideal-type as a baseline against which reality is contextualized. It is a "purely ideal *limiting* concept with which the real situation or action is *compared* and surveyed for the explication of certain of its significant components."[86] The question is not "is there democracy?" but rather "how much of democracy is realized in particular societies?" or "what features of democracy are more realized than others across societies" or even "what is democracy, as a concept, doing for politics?"

Weber is clear on how *not* to use ideal-types for social science research. Ideal-types are neither hypotheses nor descriptions: "It *is* no 'hypothesis' but it offers guidance to the construction of hypotheses. It is not a *description* of reality but it aims to give unambiguous means of expression to such a description."[87] Instead, an ideal-type "recommends itself not as an end but as a *means*."[88] As such, ideal-types cannot be evaluated on the basis of "validity," especially when validity is conceived as ideal-types "accurately" corresponding to reality. Jackson quips that "it is quite literally nonsensical to speak of an ideal-type itself as being 'valid' or 'invalid,' because in the sphere of scholarly analysis these terms cannot be applied to analytical constructs – only to applications, and then only in a technical sense."[89] We cannot apply regular standards of validity to ideal-types because "an ideal-type is by definition 'falsified' if compared to the details and nuances of an actual empirical instance."[90] There is a reason for the "ideal" in ideal-type.

Moreover, Weber specifies that ideal-types are not meant as representative cases in social science research design. An ideal-type is "neither historical reality nor even the 'true' reality. It is even less fitted to serve as a schema under which a real situation or action is to be subsumed as one *instance*."[91] In other words, an ideal-type is not a case; cases are not ideal-types either (more on this in the research design section). As such, "the ideal-type and historical reality should not be confused with each other."[92] For Weber, cases, history, reality – however one characterizes the empirical world – are necessary for motivating the ideal-type, but the construction of ideal-types "reaches beneath and beyond it for the purposes of explanation."[93] Thus, an ideal-type is a theory whose purpose is not to be representative or "make clearly explicit . . . the class or average character but rather the unique individual character of cultural phenomena."[94] Indeed, applying ideal-types is "about isolating those

---

[86] Weber 1949: 93, emphasis original.
[87] Weber 1949: 90, emphasis original.
[88] Weber 1949: 92, emphasis original.
[89] Jackson 2017: 84.
[90] Jackson 2017: 87.
[91] Weber 1949: 93, emphasis original.
[92] Weber 1949: 107.
[93] Aronovitch 2012: 358.
[94] Weber 1949: 101.

portions of a case or event that do *not* correspond to the ideal-type and helping us appreciate their significance."[95]

This point is worth emphasizing as it forms much of the confusion behind conflating concepts, typologies, and ideal-types. Conventional typologies are treated as falsifiable concepts "intended to be replaced by more detailed pictures later on."[96] By contrast,

> the whole point of using ideal-types to analyze a specific and concrete case is to distinguish between adequately and contingently causal factors (and an implicit third category of incidental, non-causal, factors) by disciplining our counterfactual imaginations; it is this disciplined imagination that generates worldly knowing about what happened in a specific case and why it happened the way that it happened. Precisely what one does *not* do is to compare actual situations to the ideal-type and then reject the ideal-type as somehow misleading or false; the question is not whether the international system "is" or "is not" anarchic, but whether the notion of anarchy captures anything important about the dynamics of that system.[97]

Ideal-types rely on "disciplining our counterfactual imaginations" by serving as a highly stylized baseline. Good ideal-types allow researchers to posit essential characteristics of social phenomena and then access that construction for better explaining reality. The goal is not to use reality to better specify an ideal-type.

Thus, the ideal-typification method is best used for distilling the essence of meaningful relationships influencing social science phenomena. An example from Weber's most widely cited contribution to IR, the definition of the state, may be useful. In particular, the definition of a state as that which has a "(successful) monopoly on the legitimate use of violence within a given territory" is drawn from a speech Weber delivered in 1919, where the purpose was to talk about politics and politicians. The definition of the state appeared as an aside early in Weber's remarks. Yet, this aside is now the most influential way of conceiving the most fundamental unit of political analysis. The state as an ideal-type, however, is given far more rigidity by its adopters than by Weber himself. Here is how Weber conceptualizes the state when he discusses ideal-types:

> When we inquire as to what corresponds to the idea of the "state" in empirical reality, we find an infinity of diffuse and discrete human actions, both active and passive, factually and legally regulated relationships, partly unique and partly recurrent in character, all bound together by an idea, namely, the belief in the actual or normative validity of rules and of the authority-relationships of some human beings towards others. This belief is in part consciously, in part dimly felt, and in part passively accepted by persons who, should they think about the "idea" in

---

[95] Jackson 2017: 87, emphasis original.
[96] Jackson 2017: 86.
[97] Jackson 2017: 88.

a really clearly defined manner, would not first need a "general theory of the state" which aims to articulate the idea. *The scientific conception of the state, however it is formulated, is naturally always a synthesis which we construct for certain heuristic purposes.*[98]

There are many dynamics of a state with "an infinity of diffuse and discrete human actions." The state as a Weberian ideal-type is not meant to capture all of these actions or ideas. Instead, it is a synthesis that heuristically privileges some principles of authority, legitimacy, monopoly, violence, and territory over others. The ideal-type of a state, just like democracy, may not exist or have ever existed. But it allows us to organize relations of authority in a way that we cannot without the ideal-type.

Thus, ideal-types are successful based on their usefulness. For Weber, "social science in our sense is concerned with practical *significance*."[99] The significance or usefulness of an ideal-type can only be brought about "by relating the empirical data to an ideal limiting case."[100] To see whether an ideal-type is significant, researchers should demonstrate that "once applied, the ideal-type is efficacious in revealing intriguing and useful things about the objects to which it is applied."[101] In other words, an ideal-type is successful when it explains or shows us something about the world that was not possible without it. Relatedly, "the worth of an ideal-type has nothing whatsoever to do with how it was generated and whether it has any empirical generality to it."[102] It is irrelevant how Weber produced his ideal-type of charismatic authority or whether it may be broadly applied to all authority relations. What matters is whether charismatic authority helps us better understand some empirical phenomena that traditional authority or rational-legal authority miss.

From this discussion, I want to highlight the distinctiveness of the ideal-type method for the rest of the book. First, ideal-types are not evaluated based on their accurate descriptions of reality as being true/false. Instead, "the appropriate scholarly verdict is insightful/not insightful, or explanatorily useful/explanatorily useless *in this instance*."[103] Second, ideal-types are general but not generalizable. While in their abstraction ideal-types have a universal quality to them, this "*logically general* notion [should not be] confused with an *empirically general* claim."[104] Third, ideal-types are contingent on their maker. Weber foregrounds that analyses are imbued with cultural values. One may analyze authority relations and forgo charismatic authority altogether. This would not be more or less "accurate" than Weber's analysis, but it may be less useful, depending on the empirical context.

---

[98] Weber 1949: 99, emphasis added.
[99] Jackson 2017: 92.
[100] Weber 1949: 94, emphasis original.
[101] Jackson 2017: 83–84, emphasis original.
[102] Jackson 2017: 92.
[103] Jackson 2017: 88, emphasis original.
[104] Jackson 2017: 84.

IDEAL-TYPES OF PUBLIC/PRIVATE HYBRIDITY

I have argued so far that public/private hybridity makes possible sovereign competence in *Lived Sovereignty*. However, public/private hybridity also creates challenges for legitimating sovereign authority in *Idealized Sovereignty* that relies on drawing clearer public/private distinctions. Now, I develop three ideal-types to show that not all public/private hybridity is the same.

The differences in public/private hybridity boil down to managing relationship entanglements. Relationships may vary on any number of dimensions, including coercion, hierarchy, familiarity, and duration. I focus on two related dimensions: formalization and recognition. Formalization is a core feature of defining a relationship *as* a relationship. For instance, a couple who started dating may decide to "take the next step" and formalize their relationship as partners or spouses. In international politics, formalization may come in different guises such as partner, contractor, agent, or member, among others. Political relations may be formalized through contracts, treaties, agreements, or membership. If formalization acknowledges the relationship, then recognition communicates the acknowledgement to others. For instance, a couple might have formalized their relationships as partners or spouses but may not have publicly recognized this relationship, perhaps for privacy concerns like with celebrities or when the costs of disclosure are high, like in infidelity.

Considering both dimensions together, I vary the levels of formal recognition to develop three ideal-types of public/private hybridity: *contractual hybridity* (high formal recognition), *institutional hybridity* (medium formal recognition), and *shadow hybridity* (low formal recognition).[105] The ideal-types vary on four analytical characteristics, summarized in Table 2.1. First, the instruments of hybridity may be formal legal contracts, informal insider rules, or side bargains. Second, the medium of conducting negotiations in hybridity may occur through official exchanges, unofficial networks, or hidden back channels. Third, the power payoffs in *Lived Sovereignty* include leveraging strategic partnerships, acquiring shared expertise, and maintaining plausible deniability. Fourth, the legitimation challenges that threaten sovereign authority in *Idealized Sovereignty* are distributed accountability, elitist exclusion, and undermined trust. I will refer to these four characteristics in the empirical chapters to set expectations for the forms, dynamics, and implications of public/private hybridity.

There are two caveats in theorizing the ideal-types. First, drawing on the discussion from the previous section, I do not use the ideal-types to generate falsifiable hypotheses to then test in the cases, nor do I regard my cases as fully

---

[105] There are also possibilities of considering the dimensions separately, as in a traditional "2 x 2" typology, and mixing across levels of recognition and formalization. For instance, one type could be high recognition and low formalization, which would be akin to a celebrity sham relationship. However, as discussed in the previous section, rather than use a standard typology, I construct ideal-types that are purposively heightened abstractions to help understand the most meaningful social relationships.

TABLE 2.1 *Characteristics of ideal-types of public/private hybridity*

	Contractual	Institutional	Shadow
Instruments	Legal contracts	Insider rules	Side bargains
Interactions	Official exchange	Embedded networks	Hidden back channels
Power payoffs	Strategic partnership	Shared expertise	Plausible deniability
Legitimation challenges	Distributed accountability	Elitist exclusion	Undermined trust

representative of the ideal-types. Instead, I view the ideal-types of hybridity as producing useful observable markers to make sense of public/private contests in sovereign power politics. I am then interested in what the ideal-types reveal about the structuring of particular hybrid relations relative to each other. When public/private hybridity features legal contracts, it helps make sense of a particular set of advantages and challenges than when public/private hybridity features insider rules or side bargains. The ideal-types allow us to observe, for instance, how the East India Company started with *contractual hybridity*, and then cycled through *institutional* and *shadow hybridity*. The ideal-types also help make sense of new contests between EIC directors and the English Crown and Parliament as their relations changed over time. But I am not interested in advancing generalizable theories that state, for instance, the conditions under which *contractual hybridity* emerges or when *institutional hybridity* might morph into *shadow hybridity* or how actors will respond to different forms of hybridity. Per my interpretive stance, such generalizable statements cannot be meaningfully theorized out of the fluidity of public/private relations.

Empirical cases will also spill over their typological cells. For instance, governance structures often feature a combination of *contractual, institutional,* and *shadow hybridity*. The analytical goal is not to impose a rigid structure on messy realities. Instead, it is to see how well the ideal-types help clarify different kinds of relational configurations. Indeed, Jackson laments that "researchers often feel compelled to 'substantiate' or 'test' their logically general claims against empirical evidence instead of demonstrating the explanatory productivity of their models by simply *putting them to work*."[106] Thus, I follow the recent "practice turn" approach to analyzing social structures "by analyzing in some detail the processes through which some relations are mobilized and appropriated rather than others [so] that we can account for the particular configuration."[107]

The second caveat is how not to reify "public" and "private" in hybridity. As global governance scholars acknowledge, even studying public/private enmeshment is

---

[106] Jackson 2017: 84, emphasis original.
[107] Sending, Pouliot, Neumann 2015: 10.

"constantly reproducing established connotations of 'the public' simply by naming it as such."[108] It is not easy to break out of this reification trap. One way to address it in this book is to emphasize that my aim is to historicize that what *counts* as public and private changes over time and that some of these changes are inspired by dealing with hybridity. This is especially evident in the early modern period where the public/private distinction was not as settled as it is now assumed. As the East India Company chapter shows, at various moments over its 274 years, the EIC's status defied fixed attributions of "public" and "private." But in the late-1700s, the EIC's claims of self-possessed sovereignty generated a reckoning within English parliamentarians who responded by invoking *Idealized Sovereignty* to draw stronger demarcations between how they understood public and private when regulating the EIC. Yet, these seemingly bright lines too were smudged in the business of conducting empire in *Lived Sovereignty*. Entities exhibiting public/private hybridity thus display a range of publicness and privateness as a result of the interplay between *Idealized* and *Lived Sovereignty*.

On the one hand, we need a stable enough version of public/private to discern *how* they relate to each other across different configurations. On the other hand, any understanding of public/private is destabilized by the hybrid relations themselves. Ultimately, the ideal-types are relational, which makes them contingent on each other and their structures. What I refer to as public/private relations are in fact relations that are *made* that way. We cannot completely evade being trapped in the categories we uphold as stable. But as Wittgenstein reminds us, concepts are generated from attempts to talk about them, however inconsistently, as "the meaning of a word is its use in the language."[109] Acknowledging public/private hybridity is the first step to tracing the emergence of "public" and "private" as analytical concepts.

The ideal-types thus advance theories of sovereignty and global governance by examining the relations constituting distinct configurations of public/private hybridity in *Lived Sovereignty* and outlining the stakes of their variation for sovereign politics. Moreover, power relations are embedded in all forms of public/private hybridity, meaning there is no reason to privilege materially powerful actors or assume the centrality of "the state" in public/private contests, as claimed in the liberal internationalist literature.[110] I now offer some illustrations of the three ideal-types.

Contractual hybridity features formally recognized performances of sovereign power in public/private contracts. A variety of sovereign functions rely on public/private contracts, including manufacturing weapons, providing healthcare, and policing schools. In *contractual hybridity*, relations are mediated primarily through formal contracts with official exchanges for sovereign competence. For instance, from 2000 to 2016, there was a 442-percent increase in contracted facilities for

---

[108] Leander 2014: 215.
[109] Wittgenstein 2009 [1953]: 43. I thank Hendrik Spruyt for this point.
[110] Milner and Moravcsik 2009.

holding detainees for US Immigration and Custom Enforcement (ICE).[111] Seventy-two percent of all ICE detainees are in contracted facilities. The US government could not perform the sovereign function of managing its border without *contractual hybridity*. After the Trump administration's controversial family separation policies amounted to putting children in cages, activists went after contractors in order to get to the government: "ICE relies on private contractors to carry out its detention operations, so one way to abolish ICE might be to make its association so toxic that it loses its collaborators."[112] But *contractual hybridity* faces a legitimation challenge of distributed accountability because public and private are treated interchangeably in governing functions without symmetric obligations in law and politics. Contractors do not face the same financial disclosure or conflict of interest rules as government employees. After a series of scandals on poor conditions at ICE contracted facilities, immigrant rights groups claimed "there is basically no meaningful accountability or oversight for the companies who are involved."[113]

Another example of *contractual hybridity* in global governance is the Internet Corporation for Assigned Names and Numbers (ICANN), which administers globally unique domain names (e.g. cnn.com).[114] The Domain Name System (DNS) connects numerical Internet Protocol (IP) addresses to domain names so that users do not have to remember a string of numbers to access the web. ICANN was set up in 1998 through a contract with the US Department of Commerce's National Telecommunications and Information Administration (NTIA). The contract enabled the United States "to bypass the lengthy and difficult process of creating a new intergovernmental organization or of harmonizing territorial jurisdiction, instead creating a private corporation empowered to issue global contracts to address the governance problems."[115] Specifically, the United States and ICANN's hybridity was formalized initially with a Memorandum of Understanding, which later turned into a Joint Project Agreement.[116] ICANN maintains oversight over the Internet's "root zone file," a master list that "definitively tracks the list of names and IP addresses of all the authoritative servers for top-level domains (e.g. .com, .edu, .org, .uk)."[117] ICANN's hybridity has raised criticisms, including "insufficient civil society participation; insufficient government authority; too much government oversight; too much American authority; questions about legitimacy; and long-standing and still ongoing concerns about its contractual relationship with the US government."[118] More broadly, states have used ICANN as an illustration to "insist on a distinction between 'public policy' and 'technical management,' reserving to

[111] Gotsch and Basti 2019.
[112] Dayen 2018.
[113] Noguchi 2019.
[114] Raymond and DeNardis 2015: 594.
[115] Mueller 2009: 185.
[116] Mueller 2009: 186.
[117] Raymond and DeNardis 2015: 595–596.
[118] Raymond and DeNardis 2015: 596.

states the former and consigning ICANN and private sector actors to the latter."[119] In response to the criticisms, in 2016 the United States surrendered oversight over ICANN to allow a genuine multistakeholder process.

Institutional hybridity features relatively less formally recognized performances of sovereign power embedded in public/private institutional linkages. Many sovereign functions operate through institutional networks, including setting trade terms, increasing defense spending, or regulating carbon emissions. In *institutional hybridity*, relations are mediated primarily through insider rules and privileges gained through embedded networks. For instance, Wall Street banks develop complex financial instruments like mortgage-backed securities (MBS) that form the backbone of credit for the American economy. The regulation of these products is largely a result of special rules that emerge from the institutional network of Wall Street with current and former regulators.[120] *Institutional hybridity* faces a legitimation challenge of exclusion because public/private hybridity is implicated in elite networks that advantage members at the expense of nonmembers. The Occupy Wall Street social movement rose out of frustration from the lack of individual (or corporate) accountability for the bankers who contributed to the 2007–8 global financial crisis by selling risky MBS. The protestors framed the issue as a crisis in sovereign legitimacy as big banks had been so deeply integrated into the US economy with insider rules that the government had no choice but to bail them out at favorable terms to the banks (unlike consumer protections for individual bankruptcy or the absence of student loan debt forgiveness).[121]

Institutional hybridity is also prevalent in the Bill and Melinda Gates Foundation, the world's largest foundation with an endowment of almost $50 billion. The Gates Foundation donates more than any other country to global health and has worked with UN agencies, including the World Health Organization, where it is the second largest funder after the United States.[122] The Foundation's resources have given it privileged access for agenda-setting and development of insider rules. Foundation staff consult with UN decision-making bodies: "Three of top-level secondments to the WHO have currently Gates Foundation connections."[123] Advocates have "focused on the invitation of Bill Gates and Melinda Gates as speakers at the World Health Assembly as a lightning rod" as well as questioned "the accountability of the organization to member states versus an unelected private actor."[124] One controversial area of agenda-setting has been vaccines, in which the Gates Foundation has long been involved by giving $750 million to set up the Global Alliance for Vaccines and Immunization (GAVI). In the race for a COVID-19

[119] Mueller 2009: 188.
[120] Lockwood 2020.
[121] Taylor 2011.
[122] Seitz and Martens 2017: 47–48.
[123] Seitz and Martens 2017: 49.
[124] Andonova 2017: 177.

vaccine in 2020, it emerged that the Gates Foundation discouraged Oxford University researchers from donating the rights to their vaccine to manufacturers to make the vaccine available for free or at low cost. Instead, Oxford sold exclusive rights to AstraZeneca.[125] Meanwhile, as of August 2021, the vaccination rate in Africa hovered at less than 6 percent compared to 90 percent in Europe.[126] The Gates Foundation is a board member not only of Gavi, but also of the Global Fund, the Partnership for Maternal, Newborn and Child Health, the Medicines for Malaria Venture, the Roll Back Malaria Partnership, the TB Alliance, the Stop TB Partnership, and many others. In the US domestic context, Gates Foundation was also behind pushing the adoption of the Common Core State Standards for K-12 education beginning in 2008 by funding and connecting think tanks, educators, associations of state officials, among other groups. Two years later, forty-five states adopted the Common Core "before the standards were even fully developed."[127] Critics derided: the idea that "the richest man in America can purchase and – working closely with the U.S. Department of Education – impose new and untested academic standards on the nation's public schools is a national scandal."[128]

Shadow hybridity features the least formally recognized performances of sovereign power in public/private shadowy bargains. Sovereign functions related to gathering intelligence, financing elections, procuring weapons, and investigating crime often operate in secrecy. In *shadow hybridity*, public/private relations are mediated primarily through side bargains in back channels that are hidden from public view. The 2019 Mueller Report on Russian interference in the 2016 US election found that a nonstate organization, the Internet Research Agency (IRA), waged a digital disinformation campaign that favored Donald Trump and disparaged Hillary Clinton.[129] It also alleged that the Russian military intelligence agency hacked into the Democratic National Committee's servers to obtain emails between Clinton and her campaign staff. The Russians handed over the emails to WikiLeaks, an NGO, which released the material. *Shadow hybridity* faces a legitimation challenge of mistrust because public/private hybridity works through behind-the-scenes deals that may undermine the public's confidence in authorities. The Mueller Report found over 100 undisclosed contacts between the Trump campaign and Russian nationals, intermediaries, or WikiLeaks. The shadow relations between the IRA, WikiLeaks, and the Trump Campaign were hidden to protect plausible deniability in service of obtaining a sovereign title. In response to the Mueller report, Trump was impeached in 2020.

---

[125] Hancock 2020.
[126] *New York Times* 2021.
[127] Callahan 2017: 161.
[128] Callahan 2017: 165.
[129] US Department of Justice 2019.

Credit rating agencies such as Moody's and Standard & Poor's (S&P) also engage in relations of *shadow hybridity*. The agencies rate around "$30 trillion worth of securities each year," ranging from best (AAA) to worst (D, for default), which "affect the interest rate or cost of borrowing for businesses, municipalities, national governments, and ultimately, individual citizens and consumers."[130] Rating agencies are "some of the most obscure institutions in the world of global finance" and boast about their ability to obtain information confidentially.[131] After rating a corporate security or a government bond, agencies continue monitoring to give future updates, including formal downgrades or informal warnings. When rating sovereign debt, the agencies maintain contacts with government officials in both the initial rating and later monitoring phases. Agencies evaluate not just the financial ability of a government, but also conduct a political analysis of its *willingness* to pay, which requires accessing a wide variety of information through backdoor contacts. When downgrading sovereign ratings, especially of countries in the Global North, agencies face potential backlash from government officials, including a withdrawal of informal access. This was the case in the late-1980s when Moody's downgraded Australia twice and the government "banned contact with Moody's officials."[132] The breakdown of shadow understandings can also spill over to public spats. When the United States was downgraded by S&P in 2011, the Treasury Secretary blasted the agency for "terrible judgement."[133] However, the agencies are also criticized for not downgrading fast enough, for instance in the case of Greek bonds that resulted in the 2010 Eurozone debt crisis.[134] In this way, "states seem to exist uneasily with rating agencies. ... The agencies helpfully offer states a vehicle through which parts of society, such as capital allocation, can be separated off as 'not political.' But they also discipline states by conducting surveillance and sending signals about policy and performance to internationally mobile capital."[135]

Of course, we can observe all three ideal-types operating in the same political structures. In summer 2010, the *Washington Post* launched a four-part series, "Top Secret America," based on a two-year investigation into the US landscape of "top secret" activities involving 1,271 government organizations and 1,931 companies in counterterrorism, homeland security, and intelligence.[136] The headline for the opening article stated: "A Hidden World, Growing Beyond Control." Of the 854,000 people with top-secret clearances, the *Post* estimated that 265,000 were contractors, arguing that "firms have become so thoroughly entwined with the

[130] Sinclair 2005: 4.
[131] Sinclair 2005: 6, 31.
[132] Sinclair 2005: 140.
[133] BBC 2011.
[134] Mallard and Pénet 2013.
[135] Sinclair 2005: 148.
[136] Priest and Arkin 2010a; Leander 2014.

government's most sensitive activities that without them important military and intelligence missions would have to cease or would be jeopardized."[137] Reflecting *contractual hybridity* of formal and relatively publicly acknowledged relations, the National Security Agency "hires private firms to come up with most of its technological innovations" for "worldwide electronic surveillance," working with at least 484 firms.[138] Three years after the *Post's* investigation, one such NSA contractor, Edward Snowden, would instigate the largest privacy scandal in recent years. Contractors at the CIA headquarters "analyze terrorist networks. At the agency's training facility in Virginia, they are helping mold a new generation of American spies."[139] Other public/private relations resemble *institutional hybridity*'s use of insider networks, such as the revolving door of recruitment, where firms "offer more money – often twice as much – to experienced federal employees than the government is allowed to pay them."[140] Companies also sponsor events for the "intelligence community," such as renting out baseball stadiums, hosting Margaritaville parties, or attending casino nights: "These gatherings happen every week. Many of them are closed to anyone without a top-secret clearance."[141] Finally, *shadow hybridity* underlies the whole operation as even top government officials are unable to fully grasp all the relations at play, claiming only God has such visibility.[142] In Leander's assessment of Top Secret America, the elusiveness of the public/private hybrid apparatus is key: "While they are seen and sensed, they slide out of view."[143]

This section developed the three ideal-types of public/private hybridity by introducing their distinguishing characteristics and illustrating how we would know when we see their relational dynamics in practice. The rest of the book delves into showing the usefulness of the ideal-types in a Weberian-inspired research design.

RESEARCH DESIGN

I put the ideal-types of public/private hybridity to use in a "world-building" research design attentive to the "softness and historical boundedness" of politics.[144] I end this chapter by highlighting my take on a Weberian methodology of social sciences for IR, which is critical for introducing a novel phenomenon in world politics, along with my data and empirical selection strategies.

[137]   Priest and Arkin 2010b.
[138]   Priest and Arkin 2010b.
[139]   Priest and Arkin 2010b.
[140]   Priest and Arkin 2010b.
[141]   Priest and Arkin 2010b.
[142]   Priest and Arkin 2010a.
[143]   Leander 2014: 206.
[144]   Almond and Genco 1977: 494.

Methodology

This book makes claims about how to interpret a set of phenomena and understand its significance.[145] I take seriously that the definitions we use in the first page of our research – for instance, by answering "what is this a case of?" – has consequences for how we analyze politics in the rest of the pages. Public/private hybridity transforms IR's foundations of unitary states. An interpretive methodology allows me to recast important aspects of international politics that are conceived as nonsovereign and a threat to sovereignty to be more usefully classified as public/private hybridity that are constitutive of sovereignty. More specifically, I adopt Weberian interpretivism, which is a dual commitment to empirically studying the specificity of the world in "understanding the characteristic uniqueness of the reality in which we move,"[146] while being reflexive enough to acknowledge that "we cannot learn the *meaning* of the world from the results of its analysis, be it ever so perfect."[147] Weber at one point refers to this as "an empirical science of concrete reality (*Wirklichkeitswissenschaft*)," as the aim is "to understand on the one hand the relationships and the cultural significance of individual events in their contemporary manifestations and on the other the causes of their being historically *so* and not *otherwise*."[148] A Weberian empirical science of concrete reality reclaims all aspects of "empirical," "science," and "reality" sometimes denied to interpretive analyses.

Weberian interpretivism acknowledges the limitations of monocausal inference, especially from observational analysis: "The number and type of causes which have influenced any given event are always infinite and there is nothing in the things themselves to set some of them apart as alone meriting attention. A chaos of 'existential judgments' about countless individual events would be the only result of a serious attempt to analyze reality 'without presuppositions.'"[149] To be clear, Weber's investigations have causal force, like when he argues the protestant ethic really did produce Western capitalism.[150] A Weberian research design, in short, combines empirical examinations on the specificity of concrete reality with an interpretive spirit of imputing meaning through ideal-typification. Weber outlined four steps on how to achieve this:

1. Determination of (hypothetical) "laws" and "factors" [or ideal-types];
2. Analysis of the historically given individual configuration of those "factors" and their *significant* concrete interaction, conditioned by their historical context, and especially the *rendering intelligible* of the basis and type of this significance;

---

[145] Yanow and Schwartz-Shea 2006; Lynch 2014; Barkin and Sjoberg 2017.
[146] Weber 1949: 72, emphasis original.
[147] Weber 1949: 57, emphasis original.
[148] Weber 1949: 72, emphasis original.
[149] Weber 1949: 78.
[150] Weber 1930.

3. Tracing as far into the past as possible of the individual features of these historically evolved configurations that are *contemporaneously* significant, and their historical explanation by antecedent and equally individual configurations;
4. Prediction of possible future constellations.[151]

This book follows these four steps. First, I develop the ideal-types of public/private hybridity in three analytical constructs of *contractual, institutional,* and *shadow hybridity,* theorized in the previous section. Second, I present detailed and system-atic analyses of concrete realities in imperial companies, interest groups, INGOs, corporations, and governments to see how the ideal-types render public/private hybrid relationships more intelligible. (I say more about my case selection and comparative strategy in the following section.) Third, I trace the ideal-types as far back as possible to see how they emerged and evolved in an early adopter and also historicize the emergence of public/private hybridity in the more contemporary cases. Finally, in the conclusion I predict, or at least ponder, the future of public/private hybridity and its consequences of power and responsibility in world politics.

This book's research design aligns with my central argument that sovereign power is produced through public/private hybridity. As a result, I do not begin with states but examine their relations with nonstate actors. I also do not overcorrect to study independent private sovereigns. Instead, I examine the phenomena appearing at first to be about private power, but are really about relations of public/private hybridity in *Lived Sovereignty.* The empirical strategy shows that what we take for granted as sovereign is in fact variable. However, this malleability comes at a cost as the tools of sovereign legitimacy are informed by the ideational structures of *Idealized Sovereignty.*

Cases

I use the empirical investigations to put the ideal-types to work in different contexts across time that show public/private hybridity in building empires, waging wars, regulating commerce, and protecting rights. As previously stated, my scope condi-tion is studying formally recognized (ostensibly) nonstate entities, which include firms, INGOs, organized criminal groups, and religious organizations, among others. The private authority literature has established this scope in studies that survey different kinds of corporate[152] and noncorporate forms[153] in international politics.

The English East India Company, Blackwater, International Chamber of Commerce, and Amnesty International are the anchors for analyzing the variations underlying public/private hybridity in *Lived Sovereignty.* In a standard design, the

[151]   Weber 1949: 75–76, emphasis original.
[152]   Cutler, Haufler, and Porter 1999.
[153]   Hall and Biersteker 2002.

four organizations might be considered building-block cases illustrating the typology and may also be regarded as too different to be meaningfully comparable.[154] However, my comparative strategy is not to hold constant one aspect across the cases, be it one type of public/private hybridity or substantive focus. A more conventional research design might evaluate different types of public/private hybridity exclusively in one substantive realm, for instance security, or examine one type of public/private hybridity, say *contractual*, across different realms in security, economy, and rights. Instead, I apply the three ideal-types to different substantive areas across times, places, and contexts. This is critical in a Weberian design that *puts the ideal-types to use*, especially in limiting cases, to judge their significance for concrete realities. Expanding the diversity of examined contexts helps reflect the usefulness of the ideal-types to the political world. Moreover, the design purposely includes an INGO to demonstrate that sovereign competence is not limited to materially powerful entities like corporations.

The case selection thus mirrors the core analytical wager of this book by inquiring: Where are the archives of sovereign power? It answers by selecting organizational archives rather than governmental archives. If we look for sovereign power exclusively in governmental records, it is of little surprise we find evidence of sovereign power in governments. Indeed, "one impoverishes the question of power if one poses it solely in terms of legislation and constitution, in terms solely of the state and the state apparatus."[155] The book thus makes use of original primary data drawn from organizational archives, particularly relying on minutes of high-level meetings and correspondence where public/private hybrid relations in *Lived Sovereignty* are likely deliberated.[156]

The English East India Company had control over a greater land size and population than Great Britain's by the nineteenth century. In India, the Company established forts and trading posts, created local currency, organized land and naval forces, collected taxes, and produced laws, all through trades in spices, textiles, and opium. Historian Philip Stern proclaimed it a "company-state modulating between positions of merchant and sovereign."[157] In IR, Andrew Phillips and Jason Sharman identify it as a "company sovereign" like other "hybrid private entities seeking profit that nevertheless also enjoyed vital sovereign prerogatives" while serving as one of the most "important non-state agents of European expansion."[158] These recent works recognize the Company's hybridity as important for sovereign competence but do

[154] George and Bennett 2005.
[155] Foucault 1980: 158.
[156] The English East India Company: India Office Records at the British Library, London; The International Chamber of Commerce: Bibliothèque National de France and the International Chamber of Commerce Documentation Center, both in Paris; and Amnesty International: The International Institute of Social History, Amsterdam.
[157] Stern 2011: 13.
[158] Phillips and Sharman 2015: 102; Phillips 2016: 39–48.

not inquire into how its hybrid forms changed over time or the consequences of such changes for sovereignty.

I use the East India Company for inductively tracing all three ideal-types of public/private hybridity.[159] I collected minutes for all its 14,400 top managerial and shareholder meetings between 1678 and 1780 (a critical century after its incorporation and before the British colonial apparatus went into high gear), reports from its field operators, parliamentary petitions, correspondence, charters, and materials from trials. In these data, the Company exhibits *contractual hybridity* in formal and frequent charter negotiations with Crown and Parliament, *institutional hybridity* in more use of political networks and fewer charter negotiations, and *shadow hybridity* in behind-the-scenes trades and infrequent charter negotiations. Navigating these hybrid forms undergird the micro-foundations of the Company's rapid growth and demise, allowing it to pursue global domination on an unprecedented scale. I also use its internal deliberations with rival powers and legal cases to highlight the transformation in the Company's self-understanding of sovereign authority shifting from a privilege, more in line with *Idealized Sovereignty*, to a self-possessed right acquired through *Lived Sovereignty*.

Blackwater had $1 million in US federal contracts in 2000. By 2007 it had more than a billion dollars and held 83 percent of the State Department's diplomatic security contracts in Iraq. The growth halted when fallout from the Nisour Square massacre forced a name change to Xe in 2009 before being sold off to form a new company, Academi, in 2010.[160] While Blackwater itself is no longer operational, Academi's contractors are involved in ongoing conflicts, including in Syria and Yemen. Academi also retains former Attorney General John Ashcroft on its Board of Directors. Meanwhile, Blackwater's founder, billionaire Erik Prince, is currently the chairman of Frontier Services Group with security training contracts in the UAE and China.[161] He remains a key figure in American politics. His sister, Betsy DeVos, was the Secretary of Education in the Trump administration. In 2017, the White House asked Prince to prepare an Afghanistan military strategy. In response, he argued for deploying more contractors and installing a viceroy like the East India Company did centuries earlier.[162]

I use Blackwater to show off the analytical usefulness of *contractual hybridity*. Blackwater is often studied in war privatization, even though it is not representative of the modal security contractor (i.e. large and providing life support) as it was relatively small and had potential for combat in diplomatic protection. However, Blackwater stands in for all war contractors in the public imagination, becoming "like Kleenex," such that "in Iraq or Yemen, they don't use the word contractors, they use Blackwater."[163] I draw on 3,462 news articles on Blackwater between 2000

---

[159]   Eckstein 1975.
[160]   In 2014, Academi merged with Triple Canopy under Constellis Holdings.
[161]   Hasan 2019.
[162]   Prince 2017.
[163]   Hasan 2019.

and 2016, Congressional hearings and reports, and legal briefs from Blackwater's criminal and civil cases in US courts through the WestLaw database. The data highlight how integral Blackwater became to the American sovereign performance in warfare in *Lived Sovereignty*. The wars in Iraq and Afghanistan are made possible because of *contractual hybridity* through official contracts between firms like Blackwater and the US government. Moreover, I follow the legitimation challenge of Blackwater's distributed accountability for conducting international violence and the ensuing bureaucratic redefinitions of "inherently governmental functions."

The International Chamber of Commerce (ICC) was founded in the aftermath of World War I in Paris to continue Allied economic cooperation from the war. More than a hundred years old, the ICC is acknowledged as the largest and most effective global business organization.[164] It lobbies governments and international organizations and provides services to members like chambers of commerce and corporations. The ICC has written some of the most widely adopted international commercial standards, including the Uniform Customs and Practices for Documentary Credits (UCP) and the International Commercial Terms for global commercial shipping (INCOTERMS), which together facilitate more than two trillion dollars of global trade annually. It is also home to the International Court of Arbitration and the International Maritime Arbitration.

I use the International Chamber of Commerce to show off the analytical usefulness of *institutional hybridity*. The ICC is well studied in international law, especially for its arbitration. But it has received scant attention in IR. I draw on minutes from its top executives' meetings between 1919 and 1973 (last available year), minutes and speeches from the annual meetings of its international congress, and all ICC news mentions in *The Financial Times* from 1981 to 2019. In *Lived Sovereignty*, the global governance of interconnected markets is made possible through the *institutional hybridity* of the ICC's issue definition and agenda-setting prowess at intergovernmental forums and through promoting corporate "self-regulation" and making a robust arbitration regime. The ICC reveals the legitimation challenge of exclusionary regulation of international trade that privileges corporate interests at the expense of labor and civil society.

Finally, Amnesty International, founded by British lawyer Peter Benenson, is regarded as the world's leading international NGO because of its longevity and capacity to shape the global human rights agenda.[165] Benenson published an article on "The Forgotten Prisoners" to expose the conditions of political prisoners in the pages of *The Observer* in 1961. The public response led to a broader "Appeal for Amnesty." Within a year, Amnesty International was formed. Amnesty was one of the first human rights organizations to produce regular field reports from repressive countries by visiting prisons, observing trials, and working with local activists. The

---

[164] Kelly 2005.
[165] Stroup and Wong 2017.

reports mobilized Western audiences to "adopt" prisoners of conscience and rally for their release. Amnesty won the Nobel Peace Prize in 1977 for its landmark Campaign against Torture and also helped pass the 1984 UN Convention against Torture. Until 2001, Amnesty's operational mandate remained narrowly focused on political rights. Recent efforts focus on a broader move to include economic, social, and cultural rights.

I use Amnesty International to show off the analytical usefulness of *shadow hybridity*. I follow philosopher John Dewey when arguing that Amnesty's sovereign competence was building a global polity for realizing human rights ideals in the postwar period. I draw on minutes from its top executive committee meetings between 1961 and 1986 (last available year), oral history interviews, correspondence, reports from its field researchers, and all news mentions in *The New York Times* from 1961 to 1980. Amnesty relied on projecting a moral purity based on impartiality and independence from governments. However, the data show that international human rights were made possible from Amnesty's *shadow hybridity* with governments through back channels for funding and country access in its first two decades. Amnesty's side bargains raise the legitimation challenge of mistrust related to guaranteeing human rights transnationally. Moreover, Amnesty shows that even those with a stated mandate to promote sovereign responsibility can fall prey to the hybrid dynamics of producing sovereign power.

The four cases are conceived typically as "sovereignty challengers," where their private actions diminish public sovereign power. In contrast, I demonstrate they are cases of public/private hybridity producing sovereign power in the world, but without sovereign authority. The English East India Company gave birth to the most powerful global empire. Blackwater supported the most powerful military. The International Chamber of Commerce organizes the most powerful capital. Amnesty International protects the most powerful rights. As discussed in Chapter 1, sovereign functions have broadly emerged in the domains of violence, markets, and rights. In selecting these cases, I intend to cover the wide variety of sovereign experience without treating the cases as standing-in for *all* experiences of public/private hybridity in these domains. Moreover, these specific cases do not all implicate their entire organizational forms. INGOs like Amnesty also engage in *contractual* and *institutional* hybridity and businesses like Blackwater or associations like the ICC also engage in *shadow hybridity*. Finally, while the cases are typically depicted as independent transnational private authorities, I show they are not simply transnational private actors acting as sovereigns or possessing sovereignty, conventionally understood. Instead, the empirics reveal that sovereign power is produced through collective efforts across the public/private boundary, which call into question previously accepted ideas about *Idealized Sovereignty*. In this way, *Lived Sovereignty* and *Idealized Sovereignty* coevolve with each other. Indeed, as the previous chapter highlighted, Amnesty's expansion of the sovereign compact underscores that lived experiences inform how sovereignty is idealized over time, including in the last century.

CONCLUSION

If Chapter 1 was the theoretical core of this book in promoting a new framework on hybrid sovereignty, this chapter is the analytical heart of the book. I developed the dynamics of public/private hybridity in *Lived Sovereignty* by situating it in the global governance literature, introduced three ideal-types of public/private hybridity, and outlined a Weberian-inspired research design to show off the ideal-types in the rest of the chapters that follow. This chapter serves to inform the reader's expectations on how to interpret the claims of this book. The payoff is to take seriously the social construction of public/private hybridity as an analytical phenomenon in world politics that deserves its own mode of political study. I have tried to be explicit about the aims, assumptions, and framework that ground this study. It is time now to put the theories and analytical constructs in the preceding chapters to work.

3

Hybrid Sovereign Empire in the English East India Company

> Since the reign of Aurungzeb, their [Hindu] empire has been dissolved, their treasures of Delhi have been rifled by a Persian robber, and the richest of their kingdoms is now possessed by a company of Christian merchants, of a remote island in the Northern ocean.[1]

The beginning of the seventeenth century offered a unique opportunity for an experiment in transnational ordering. The Spanish and Portuguese had thus far monopolized trade in the "East Indies," consisting of spices and textiles for the European market. However, a sharp decline in Portuguese dominance set off a race to take over their market share. The Dutch, with deep financial pockets and advanced naval technology, were poised to assume this position. The English, who stalled in efforts during the preceding century, had to try something new in order to compete. The result after much negotiation between Queen Elizabeth I and London merchants was the establishment of the English East India Company (hereby "the Company" or EIC) by royal charter on December 31, 1600. Initially, the Company was financed one voyage at a time without any stable stockholders. However, after figuring out sea routes and establishing local contacts in the Indies, the Company negotiated steady financing by the mid-1650s. The Company then experienced rapid growth as its trade volume, number of ships, and access to ports grew exponentially.[2] The English market share of all Asian trade went from nonexistent in 1590 to a quarter by 1650, a third by 1780, and two-thirds by 1820.[3]

By the nineteenth century, the Company ruled one-fifth of the world using a larger military than Great Britain's. In 1788, philosopher and parliamentarian Edmund Burke famously referred to the Company as "a state in the disguise of a merchant."[4] Moreover, as the epigraph states, the Company pilfered massive

---

[1] Gibbon 1996 [1856]: 853, as quoted in Milanovic 2016: 243, en14.
[2] Chaudhuri 1978: 82.
[3] Bogart 2017b: 5. As measured by shipping tonnage.
[4] Stern 2011: 3.

wealth from the Indian kingdoms: "There are more Mughal artefacts stacked in a private house in the Welsh countryside [Powis Castle] than are on display in any one place in India – even the National Museum in Delhi."[5] The Company's economic presence was unmatched: "Every seventh pound of goods brought into Britain would be carried on Company ships, unloaded at Company docks and sold in Company auctions."[6] The Company's profits and loot reversed capital flows from the West to the East, making possible the Industrial Revolution.[7] Meanwhile, the Company's influence on English society was immense, as it seemed "almost everyone in eighteenth- and nineteenth-century England was connected" to it.[8]

In Asia, the Company established forts and trading posts, organized land and naval forces, minted currency, collected taxes, and administered justice, all through a trade in spices, textiles, and opium. Yet most scholars of global politics do not consider the Company as sovereign, nor is it included as a major player in analyses of international politics of that time (with Phillips and Sharman as one rare exception). The Company not only occupies two and a half centuries of international history, much longer than most states today, but it also flourished during the immediate post-Westphalian period, precisely when we should have seen it disappear.[9] This treatment is symptomatic of a broader bias where sovereignty is idealized as indivisible public authority, covered in the previous chapters. However, if IR scholars existed in the time of the Company, we would treat it like contemporary China with an unparalleled obsession over categorizing it and debating whether or not the Company was a great power and how to fit its authority within conventional notions of sovereignty. Indeed, "a peculiar amnesia continues to hang over the role that corporations such as the East India Company had in the creation of the modern world."[10] Moreover, the Company sheds light on the origins of sovereign power politics, helping fill a post-Westphalian gap in international history.[11]

Recent interest in European charter companies excavates some of the Company's sovereign influence. In IR, Andrew Phillips and Jason Sharman identify "company sovereigns" as "hybrid private entities seeking profit that nevertheless also enjoyed vital sovereign prerogatives" while serving as one of the most "important non-state agents of European expansion."[12] The Company as a "corporate thalassocracy" was "neither just an instrument of the English state nor a state itself."[13] Historian Philip Stern argues that the EIC as a "Company-State," was "possessed of political institutions and underscored by coherent principles about the nature of obligations of

---

[5] Dalrymple 2019: 1.
[6] Robins 2006: 29.
[7] Erikson 2014: 32–34, 173.
[8] Robins 2006: 9.
[9] Spruyt 1994; Thomson 1994.
[10] Robins 2006: xii.
[11] Buzan and Lawson 2015; Sharman 2019.
[12] Phillips and Sharman 2015: 102; Phillips 2016: 39–48. On the Dutch VOC, see Blachford 2020.
[13] Phillips and Sharman 2015: 113.

subjects and rulers, good government, political economy, jurisdiction, authority, and sovereignty."[14] For Lauren Benton, the EIC emerged during a time when "composite forms of state, empire, and sovereignty were central to the constitution of political power."[15] One-way travel between Europe and Asia took five months on average. In the Indian Ocean, sovereign prerogatives were delegated to a variety of actors such as "ship captains, leaders of reconnaissance voyages, trading companies, municipalities, colonial governors or viceroys, and garrison commanders."[16] The resulting orders were "multicentric" and the "layered systems of law and sovereignty [did not] correspond to neat hierarchies of authority."[17]

My research is inspired by this literature to study the EIC's transformation into a corporate empire as one of the earliest forms of public/private hybridity in world politics. Hybridity was baked into the Company's founding since it could not exist without "a special privilege granted by the Crown (and later Parliament)."[18] However, the Company also became important as a hybrid source for Britain's sovereign power through its imperial extractions. In this chapter, I advance the scholarship in two ways. First, I conduct a systematic inquiry into the Company's hybridity and the variation in forms and dynamics of sovereign power. I ask: Did the Company exhibit the same form of hybrid relations in *Lived Sovereignty* over its tenure? If not, how can we tell? Second, I examine how the Company's sovereign competence impacted English sovereignty. Between 1500 and 1800, mutually inclusive delegated authority from state sovereigns to other actors was not obviously hierarchical such that states would retain "ultimate authority" (variously defined).[19] Instead, sovereignty was "widely understood as a work in progress."[20] But after 1800, the international system shifted to "an ever more restrictive one in which prerogatives of government were presumed to lie exclusively with sovereign states."[21] I trace how the EIC's public/private hybridity had a role to play in this late modern shift as the Company's *Lived Sovereignty* clashed with English *Idealized Sovereignty*.

This chapter uses extensive archival data to construct a hundred-year political history of the Company. The research focuses on the EIC as it began with more arms-length state relations than its main counterpart, the Dutch VOC.[22] After 1600, the EIC incorporated (1657), merged with a rival (1709), conquered Bengal (1757), began taxing ten million Bengalis, double England's population[23] (1765), entered a financial crisis (1770), was bailed out by Parliament with increased oversight (1773)

[14] Stern 2011: 13; Erikson 2014.
[15] Stern 2008: 260.
[16] Benton 2009: 31.
[17] Benton 2009: 32, fn89.
[18] Robins 2006: 27.
[19] Costa Lopez et al. 2018.
[20] Benton 2009: 38.
[21] Phillips and Sharman 2020: 212.
[22] Erikson 2014: 76; Sharman 2019: 178.
[23] Phillips and Sharman 2015: 173.

that became stricter (1784), ceased to trade and became a territorial administrator (1833), relinquished India's administration to the British government (1858), and was dissolved (1874). The period between incorporation in the late-1600s and regulatory scrutiny in late-1700s is pivotal for both the EIC's emergence as a company-state and the delegitimization of nonstate actors from the international system.[24] The Company had no singular chief executive. Instead, its twenty-four directors met thrice a week to run the organization and shareholders held quarterly meetings. The research draws on all 14,400 EIC managerial and shareholder meetings between 1678 and 1780. This unprecedented data collection was made possible by materials recently being allowed to be photographed in the British Library.[25] In addition to minutes, the data feature drafts of correspondence and petitions, along with summary statistics on finances and operations. Rather than observe sovereignty by locating the term itself in the EIC records, an inductive analysis reveals that the Company's invocation of sovereignty appeared primarily through the language of "rights."[26] This conceptualization of early sovereignty fits the juridical view at the time, referenced in Chapter 1.

The data show two key transformations. First, the Company did not hold the same form of public/private hybridity over its tenure. It began with *contractual hybridity*, which involved formal and frequent contract negotiations with the Crown and Parliament, moved into *institutional hybridity* by embedding in political networks, and slithered into *shadow hybridity* through behind-the-scenes side bargains. I mobilize new data sources and reinterpret older ones to depict the EIC's distinct practices in each ideal-type. Cycling through the ideal-types allowed the Company to grow its sovereign competence in *Lived Sovereignty*. The upshot of systematically studying a pivotal century in the EIC's hybridity through the archival material is that it allows substantial rich, longitudinal data from which to inductively derive the ideal-types introduced in the previous chapter. In this chapter, I focus on identifying the observable indicators and instruments proposed in Table 2.1. In the next three empirical chapters, I dive deeper into each ideal-type separately to analyze their unique power payoffs and legitimation challenges.

Second, the Company's self-understanding of its sovereign authority shifted from a privilege to a right. The Company initially derived its sovereign authority within *Idealized Sovereignty* as a privilege granted by the Crown and Parliament. However, over the course of the century, the Company began claiming a self-possessed right based on its sovereign competence within *Lived Sovereignty*. The Company's sovereign awakening redefined the EIC's challenge to the English state. Existing literature posits that Company misrule led to more demarcations of public and private such that by the 1800s company-states were no longer "indispensable substitutes for

---

[24] Spruyt 1994; Thomson 1994.

[25] While I have digital photocopies of the data, a combination of document quality and old handwriting makes these image files unreadable by software. As a result, I hand-transcribed the meeting minutes.

[26] For additional context on data collection and analysis, see Srivastava 2022b.

sovereign state power."[27] However, my research shows that it was not just mismanagement, but self-possessed Company sovereignty that sparked a reckoning within Crown and Parliament. Until the late-1700s, the English state had tolerated ambiguity in Company sovereignty under the purview of nonhierarchical, mutually inclusive layered sovereignty.[28] But self-possessed nonstate sovereignty claimed from the core of the state became too much. The state responded by anchoring its sovereignty along more indivisible, hierarchical foundations espoused by theorists centuries prior. Thus, as discussed in Chapter 1, *Lived Sovereignty* informed the contours of *Idealized Sovereignty*.

The EIC's transformations have implications for the social construction of sovereignty. IR constructivists have long argued that "rather than proceeding from the assumption that all states are sovereign, [they] are interested in considering the variety of ways in which states are constantly negotiating their sovereignty."[29] Studying the EIC exemplifies how the Company's self-possessed sovereignty was constructed in moments of contestation with other sovereigns. The EIC further shows that states also confronted company-states as sovereign rivals and wrestled with nonstate sovereignty. As already mentioned in Chapter 1, Richard Ashley observes that sovereignty's "empirical contents are not fixed but evolve in a way reflecting the active practical consensus among coreflective statesmen who are ever struggling."[30] While the English loss of the American colonies is recognized as setting a new practical consensus of sovereignty,[31] I argue the EIC's self-understanding as "statesmen" should be regarded as equally important.

In this chapter, I first contextualize the Company's sovereign competence within standard accounts, then move to examine the two transformations of EIC cycling through ideal-types of public/private hybridity and asserting a self-possessed Company sovereignty, and finally contend with the contests generated between *Idealized* and *Lived Sovereignty* when the EIC's corporate empire was put on trial.

SEEING LIKE A COMPANY-STATE

There are two standard accounts to help contextualize the Company's sovereign status. First, state formation theorists trace the gradual emergence of a consolidated public sovereign authority in Europe after 1648. As mentioned in Chapter 2, states did not have exclusive control over governance in early modern Europe. Instead, mercantile companies, mercenaries, and privateers were engaged in hybrid relations with rulers to build sovereign competence in trade and violence.[32] Over time, states

---

[27] Phillips and Sharman 2020: 111; Dirks 2008: 197.
[28] Benton 2009: 148.
[29] Biersteker and Weber 1996: 11.
[30] Ashley 1984: 272, fn101.
[31] Wood 1998 [1969]; Dirks 2008; Benton 2009; Dalrymple 2019.
[32] Tilly 1990; Spruyt 1994; Thomson 1994.

consolidated by phasing out "private" actors from the functions of statehood.[33] The disappearance of private actors occurred because their sovereign-generating functions were no longer recognized as legitimate by the Westphalian state system.[34] Key to this process was the legitimation challenge derived from *contractual hybridity* distributing accountability across state and nonstate agents. Privateers and mercenaries complicated state alliances and neutrality obligations. Since states could not ultimately be held accountable for actions taken under their name by nonstate agents, their sovereign legitimation was threatened.

So far, the standard story tracks with the framework I introduced in Chapters 1 and 2. But the implications differ for international politics. In arguing that nonstate actors eventually disappeared from global sovereign politics, the state-formation scholarship ultimately confirms the Westphalian myth of an independent public and an eschewed private in *Idealized Sovereignty*. Nonetheless, these scholars would agree that "the Peace of Westphalia did not establish the 'Westphalian system' based on the sovereign state. Instead, it confirmed and perfected something else: a system of mutual relations among autonomous political units that was precisely not based on the concept of sovereignty."[35] The analytical construct of public/private hybridity is attentive to the legitimation challenges posed by nonstate participants to *Idealized Sovereignty* while not erasing nonstate existence in *Lived Sovereignty*.

Second, most Company histories claim the EIC remained a purely commercial venture, "just for trade," until the mid-eighteenth century when it became "more colonial."[36] For William Dalrymple, "1765 was really the moment that the East India Company ceased to be anything even distantly resembling a conventional trading corporation ... and became something altogether much more unusual."[37] Many ascribe the dramatic rise and fall of the Company to corruption. The British Parliament's website affirms this account: "Parliament had to determine its relationship with this private trading company *once it became a territorial and political power* in India, arising from its military victories at Plassey (1757) and Buxar (1764). ... The Company was badly administered, with corruption among its officials in Britain and India."[38] Two points stand out. First, the Parliament had to "determine its relationship" with the Company foregrounds the relational approach to sovereign politics I advance here. Second, it parrots the standard account that the Company was only a political power after 1757 and that corruption played a big role in the eventual government takeover.

Recent studies have complicated the standard histories by showing that the Dutch, French, and English East India Companies had sovereign functions built

---

[33] Spruyt 1994: 16.
[34] Thomson 1994.
[35] Osiander 2001: 270.
[36] For classic treatments of the Company, see Chaudhuri 1978; Lawson 1993.
[37] Dalrymple 2019: 2–3.
[38] U.K. Parliament. "Parliament and the East India Company."

into their operating cores.[39] The EIC lasted the longest amongst its rivals as a company-state:

> With its roots planted in both hemispheres, the Company's constitution could be volatile and fragile, dependent as it was on constantly changing regimes in both Europe and Asia as well as its own inchoate and often resource-starved political institutions and practices. At the same time, the ability to borrow and balance these various sources of authority and legitimacy potentially offered a remarkably flexible and robust form of political power. Unlike a monarchical state, the Company could modulate between positions of deference and defiance, between claims to be "mere merchant" and an independent "sovereign."[40]

Stern emphasizes that standard histories overestimate the Company's vulnerability and underestimate its power. The complicated blend of merchant, sovereign, subject, and authority was a huge accomplishment and also posed many problems for the Company. However, Stern ultimately does not wrestle with the consequences of a "company-state" occupying the international system for centuries, such as tracing the resulting contests between *Idealized* and *Lived Sovereignty*. Thus, I build on this research to detail the emergence of sovereign competence in the Company and its transformative implications for sovereign politics.

Emergence of Sovereign Competence in the Company

The Company's sovereign competence was originally based on a charter, first by royal sanction and then by parliamentary acts. A charter was an exemption that the company required because the three things it needed to trade were illegal: trade with non-Christians, a trade monopoly, and exporting gold and silver. Bruce Carruthers contextualizes: "Since there were no general laws of incorporation, the establishment of each company required a distinct political act on the part of the sovereign or legislature. They enjoyed special rights and powers that were delegated to them and no one else, and in return provided loans and other kinds of support."[41] In addition to the trade monopoly, the Company also negotiated to extend its sovereign functions in the charters. These included controlling and regulating military, territory, laws, commerce, and money. I examined all the fifty-three Company charters between 1600 and 1780, of which thirty-seven specifically related to the Company's sovereign functions. I plot these thirty-seven charters in Figure 3.1. The distribution shows that the majority of the Company's sovereign functions were in place before 1700. This puts into question the standard histories of a purely commercial enterprise until 1757 as well as the state-formation accounts of sovereignty consolidating in public authority after 1648.

---

[39]   Stern 2008; 2011; Phillips and Sharman 2015; 2020.
[40]   Stern 2011: 13.
[41]   Carruthers 1996: 137.

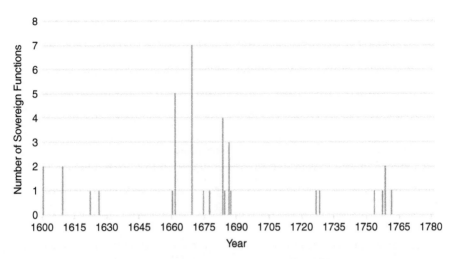

FIGURE 3.1 Number of sovereign functions in EIC charters, 1600–1780

I further coded the Company's sovereign functions as falling under five cat-egories: laws (creating and administering laws and justice), military (creating and regulating armed forces), territory (taking control of territory), money (creating and regulating money), and private trade (creating trading licenses and regulating private trade). Figure 3.2(a–e) shows these specific sovereign functions that appeared in the thirty-seven charters between 1600 and 1780. In the first charter in 1600, the Company had liberty to "make laws and impose penalties on offenders," as long as they were not "repugnant to the Laws of England." The Company could also grant a "licence to any persons to trade to or from the East-Indies." While the Company could wage war using the Crown's ships from its founding, in 1661 the Company could raise its own military forces. Specifically, it could "send out ships of war, men or ammunition for security and defense"; it could choose its own commanders and officers; and it had "power and authority to continue or make peace" with non-Christians. Soon thereafter, in 1669 the Company had sovereign control over a territory in Bombay. Crucially, this was also the first mention of sovereignty in the charters: "Cede Bombay together with all the Rights, Profits, Territories and Appurtenances thereof, and as well the Property as the direct, full and absolute Dominion, and Sovereignty of the said Port and Island." In 1677, the Company had control over its own money, to stamp and coin gold, silver, copper, tin, or lead. Finally, tax collection was granted to the Company in 1765 by the Mughals in an "act of involuntary privatization."[42]

Behind the evolution of these sovereign functions in the Company's charters were dynamics of public/private hybridity that established the EIC's sovereign

---

[42] Dalrymple 2019: 2.

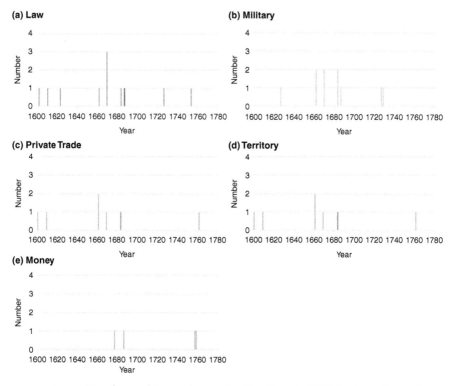

FIGURE 3.2 Number and types of sovereign functions in EIC charters, 1600–1780

competence in *Lived Sovereignty*. Meanwhile, the Company's sovereign status under *Idealized Sovereignty* was subject to intense scrutiny, contestation, and change:

> Given the contingent nature of the rights enjoyed by joint-stock companies [like the Company] (what the King gives, the King can also take away), their relationship with the Crown was a crucial and problematic one of mutual dependence. The balance of power obviously favored the King but at times he had to lean very heavily on his merchant constituents for crucial monetary and political support. It was also a very public relationship, easily visible to rivals in the merchant community as well as opponents of the Crown.[43]

The Company's public/private hybridity was formalized in the royal charter and its relationships with the Crown were often "easily visible to rivals." But this was not always so. The Company's hybrid relations varied in their formal recognition over time to maintain the EIC's sovereign competence. These changes, in turn, underlie the first transformation emergent in the data.

[43] Carruthers 1996: 148.

FIRST TRANSFORMATION: EIC CYCLING THROUGH IDEAL-TYPES
OF PUBLIC/PRIVATE HYBRIDITY

This section shows the different public/private configurations in the Company's hybridity by layering various data over 102 years. My aim is to derive the characteristics of ideal-types specified in the previous chapter (Table 2.1) through interpretive analysis and descriptive quantification. I trace the observable characteristics of the ideal-types as seen through formal contracts in official exchanges, insider rules in embedded networks, and side bargains in hidden back channels. Two caveats before I proceed. First, it is important to reiterate that the Company was not enacting these hybrid relations in completely distinct periods of *contractual, institutional,* and *shadow hybridity.* However, to show the usefulness of ideal-types, I regard some of the Company's modes of interactions as relatively more dominated by *contractual, institutional,* and *shadow* logics of hybridity. Second, the sequence of emergence of the ideal-types I observe here, from *contractual* to *institutional* to *shadow,* is not a generalizable "track" for other hybrid relationships. Instead, the evolution of hybrid configurations is specific to the *contractual* origins of the Company. As such, other hybrid relations may just as easily start with *shadow* and move to *contractual hybridity,* for instance.

To begin, the Company's continued trade monopoly was contingent on its charter. There were ten "main charters" between 1678 and 1780 that specifically extended the Company's monopoly overseas. I treat these main charters as focal points around which the Company staged sovereign negotiations. Figure 3.3 shows the distribution of these main charters, where the vertical lines represent whether or not there was a charter in that year. Paying attention to the density over time in Figure 3.3, the number of main charters decreased and their duration increased.

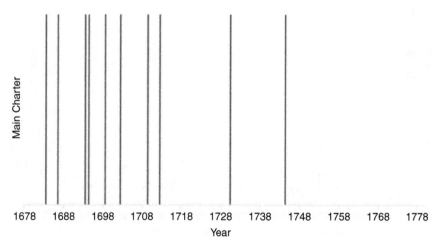

FIGURE 3.3 Main EIC charters in year, 1678–1780

The number and distribution of charters tell us that formal contract negotiations were more common earlier in this period. As the Company's sovereign competence evolved, it asked for more special rights and powers in its charters. As the charters increased in duration, the EIC's formal focal points for expanding its sovereign powers became limited. Indeed, the period after 1750, when Company histories dictate it finally became more than "just for trade," features no main charters that extend the EIC's sovereign powers beyond what was previously negotiated. The decreasing trend gives a clue that the Company does not exhibit the same type of public/private hybridity, for example *contractual hybridity*, over time.

To capture more varied hybrid relations, out of the 14,400 meetings I singled out special sessions for Company shareholders. The shareholders met in quarterly special sessions in March, June, September, and December. The directors could call additional special sessions for discussions related to charters or stock. Company bylaws required that all charters and policy changes had to be approved by the shareholders. There were 812 special sessions between 1678 and 1780, of which 212 were for elections and 600 were nonelection special sessions. Any charter or other sovereign negotiations should then be in these 600 special sessions. Figure 3.4 shows the distribution of the 600 general court special sessions per year from 1678 to 1780. The trend line shows volatility in the number of special sessions per year. Focusing chronologically on the years with more than twice the required four sessions, there were ten special sessions in 1693, fifteen in 1698, thirteen in 1708, eight in 1732, ten in 1749, twenty-six in 1767, forty-two in 1773, seventeen in 1776, and seventeen in 1779. The last spikes in particular follow parliamentary scrutiny culminating in the 1773 Regulating Act that preceded Pitt's India Act (1784). Comparing the special session spikes in Figure 3.4 and the presence of charters in Figure 3.3 suggests a fairly close

FIGURE 3.4 EIC general court special sessions, 1678–1780

relationship where it was likely that a charter year would have higher than average special sessions. This is the sort of relationship undergirding *contractual hybridity*: formalized and publicly recognized negotiations as the basis for sovereign competence.

To observe networked linkages, I collected data on the number of Members of Parliament (MP) who were also Company directors. It was understood that "men went out to India to make their fortunes and returned intent on a seat in Parliament, either as a symbol of their newly-acquired wealth or as a safeguard against official inquiries into their conduct."[44] Thus, corruption played a role in gaining parliamentary seats. Senior Company officers in India ("Nabobs") "generally sought out boroughs which were amenable to the influence of money."[45] I focus then only on Company directors, who were powerful London merchants and bankers, rather than all Company officers. The data come from keyword searches of the biographies of MPs online.[46] I count MPs who were at the time or had in the past been EIC directors in a given year. For instance, Zachary Philip Fonnereau became an EIC director in 1753, while he served as an MP from 1747 to 1774. I count only 1753–74 as Fonnereau's tenure as MP-Director. Figure 3.5 plots the number of MP-Directors by year from 1678 to 1780.[47] The average number of MP-Directors in a year is eleven.

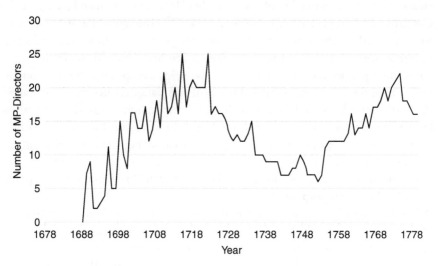

FIGURE 3.5 Number of EIC MP-directors by year, 1678–1780

---

[44] Namier and Brooke 1964.
[45] Namier and Brooke 1964.
[46] Historyofparliamentonline.org. Specifically, I used the keyword "E. In. Co." – a standardized term in the biographies to refer to the old and new East India Company – in the offices held section.
[47] There is a gap from 1680 to 1688 when Parliament was suspended.

The distribution shows a variable climb starting when the two political parties, the Whigs and Tories, became more established in British politics at the turn of the eighteenth century (1688–1700) to reach the twin zeniths of twenty-five MP-Directors in 1715 and 1722. There is a decline starting in the mid-1720s with some minor volatility to reach a low of six MP-Directors in 1752. Finally, the trend climbs back steadily over three decades to another peak of twenty-two MP-Directors in 1774, right after the first EIC Regulatory Act passed.

I bring these data together to paint an overall portrait of the Company's hybridity over 102 years. Figure 3.6 overlays the presence of main charters in a given year (Figure 3.3), the number of special sessions per year (Figure 3.4), and the number of MP-Directors per year (Figure 3.5) from 1678 to 1780. Figure 3.6 thus interacts focal points in the main charters with charter negotiations in the special sessions and institutional effects in the MP-Directors. I will refer to Figure 3.6 as I trace the first transformation of shifting hybrid types in the remainder of this section.

Contractual Hybridity

As Figure 3.6 depicts, from 1678 until 1712, there were lots of main charters and a high number of special sessions, in the 1690s in particular. The Company's first charter in 1600 was limited to fifteen years, but "by 1607 the Crown had agreed the Company could expect a 'perpetual succession.'"[48] Throughout the 1600s, charters were renewed at fifteen-year intervals on average, but sometimes renewal came sooner as seen at the end of the seventeenth century. Thus, in the beginning of the studied period, the EIC achieved its sovereign competence through public/private hybrid relations in formal and frequent negotiations as in *contractual hybridity*. Formalizing hybrid relations in a chartered corporation was an English particularity and even continues today with the British Broadcasting Corporation (BBC). Moreover, the Company charters were public because they were "awarded only for ventures that mixed private interest with a broader public. . . . The Company was a 'national object' and 'the members of it bound to attend to the interest of the public as well as their own purpose.'"[49]

The Company's *contractual* relations were dominated by formal and frequent charter negotiations with the Crown and Parliament. The primary means of negotiating relations was through the exchange of formal contract privileges with forced loans or government fiscal extractions. Forced loans were when the Company gave a loan to the government at below market interest rates, which sometimes were lowered even still over the course of repayment. Some forced loans were never repaid. Fiscal extractions included taxes and special customs duties. In 1697, as the

---

[48] Stern 2011: 10.
[49] Robins 2006: 27.

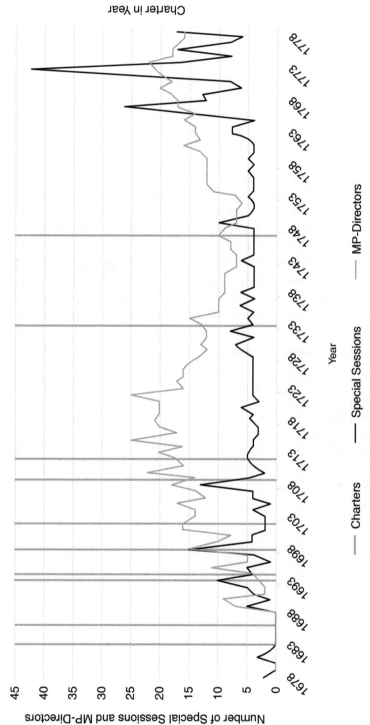

FIGURE 3.6 EIC special sessions, MP-directors, and main charters, 1678–1780

——— Charters   ——— Special Sessions   ——— MP-Directors

pressure for a second East India Company mounted, the Company offered a forced loan to the Crown:

> Governor represented unto the Court the present state of company affairs and the difficulties they were under in carrying on their trade, by reason of the number of interlopers daily set forth and that there had been several discourses of late touching this company as procuring a parliamentary establishment: that by setting the East India Company, a loan of 700,000 pounds may be made to his majesty.[50]

Adjusting for inflation, this forced loan would be worth £122 million today. I searched for all EIC forced loans and fiscal extractions to the Crown between 1678 and 1780 in the records. I supplement data collected by the economist Dan Bogart[51] with Company meeting minutes rather than use standard data on sovereign lending. Figure 3.7 shows the distribution where the vertical lines represent whether there was a forced loan or fiscal extraction in that year. In Figure 3.7, the clustering of loans and extractions toward the early period is indicative of formal transactions in *contractual hybridity*. Moreover, these new data go against a key state-formation claim that sovereign borrowing ceased in 1695, which led to more accountable institutions.[52]

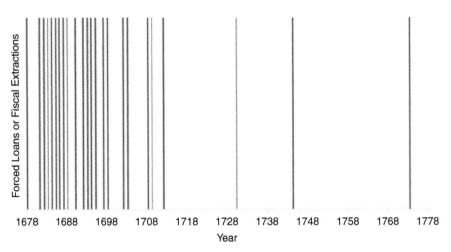

FIGURE 3.7 EIC forced loans or fiscal extractions in year, 1678–1780
Note: Data sources include Bogart (2017b) supplemented with author's compilation.

50 IOR-B.41: 272.
51 Bogart 2017b: 28–33; 36–38; 39–40.
52 Tilly 1990.

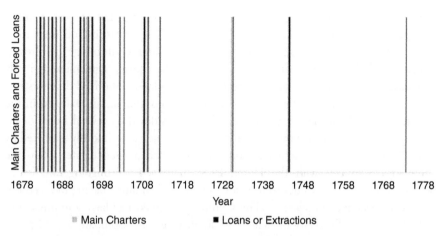

FIGURE 3.8 EIC forced loans/fiscal extractions and main charters in year, 1678–1780

To further highlight the transactional quality of *contractual hybridity*, I link the grant of sovereign privileges with monetary payments. Figure 3.8 overlays the main charters (Figure 3.3) with the forced loans and fiscal extractions (Figure 3.7) to show a close relationship between a loan or extraction and charter negotiation. In fact, in *every* year there was a main charter, there was also a major forced loan or fiscal extraction. In *contractual hybridity*, we expect to see publicized loans and fiscal extractions as standard payments for sovereign privileges. While these payments slowed down over the 1700s, the logic of payment still showed up in more limited guises. After the Company captured the Bengal treasury in 1765, Parliament imposed an annual fee of £400,000 in 1767.[53] But just two years later, the Company was in default and was unable to pay. The 1773 Regulatory Act then formalized the explicit leasing of the Company's sovereign privileges for £10,000 a year.

Examining the Company's territorial gains also reveals relations of *contractual hybridity* outside formal charter negotiations. The Company's first sovereign possession, Bombay, was granted by Charles II in 1668, who received the territory as part of his dowry from the King of Portugal. Bombay is where the Company's first mint was established. Then, in 1673, Charles II made another gift of St. Helena, an island in the South Atlantic and an important servicing station for the Company's voyages. However, the Company's territorial expansion in India from the 1720s onward was obtained by conquest rather than sovereign grants, culminating in its control of Bengal (1767), which I cover at greater length later in the chapter. Crucially, while the Company's territorial gains were increasingly acquired through force rather than grants, peace was still formally negotiated *on behalf* of the Crown. In 1754, the EIC and the French East India Company were negotiating a peace agreement to conclude the Second Carnatic War (1749–54) in South India. Article 11 stated: "The two

53   Robins 2006: 89.

companys agree an humble application shall be made by each of them to their respective sovereigns, that they would be graciously pleased to extend their royal favor and protection toward them, by approving and confirming the present agreement."[54] Thus, the final authority to conclude a peace agreement formally remained with the Crown. This was no ceremonial clause. The EIC directors had kept the Crown appraised throughout the negotiations and, as summarized in the minutes, the draft of the agreement "had been considered by several Lords of his majesty's council, and after making some alterations, was unanimously approved by them."[55] The same contractual arrangement recurred a decade later when the Company negotiated with the Dutch VOC regarding an ongoing conflict in Bengal. In 1762, the two sides were ready to make a deal after "having induced our respective sovereigns to agree."[56] The Company retained regular communications with the Crown's Secretary of State.[57] In short, when the Company signed peace agreements with foreign powers, it also displayed elements of *contractual hybridity*.

Thus, charters and formal contracts remained important to the Company. When exploring other forms of hybridity over the eighteenth century, I do not suggest that the Company moved away from contract-based negotiations. Quite the contrary. The Company pursued contracts outside England, especially in the Mughal *farman*, for sovereign grants well into the late-1700s: "Like the charter, the *farman* provided certain protections and exceptions from legal and financial obligations and impositions, such as customs duties or restrictions on the movement of people and goods. Like the *farman*, the charter was a tool that could establish political legitimacy and provide leverage against rivals."[58] Moreover, when Parliament began renewing the charter instead of the Crown, "paying bribes to parliamentarians were simply part of the fundamental costs of business."[59] Thus, *contractual hybridity* was foundational for establishing the Company's trade monopoly and securing new sovereign functions. But what did change was an *exclusive* reliance on the main royal or parliamentary charters as the primary instrument for sovereign negotiation.

Institutional Hybridity

Let us return to Figure 3.6. From 1712 onward, the Company managed its sovereign competence via royal commissions and letter patents, which were issued much more frequently and negotiated through institutional networks. As such, this period has fewer main charters and a rise in MP-Directors, which coincides in 1712 with the Company's longest-lasting charter thus far until 1730. The Company's sovereign

---

[54] IOR-B.72: 497.
[55] IOR-B.72: 493.
[56] IOR-B.78: 129.
[57] IOR-B.85: 155.
[58] Stern 2011: 13.
[59] Robins 2006: 28.

competence was maintained primarily through public/private hybrid relations characterized by fewer formal negotiations and more use of institutional networks in *institutional hybridity*. The Company now sought to shape insider rules, such as "winning sizeable tax breaks, placing it at a distinct advantage compared with local traders."[60] Institutional linkages also created advantages compared to the EIC's European rivals, mainly the Dutch and French East India Companies, as the Company expanded faster to new markets when moving from spices to textiles to tea to opium over the course of the 1700s. Moreover, the institutional linkages did not just secure insider rules for the EIC's sovereign competence, but also served as a patronage network for politicians. Indeed, many MPs were Company shareholders: "Alongside the dividend, shareholding also gave investors access to the Company's vast network of economic opportunities, notably jobs. The 24 directors controlled the Company's system of patronage, enabling them to place friends, relatives and business partners in key positions, a gift that became increasingly valuable in the second half of the eighteenth century."[61] Thus, *institutional hybridity* was vital for the Company's continued maintenance of sovereign ordering in India and leveraging regulation for expanding its trade.

The Company's *institutional* relations were guided by more sophisticated lobbying and securing political representation, which coincided with the emergence of the Tories and Whigs as prominent political parties. The Company's close ties with the Crown in *contractual hybridity* became a liability after King James II was overthrown in the Glorious Revolution in 1688 and power shifted from the Tories to the Whigs and the Crown to the House of Commons. These changes resulted in a temporary dissolution of the Company's charter, which

> had constitutional implications since one key question was whether a company could legitimately possess monopolistic trading privileges on the basis of a royal charter alone, or if it needed parliamentary sanction. As power shifted to the Commons in the aftermath of the Glorious Revolution, it became clear that the old East India Company needed to consolidate its position with an Act of Parliament.[62]

After Parliament approved the creation of the new East India Company in 1698, the old Company found itself lacking political leverage when the Tories lost the house majority. Indeed, by one analysis of London city leaders during this time, two-thirds of the old Company directors were Tories while 80 percent of the new Company directors were Whigs.[63] The Company thus aimed for more stable and taken-for-granted sovereign competence without requiring formal and frequent exchanges in short-lived charters.

---

[60]　Robins 2006: 28.
[61]　Robins 2006: 31.
[62]　Carruthers 1996: 148.
[63]　Carruthers 1996: 150.

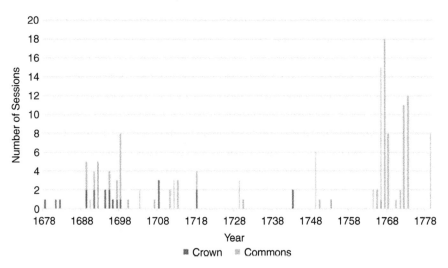

FIGURE 3.9 Number of crown and commons special sessions, 1678–1780

Figure 3.9 depicts the number of special sessions, out of 600 total, that were explicitly about public relations with the Crown or the House of Commons. In the late-1600s, there were an above average number of sessions concerning the Crown, where the Company would negotiate its charter directly with the monarch in exchange for sovereign privilege, as expected in *contractual hybridity*. In the early- to mid-1700s, the gaps between special sessions widen as the Company refocused its informal arrangements with the Commons, which is more reflective of *institutional hybridity*. In particular, after the merger with the new Company in 1709, the United Company sought its longest charter through a parliamentary act in 1712 by paying £1.2 million in the form of a grant to Parliament rather than a forced loan to the Crown. Another spike in parliamentary discussions happened in 1720, when the South Sea Company's share bubble burst. The next discussions were surrounding the 1730 charter, a special situation I discuss later in the chapter. Parliamentary scrutiny surrounding the Company's control of Bengal's treasury (1765) and a financial crisis brought an unprecedented wave of discussions from mid-1760s until the passage of the first Regulatory Act in 1773.

In *institutional hybridity*, the Company was "a corporate battleground for Whigs and Tories."[64] These partisan contests spilled over to the special sessions: "Not for nothing were the annual meetings of the shareholders described as 'little parliaments' by William Pitt the Elder."[65] As one parliamentary historian observed:

In 1754 the East India Company was a business organization trading to India and China, and enjoying monopoly rights under a charter from the Crown. By 1790, in

[64]   Carruthers 1996: 151.
[65]   Robins 2006: 31.

addition to its commercial interests, it had acquired sovereignty over a large part of India, which it exercised under the direction of the British Government. The story of how this change was brought about does not belong to this survey, but many of the men who helped to shape the destiny of India during these years sat in the House of Commons and the affairs of the Company became increasingly the concern of Parliament. As a political problem India ranked second only to America.[66]

The Company experimented with many kinds of relations with Parliament, some with limited success. When Parliament was considering giving a license to trade to the new Company as early as 1693, a Company director, Thomas Cooke, "tried to co-opt key members of the opposition by secretly giving them company stock, and engaged in widespread bribery of politicians. The latter strategy backfired when it came to light in 1695 and was fully exploited by the Whigs to create a public scandal."[67] The Thomas Cooke Affair, as it came to be known, served as a reminder of the costs of unofficial exchanges in public/private hybridity.

The Company next learned a lesson to maintain closer parliamentary linkages for regulating trade when, following protests by London weavers about Indian cloth imports in 1697, Parliament prohibited Indian silks in 1700. The Company quickly moved to form a parliamentary caucus. The Company's governing structure included official subcommittees. As of 1695, the subcommittees were all of commercial nature[68] with none on government relations.[69] In 1698, the Company formed an ad hoc Parliament pressure committee "to solicit the Members of Parliament for preserving to the Company their just Rights, Privileges, and Inheritance."[70] In 1704, to prevent another damaging bill on trade barriers, the Company recommended that shareholders "solicit their Friends in this affair, and to use their best endeavors to *prevent passing* the said Bill."[71] At this point, the call was for prevention of passing the bill. In 1718, the Company created an official subcommittee "For the House."[72] The Company again recommended shareholders "solicit their Friends *in case* such Bill be brought into Parliament."[73] Now the call was to prevent having damaging bills brought up in the first place.

The Company thus shifted its institutional strategy to a more sophisticated lobbying, which also accounts for the rise of MP-Directors during this time (Figure 3.5). Recall that the average number of MP-Directors in a year was eleven. By 1707, there were fourteen MP-Directors, which climbed to a peak of twenty-five

---

[66] Namier and Brooke 1964.
[67] Carruthers 1996: 149.
[68] Namely: Treasury; Shipping and Private Trade; Buying of Goods; Warehouses; Company Books and Accounts; House Keeper Accounts; Law Suits and Debts; Husbands Accounts; Secretaries Accounts; and Writing of Letters.
[69] IOR-B.41: 6.
[70] IOR-B.41: 286.
[71] IOR-B.44: 180; emphasis added.
[72] IOR-B.55: 9; emphasis added.
[73] IOR-B.55: 135.

MP-Directors in 1715 and again in 1722. The next decade saw a decline to a below average ten MP-Directors in 1735 and the count remained under ten between 1738 and 1753. Nonetheless, from 1695 until 1780 there was no year in which there were not at least five MP-Directors in Parliament. The consistency is significant as institutional linkages continued after MP-Directors were out of office. Some MP-Directors served long terms and became anchors for the Company's continued relations with Parliament. During this period, the longest-serving MP-Directors were John Page with thirty-three years (1730–68); Samuel Shepheard with thirty-one years (1717–22; 1724–48), and Sir Gilbert Heathcote with twenty-nine years (1701–10; 1715–33). Henry Crabb Boulton, another director and Chairman, had a long stint as MP-Director, serving twenty years in Parliament from 1754 until his death in 1773. Among the governors in India, Robert Clive (Bengal) maintained his MP seat for sixteen years (1754–5; 1761–74) and George Pigot (Madras) for thirteen years (1765–77). The data on MP-Directors only captures the publicly visible forms of public/private hybridity between the Company and Parliament. We know from Company records that lobbying also occurred through back channels. I discuss this aspect more in relations of *shadow hybridity*.

The institutional linkages paid off in protecting the Company's monopoly from rivals and interlopers, including from the government. Early on, the Company was committed to maintaining the long-standing legal distinction between the

> Company's jurisdiction in the East Indies and the Crown's authority in the Atlantic. In 1708 they successfully lobbied Parliament to have a clause added to the "Act for the Encouragement of the Trade to America" governing privateering and impressment in the Atlantic to restrict the commissioning of privateers to "within the space of One hundred Leagues of any Part of Asia or Africa."[74]

In 1718, the Company secured a parliamentary act banning "British subjects traveling under the auspices of foreign East India Companies."[75] During this time, the Company also used parliamentary linkages for tax breaks on bullion, which was crucial for securing trade in Bengal from the Mughals. A "combination of strong demand and tight regulations meant that the terms of trade for the European traders drawn to Bengal were tough. Only bullion would do, and between 1708 and 1756 three-quarters of the Company's imports into Bengal were in the form of silver."[76]

Increased linkages from the early-1700s made it easier to exchange favors for money, unlike in the Thomas Cooke Affair. As the Company's charter came up for renewal in 1730, a proposal was "put forward to replace the Company's joint stock with a regulated company, which would manage the common infrastructure of the India trade, in return for a commission on all imports and exports; independent traders would then operate freely under this umbrella."[77] The Company made a gift of

[74]   Stern 2011: 193.
[75]   Stern 2011: 196.
[76]   Robins 2006: 63.
[77]   Robins 2006: 57.

"two hundred thousand pounds to be paid by the Company for the use of the Publick – without any interest or addition to their Capital."[78] The charter was renewed until 1766 and the Company's trade monopoly was not threatened until 1793. Note that £200,000 was far less than the £1.2 million the Company paid in 1712 when its institutional networks were still getting established. The Company's institutional investments also helped stave off the most restrictive regulatory reforms pressed by Prime Minister North from the late-1760s onward. North negotiated directly with Company directors. He did not often agree to their protests or petitions, but he would be in frequent meetings with representatives of the directors and kept tabs on upcoming special sessions.[79] As discussed later in the chapter, when structuring Parliament's oversight in India in the 1773 Act, the Company retained a de facto majority on the new governing council. It was also able to appoint its own administrators and maintained control over territorial revenues in Bengal, Bihar, and Orissa.[80] These would all be the subject of major reforms a decade later in the 1784 India Act.

Shadow Hybridity

Back to Figure 3.6, the last main charter with a formal sovereign grant during this period was in 1747. But discussions of sovereign competence among the directors continued with ten special sessions in 1749, eight special sessions in 1764, and twenty-six special sessions in 1767. The number of MP-Directors also shows a steady increase, meaning institutional linkages remain important. However, formally recognized negotiations to manage the Company's sovereign competence subdued. Instead, this period saw the rise of the Company's Secret Committee with "broad powers to manage sensitive political business."[81] The Secret Committee led informal behind-the-scenes discussions with both Crown and Parliament. In fact, as discussed later in the chapter, Parliament created its own secret committee to deal with the Company's Secret Committee. The Company's sovereign competence was increasingly maintained through public/private hybrid relations characterized by no formal charters and an increased use of back channels for reaching side bargains, indicative of *shadow hybridity*. One of the major consequences of *shadow hybridity* was the opening of a new front in European wars. In India, the Company's Carnatic Wars (1746–63) with the French East India Company in South India gained steam. During this time, "both companies began to pursue alliances with southern and eastern Indian powers, which served to extend the European conflict into proxy wars in South Asia."[82] The Company's discussions with Crown and Parliament were conducted through its Secret Committee as the wars violated neutrality agreements when England and

---

[78] IOR-B.60: 435.
[79] IOR-B.259: 177, 224.
[80] IOR-B.258: 323.
[81] Stern 2011: 71.
[82] Stern 2011: 197.

France were officially at peace outside the War of Austrian Succession (1744–8) and the Seven Years' War (1756–63). Hence, *shadow hybridity* was crucial for extending the empire through violence against rivals.

In *shadow hybridity*, the Company's relations were dominated by nonformalized and nonpublicized side bargains with the Crown and Parliament, largely through the use of secret committees. In 1718, the Company created an ad-hoc "secret committee to prevent the progress of a new trade to the east indies under the colour of foreign commissions."[83] It took another twenty-three years before such a committee was introduced as an official EIC subcommittee. In 1741, the Company formed the Committee on Secrecy, also known as the Secret Committee.[84] The Secret Committee "defined the Company's political and military strategy in times of war."[85] For instance, it was responsible for negotiating the aforementioned 1754 agreement with the French East India Company during the Second Carnatic War.[86] However, the Secret Committee's bounds extended beyond times of war to envelop ordinary operations of the Company. By 1762, "the Secret Committee ... recommending ... the observance of an inviolable secrecy as to their contents," referred to receiving direct communications from Parliament.[87] Moreover, communications with the royal Secretary of State Weymouth were also "transmitted through confidential communication."[88] These secret communications were not simply rerouting messages meant for managers or shareholders, they were back channels properly understood.

In fact, all major Company internal discussions that dealt with its sovereign functions from the mid-1700s originated from and were tasked to the Secret Committee. Previously, such work was delegated between the other subcommittees and was coordinated by the Subcommittee on Correspondence. Moreover, Parliament also adopted this form of governance by installing its own shadow apparatus. In 1765, the Company's Secret Committee was made aware of a "parliamentary Enquiry on the committee and company affairs."[89] Parliament, in an unprecedented move, created its own secret committee to investigate the Company's Secret Committee and shadow dealings. However, in an amusing turn of events, the Company had access to the Parliament's secret committee and obtained a list of its members by the end of day. Moreover, the Company made use of the parliamentary secret committee to make appeals outside the more visible institutional process of petitioning and contractual process of charter negotiations. For instance, just after the creation of the parliamentary secret committee, the Company's Secret Committee informally asked to extend their trade monopoly to

[83] IOR-B.55: 133.
[84] IOR-B.66: 269.
[85] Robins 2006: 32.
[86] IOR-B.72: 493.
[87] IOR-B.78: 337.
[88] IOR-B.85: 160.
[89] IOR-B.81: 388.

Europe, which would profoundly alter the formal charter: "If this company did not import a quantity of goods from the East India sufficient for the supply of the African trade, they should be allowed to import such goods from any part of Europe."[90] The request did not succeed, but it highlights that the Company was willing to circumvent the more formal arrangements for negotiating sovereign competence in the shadows.

The Company also did not hesitate to use secrecy against Parliament when it served its interest. The Company was made aware on December 1, 1772, of growing parliamentary inclinations to stricter Company oversight in India, discussed later in the chapter. In its response to Parliament two days later, the Company protested the nature of secrecy:

> That notwithstanding the firm reliance of your petitioners on the protection of Parliament, they cannot avoid being alarmed at the appointment of a committee of secrecy as an uncommon mode of proceeding and which they are informed has not hitherto been instituted unless upon some act of delinquency charged or some special fact stated in the house. . . . Your petitioners therefore most humbly pray, with all deference to the wisdom of Parliament, that their affairs may be publickly examined.[91]

The directors were of course aware of the possibility of a parliamentary inquiry since 1765 and had engaged in numerous exchanges with the parliamentary secret committee. Now that the stakes were higher, the EIC publicly criticized Parliament's use of secrecy for protecting the inquiry from leaks, secrecy which failed anyway because of the continuing linkages between EIC and Parliament through *institutional hybridity*.

Another indicator of growing shadow relationships was the lack of official exchanges of sovereign functions for money or other favors. Recalling Figure 3.7, which depicted all EIC forced loans or fiscal extractions, it is clear that the Company avoided formal payment during a vast portion of its *shadow hybridity*. Even more surprising is that while the Company was forced to lend to the government in each of the wars up to 1750, it did not make any forced loans or fiscal extractions during the crucial Seven Years' War from 1756 to 1763. Moreover, during the 1767–8 discussions about restructuring the Company's dividends, the directors considered "the propriety of offering [£400,000] to government."[92] Even at the height of Company–Parliament tensions during the passing of the 1773 and 1784 regulatory acts, Prime Ministers North and Pitt entertained delegations from the Company's Secret Committee for meetings.

Studying the Company's public/private relations over 102 years helps trace the coevolution of *contractual, institutional*, and *shadow hybridity* in a single entity. Determining and changing relationships in the various hybrid forms were central to

[90] IOR-B.80: 393.
[91] IOR-B.258: 81–83.
[92] IOR-B.83: 55.

the Company's survival, and it also muddied who counted as public and private in the process. While embedded in this period are accounts of changing British politics, property rights, and military might, one other compelling narrative is internal to the tensions between the Company's growing *Lived Sovereignty* nestled within English *Idealized Sovereignty*. For Stern, the Company's

> legitimacy rested in a complex amalgam of English charters, Asian grants, and its own deliberate and aggressive political behavior, constantly negotiated with its subordinates, allies, rivals, and subjects. In forging this political system, Company leadership were guided by a coherent, if composite, set of political ideas about the duties of subjects and rulers and the nature and extent of political authority.[93]

My research validates Stern that the Company's sovereign legitimacy was constantly negotiated through charters and bargains with rulers and rivals. However, it departs from Stern in assuming the Company's leaders were possessed by a "coherent set of political ideas … on the nature and extent of political authority." Instead, the Company's self-understanding of sovereign authority shifted from a privilege granted under indivisible *Idealized Sovereignty* to a right cultivated through sovereign competence in *Lived Sovereignty*. I move to examining this transformation next.

SECOND TRANSFORMATION: COMPANY SOVEREIGNTY SHIFTS FROM PRIVILEGE TO RIGHT

The Company was originally authorized by the Royal Charter to set up trading posts and generally act as it saw fit on foreign lands. Thus, the EIC was "subject to the English Crown in one sense but possessed of a supreme rule abroad in another."[94] Beyond a simple principal–agent relationship, this meant the Company was initially constituted by the Crown's sovereign authority in *Idealized Sovereignty*, but in asserting its own sovereign competence *as* authority in *Lived Sovereignty*, it could supersede the Crown: "If the Crown had indeed created a grant that rendered the Company something other than a direct agent or ambassador for the monarch, it could never be withdrawn."[95] So, could the Company "'argue the king by his prerogative out of his prerogative?'"[96] The second transformation of the Company's sovereign status depended on the answer to this question and provided impetus for the Company's experimentation with embracing *Lived Sovereignty* as the basis of its sovereign status.

---

[93] Stern 2011: 6.
[94] Stern 2011: 26.
[95] Stern 2011: 54.
[96] Stern 2011: 54.

Emerging Desires for Self-Possessed Company Sovereignty

The Company's self-understanding of its sovereign authority appears at first in legal cases. I searched all cases in which the Company was named as plaintiff or defendant between 1650 and 1880 in *Hein Online*. I found 107 total cases, of which the Company was the plaintiff in 44 cases. It is useful to see which legal claims the EIC itself initiated. I coded the forty-four legal cases of EIC as plaintiff into four broad categories of claims: private trade, like going after unlicensed traders; payment, like collecting debts; property, like building new headquarters or warehouses; and procedural, like setting standards on what is a late payment.[97] Figure 3.10 plots these forty-four cases by type per year. Private trade and procedural types account for a third each of all the legal cases, while a quarter were payment-related and 7 percent were property cases. The historical development of these cases suggests the Company pursued more private trade claims earlier and more procedural cases later. The Company thus enforced a trade monopoly through English courts until the middle of the eighteenth century, after which its territorial and military gains in India helped secure the monopoly.[98]

One early case that the EIC pursued against unlicensed traders – or interlopers – shows the Company in the rare position of publicly justifying its sovereign authority. By the late 1670s, interloping was a familiar topic of concern in London. The Company rewarded intelligence on suspected interlopers, boarded ships, detained unlicensed traders, and brought them to English courts. One such interloper was

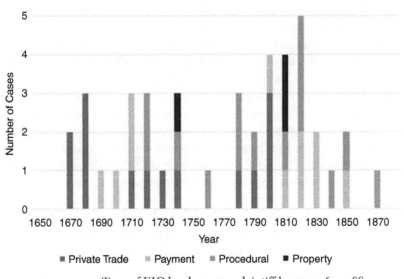

FIGURE 3.10 Type of EIC legal cases as plaintiff by year, 1650–1880

---

97 *East India Company v. Evans* (1684); *East India Company v. Boddam* (1804); *East India Company v. Vincent* (1740); *East India Company v. Chitty* (1789).
98 I thank Sammy Barkin for this point.

Thomas Sandys, who in 1682 was preparing to make an unlicensed trip to India. The Company had Sandys' ship stopped by the Admiralty on the Thames and brought him to the Court of Chancery to have his goods forfeited.[99] Sandys, unlike other interlopers,

> challenged the Admiralty's right to seize his ship, arguing that its civil law jurisdiction extended only to the high seas. Before the Chancery, he similarly made no effort to deny he planned an eastward voyage. He insisted instead that, according to common law, he had every right to do so, since the Company's charter, being for a monopoly, was "in itself void."[100]

The resulting case, *East India Company* v. *Sandys*, also known as "the Great Case of Monopolies," was argued by London's most prominent lawyers.

There were three main arguments to adjudicate. First, EIC lawyers maintained that Asian trade would not exist were it not for the Company: "It is well known, that if this Company had not settled and established a trade in the Indies, Mr. Sandys, nor none of these gentlemen could have had an opportunity to do it."[101] According to the Company, trade against non-Christians was "inconvenient and mischievous" – which is why it was prohibited without a trade monopoly – and thus could not exist without the Company's agents, who maintained all the diplomatic connections necessary to secure access to ports. I interpret this as an assertion of *Lived Sovereignty*. The Company also claimed that since it inaugurated the trade to Asia, it was not depriving others of the right that existed before: "They cannot make out that they were in possession of this trade before, therefore this charter does not restrain them of any freedom they had."[102] Sandys' defense retorted: "Generally speaking, merchandizing was always reckoned a lawful trade; every man might use the sea, and trade with other nations as freely as he might use the air. And for this trade to the East Indies, it was lawfully used before there was a Company, or else there had never been a Company."[103]

Second, the Company invoked *Idealized Sovereignty* to claim umbrella protection under the Crown's sovereign authority: "There is a great deal of difference between trading in a company, and trading out of a company: if they trade in a company, they trade under the government of England; if they trade out of a company, then they trade out of the government of England, and *out of its protection*."[104] This umbrella authority extended to the Company's privileges, including prosecuting interlopers. However, Sandys' lawyers turned this umbrella privilege on its head and questioned the Company's standing to sue. For Sandys, since "the defendant trades there without licence, this may subject him to penalty at the suit of the king, but this gives no title to levy money upon the defendant for trading without licence, there is no privity, no cause

[99] Howell and Howell 1816, Vol. 10: 385.
[100] Stern 2011: 46.
[101] Howell and Howell 1816, Vol. 10: 377.
[102] Howell and Howell 1816, Vol. 10: 380.
[103] Howell and Howell 1816, Vol. 10: 386–387.
[104] Howell and Howell 1816, Vol. 10: 379–380; emphasis added.

of action."[105] Furthermore, the defense claimed that Sandys did not impose considerable damages on Company profits. The Company agreed on this point, but in asserting "that interloping was more an offense against jurisdiction than commerce, Company advocates maintained that Sandys' crime was not his trade per se but his intent in the first place to traffic into the East Indies without the Company's permission to do so."[106]

Finally, Sandys' defense questioned the legitimacy of the Crown in *Idealized Sovereignty*. The Company had claimed it required an exclusive monopoly in the charter as "the subjects of a Christian prince going to trade with Infidels ... may be dangerous to the state and religion; so that it must necessarily be in the power of the king to control it."[107] The defense turned this around: "The [king's] prerogative is great; but it has this general and just limitation, that nothing is to be done thereby that is mischievous or injurious to the subject."[108] The defense argued two kinds of injury that threatened the Crown's sovereign legitimacy. First, the Crown allowed trade with non-Christians, which went against another authority: "There is not nor can be any peace, treaty or intercourse between the English and the Indians, but a constant never-ceasing state of war; and especially if it be founded upon a Divine precept: for whatsoever prerogative the king may have, he cannot have a prerogative to dispense with the canon of the scripture."[109] Second, the Crown granted a monopoly to the Company that was injurious to the public good: "The [Statute of Monopolies] indeed in the preamble says, it is for public good, but it is the public good of the EIC."[110]

Ultimately, the case was ruled in favor of the Company in 1688. But the verdict was more of a defense of the Crown's *Idealized Sovereignty*: "The King hath the sole power of this trade, as of war and peace; and by declaring a war, he may determine a public trade, though settled by the act of parliament. No parliament ever looked on this as a monopoly, nay, so far from it, as this Company are said to be an advantage to the public."[111] On the legitimacy of trading with non-Christians: "The prerogative of making leagues is in the king, and he may make them as he pleases."[112] More broadly, "for surely the King may restrain his subjects from going beyond sea, and is not bound to give any reason for his doing so."[113] Thus, even though the Company won, the prominence of the "Great Case" publicly challenged the basis of its sovereign authority in a profound way. The case also showed that by the late-1600s the Company viewed even a single interloper as a disavowal of its authority secured in *Lived Sovereignty*. The aggressive pursuit of interlopers by the Company, especially the resources employed in the *Sandys* case, was not simply for the protection of

---

[105] Howell and Howell 1816, Vol. 10: 403.
[106] Stern 2011: 56–57.
[107] Howell and Howell 1816, Vol. 10: 375.
[108] Howell and Howell 1816, Vol. 10: 386.
[109] Howell and Howell 1816, Vol. 10: 391–392.
[110] Howell and Howell 1816, Vol. 10: 398.
[111] Howell and Howell 1816, Vol. 10: 517.
[112] Howell and Howell 1816, Vol. 10: 518.
[113] Howell and Howell 1816, Vol. 10: 518.

its commercial profits, but also for its hard-won sovereign jurisdiction abroad (which of course fed back into profits). Over the next century, the Company would act in even more aggressive ways to claim this authority as a right rather than a privilege. Perceptively, the *Sandys* judgment ended by citing legal theorist Grotius, also a lawyer for the VOC, to predict: "The company hath been in possession of this trade near one hundred years, and that possession will in time give a right."[114]

Establishing Self-Possessed Company Sovereignty

Two years after the *Sandys* verdict, Company directors privately regarded the Crown and Parliament's sovereignty to extend "no farther than 'the Kingdoms of England, the Dominion of Wales, and the Town of Barwick upon Tweed.'"[115] The directors wrote to the Bombay Council that increasing revenues

> is no less the subject of our [concern] & must always be yours, as much as our trade; 'tis that must make us a nation in India, without that we are but as a great number of Interlopers, united by his Majesties Royall Charter, fit only to trade where no body of power thinks it their interest to prevent us.[116]

In 1691, the directors invoked the VOC as a model "to create a self-sustaining political and military establishment in India founded upon the raising of local revenue, of the sort that 'enables [the Dutch] to secure ... their soveraigne state in India.'"[117] Unlike the Dutch, the EIC intended its self-sustaining sovereign state to be free of delegation. The Company's desire would be fulfilled in Bengal, not Bombay, and its pronouncements of self-possessed sovereignty would become louder after successes in eighteenth-century war-making.

The Company fought many wars with European and Asian powers, including the Dutch (1618–25; 1653–74), French (1746–8; 1749–54; 1758–63; 1778–83), Mughals (1688–90), Mysoreans (1767–9; 1780–4; 1789–92; 1798–9), Rohillas (1773–4; 1794), and Marathas (1775–82). Figure 3.11 plots the frequency of all major Company wars from 1600 to 1800. The vertical lines indicate whether there was a major EIC war that year. Focusing on the density over time, the early- to mid-eighteenth century was a relatively peaceful period. By contrast, starting with the First Carnatic War in 1748, there was barely a year when the Company was not at war.

Of all the wars, the Company's campaigns in Bengal proved pivotal. By 1690, the Company set up a trading post and established Fort William in Calcutta. In 1717, it negotiated a trade license with Mughal Emperor Farrukhsiyar. A decade later, Bengal's exports made up 70 percent of the Company's trade. The Company then conflicted with the Nawab of Bengal in a series of escalations, including dismissing its entire

---

[114] Howell and Howell 1816, Vol. 10: 520.
[115] Stern 2008: 279.
[116] Stern 2008: 279.
[117] Stern 2008: 280.

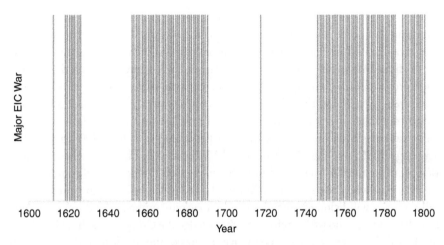

FIGURE 3.11 Frequency of major EIC wars by year, 1600–1800

Bengal Council in 1732. The crisis came to a head under a different Nawab, Siraj ud-Daulah, who attacked Fort William in 1756 with the French, resulting in a siege of Calcutta. By January 1, 1757, the Company, led by Robert Clive, recaptured Calcutta and then won Bengal in the Battle of Plassey on June 23, 1757. Clive was appointed Bengal's president and governor in 1759, returning to a second term in 1765. Plassey led to big military and financial gains (£232 million today), allowing the Company to force control over the right to tax collection (*Diwani*) from the Mughals in 1765, leading "directly to the Company's accession to the position of de facto territorial sovereign of Bengal."[118] In addition to conquering the East, the Company consolidated control over the South in 1763 by ending the Carnatic Wars with the French East India Company.

Bengal, acquired by conquest rather than a grant like Bombay, launched more aggressive claims of self-possessed Company sovereignty. In 1765, Clive wrote to the directors:

> Princes of Indostan must conclude our Views to be boundless ... We must indeed become the Nabobs ourselves in Fact, if not in Name, perhaps totally without Disguise. ... Let us, and without delay, compleat our three European Regiments to one thousand each. ... If Riches and Stability are the Objects of the Company, this is the Method, the only Method we now have for attaining and securing them."[119]

Clive invoked war as the source of Company sovereignty. As shown earlier, the Company had already warred for more than a century. Yet, after 1750, "the dissolution of the Mughal Empire, the emergence of post-Mughal successor kingdoms, and Anglo-French global warfare created a volatile context in which British and EIC forces in South Asia became entangled in indigenous political and military affairs."[120]

[118] Erikson 2014: 65.
[119] Dirks 2008: 174–175; Vaughn 2019: 190.
[120] Vaughn 2019: 5.

While previous wars were fought for commercial rights and ports, Bengal gave the Company a source of territorial revenues and helped make a state for better extraction.[121] Within this context, Bengal also entangled the Company in peace negotiations that forced it to articulate Company sovereignty vis-à-vis Indian powers and European rivals. During the EIC's secret negotiations to end the Second Carnatic War (1749–54) with the French East India Company, the two sides divided territory, recognized other sovereigns, and exchanged prisoners of war and deserters.[122] The same pattern played out as the Company negotiated with the VOC in Bengal,[123] agreeing in 1763 that the Dutch-preferred Mir Jafar would be restored as Nawab of Bengal, while the EIC maintained functional control.[124] Discussing the arrangement with the directors, Clive said Mir Jafar would be a fig leaf for Company sovereignty, as "all revenues will belong to the Company," to avoid "umbrage" and loss of revenue from Europeans, who would refuse to acknowledge the Company as the sole "Nawab of Bengal."[125] However, by 1769, Clive removed the fig leaf and declared in Parliament:

> The East India Company are at this time sovereigns of a rich, populous, fruitful country in extent beyond France and Spain united; they are in possession of the labour, industry, and manufactures of twenty million of subjects; they are in actual receipt of between five and six millions a year. They have an army of fifty thousand men.[126]

Importantly, Clive did not link Company sovereignty to any delegation; the claim stood on the EIC's own sovereign agency.

After Bengal, Company directors also adopted Clive's declaration of self-possessed sovereignty. Figure 3.12 plots the number of discussions of Company sovereignty in director meetings between 1750 and 1775.[127] The inductive analysis does not rely solely on mentions of "sovereign" or "sovereignty" since these terms were not well established. Instead, directors often invoked "rights" broadly to make claims about Company sovereignty.[128] The distribution shows spikes related to peace agreements with the French (1753, 1765), the VOC (1761), and the Levant Company (1764–65). The grant of *Diwani* felicitated heightened talks (1765–7) and the 1773 Act yielded the most discussion.

The substance of the discussions highlights that the Company's growing sovereign competence in *Lived Sovereignty* reverberated in England. Both Crown and Company troops fought the French during the Third Carnatic War (1756–63). In

---

[121] Tilly 1985.
[122] IOR-B.72: 493–494.
[123] IOR-B.78: 47.
[124] IOR-B.78: 134.
[125] IOR-E.4.27: 32–33.
[126] Dirks 2008: 177–178.
[127] "Discussion" is counted as one agenda item in the minutes per meeting session. Sometimes directors met twice a day in a director session and a shareholder session. I counted these as separate discussions.
[128] This inference emerged from reading the 600 special shareholder sessions fully.

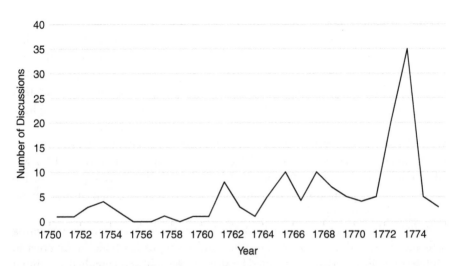

FIGURE 3.12 Frequency of discussion of EIC's sovereign rights in director meetings by year, 1750–1775

1757, when determining how to divide the spoils of wars, "the Crown's advocate, attorney, and solicitor generals implied that, legally speaking, there were in fact two wars going on simultaneously."[129] After EIC assumed the *Diwani*, in 1769, the Crown asked that the commander of a royal ship to India contracted by the Company get a vote at the Indian governing councils. The request centered on "the powers it may be proper for the company to give the crown."[130] While the EIC was established by royal charter so it could borrow sovereign authority to legitimize its monopoly and powers, now Company sovereignty was necessary to legitimate the Crown's sovereign powers in India. After debating, the directors ruled out a Crown vote on Company war- and peace-making but granted the Crown's officer "a share in the deliberations and resolutions of the Company merely with regard to the two objects of making peace and declaring war when his majesty's forces are employed."[131]

Thus, by the middle of the eighteenth century, the Company routinely performed sovereign functions of building an empire through making war and agreeing to peace. But the EIC's *Lived Sovereignty* created conflicts for the English state's *Idealized Sovereignty*, which became evident in a series of parliamentary interventions.

In 1767, the directors separated trade profits, subject to public payment through dividends, from the *Diwani*'s territorial revenues, whose share the directors claimed the public or government was not entitled to receiving.[132] A parliamentary inquiry

---

[129]   Stern 2011: 197.
[130]   IOR-B.85: 171.
[131]   IOR-B.85: 212.
[132]   IOR-B.82: 430.

ensued. A Select Committee argued that "the armies [the Company] maintained the alliances they formed and the revenues they possessed procured them consideration as a sovereign and politic, as well as a commercial body."[133] But MP Lord Chatham claimed "that the legal right to the Company's recently acquired territories and rights in Bengal lay with the Crown rather than the Company."[134] Another committee inquired into who could lay claim to Bengal given it was the Mughals, and not the Crown, that granted the *Diwani*. MP Edmund Burke, a Company supporter at the time, "was concerned that the ministry was attempting to infringe on the Company's basic chartered privileges."[135] The inquiry revealed the EIC was "deliberately ambiguous on the question of sovereignty."[136] The Company agreed to pay £400,000 (£46 million today) annually to Parliament in lieu of a claim on *Diwani* right or revenue.[137]

By 1770 the Company became unable to pay the annual sum after entering a financial crisis due to corruption, wars, and losing its tea trade in America to Dutch smuggling. Parliament readied for stricter oversight and launched a criminal investigation into Clive's wealth. William Bolts, a former Bengal officer turned MP, published *Considerations on Indian Affairs* in 1772, criticizing the mismanagement of company's affairs:

> There is something excessively ridiculous in the very idea of vesting a body of mere traders with unlimited sovereign authority, and setting them between the real Sovereign and people of this kingdom, and two mock Sovereigns and the whole people of the Bengal provinces, to play securely their own game of advantage, to the prejudice of all the other parties.[138]

An anonymous tract argued that "only the king was the 'supreme Arbiter, by the British constitution, of all matters of war and peace.'"[139] MP John Burgoyne's motion that "all territorial acquisitions made by subjects belonged to the Crown" passed by a wide margin.[140] However, the battle between the Company's claims in *Lived Sovereignty* and the English state's notions of *Idealized Sovereignty* was just getting started.

In 1772, Prime Minister North audited the Company and proposed a bill to appoint a Governor-General in India to oversee the Company in exchange for a £1.5 million bailout. The Company had borrowed from the government before without oversight. The directors petitioned against "the intention of Parliament to infringe those sacred rights which the East India Company have hitherto enjoyed

---

[133] Bowen 1991: 9–10.
[134] Dirks 2008: 178–179.
[135] Dirks 2008: 179.
[136] Dirks 2008.
[137] Dirks 2008: 179–180.
[138] Bolts 1772: 219–220.
[139] Phillips and Sharman 2020: 145.
[140] Dirks 2008: 181.

and exercised with the greatest and most extensive advantages to the commerce and revenue of this kingdom."[141] When the directors petitioned Parliament in 1698 against the rival East India Company, they claimed the new Company would infringe on the EIC's "rights, privileges, and inheritances."[142] Now, the Company jettisoned "privileges and inheritances" and stuck with "rights" exclusively. The directors were most aggressive when defending their right to appoint personnel in India. Retaining control over appointments was important as two-way correspondence between India and England took ten months on average. By that time, whole wars would have been initiated and peace terms concluded. The directors had to ensure they had a final say in who acted on their behalf:

> That the company do with all humility conceive it to be their undoubted legal right to send out any persons whom they judge proper to enforce and execute such regulations (agreeable to the powers of their charters) as the said company shall think necessary for the good government of their several settlements in India or for correcting such abuses as may have prevailed therein.[143]

Moreover, the Company's sovereignty claim was still based on the charter, but now the charter's authority itself did not rely exclusively on delegated authority from Crown or Parliament: "The Company therefore do with all humility claim the benefit of the Law of the Land, and the public faith of the Nation, for the free enjoyment and exercise of the rights and powers which they hold."[144] The Company thus fulfilled the prediction made in the *Sandys* verdict by claiming a sovereign right because of its long experience with *Lived Sovereignty*.

Meanwhile, the Company also contributed to the Great Bengal Famine (1769–73) by switching food crops to opium, leading to an estimated loss of ten million lives. The negative attention brought a drop in the Company's share price, which exacerbated the Company's financial woes. The famine also threatened "the Company's ability to maintain a basis of trust with society at home and abroad that decided its fate – and once this trust was broken, protest, rebellion and, ultimately, removal would follow."[145] Prime Minister Lord North argued in March 1773: "I think, Sir, it is allowed that Parliament have a right over the India Company."[146] Parliament passed another resolution on May 10, 1773, that specifically addressed its grievances under *Idealized Sovereignty* with the Company's public/private hybridity in *Lived Sovereignty*:

> That all acquisitions made under the influence of a military force or by treaty with foreign princes do of right belong to the State;

---

[141]   IOR-B.258: 81–82.
[142]   IOR-B.41: 286.
[143]   IOR-B.258: 81–83.
[144]   IOR-B.258: 81–83.
[145]   Robins 2006: 34.
[146]   Robins 2006: 106.

That to appropriate acquisitions so made to the private emolument of persons entrusted with any civil or military power of the state is illegal;

That very great sums of money and other valuable property have been acquired in Bengal from Princes and others of that country by persons entrusted with the military and civil powers of the state by means of such powers, which sums of money and valuable property have been appropriated to the private use of such persons.[147]

Parliament asserted that the Company's territory, military, treaty commitments to foreign princes, money and property, and most of all its "military and civil powers" "of right belong to the State."[148] In other words, Parliament questioned both the basis of the Company's sovereign competence independent of the "state's" military and civil powers in *Lived Sovereignty* and any basis of sovereign right to this competence in *Idealized Sovereignty*.

The Company responded that it would rather refuse the bailout than agree to the terms.[149] The directors claimed Company sovereignty as "nothing less than the preservation of their essential rights"[150] and framed their fight against abuse of "powers of the State."[151] The Company's sticking point remained the appointment of officers, arguing it would be nonsensical if appointees of Parliament or Crown "be vested with the whole civil and military authority of the Presidency of Bengal, Bihar, and Orissa."[152] The directors asserted the Bill "under the colour of regulation will annihilate at once the powers of the East India Company and virtually transfer them to the Crown."[153] In the *Sandys* trial, the Company's self-understanding of its sovereign authority recognized the umbrella protection of the Crown as a privilege in *Idealized Sovereignty*. Now, after close to a century of sovereign competence exercised within *Lived Sovereignty*, the Company asserted its sovereign authority as an essential right that it did not want transferred to the Crown.

The Company leveraged its institutional connections, including with the Mayor of London, and used shadow back channels[154] to negotiate with North, who ultimately "decided not to push the constitutional argument about who owned Bengal, and also shied away from touching the Company's monopoly, realising that this was the prime mechanism for returning Indian tribute to Britain."[155] Moreover, Parliament cleared Clive of all charges and retained Warren Hastings, who was previously governor of Calcutta, as the new Governor-General. Importantly, the Company held a majority on his executive council and appointed its own president

[147] IOR-B.89: 116.
[148] IOR-B.89: 116.
[149] IOR-B.258: 211.
[150] IOR-B.258: 211.
[151] IOR-B.258: 211.
[152] IOR-B.258: 242.
[153] IOR-B.258: 242.
[154] IOR-B.258: 254.
[155] Robins 2006: 107.

and council in Bengal, Madras, and Bombay.[156] The 1773 reforms affirmed the Company's claims in *Lived Sovereignty* by letting it largely carry on as before in India.

In sum, the Company's self-understanding of its sovereign authority transformed from a privilege granted by Crown and Parliament within *Idealized Sovereignty* to an essential right derived from *Lived Sovereignty*. Parliament reacted to the Company's sovereign awakening by asserting more indivisible claims of *Idealized Sovereignty* in the lead-up to the 1773 Regulatory Act, but ultimately fell short of meaningful regulation given the EIC's hybrid relations and influence. However, the English state's sovereign reckoning with the EIC would erupt in even more dramatic fashion in the trial of the century: the impeachment of Warren Hastings.

CLASHES OF *IDEALIZED* AND *LIVED SOVEREIGNTY* IN EIC'S CORPORATE EMPIRE ON TRIAL

Following the 1773 Regulatory Act, Hastings' mandate as Governor General of Bengal was to establish a bureaucratic structure for revenue collection.[157] He succeeded in creating a revenue board and two courts, but argued that "the collection of revenue was the task of a state rather than a trading company, requiring greater executive authority and power."[158] Hastings advocated that the "'sovereignty of this country [be] wholly and absolutely vested in the Company,' and that he be the sole 'instrument' of this sovereignty."[159] However, he proposed establishing this supreme sovereignty from "clearer ties with the Crown,"[160] which was now at odds with the directors. Meanwhile, Hastings "began to take a more old-fashioned, pseudo-monarchical and even despotic idea of his powers."[161]

In June 1782, Parliament called on the EIC directors to remove Hastings for what it deemed as unlawful imprisonment of the Raja of Benaras.[162] In August, the directors agreed that Hastings engaged in improper conduct and would remove him.[163] After learning of his removal, Hastings intended to resign. In a scathing letter to the directors, he called out their lack of financial support for the Company's wars.[164] Hastings also discussed the source of his sovereign authority:

> There was indeed an interval, and that of some duration, in which my authority was wholly destroyed; but another was substituted in its place, and that, though,

[156] IOR-B.258: 323.
[157] Bowen 1991: 113.
[158] Bowen 1991: 184.
[159] Bowen 1991: 187.
[160] Bowen 1991.
[161] Dalrymple 2019: 312.
[162] IOR-B.260: 210.
[163] IOR-E.4.627: 530.
[164] IOR-E.4.40: 385–386.

irregular, was armed with the public belief of an influence invisibly upholding it, which gave it a vigor scarce less effectual than that of a constitutional power.[165]

Although Parliament "destroyed" the "constitutional" source of Hastings' authority when calling for his removal, he "substituted" another source "armed with the public belief" of equal "vigor." In the interim, Hastings had gained ground in the first Anglo-Maratha war (1775–82) after the EIC suffered nearly complete defeat. In October 1783, the directors rescinded their removal of Hastings, arguing it would be improper "at a period so critical."[166] After the directors refused to remove Hastings, Prime Minister North told them that Parliament had taken up the Company's affairs into consideration again.[167]

As a new draft bill to regulate the Company circulated in November 1783, parliamentarian Edmund Burke now wondered: "What did it mean for the Company to 'possess' India, whether by Parliamentary right, sheer force, or local treaty?"[168] The year prior, Burke argued that the nation was "not an idea only of local extent, and individual momentary aggregation; but it is an idea of continuity, which extends in time as well as in numbers and in space."[169] For Burke, national sovereignty "is a deliberate election of ages and generations; it is a constitution made by what is ten thousand times better than choice, it is made by the peculiar circumstances, occasions, tempers, dispositions, and moral, civil and social habitudes of the people, which disclose themselves only in a long space of time. It is a vestment which accommodates itself to the body."[170] For Historian Nicholas Dirks, Burke's views were "changed greatly from those he had held in younger years" and "it cannot be accidental … that Burke was spending most of his time thinking about Company abuses in India, wondering whether Warren Hastings was undermining universal principles and national reputations."[171]

In December 1783, the directors petitioned Parliament that the impending bill would be "subversive of your petitioner's constitution, divesting them of their rights and privileges, seizing their property and continuing a trade at their risk but without their consent or control."[172] Later, the directors said they would concede to some of the proposals as long as "the government in India be carried on in the name of the company by a Governor and three counsellors, at each of the presidencies of Madras and Bombay."[173] But the directors queried:

> Will there remain with the executive body of any decisive or conclusive authority respecting the commercial affairs of the company? Will the heads of the intended

[165] IOR-E.4.40: 387.
[166] IOR-B.260: 219.
[167] IOR-B.99: 563.
[168] Dirks 2008: 167.
[169] Dirks 2008: 193–194.
[170] Dirks 2008: 194.
[171] Dirks 2008: 195.
[172] IOR-B.260: 298.
[173] IOR-B.260: 309.

bill go to the annihilation of the company's authority in India, and will all the power and authority of the company be vested in the governors and council to be named by the crown?"[174]

Pitt's India Act (1784) aimed to resolve these questions with six Commissioners for the Affairs of India, also referred to as the Board of Control, as an arm of Parliament to establish "dual control" over India alongside the Company, with the intent to leave "ultimate authority" in the British government. The Act forbade the Company to "pursue schemes of conquest and extension of dominion in India."[175]

Yet, Hastings continued with self-authorized wars.[176] The directors too gave mixed signals on how to implement the 1784 Act. They told Hastings they were unable to maintain proper oversight over which offices in India to reduce:

> We found ourselves under difficulties to ascertain by a just decision many circum-
> stances of detail, which must be familiar to you; we found it difficult and in many
> cases impossible to discover the real present value of such offices. . . . We have come
> to the conclusion of leaving the first detail of it in your hands, reserving to ourselves
> the final examination and approbation of the establishment made up by you.[177]

The directors also relayed to Hastings that while the Act established guidelines for administering justice in India, they "recommend it is your particular consideration how far it may not be practicable to owe the offices you may find it necessary to keep up. . . . We are sensible that in the application of this principle, modifications and exceptions may become necessary."[178] In late 1784, Hastings reiterated his wish to resign, alluding to deteriorating health.[179] The directors allowed him to leave in February 1785.[180]

Following Hastings' departure and the new Act, the Bengal Council protected the Company's self-possessed sovereignty. In July 1785, the Council noted when dealing with Maratha ruler Mahadji Shinde that they

> had taken pains to publish to the native powers those principles of a publick system
> which have been so wisely established in the last act of the British legislature, but it
> was proper also to be publickly understood that these were not to be perverted to any
> interpretation that could weaken your actual authority or reflect discredit instead of
> honor on your management of it.[181]

Company administrators continued to assert their "actual authority" regardless of the London machinations. The EIC's Maratha representative also conveyed that "after his remonstrance was made publick in Sindia's *durbar* [court], he received

[174] IOR-B.260: 313.
[175] Lawson 1993: 128.
[176] Dirks 2008: 188.
[177] IOR-E.4.629: 207–208.
[178] IOR-E.4.629: 210–212.
[179] IOR-E.4.42: 257.
[180] IOR-B.100: 954.
[181] IOR-E.4.43: 136.

visits from the *vakeels* [regents] of the different states of India, who attended the
Shaw and Maratta camps, and offered to join the English against Sindia."[182] Thus,
the Company's reassertion of "actual" sovereign authority signalled their military
credibility to the Indian powers balancing against the Marathas.

Hastings arrived back in England in June 1785 and was unanimously thanked by
the directors for his "long, faithful and able services."[183] Throughout the year, he
corresponded with them on plans for military establishments in India.[184] In
February 1786, Burke launched an impeachment inquiry into Hastings[185] and
made numerous requests to the Company for records, correspondence, and
minutes.[186] That summer, the House of Commons voted to impeach Hastings.

Hastings' impeachment trial began in February 1788 and lasted seven years in the
House of Lords. It was the event of the season with tickets going "for as much as £50
(£5,250 today)."[187] The trial was "not just the greatest political spectacle in the age of
George III, it was the nearest the British ever got to putting the Company's Indian Empire
on trial."[188] In an impassioned opening argument, Burke identified the Company's
rapaciousness as "more like an army going to pillage the people, under the pretence of
commerce than anything else."[189] He challenged the English public to "realize that the
crisis of legitimacy in India could lead to a crisis of legitimacy in Britain."[190]

Burke surveyed that the EIC

> was no longer merely a mercantile company, formed for the extension of the British
> commerce; it more nearly resembled a delegation to the whole power and sover-
> eignty of this kingdom, sent into the East. From that time the Company ought to be
> considered as a subordinate sovereign power; that is, sovereign with regard to the
> objects which it touched, subordinate with regard to the power from whence its
> great trust was derived.[191]

After assuming the *Diwani*, Burke argued, the Company ceased behaving like a subordinate power. He read aloud Hastings' claims of self-possessed Company sovereignty:

> The sovereignty which they assumed fell to my lot, very unexpectedly, to exert; and
> whether or not such power, or powers of that nature, were delegated to me by any
> provisions of any Act of Parliament, I confess myself too little of a lawyer to
> pronounce. I only know that the acceptance of the sovereignty of Benares, &c., is
> not acknowledged or admitted by any Act of Parliament; and yet, by the particular

[182]   IOR-E.4.43: 136–137.
[183]   IOR-B.101: 178.
[184]   IOR-B.101: 331, 336, 424, 644.
[185]   IOR-B.102: 797.
[186]   IOR-B.102: 799, 800–802, 911–913, 936–937, 983, 996; IOR-B.103: 142, 147, 1066, 1073; IOR-B.104:
       1038–1040, 1051, 1066, 1072–1073, 1095, 1103–1104, 1126, 1129.
[187]   Dalrymple 2019: 307.
[188]   Dalrymple 2019: 308.
[189]   Dalrymple 2019: 93.
[190]   Dirks 2008: 190.
[191]   Burke 1909: 19.

interference of the majority of the council, the Company is clearly and indisputably seized of that sovereignty. If, therefore, the sovereignty of Benares, as ceded to us by the vizier, have any rights whatever annexed to it (and be not a mere empty word without meaning), those rights must be such as are held, countenanced, and established by the law, custom, and usage of the Mogul empire, and not by the provisions of any British Act of Parliament hitherto enacted. Those rights, and none other, I have been the involuntary instrument of enforcing. And if any future act of Parliament shall positively, or by implication, tend to annihilate those very rights, or their exertion, as I have exerted them, I much fear that the boasted sovereignty of Benares ... will be found a burden instead of benefit, a heavy clog rather than precious gem to its present possessors.[192]

Hastings declared that Company sovereignty over conquered territories, like Bengal and Benares, were not delegated by English authority and operated instead within the Mughal sovereign system. Hastings also claimed that Company sovereignty was absolute, otherwise sovereignty would be as useless as a "heavy clog." These thoughts echoed Hastings' alternative sovereign authority in his resignation letter.

Burke countered that no legitimate government can delegate absolute sovereignty: "absolute, supreme dominion was never conferred or delegated by [Parliament]."[193] He continued:

Before Mr. Hastings none ever came before his superiors to claim it; because, if any such thing could exist, he claims the very power of that sovereign who calls him to account. ... Such a claim is a monster that never existed except in the wild imagination of some theorist. ... No country has wholly meant, or ever meant, to give this power.[194]

Burke often invoked the supreme sovereignty of the Crown ("here we see virtually in the mind's eye that sacred majesty of the crown, under whose authority you sit, and whose power you exercise")[195] and Parliament ("[Hastings] had sent even the plan of an Act of Parliament, to have it confirmed with the last and most sacred authority of this country").[196] He denied that non-Europeans had a different conception of sovereignty: "The supreme power of the state in the Mogul empire did by no means delegate to any of its officers the supreme power in its fulness."[197] Thus, "in Asia as well as in Europe, the same law of nations prevails; the same principles are continually resorted to; and the same maxims sacredly held and strenuously maintained."[198] Burke's idea of indivisible absolute sovereignty as a "law of nations" recalled Bodin's doctrine two centuries prior.

[192] Burke 1909: 112–113.
[193] Burke 1909: 122.
[194] Burke 1909: 123–124.
[195] Burke 1909: 283–284.
[196] Burke 1909: 199.
[197] Burke 1909: 141–142.
[198] Burke 1909: 143.

In 1795, Hastings was acquitted, which Burke had anticipated given the EIC's institutional reach and rampant corruption.[199] Yet, the trial created political space to "demonstrate that the Company's many misdeeds were answerable to Parliament, and it helped publicise the corruption, violence and venality of the EIC, so setting the stage for further governmental oversight, regulation and control."[200] In the early-1800s, Parliament complained: "Were it not, indeed, that the locality of its wealth is at so remote a distance, the very existence of such a body would be dangerous, not merely to the liberty of the subject, but to the stability of the state."[201] By 1858, the English state would take over direct rule and start the Raj in India. The EIC's divisible sovereignty was stripped away and it was no longer acceptable that company-states functioned as they had.[202] Eliminating the use of nonstate actors for sovereign functions was critical for institutionalizing nonintervention norms among late modern European states.[203] This section underscores that states also confronted nonstate sovereign rivals that could no longer be left unchecked. Thus, the impeachment trial made apparent that the EIC's self-possessed sovereign claims were undergirded by practices of *Lived Sovereignty*; while dealing with the EIC's claims fueled the next iteration of *Idealized Sovereignty* discourse.

CONCLUSION

This chapter on the English East India Company concretized the theoretical and analytical arguments of the first two chapters. I showed that key to the Company's success were public/private hybrid relations ranging from contractual, institutional, and shadow configurations. *Contractual hybridity* was visible through formal and frequent charter negotiations and public exchange of forced loans and other fiscal extractions. *Institutional hybridity* was evident through the EIC benefiting from insider rules and the rise of MP-Directors as well as more sophisticated informal lobbying. *Shadow hybridity* materialized through side payments, captured in the lack of EIC public forced loans even during expensive wars, and the presence of back channels through the Secret Committee. Importantly, the EIC's public/private hybridity advanced the British Empire. *Contractual hybridity* created a monopoly for the lucrative East Indies trade; *Institutional hybridity* consolidated commercial advantages; and *Shadow hybridity* expanded imperial territories through plausible deniability. The analysis demonstrated that while hybrid relations are fluid, we can still trace their variation across time. In the forthcoming chapters, I dive deeper into the power payoffs and legitimation challenges of each ideal-type also theorized in Chapter 2.

[199] Dirks 2008: 201.
[200] Dalrymple 2019: 314.
[201] Bowen 2005: 16–17.
[202] Phillips and Sharman 2020: 212.
[203] Thomson 1994.

The EIC also provided empirical leverage to examine the dynamic relationship between *Idealized* and *Lived Sovereignty* introduced in Chapter 1. The EIC's self-understanding of sovereign authority shifted from a privilege understood within *Idealized Sovereignty* to a self-possessed right from extensive enactments of *Lived Sovereignty*. Meanwhile, the Company's sovereign awakening revealed problems with nonhierarchical early modern layered sovereignty that were thus far ignored. After the Company's assumption of the Bengal *Diwani*, the stakes of the Company's *Lived Sovereignty* escalated. The English state introduced more hierarchical relations through the 1773 Act's oversight, the 1784 Act's Board of Control, and the rebukes in Hastings' impeachment. Ultimately, these exchanges clarify that the social production of sovereignty occurs through a historical process that includes wrestling with public/private hybridity. Indeed, sovereignty was born in empire and forged by nonstate actors, even though we now associate it with the modern international system of states.

4

Contracting American Wars through Blackwater

The war will be won in large measure by forces you do not know about, in actions you will not see and in ways you may not want to know about, but we will prevail.[1]

For the first time in major American wars, as many contractors as troops were used in Afghanistan and Iraq (Table 4.1).[2] More contractors than troops have died since 2001.[3] Of these, armed security contractors are of particular interest in this chapter. A third of all Iraqi reconstruction funds went to security contractors, funds that amounted to the combined payments of "more than 90 percent of all U.S. taxpayers."[4] The trend led practitioners to observe that "in Iraq, the postwar business boom was not oil, it was security"[5] and scholars to examine the "growing market for force [that] now exists alongside, and intertwined with, state military and police forces."[6] The epigraph quotes the Central Intelligence Agency's (CIA) then number three official, Buzzy Krongard, whose reference to "forces you do not know about" could be a general nod to unknown events. But Krongard's statement also foreshadows an unprecedented contractor force in American wars. One member of the contractor force was Blackwater, whose 2007 Nisour Square civilian massacre opened this book. Blackwater was once the largest contractor for the US State Department in Iraq and performed over 100,000 missions.[7] Its founder, Erik Prince, has stated his goal was "to do for the national security apparatus what FedEx did to the postal service."[8]

Prince established Blackwater in 1997 as a military training facility, receiving a Federal Bureau of Investigation (FBI) contract to train police officers after the Columbine school shootings and a Navy contract for counterterrorism after the 1999

[1] Mercury 2001.
[2] These numbers are notoriously difficult to pin down, as I discuss in a later section on oversight.
[3] About 6,870 US troops and 7,402 US contractors in Afghanistan and Iraq, October 2001–October 2019. Neta Crawford and Catherine Lutz, "Human Cost of Post-9/11 Wars," Costs of War, as of 11/13/2019.
[4] Bartlett and Steele 2007.
[5] Hider 2004.
[6] Avant 2005: 253.
[7] Hasan 2019.
[8] Erik Prince speaking at a conference, January 11, 2006, as quoted in McFate 2014: 10.

TABLE 4.1 *Ratio of contractors to troops in major American wars*[9]

War	Contractors	Troops	Ratio
American Revolution	1,500	9,000	1:6
Mexican/American	6,000	33,000	1:6
Civil War	200,000	1,000,000	1:5
World War I	85,000	2,000,000	1:20
World War II	734,000	5,400,000	1:7
Korean War	156,000	393,000	1:2.5
Vietnam War	70,000	359,000	1:6
Iraq War I	50,400	541,000	1:10
Afghanistan	104,000	64,000	1.6:1
Iraq War II	190,000	160,000	1.3:1

bombing of the USS Cole destroyer. Following the 9/11 attacks, the FBI extended its contract to include counterterrorism. After stepping down from the CIA, Krongard worked as an executive at Blackwater and brokered its first major war contract for the CIA station in Kabul in 2002.[10] The State Department then contracted to protect Paul Bremmer, the top American diplomat in Iraq, in 2003. J. Cofer Black, the State Department's head of counterterrorism and leader of the hunt for Bin Laden, joined Blackwater in 2004 as the company's vice chairman.[11] Blackwater also trained the Afghan border police on a Pentagon contract.[12] In 2005, Joseph E. Schmitz, the Pentagon's Inspector General, and "the top U.S. official in charge of directly overseeing military contractors in Iraq and Afghanistan," resigned to serve as the Prince Group's chief operating officer and general counsel.[13] By 2005, Blackwater had more than half a billion dollars in federal contracts, and in 2007 it had more than a billion (Figure 4.1). After Nisour Square, Blackwater changed its name to Xe and then sold the company, now known as Academi. Prince is currently the chairman of Frontier Services Group with security contracts in the UAE and China.[14] In 2017, he advocated for deploying an "East India Company"-style contractor force with a viceroy in Afghanistan.[15]

Blackwater exhibits public/private hybridity in American wars as its employees "carried weapons, had their own helicopters and fought off insurgents in ways that were hard to distinguish from combat."[16] Indeed, in 2006, the United States

---

9   Adapted from: Zamparelli 1999: 12; Isenberg 2008: 4.
10   Pelton 2007: 36–37.
11   Jackson 2004.
12   Hasan 2019.
13   Scahill 2008: 366–367.
14   Hasan 2019.
15   Prince 2017.
16   Avant 2005: 21.

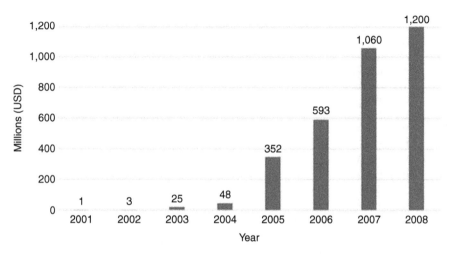

FIGURE 4.1 Value of Blackwater federal contracts in millions (USD), 2001–2008

included contractors like Blackwater in the Pentagon's "Total Force," defined as "its active and reserve military components, its civil servants, and its contractors" that "constitute its warfighting capability and capacity."[17] Many scholars have examined security contractors in twenty-first-century wars[18] and wars of the past.[19] The rise in security contracting across the world is usually attributed to the end of the Cold War, which "gave states a reason to downsize their military forces, freeing up millions of former military personnel from a wide variety of countries, many of them Western. At the same time, the end of the Cold War lifted the lid on many long-simmering conflicts held in check by the superpowers."[20] Security contractors filled the vacuum for peripheral conflicts when the United States and others turned a blind eye. In "weak states" like Sierra Leone "contracting may buy the state the means to defend its territory in the short run."[21] But even in "strong states" like the United States, contractors help implement American grand strategy to maintain a "role of guarantor of global stability at a time when the American public is unwilling to provide the resources necessary."[22] As such, the use of contractors highlights "global security assemblages" where the state "is located within networks that cut across and through it, and where public and private, global and local intersections and connections provide multiple sites for political engagement."[23] But there are costs. Contracting

---

[17] Department of Defense 2006.
[18] Singer 2003; Avant 2005; Leander 2005; Kinsey 2006; Krahmann 2010; Abrahamsen and Williams 2011; McFate 2014; Dunigan and Petersohn 2015; Fitzsimmons 2015; Eckert 2016; Mahoney 2017.
[19] Thomson 1994; Percy 2007.
[20] Isenberg 2008: 1.
[21] Avant 2005: 59.
[22] Isenberg 2009: 5.
[23] Abrahamsen and Williams 2011: 225; Leander 2005.

"sovereign services in strong states is likely to lead to some functional loss."[24] A contractor force also distorts ethical justifications for war where proportionality is a major consideration.[25] Finally, contracting complicates "ideal models of the democratic state, the citizen and the soldier."[26]

This chapter builds on such scholarship to examine how *contractual hybridity* orders global violence through the case of Blackwater. Chapter 2 mentioned that Blackwater is not a modal war contractor – that is, a large logistics firm – nor does Blackwater solely exhibit contractual relations. Blackwater had extensive institutional linkages with politicians (e.g. Krongard, Black, Schmitz) and also operated through off-the-books shadow relations with the CIA.[27] But Blackwater best shows the usefulness of the ideal-type of *contractual hybridity* and the resulting trade-offs for *Idealized* and *Lived Sovereignty*. Blackwater was distinct from its main competitors in security provision, DynCorp and Triple Canopy.[28] Compared to these firms, Blackwater participated in "both explicit and implicit attempts to shape foreign policy … [and its] size [was] such that its attempts to affect foreign and military policy [were] positioned to have an impact."[29] Iraqis too "harbored resentment toward the contractors themselves and Blackwater as a whole."[30] Thus, Blackwater's aim to privatize sovereign power and its public perceptions make the stakes of *contractual hybridity* clearer than other security contractors. Since I could not obtain access to Blackwater's internal documents, as I do for the rest of the organizations in this book, I draw on an originally assembled archive of 3,462 news articles from seven sources[31] on Blackwater between 2000 and 2016, Congressional hearings, and 153 motions and memos from Blackwater's legal cases. From these materials, this chapter makes two contributions to the relationship between sovereignty, contractors, and governance.

First, I examine how Blackwater's strategic partnership with the United States in *Lived Sovereignty* led to legitimation challenges of distributed accountability for *Idealized Sovereignty*. In *contractual hybridity*, state and nonstate are treated interchangeably without symmetric obligations in finance, law, and politics. While the deployment of war contractors may enable a particular fulfillment of American grand strategy with limited political costs, contractor unaccountability has the potential to inspire public backlash against the government. Moreover, in contracting violence, "individual states may gain power even as their actions erode the sovereign system."[32] Contractors challenge the purpose of sovereign authority as "a government dependent

---

[24] Avant 2005: 58.
[25] Eckert 2016.
[26] Krahmann 2010: 3.
[27] I thank Deborah Avant for this point.
[28] Fitzsimmons 2015: 146.
[29] Dunigan 2011: 18.
[30] Dunigan 2011: 72.
[31] *The New York Times, The Washington Post, The Wall Street Journal, The Los Angeles Times, Associated Press, Reuters,* and *The Virginia-Pilot.*
[32] Avant 2005: 258.

on contractors to function too easily loses sight of those things that only government can do well."[33] Thus, *contractual hybridity* in war-making both sustains sovereign competence in *Lived Sovereignty* and undermines sovereign legitimacy in *Idealized Sovereignty*.

Second, I question the taken-for-granted notion of "things that only governments can do well." Over the past half-century, American bureaucrats have debated the boundaries of the state in light of contracting. This chapter uses all executive branch memos, legislative reports, and hearings on American contracting from 1950 onward to trace increasingly complex definitions and tests for determining "inherently governmental functions." For some media commentators, the 2003 Iraq War was indicative of how "almost no thought had been given to an overall strategy to determine which jobs and functions should be handled by the government, and which could be turned over to private companies."[34] The archival records show that, contrary to expectations, a lot of thought went into defining inherently governmental versus commercial functions. Bureaucrats created new categories of government functions, revised examples of necessary governmental authority, and prohibited particular types of contracting relations that affected all facets of governance. Thus, the research highlights how public/private hybridity forces a rearticulation of core sovereign functions in the social construction of sovereignty.

In the rest of this chapter, I give an overview of contracting in the United States, examine *contractual hybridity* first in theory and then in practice in Blackwater, and follow how the contests between *Lived* and *Idealized Sovereignty* informed American bureaucratic debates over "inherently governmental functions."

SOVEREIGNTY UNDER CONTRACT

Contracting is not an unusual phenomenon. Governments face a "make or buy" decision when industry is capable of providing comparable goods or services. Former New York governor Mario Cuomo stated: "It is not the role of governments to provide services. It is the role of government to see to it that services are provided."[35] The US federal government consists of 2.1 million employees, excluding uniformed military personnel, the postal service, and select intelligence agencies.[36] In 2016, the Office of Management and Budget (OMB) estimated that 43 percent of them are engaged in "commercial functions" that may be contracted.[37] But American contracting has varied. Figure 4.2 plots US federal contract spending in inflation-adjusted billions from 1984 to 2018.[38] After 1985, spending had a downward trend with some spikes until 2001. Contract

---

[33]   Stanger 2009: 8.
[34]   Risen 2008.
[35]   House of Representatives 2016: Palatiello testimony.
[36]   Congressional Research Service 2021: 1.
[37]   House of Representatives 2016: Palatiello testimony.
[38]   Bloomberg Government 2019.

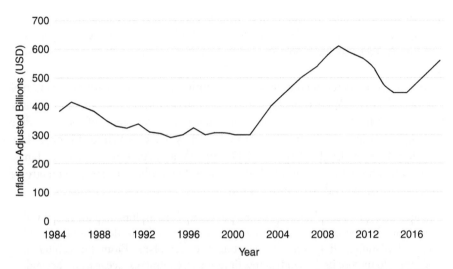

FIGURE 4.2 US government prime contract spending in inflation-adjusted billions (USD), 1984–2018

spending doubled between 2000 and 2008. At its peak in 2009, the United States spent $612.4 billion on contracting, amounting to more than "40 cents of every discretionary dollar."[39] However, a 2010 moratorium on new contracts led to steady decline until 2015, after which spending increased again. The big uptick after 2002 was due to the rise in war contracting, the seeds of which were sown a decade earlier.

In 1992, Secretary of Defense Dick Cheney commissioned a study from Halliburton on how to quickly privatize the military bureaucracy. Cheney's "idea was to free up the troops to do the fighting while private contractors handled the back-end logistics."[40] During his tenure, Cheney reduced the number of troops from 2.2 million to 1.6 million. After his term ended, Cheney went on to lead Halliburton.[41] In 1995, a Defense Science Board report suggested that "the Pentagon could save up to $12 billion annually by 2002 if it contracted out all support functions except actual warfighting."[42] In 1996, President Bill Clinton sent contractor Military Professional Resources Incorporated (MPRI) to train the Croatian military against Yugoslavia, "a contract that ultimately tipped the balance of that conflict."[43] DynCorp "supported every major U.S. military campaign since Korea"[44] and represented "virtually all U.S. contributions to international civilian police units in the 1990s."[45] The United

---

[39]   House of Representatives 2007b: 1.
[40]   Briody 2004: 195–196.
[41]   Scahill 2008: 51.
[42]   Isenberg 2008: 2.
[43]   Scahill 2008: 52.
[44]   Isenberg 2008: 2.
[45]   Avant 2005: 20.

States used contractors "in both the 1990–1991 Iraq War and the Balkans conflicts in the mid-1990s, but the majority of the companies involved in these conflicts were employed to perform logistical functions, not security services."[46] This changed in the new millennium.

By 2000, American war contracting was in position for a boom with the election of George W. Bush. Apart from Cheney, the Bush administration appointed many former executives of defense contractors, like Under Secretary of Defense Pete Aldridge (Aerospace Corporation), Army Secretary Thomas White (Enron), Navy Secretary Gordon England (General Dynamics), and Air Force Secretary James Roche (Northrop Grumman).[47] A day before September 11, 2001, Secretary of Defense Rumsfeld laid out a new doctrine:

> The topic today is an adversary that poses a threat, a serious threat, to the security of the United States of America. This adversary is one of the world's last bastions of central planning. It governs by dictating five-year plans. From the capital, it attempts to impose its demands across time zones, continents, oceans, and beyond. It disrupts the defense of the United States and places the lives of men and women in uniform at risk. ... The adversary's closer to home. It's the Pentagon bureaucracy.[48]

Rumsfeld went on to argue that the Pentagon "must behave less like bureaucrats and more like venture capitalists."[49] After the terrorist attacks, Rumsfeld's vision came to fruition. The military moved to expand the 1985 Logistics Civil Augmentation Program, or LOGCAP, under which "contractors provided services ranging from building bases to cooking food and doing laundry."[50] The United States then awarded a ten-year $32 billion LOGCAP contract to Halliburton for the "war on terror."

The Post-9/11 Contractor Force

In a post-9/11 world, Krongard's "contractor force" was taking shape. The United States admits spending $85 billion on Iraqi contracts between 2003 and 2007.[51] However, *The Financial Times* estimates the figure to be at least $138 billion.[52]

There were three important differences in war contracting after 2001. First, while "life support" contracts like setting up bases remained important, contracting also included mission security, like protecting diplomats or convoys that had potential for combat. In 2002, the State Department's Bureau of Diplomatic Security began

[46]   Dunigan 2011: 3.
[47]   Scahill 2008: 53.
[48]   Dunigan 2011: 11.
[49]   Rumsfeld 2002.
[50]   Department of Defense 2009b: 40.
[51]   Congressional Budget Office 2008: 1.
[52]   Fifield 2013.

a Worldwide Personal Protective Services contract, "envisioned as a small-scale bodyguard operation to protect small groups of U.S. diplomats and other foreign officials. In Iraq, the administration turned it into a paramilitary force several thousand strong. Spending on the program jumped from $50 million in 2003 to $613 million in 2006."[53] In 2007, Ambassador Ryan Crocker stated, "there is simply no way at all that the State Department's Bureau of Diplomatic Security could ever have enough full-time personnel to staff the security function in Iraq. There is no alternative except through contracts."[54] Even though security contractors like Blackwater constituted about 15 percent of all Iraqi contractors, they received 30 percent of the reconstruction funds.[55] Furthermore, "changes in the nature of conflicts led tasks less central to the core of modern militaries (such as operating complex weapons systems and policing) to be closer to the front and center of maintaining security, and private security companies provide[d] these services readily."[56] Thus, "in a war zone with no front, these companies [were] becoming more deeply enmeshed in combat, in some cases all but obliterating distinctions between professional troops and private commandos."[57]

Second, contractors in Iraq and Afghanistan were not "formally integrated into the military structure, as is the case with, for instance, French Foreign Legion troops and the French military. Security contractors' position in the military chain of command [was] therefore constantly in question, which, among other things, [led] to a host of potential coordination problems."[58] In Iraq, many security firms coordinated and subcontracted with each other. The resulting self-regulation worried politicians that "the fastest-growing component of government is the 'shadow government' represented by private companies doing public work under federal contract."[59] One government official observed that "each private firm amounts to an individual battalion. Now they are all coming together to build the largest security organization in the world."[60] In short, "the U.S. had created a fifth branch of the military" using contractors.[61]

Third, high-profile scandals, like Blackwater's Nisour Square massacre and the involvement of CACI and Titan contractors in the 2004 Abu Gharib prisoner abuse, resulted in more public discussions of war contracting.[62] In a 2007 study from the Project for Excellence in Journalism, less than 0.25 percent of coverage about Iraq in a sample of 100,000 news stories between 2003 and 2007 mentioned contractors.[63]

[53] Scahill 2007.
[54] Parker (J) 2007, emphasis added.
[55] Congressional Budget Office 2008: 2.
[56] Avant 2005: 3.
[57] Barstow et al. 2004.
[58] Dunigan 2011: 3.
[59] House of Representatives 2007b: 2.
[60] Priest and Flaherty 2004.
[61] Fifield 2013.
[62] Avant 2005: 2.
[63] Project for Excellence in Journalism 2007.

More recently, Avant and Neu introduce a Private Security Events Database that "traces the involvement of private military and security companies (PMSCs) in 1,288 events in Africa, Latin America, and Southeast Asia from 1990 to 2012."[64] They find that reporting on security contractors has increased over time, though most reports are largely about contractors "performing their prescribed activities or responding to crime" with fewer reports on contractors "involved in contentious events and most events were not accompanied by allegations of abuse."[65] Yet, incidents of contractor abuse have occurred across types of contractors: "Aegis guards, for example, have been allegedly involved in drive-by shootings; Zapata Engineering employees have been held by the armed forces for firing on a Marine observation post; and Triple Canopy contractors have been dismissed for targeting civilians 'for amusement.'"[66]

Two other developments happened at this time. First, by 2006, the size of the US federal workforce had remained the same since 1963.[67] However, the federal budget had grown threefold. Each federal employee was now responsible for overseeing a million dollars more with the same resources. Critically, the human capital shortfall also sustained the demand for contractors while making it more difficult to oversee them. Despite the post-9/11 contracting boom, "the number of contract specialists – an occupation critical to the execution of contingency contracting – rose by only 3 percent government-wide between 1992 and 2009."[68] This created situations where contractors were overseen by other contractors. In 2004, the United States awarded a $293 million contract to Aegis in Iraq to "coordinate and oversee the activities and movements of the scores of private military firms in the country servicing the occupation, including facilitating intelligence and security briefings."[69]

Second, tracking contractors became difficult. In December 2006, two different government groups came up with wildly different counts of contractors in Iraq. The Congressional Iraq Study Group estimated 5,000; the Pentagon's central command estimated 100,000. It was difficult to track contractors because of different definitions and off-the-book contracts. But the biggest reason was subcontracting. A contract can go through as many as three layers of subcontracts, which firms can refuse to disclose for proprietary reasons. Also, contractor deaths are not counted the same as military deaths. While the Pentagon keeps track of military fatalities releasing details to the press as they occur, contractor deaths are tracked by the Department of Labor, which regards them as workplace fatalities and does not share them as they happen. Finally, media investigations on contracting were often restricted by blocks to Freedom of Information Act (FOIA) requests. Some activities of security contractors would have

64 Avant and Neu 2019: 1.
65 Avant and Neu 2019: 9.
66 Krahmann 2010: 209–210.
67 Stanger 2009: 13.
68 Commission on Wartime Contracting 2011: 2.
69 Priest and Flaherty 2004.

been covered by the Arms Export Control Act, opening contractors to public disclosure and Congressional approval. However, many contractors circumvented the export regime by working under the Foreign Military Sales Program, where they were employed as Pentagon liaisons to foreign governments. This program avoided export controls and also denied FOIA requests.[70]

Blackwater in American Total Force

Meanwhile, Blackwater was seen as a core part of the American war effort. As mentioned in this book's Introduction, during the Nisour Square sentencing trial, one witness observed: "Blackwater had power like Saddam Hussein. The power comes from the United States."[71] The statement speaks to a concern from Representative Elijah Cummings "that the ordinary Iraqi may not be able to distinguish military actions from contractor actions. They view them all as American actions."[72] Erik Prince positioned Blackwater as "a patriotic extension of the U.S. military, and in September 2005 he issued a company-wide memorandum requiring all company employees and contractors to swear the same oath of loyalty to the U.S. Constitution as the Pentagon, State Department and intelligence agencies."[73] When Congress asked why there was no clause in Blackwater's bylaws forbidding it to work for American enemies, Prince replied:

> This idea that we have this private army in the wings is just not accurate. The people we employ are former U.S. military and law enforcement people, people who have sworn the oath to support and defend the Constitution against all enemies, foreign and domestic. They bleed red, white and blue. So the idea that they are going to suddenly switch after having served honorably for the U.S. military and go play for the other team, it is not likely.[74]

Key to Prince's sell was to move away from the language of mercenaries to "part-ners." Sarah Percy argues that over the 1990s a strong anti-mercenary norm shifted the discourse around private military and security contractors to displace "mercen-aries" from their branding.[75] In this vein, Prince argued, "the Oxford Dictionary defines a mercenary as a professional soldier working for a foreign government. And Americans working for America is not it."[76] The efforts paid off as legislators began referring to Blackwater as "our silent partner in this struggle."[77]

---

[70]　Avant and Sigelman 2010: 244.
[71]　Apuzzo 2015.
[72]　House of Representatives 2007a: 61.
[73]　Scahill 2008: 58–59.
[74]　House of Representatives 2007a: 100.
[75]　Percy 2007: 206–207.
[76]　House of Representatives 2007a: 91.
[77]　Barstow et al. 2004.

In 2017, when establishing jurisdiction for the criminal prosecution of Blackwater guards for the Nisour Square shootings, the US government argued three ways in which Blackwater's functions related to the Pentagon's mission in Iraq. First, "the State Department was an important part of the rebuilding effort the Defense Department was engaged in; its diplomats were helping the Iraqis restore their country. Blackwater employed the defendants to provide security for the diplomats whose work plainly supported the DOD mission."[78] Second, "Blackwater employees were assigned to assist distressed military units during firefights, train Army security escorts and provide escorts to Provincial Reconstruction Teams when Army escorts were unavailable." Third, "the Defense Department was 'able to reduce the amount of [its] platoons ... dedicated for Department of State security convoy missions' as 'Blackwater took the majority of those tasks.'" In constructing these links, the US government made explicit that public/private relations in *contractual hybridity* were necessary to conduct American wars.

There were a few early calls for contractor accountability before Nisour Square. In a 2004 editorial on "Privatizing Warfare," *The New York Times* began: "It's one thing for the military to outsource food and laundry services to private firms, as it started doing aggressively in the 1990s, but it's quite another to outsource the actual fighting. ... The Pentagon seems to be outsourcing at least part of its core responsibilities for securing Iraq instead of facing up to the need for more soldiers."[79] The same year, *The Washington Post* reported on the conflicts of interest between security contractors and regulators that affect oversight.[80] *The Associated Press* reported in 2006 that "Iraqi officials accuse many of the companies providing protection in violence-plagued Iraq of being a law unto themselves, prompting a flurry of attempts to better regulate an industry that is expanding rapidly around the world."[81] Blackwater commented then: "Failure in this industry comes soonest to those who openly violate sound business principles and disregard the moral, ethical and legal high ground."[82] *The Virginian-Pilot*, the local paper for Blackwater's headquarters and one of its earliest critics, quoted Amnesty International on contractor impunity in 2006: "It sends the message that you can do whatever you want over there and get away with it."[83] Finally, *The Los Angeles Times* was the first to run some numbers and reported in July 2007 that contractors outnumbered troops in Iraq and that contractor accountability was severely lacking.[84]

[78] *United States v. Nicholas Abram Slatten*, District of Columbia Circuit Court of Appeals. August 4, 2017.

[79] *New York Times* 2004.

[80] O'Harrow Jr. and McCarthy 2004.

[81] Zavis 2006.

[82] Zavis 2006.

[83] Sizemore 2006.

[84] Miller 2007.

In one of these early warnings, Daniel Bergner profiled the founders of Triple Canopy and shadowed their contractors in Iraq for a long feature titled "The Other Army" for *The New York Times Magazine*.[85] Bergner set the scene by quoting Lyle Hendrick, a contractor for an unnamed firm and former Special Forces captain:

> At best you've got professionals doing their best in a chaotic and aggressive environment. At worst you've got cowboys running almost unchecked, shooting at will and just plain O.T.F. (Out There Flappin'). [They looked] like extras in Mel Gibson's Road Warriors. There was no instruction, no sit-down, no here's how we operate; it was, throw your stuff on the truck and let's go.[86]

Similarly, Blackwater's

> high-speed, get-out-of the-way-or-die motorcades have become the stuff of legend in Baghdad. By many accounts, the convoys are so deeply resented that they are setting back the overall US military effort to win Iraqi hearts and minds. Blackwater's aggressive tactics drew no complaints from the officials ferried from Baghdad's Green Zone to appointments in the Red Zone that is the rest of Iraq.[87]

Ann Starr, a former Coalitional Provisional Authority (CPA) advisor, concurs: "What they told me was, 'Our mission is to protect the principal at all costs. If that means pissing off the Iraqis, too bad.'"[88] Even though contractors may see combat, they are not part of the military's chain of command. Specifically, "contractors' duties are set out in their contract, which is managed by a government contracting officer, not the military commander."[89] Berger interviewed a Triple Canopy manager who spoke about the lack of oversight:

> D.O.D. doesn't want anything to do with it. They don't have time. They don't have the numbers. And State can't investigate incidents. They don't have the investigators. So there's Iraqi law. Not that Iraqi law really exists. Am I going to give up my weapons to Iraqi police? I don't think so. That could get me killed.[90]

From a contractual perspective, Blackwater was "actually getting our contract exactly as we asked them to [and] at the same time hurting our counterinsurgency effort"[91] by alienating Iraqis who rely on American support and jeopardizing US servicepersons because of contractor backlash.

Media reports in the mid-2000s reveal that *contractual hybridity* was key to ordering violence in the major American wars of the twenty-first century as part of *Lived Sovereignty*, but also led to legitimation challenges for the United States in

---

[85] Bergner 2005.
[86] Bergner 2005.
[87] Debusmann 2008.
[88] Singer 2007: 6.
[89] Congressional Budget Office 2008: 2.
[90] Bergner 2005.
[91] House of Representatives 2007a: 78.

Idealized Sovereignty. Specifically, security contractors were considered as part of the government for sovereign privileges like international legal immunity in a "Total Force," but were not part of the sovereign obligations to be included in war fatalities or disclose their finances or be held legally liable. I deal with these sovereign dilemmas next.

SOVEREIGN DILEMMAS IN *CONTRACTUAL HYBRIDITY*

War contracting challenges the dimension of sovereign authority in *Idealized Sovereignty* where the legitimate use for force is exclusively reserved to a sovereign state. Max Weber argues that the state "(successfully) claims the monopoly of the legitimate use of physical force within a given territory."[92] This definition is often interpreted to mean that any outsourcing of violence undermines the monopoly (which I complicated in Chapter 2). Former American Ambassador to Iraq, Joe Wilson, exemplifies this concern: "I think it's extraordinarily dangerous when a nation begins to outsource its monopoly on the use of force and the use of violence in support of its foreign policy or national security objectives."[93] This section argues that security contractors' implications for sovereignty are more nuanced than an obvious loss of Weberian control. Instead, the challenge is to Weberian legitimacy as seen in the potential to hold states responsible for contractor abuse in *Lived Sovereignty*, which is exacerbated by distributed accountability and has political implications for *Idealized Sovereignty*.

Weber and the Monopoly over Legitimate Use of Force

Weber looms large in the literature on security contractors.[94] Deborah Avant begins her landmark study on the international market for force by asserting, "Weber's definition of the state is the obvious starting point in most investigations."[95] She acknowledges that Weber's claim on the state's monopoly on force "was exaggerated from the start and there has been a role for the private sector in security for some time."[96] Nonetheless, Avant's conclusion is that a "transnational market for force now exists alongside the system of states and state forces."[97] By conceptualizing the contractor force as external to the state system, Avant inquires the implications for state control:

> Does the privatization of security undermine state control of violence? Can the privatization of security enhance state control of violence? Does the privatization of

---

92   Weber 2004 [1919]: 32.
93   Scahill 2008: 45.
94   In theorizing security assemblages, Abrahamsen and Williams (2011: 9) rely on Pierre Bourdieu's variation on Weber instead as it allows them access to conceiving the state as "a field of power" that is not reducible to physical coercion.
95   Avant 2005: 1.
96   Avant 2005: 2.
97   Avant 2005: 3, emphasis added.

security chart new ways by which violence might be collectively controlled? How does private security affect the ability to contain the use of force within political process and social norms?[98]

Avant finds that "the control of force has been most stable, effective, and legitimate when all three aspects have reinforced one another – when capable forces have been governed by accepted political processes and operated according to shared values."[99] State capacity is an intervening variable. "Strong states" that are "coherent, capable, and legitimate to begin with" are "best able to manage the risks of privatization and harness [security contractors] to produce new public goods."[100] Meanwhile, Avant cites Weber on patrimonial authority to posit that for weak states outsourcing violence is a "desperate state-building gambit"[101] as "contracts become just another tool for maintaining a corrupt leader's rule or protecting private interests."[102]

My analytical construct of public/private hybridity differs from Avant's starting point of separate contractor and state forces acting alongside each other. But I build on Avant in weaving Weberian legitimacy into the implications of contracting. In *Idealized Sovereignty*, "states have primary responsibility for and monopoly over legitimate security services."[103] It is in this context that Avant argues that strong states "have the most to lose if privatization tips the ledger and undermines the capacities of public forces or legitimacy of foreign policy."[104] Even when states regulate contractors, their resulting "'engage[ment]' of [contractors] as legitimate purveyors of military services . . . flies in the face of the international norm that security should be the exclusive realm of states. Many have held that states' collective monopoly of the legitimate use of force is a fundamental feature of the modern state system."[105] I take this a step further by arguing that the key Weberian dilemma is not about overall state control but about maintaining legitimate control for reinforcing *Idealized Sovereignty*.

Indeed, what is at stake in the Weberian dilemma for contractual hybridity is not the outsourcing of violence itself – by delegating functions in war, the state may still maintain a monopoly of control. In fact, war contracting bolsters American sovereign competence in *Lived Sovereignty*. Representative John Tierney observed: "The all-voluntary professional force after the Vietnam War employed the so-called Abrams Doctrine. The idea was that we wouldn't go to war without the sufficient backing of the Nation. Outsourcing has circumvented this doctrine. It allows the administration to almost double the force size without any political price being paid."[106] Contracting

---

98   Avant 2005: 3.
99   Avant 2005: 6.
100   Avant 2005: 7.
101   Avant 2005: 59.
102   Avant 2005: 59.
103   Avant 2005: 69.
104   Avant 2005: 7.
105   Avant 2005: 69.
106   House of Representatives 2007a: 17.

also allows governments to do more in war. Prince recalled how "Blackwater's work with the CIA began when [Blackwater] provided specialized instructors and facilities that the Agency lacked. In the years that followed, the company became a virtual extension of the CIA because we were asked time and again to carry out dangerous missions, which the Agency either could not or would not do in-house."[107] Contractors subverted the "need to build a 'coalition of the willing'" by renting "an occupation force."[108]

Thus, I recast the Weberian dilemma as meaning whether the use of force can be adjudicated legitimately.[109] In other words, Weberian legitimation relies on making the state accountable for its use of violence, whether contracted or not. This echoes the nineteenth-century process of delegitimizing privateers and mercenaries from the international system once states were forced to take accountability for their use of violence. According to Janice Thomson, "if we take states themselves as the assessors of legitimacy, it is clear that the state is the legitimate deployer of coercion."[110] The Weberian legitimacy claims are not "the ends to which the state deploys violence [but that . . .] from the point of view of statesmen, the legitimate deployer of violence is the state."[111] Crucially, Weberian "states are not merely authorized to do these things; they are expected to do them."[112] Thus, Thomson argues that "state authority was made coterminous with territorial boundaries, and states were held accountable for the transborder coercive activities of individuals residing within their borders. Violence, which for three or four centuries was an international market commodity, was by 1900 taken off the market."[113]

Weberian legitimation is then part of the accepted discourse in *Idealized Sovereignty* that set up the stakes of irresponsible contractors in *Lived Sovereignty*. Weberian states are expected to build a legitimate claim for the use of force. Security contracting can threaten this legitimacy:

> The firms that make up the American market for force have emerged as perhaps the most capable and willfully independent private armed forces in the world, which have regularly ignored regulations imposed by their chief client: the government of the United States. It is, therefore, unsurprising that their behavior has undermined the United States' monopoly on force and the provision of security as a public good in its operations abroad.[114]

What matters for Weberian legitimacy in this instance is that contractors "regularly ignored regulations" from the US government, which reflects poorly on the maintenance of American *Idealized Sovereignty*. After Nisour Square, journalists accused

[107] Lake 2013.
[108] Scahill 2008: 46.
[109] I thank Sammy Barkin and Hendrik Spruyt for helping explore this point.
[110] Thomson 1994: 8.
[111] Thomson 1994: 16.
[112] Thomson 1994: 17, emphasis in original.
[113] Thomson 1994: 19.
[114] Fitzsimmons 2015: 145.

Blackwater of building "a privatized parallel structure to the U.S. national security apparatus."[115] Politicians questioned "whether [Blackwater] created a shadow military of mercenary forces that are not accountable to the U.S. Government or to anyone else."[116] Scholars worried that "systemic privatization" shrinks the state[117] and "changes who guards the guardians."[118] Thus, perceptions of American unaccountability for Blackwater's actions in *Lived Sovereignty* matters for the construction of *Idealized Sovereignty*. Moreover, expectations of accountability are strongest in *contractual hybridity* as it is the most formally recognized relationship in the ideal-types of public/private hybridity. In theory, *contractual hybridity* is both a strategic asset for Weberian sovereign competence in *Lived Sovereignty* and a liability for Weberian sovereign legitimacy in *Idealized Sovereignty*. I now tease out specific legitimation challenges from Blackwater's practices.

Distributed Accountability

Contractual hybridity's formalized and publicized characteristics make it amenable to oversight that could prevent sovereign abuses for which the United States is expected to be held responsible. But public/private contractual relations also distribute accountability, especially when oversight is limited.

Insufficient oversight in security contracting contributed to monopolistic behavior and financial abuse by firms. Of Blackwater's total contracts, less than 5 percent were obtained under open competition, meaning the contract was awarded when more than one competitor made a bid. Less than 9 percent were under partial competition, meaning the contract was awarded with open competition but no other competitors made a bid (which happens with extremely tight deadlines). A third of all contracts were awarded under no competition, meaning the contract was closed to bids from other competitors.[119] Given these practices, it is no surprise that Blackwater held 84 percent of all State Department diplomatic protection contracts around the world in 2007.[120] Monopolies make it difficult to terminate a contract when things go wrong. This was the case when the State Department retained Blackwater even after the Nisour Square shootings, otherwise there would have been a security vacuum. Monopolies also grant bargaining leverage for pricing to contractors, which may lead to financial abuse.[121] A 2011 Congressional bipartisan study conservatively estimated waste of $31 billion to

[115] Scahill 2008: 43–44.
[116] House of Representatives 2007a: 20.
[117] Feigenbaum and Henig 1994.
[118] Avant 2005: 6.
[119] Data obtained from the Federal Procurement Data System and legal briefs filed on behalf of Blackwater in civil trials. Data are missing for more than half of Blackwater contracts worth $500 million.
[120] Blackwater legal brief, May 1, 2008.
[121] Mahoney 2017: 41.

$60 billion out of the $206 billion paid to contractors in Iraq and Afghanistan.[122] The broad range indicates a major obstacle in better contractor oversight: "A forensic compilation of wasted dollars derived from individual projects and programs is not possible because it would need to be recreated over the last 10 years and, in far too many cases, the necessary documentation does not exist."[123]

The reasons behind financial waste range from poor planning and limited oversight to kickbacks for civilian officials and payments to insurgents. Blackwater's 2004 contract with the State Department, which was originally $229.5 million for five years, became $321 million by June 2006. Then, "the estimated value of the contract through September 2006 was $337 million. By late 2007, Blackwater had been paid more than $750 million under the contract."[124] Why did the contract cost the government over twice its original value? One reason is subcontracting. In a typical relationship, Blackwater's subcontracting charges of a $600 daily rate per contractor increased by more than three times as the main contractor charged the government $2,500 for the same job.[125] It is not easy for regulators to uncover subcontracts. In 2004, four Blackwater guards were murdered in Fallujah. Their families filed a wrongful death suit against Blackwater, stating the guards had inadequate protection, including vehicles without armor, which the families claimed was against their contract. Congress tried to determine whose contract Blackwater was operating under, which turned out to be with Halliburton. Halliburton denied subcontracting with Blackwater and it took regulators three years to figure out whether Blackwater violated its contract.[126]

Financial waste also occurs when contractors poach military personnel. Contractors present a cost-effective option for governments to buy rather than make because of the cost savings from not training and giving benefits to military personnel. However, the savings evaporate when taking into account that contractors employed by Blackwater, who were more likely to see combat, are usually trained by the US military and remain on government benefits. Representative Yarmouth questioned Prince on such government double spending:

> But in this situation, the American taxpayers are bidding against themselves. Because we trained Navy SEALs, Navy SEALs then go into your employ, then the Navy has to bid, as I understand, in one report, $100,000 to get them back. But we are bidding against ourselves, aren't we? We are not bidding against another external competitor.[127]

Double spending, no-bid contracts, and subcontracting distribute accountability for financial abuse across a complex web of relationships in *contractual hybridity*.

[122]   Commission on Wartime Contracting 2011: 1.
[123]   Commission on Wartime Contracting 2011.
[124]   Scahill 2008: 229–230.
[125]   House of Representatives 2007a: 3.
[126]   House of Representatives 2007a: 5.
[127]   House of Representatives 2007a: 90.

Contractors also distribute accountability by taking advantage of legal gray zones. Security contractors "are not quite civilians, given that they often carry and use weapons, interrogate prisoners, load bombs, and fulfill other critical military roles" and "yet they are not quite soldiers."[128] Security contractor obligations under international humanitarian law remain muddy in questions concerning "state responsibility for the actions of those acting in their name."[129] Contractors do not fit the "lawful combatant" definition under the United Nations (UN) Geneva Conventions because they do not wear military uniforms or answer to a military hierarchy. Nor do contractors fit the "mercenary" definition because they do not always have foreign national status. Contractors may align with the Bush administration's "illegal enemy combatant" status deployed for Guantanamo Bay detainees. Amy Eckert proposes the term "civilian combatant" to consider "the possibility for holding corporations responsible for their immoral or illegal acts [where] they may share responsibility for those acts alongside the individuals they employ and the state actors who hire them."[130]

A lack of accepted legal status makes imposing responsibility under international law difficult. It also deprives rights to contractors under international law, for instance obtaining prisoner of war status. In 2008, a multi-stakeholder process with the help of the International Committee for the Red Cross and the Swiss government culminated in the Montreux Document for "pertinent international legal obligations and good practices for states related to operations of private military and security companies during armed conflict."[131] The Montreux Document offers states practical guidance to existing international law for executing security contracts. While useful, it does not impose new legal obligations for regulating contractors and buck-passes some thorny issues. It states that contractors "are obliged to comply with international humanitarian law or human rights law imposed upon them by applicable national law."[132] However, this passes the international obligations to national law, where legal clarity is also lacking.

The status of security contractors under US laws is similarly complicated. At the start of the wars in Afghanistan and Iraq, contractors remained outside the Pentagon's Uniform Code of Military Justice (UCMJ). Their in-between legal status was most evident in 2006 when a drunken Blackwater contractor shot and killed a bodyguard for the Iraqi vice president. As referenced in this book's Introduction, instead of criminal proceedings, he was fined and sent home. An exchange between Erik Prince and Representative Maloney highlights the accountability gap:

> Prince: Look, I am not going to make any apologies for what he did. He clearly violated our policies.

[128] Singer 2005: 126.
[129] de Nevers 2009: 488.
[130] Eckert 2016: 118, 136.
[131] ICRC 2008: 1; Avant 2016.
[132] ICRC 2008: 14.

130 *Hybrid Sovereignty in World Politics*

Maloney: OK. All right. Every American believes he violated policies. If he lived in America, he would have been arrested, and he would be facing criminal charges. If he was a member of our military, he would be under a court martial. But it appears to me that Blackwater has special rules. That is one of the reasons of this hearing.[133]

In 2007, the Pentagon made a change to the UCMJ that allowed for the code to apply to contractors. However, there was a caveat: "Defense contractors can be prosecuted in U.S. courts for crimes committed overseas, but because of a legal loophole, contractors for other agencies can only face charges if their work assignments supported the Defense Department."[134] In other words, because some contractors like Blackwater were on a State Department contract, the UCMJ would still not apply.

Meanwhile, a patchwork of contractor protections developed in the Iraq War. In 2004, the CPA's Order 17 stated that "contractors shall be immune from Iraqi legal process with respect to acts performed by them pursuant to the terms and conditions of a Contract or any sub-contract thereto."[135] Order 17's immunity effectively barred the Iraqi government from prosecuting contractors. As mentioned earlier, in 2006, Rumsfeld classified contractors as part of the Defense Department's "Total Force." Blackwater jumped on Rumsfeld's language in its legal battles, claiming immunity from the wrongful death suit brought by the Fallujah families by arguing Blackwater was "performing a classic military function – providing an armed escort for a supply convoy under orders to reach an Army base – with an authorization from the Office of the Secretary of Defense" and that "any other result [than immunity] would amount to judicial intrusion into the President's ability to deploy a Total Force that includes contractors."[136] Blackwater was successful in dismissing the suit in favor of forced arbitration, which was appealed by the families, who later settled.

In April 2004, *60 Minutes* broadcasted abuse in the Abu Ghraib prison occurring since 2003, citing a classified US Army investigation on torture, including sexual assault, and showed degrading photos of military service members with detainees. The extent and horror of Abu Ghraib, called a "new gulag" by foreign observers,[137] generated a national reckoning, as lawmakers asked: "Given the catastrophic impact that this scandal has had on the world community, how can the United States ever repair its credibility?"[138] CACI and Titan contractors who worked as interpreters and interrogators were implicated in almost a third of the physical and sexual abuse incidents (ten out of the thirty-two incidents).[139] But the Pentagon claimed that under the Military Extraterritorial Jurisdiction Act (MEJA), it had "no jurisdiction

[133] House of Representatives 2007a: 58.
[134] Department of Defense 2006a.
[135] Department of Defense 2004.
[136] Blackwater appellate brief, October 31, 2005.
[137] Blumenthaul 2004.
[138] Senate Armed Services Committee Hearing 2004.
[139] Fay 2004: 71–87.

over the civilian contractors. The military can make recommendations, but it is going to be up to the employer to decide what measures to take."[140] In response, Congress amended MEJA to apply to non-DoD contractors, whose function "relates to supporting" DoD's overseas mission. Three years later, Blackwater's Nisour Square massacre prompted the first application of criminally prosecuting security contractors under US law, as discussed in the next section.

Meanwhile, there were conflicts within the State Department. In August 2007, the Department began an investigation into Blackwater's operations in Iraq. Jean Richter, the chief investigator, filed a memo reporting that Blackwater's top manager threatened "he could kill" Richter and "no one could or would do anything about it as we were in Iraq."[141] A second individual compared Blackwater's environment in Iraq to O.K. Corral, where a gunfight occurred between a loose group of outlaws and self-appointed lawmen in 1881. To Richter, "it was immediately apparent that the Blackwater contractors believed that they were the de facto authority and acted accordingly, in an alarming manner."[142] Moreover, the "hands off" managerial style from Washington DC "served to create an atmosphere where the contractors, instead of Department officials, are in command and control."[143] However, following the report, American Embassy officials in Baghdad "told the investigators that they had disrupted the embassy's relationship with the security contractor and ordered them to leave the country."[144] The *Associated Press* called out Blackwater: "They operate with little or no supervision, accountable only to the firms employing them."[145] Next month, Blackwater's civilian shootings would have major political ramifications related to such distributed accountability.

Politics of Distributed Accountability

On September 16, 2007, four Blackwater trucks were on their way to the site of a car bomb in Baghdad. As the convoy approached the crowded Nisour Square, guards stopped traffic to make way for the trucks. One car did not slow down. Blackwater guards fired upon the car, which kept moving when the driver was fatally shot in the head. Guards set off grenades and then continued firing rounds into the fleeing crowds, leading to a firefight with Iraqi police and soldiers. There were seventeen civilian deaths and twenty casualties. The FBI later found that fourteen of the seventeen civilians fatally shot were unjustified killings with no evidence supporting Blackwater's assertions they were fired upon.[146] In 2010, three Blackwater witnesses agreed with the FBI's assessment, claiming the "unarmed civilians shot and killed

[140] Stockman 2004.
[141] Richter 2007; Risen 2014.
[142] Richter 2007.
[143] Richter 2007.
[144] Risen 2014.
[145] Hastings 2007.
[146] Jordan 2007.

were clearly no threat to anyone."[147] The Nisour Square aftermath shows the political fallout from Blackwater's *Lived Sovereignty* compromising the United States' position in Iraq and the Middle East. The crisis also starkly highlights the illusion of an American monopoly on the legitimate use of force assumed in *Idealized Sovereignty*.

The day after the shootings, Iraqi Prime Minister Nouri al-Maliki asserted that Iraq's sovereignty was violated and revoked Blackwater's contract.[148] Maliki's spokesperson asserted: "The forces operating in Iraq, including the security companies, should respect the sovereignty of Iraq."[149] The United States quickly banned diplomats and other civilian employees from traveling outside Baghdad's Green Zone. One diplomat warned: "People have to get out. There is no point of having a diplomatic mission in a country if you don't get out."[150] Meanwhile, Iraq's cabinet drafted a new measure to rescind Bremmer's Order 17: "These firms will be under the grip of Iraqi law . . . and will be punished decisively for every breach."[151] But Iraqi security forces realized it was not easy to be rid of Blackwater. One spokesperson reflected on the reliance on *contractual hybridity* for sovereign competence in Iraq while also asserting a need for laws to grant legitimacy to that hybridity:

> If Blackwater left at this moment, it might leave a security gap because most of the embassies and most of the foreign organizations that are working in Iraq rely on Blackwater. This will create a security imbalance. That's why the Iraqi government preferred to be patient on activating this decision to stop them. But the government is still serious in finding certain rules. . . . We would like to have some laws.[152]

Meanwhile, Blackwater's President Gary Jackson retorted: "We don't need a new law, we need to enforce the ones we have."[153]

The US government scrambled to contain the fallout. The American Ambassador to Iraq, Ryan Crocker, agreed that he did not foresee security contractors as "a disaster waiting to happen" and still held Blackwater guards, in charge of his protection, in "high regard."[154] But another American diplomat acknowledged that "growing frustration over the Americans' failure to rein in the security firms had transformed Sunday's shooting into a symbol of abuses committed over the years: 'It's amazing the Iraqi government [revoked Blackwater's license], but they did it because we wouldn't.'"[155] The statement captures the Weberian dilemma confronting the United States' sovereign authority to wage war. The shooting was "a

---

[147]　Risen 2010.
[148]　Reid 2007.
[149]　Zakaria 2007.
[150]　Parker (N) 2007.
[151]　Gerstenzang and Zavis 2007.
[152]　Rubin and Kramer 2007.
[153]　Parker (N) 2007.
[154]　Hurst 2007.
[155]　Parker (N)2007.

symbol of abuses committed over the years," which the United States had thus far largely ignored. The refusal to revoke Blackwater's license over previous abuses had now blown to a full crisis of legitimacy for the United States' ability to contract out the use of force.

A week later, Prime Minister Maliki was in New York for the opening of the UN General Assembly. In an interview with the *Associated Press*, he claimed: "The Iraqi government is responsible for its citizens, and it cannot be accepted for a security company to carry out a killing. There are serious challenges to the sovereignty of Iraq."[156] The *Associated Press* contextualized that Maliki "used the Arabic word *tajawiz*, which can be translated either as affronts or challenges" to Iraqi sovereignty.[157] Maliki also met with President George W. Bush. Bush's national security advisor Stephen Hadley agreed there was "a general discussion of the importance of recognition of Iraqi sovereignty [and] . . . taking into consideration Iraqi sovereignty and the needs of protecting State Department personnel."[158] A senior Iraqi official narrated that Maliki told Bush the shootings were "an embarrassment for us and you before the Iraqi people."[159] Bush's response was to ask Maliki to "provide him with a list of violations and the number of such incidents while noting that those who were convicted of crimes in the Abu Ghraib prisoner abuse scandal in 2004 were held accountable and are in prison."[160]

While media reports focused on Iraqi sovereignty, the Nisour Square shootings also had implications for American *Idealized Sovereignty*. Specifically, by calling repeated attention to violations of Iraq's international legal sovereignty and the absence of contractor regulations and accountability – for instance by stating "we would like to have some laws" – Iraq was openly questioning the United States' Weberian claim over its monopoly to the *legitimate* use of force. This was the meaning behind Maliki's statement to Bush that Blackwater's shootings were "an embarrassment for us and you." Just as privateers and mercenaries were delegitimized in late modern Europe because they distributed accountability away from states and undermined *Idealized Sovereignty*, the same logic was at work here.

The United States mobilized a response both publicly and in internal bureaucratic debates (covered more extensively in the next section). Publicly, Defense Secretary Robert Gates broke with Rumsfeld's "Total Force" doctrine by stating that "contractors are at 'cross purposes' with military goals, and suggested they be put under his authority."[161] The State Department issued new rules for Blackwater, including cameras and other recording devices on its convoys, and launched an investigation.[162] But other public efforts only strengthened the challenge to

[156] Rubin and Kramer 2007.
[157] Abdul-Zahra and El-Tablawy 2007.
[158] Gerstenzang and Zavis 2007.
[159] Abdul-Zahra and El-Tablawy 2007; emphasis added.
[160] Abdul-Zahra and El-Tablawy 2007.
[161] DeYoung 2007.
[162] Pleming 2007.

American sovereign legitimacy. A team led by diplomat Patrick Kennedy concluded that they were "unaware of any basis for holding non-Department of Defense contractors [like Blackwater] accountable under U.S. law."[163] For the amended MEJA to apply, the government had to prove that Blackwater was essential to DoD functions. In addition to immunities under Order 17, the State Department offered immunity to Blackwater contractors willing to cooperate with the investigation without prior authorization from the Department of Justice. Leaked emails revealed that the State Department knew "ambiguities in U.S. law allowed contractors to escape criminal prosecution."[164] After a House Committee launched an investigation, the State Department sent a letter to Blackwater, ordering it "to make no disclosure of the documents or information" about its work in Iraq without permission from the administration.[165]

As the State Department confirmed their offer of immunity, the Iraqi cabinet voted for a draft legislation to overturn Order 17.[166] Under the legislation, Iraq would require that all contractors' weapons and equipment like helicopters and armored vehicles be registered in Iraq. As the Iraqi Parliament considered the measure, one MP remarked: "The Iraqi Parliament is enthusiastic about controlling these companies and will not allow them to have a free hand, especially after the massacre of Nisour Square. ... We can no longer deal with the security firms in this way."[167] Another MP was blunter: "We cannot continue to have the Iraqi-American relationship solely on the basis of Order 17."[168]

In political discourse, the shootings drew attention to how the United States was "too hooked on hired help."[169] Public scrutiny on the nature of contracting followed from Americans: "Why does the world's mightiest military power need civilians to fight its wars and guard its diplomats?"[170] Media reports mounted that "American officials refused to explain the legal authority under which Blackwater operates in Iraq."[171] Presidential candidate Barack Obama said on the campaign trail from the Democratic Primaries: "Most contractors currently act as if the law doesn't apply to them, because it doesn't. That has to end."[172] Iraqi security forces murmured about the close relationship between the State Department and Blackwater: "They draw the wagon circle. They protect each other. They look out for each other. I don't know if that's a good thing, that wall of silence. When it protects the guilty, that is definitely not a good thing."[173] A State Department official begrudgingly agreed: "Oversight

[163] Scahill 2008: 36.
[164] Schakowsky 2007.
[165] Spiegel 2007.
[166] Rubin 2007.
[167] Rubin 2007.
[168] Shishkin 2007.
[169] Debusmann 2007.
[170] Debusmann 2007.
[171] Reid 2007.
[172] Reid 2007.
[173] Parker and Raheem 2007.

has perhaps not been as good as it could be."[174] The Pentagon too leaked a classified report expressing frustrations from US military commanders towards Blackwater: "There is a feeling that they are untouchable, a perception that they can do whatever they want with impunity."[175] Internationally, the UN rebuked: "When you kill 17 people like that, it's a crime against humanity if it is proven that it was done in cold blood."[176]

Questions zeroed in on implications for Weberian legitimacy. After the State Department's offer of immunity was revealed, an editorial in the *Los Angeles Times* asked: "Certainly Blackwater seems to have unwarranted influence in Washington, as evidenced by the letter it procured from the State Department ordering it not to disclose information to Waxman's committee. Who's in charge here, the U.S. government or Blackwater?"[177] The *Virginian-Pilot* proclaimed: "Washington has unwanted armed Americans operating in another country, and no interest in how that might look."[178]

Congress did worry about how this looked. During the October 2007 hearings on Blackwater, a report produced evidence related to the Fallujah wrongful death suits that Blackwater had shunned armored vehicles because of their cost: "These actions raise serious questions about the consequences of engaging private, for-profit entities to engage in essentially military operations in a war zone."[179] Representative Elijah Cummings responded to Erik Prince's repeated assertions of Blackwater's success rate in protecting diplomats: "It's not about what you do well, it's a question of when things go wrong where is the accountability?"[180] There were calls for clearer demarcations of public and private:

> We need more accountability. We need to clarify and update our laws. We need to restore the Government's ability to manage any such contracts. We need to punish corporations that commit fraud or undermine our security. Basically, we need to reconsider which jobs should be private and which jobs should remain in the public sector.[181]

All of this uproar was, as Representative David Price deduced, crucial: "If we do not hold contract personnel accountable for misconduct, as we do for our military, we are undermining our nation's credibility as a country that upholds the rule of law."[182]

The legal process to hold Blackwater accountable stretched across three presidential administrations. Blackwater's contractual terms with the State Department

---

[174] DeYoung 2007.
[175] DeYoung and Tyson 2007.
[176] Kratovac 2007.
[177] Kratovac 2007.
[178] *Virginian-Pilot* 2007.
[179] Kessler and DeYoung 2007.
[180] House of Representatives 2007a: 63.
[181] House of Representatives 2007a: 17–18.
[182] Meyer and Barnes 2007.

complicated the proceedings in part. The first trial in 2009 against four Blackwater guards was dismissed as the State Department's mandatory debriefings with contractors following the shooting were regarded as compelled testimony that tainted witness statements.[183] Following a second trial, all four contractors were convicted in 2014 and sentenced in 2015. However, in 2017, a federal appeals court ruled to resentence three of the guards citing "cruel and unusual punishment" and threw out a murder conviction while ordering a new trial for the fourth one. After a third trial in 2018, that guard was reconvicted of murder and sentenced to life in prison. In 2019, the sentences of the remaining three guards were cut in half. Then, before Trump left office in 2020, he pardoned all four Blackwater guards. The UN responded with dismay: "These pardons violate U.S. obligations under international law and more broadly undermine humanitarian law and human rights at a global level." Former General David Petraeus and Ambassador Ryan Crocker also criticized the pardons as "hugely damaging, an action that tells the world that Americans abroad can commit the most heinous crimes with impunity."[184]

Meanwhile, political ramifications impacted American leverage in the War in Iraq. The year following the shootings, the United States and Iraq were negotiating a new Status of Forces Agreement, which Bush intended to complete by July 2008 after a UN mandate was set to expire at the end of the year. The United States was hoping to establish more than fifty long-term bases in Iraq. However,

> [n]egotiations are intense, particularly over the longevity of military bases, control of Iraqi airspace and the legal status of civilian contractors such as the Blackwater security guards involved in a deadly confrontation that killed 17 Iraqi civilians last September. Public critics in Iraq worry the deal will lock in American military, economic and political domination of the country. Iraqis also widely view the U.S. insistence that American troops continue to enjoy immunity under Iraqi law as an infringement on national sovereignty.[185]

The renewed attention to Iraqi sovereignty made it impossible to proceed with both the bases and contractor immunity in Order 17. The United States thus conceded on removing the "immunity from prosecution for American contractors. Under the latest version of the pact, they could be subject to Iraqi law."[186] Ambassador David Satterfield, the State Department's Iraq coordinator, "acknowledged that the killing of 17 Iraqis by Blackwater staffers last September has made the issue of security contractors a 'sensitive' subject."[187] Even other contractors agreed that the immunity deal was too good to last, as the head of Triple Canopy mused: "My own personal opinion was that immunity turned into impunity, and that was bad for the entire

[183] A 2011 federal appeals court upheld the decision.
[184] Reuters 2020.
[185] Gearan 2008.
[186] Rubin 2008.
[187] Chon 2008.

industry."[188] Iraq officially ended the Order 17 immunity for contractors on December 31, 2008, in its Status of Forces Agreement with the United States.[189]

The damage to American legitimacy continued even after the end of Order 17, as Blackwater remained in Iraq. Right after the shooting, commentators had predicted that "what had been a close and apparently very happy marriage between Blackwater and the State Department has gone sour. Signs point to a divorce in May. That's when the company's contract expires."[190] But there was not even a real separation. Blackwater operated in Iraq for a full two years after it lost its license to operate there. Despite the Iraqi ban, the State Department renewed its contract with Blackwater in April 2008.[191] An editorial called it the "diplomatic equivalent of showing a stiff middle finger to the Iraqi government."[192] Meanwhile, former Blackwater executives admitted to authorizing secret payments of $1 million to silence Iraqi officials three months after the shooting, although it was not known whether the cash was delivered.[193] After a US court dismissed charges against the Blackwater guards in 2010, one of the injured victims exclaimed: "Why do they have the right to kill people? Is our blood so cheap? For America, the land of justice and law, what does it mean to let criminals go?"[194]

Nisour Square ricocheted throughout conflicts in the Middle East. Blackwater's "violent and willfully independent nature has made it difficult, at times, for American military commanders to maintain political control over the use of force in overseas conflict zones."[195] In 2010, Afghanistan began disarming security contractors, with President Hamid Karzai calling them "thieves during the day and terrorists during the night."[196] (Ironically, Karzai had been kept alive when the United States hired DynCorp and later Blackwater for his protection in the early phases of the war in Afghanistan.) Aid donors and life-support contractors complained that they "will not be able to find insurers if they are forced to give up private security. Some have already been winding down projects early because they feared they would not be able to protect their workers."[197] In response, Afghanistan pushed back the deadline to 2012. Over in Iraq, one month after the American troop withdrawal in December 2011, the government detained hundreds of American contractors, from a few hours to three weeks, on improper documentation, including visas, weapons permits, and other authorizations. Latif Rashid, a senior advisor to the Iraqi president, said that "the Iraqis' deep mistrust of security contractors had led the

---

[188]   Cole 2008.
[189]   Department of Defense 2009b: 18.
[190]   Debusmann 2007.
[191]   Lee and Baker 2009.
[192]   Debusmann 2008.
[193]   Mazzetti and Risen 2009.
[194]   Williams 2010.
[195]   Fitzsimmons 2015: 159.
[196]   Trofimov 2010.
[197]   Riechmann 2010.

government to strictly monitor them: 'We have to apply our own rules now. . . . There is a general bad feeling towards the security contractors among the Iraqis and that has created bad feelings towards them all.'"[198] The bad feeling migrated to Pakistan, where anti-US sentiment led to a blacklist of 180 US government visa requests in 2009 after local media reported that the US Embassy hired Blackwater, then known as Xe, "to spy on and seek to kill insurgent leaders. . . . One Pakistani commented: 'It's like history repeating itself, from the time the East India Company came out here.'"[199]

This section traced the political challenge of Blackwater's *contractual hybridity* to Weberian legitimacy. When Daniel Bergner shadowed Triple Canopy contractors in 2005, he raised the question of authority: "It is hard to discern who authorized this particular outsourcing as military policy. No open policy debate took place; no executive order was publicly issued. And who is in charge of overseeing these armed men?"[200] This bothered him: "We may not know what to think of ourselves if service and sacrifice are increasingly mixed with the wish for profit. We may know less and less how to feel about a state that is no longer defended by men and women we can perceive as pure."[201] The Pentagon assured him: "Private Security Contractors are not being used to perform inherently military functions."[202] The statement echoed congressional demands that "contracts for the use of force in war also pose legitimate questions about the propriety of hiring private firms to perform such a public, some would say inherently governmental, function."[203] The meaning of the phrase "inherently governmental," however, was part of another ongoing battle.

CONSTRUCTING "INHERENTLY GOVERNMENTAL"

The analysis so far interpreted Blackwater's experiences in *Lived Sovereignty* as challenging the Weberian construction of the legitimate use of force in *Idealized Sovereignty*. Now, I describe how in response to this legitimation challenge the American bureaucracy embarked on the perpetual construction of "inherently governmental" functions to reassert its sovereign authority.

The Bureaucratic State of American Contracting

Accompanying the rise in American contracting are increasingly complex bureaucratic guidelines about what the government may contract.[204] The US Code of

---

[198] Schmidt and Schmitt 2012.
[199] DeYoung and Constable 2009.
[200] Bergner 2005.
[201] Bergner 2005.
[202] Bergner 2005.
[203] House of Representatives 2007a: 13.
[204] Krahmann 2010 contrasts the privatization debates in United States with the United Kingdom and Germany, highlighting the particular neoliberal tendencies of the United States.

Federal Regulations states: "Contracts shall not be used for the performance of inherently governmental functions."[205] Typical examples of commercial activities include "audiovisual products and services, automatic data process, food and health services, management support services, system engineering, and transportation."[206] Contractors refer to this as the "yellow pages test," where "if you can find firms in the Yellow Pages of the phone book providing contracts or services that the government is also providing, then the government service should be subject to market competition."[207] Unsurprisingly, confusion still reigns in defining commercial functions. However, the efforts to demarcate governmental from commercial functions help us see the makings of "sovereign" competence.

Early American bureaucratic discussions of contracting included a 1932 special House of Representatives Committee on "government competition with private enterprise." By 1953, the Intergovernmental Relations Subcommittee of the House Committee on Government Operations "reported that the number of [commercial and industrial] activities conducted by Government agencies posed a real threat to private industry and imperiled the tax structure," recommending that "a permanent, vigorous, preventive and corrective program be inaugurated."[208] Two reports from the Commissions on Organization of the Executive Branch of Government in 1949 and 1955 developed twenty-two recommendations aimed at moderating government competition with the private sector.[209]

A breakthrough came in 1955 under President Eisenhower when the Bureau of the Budget, the predecessor of the Office of Management and Budget (OMB), issued Bulletin Number 55-4: "It is the general policy of the administration that the Federal Government will not start or carry on any commercial activity to provide a service or product for its own use if such product or service can be procured from private enterprise through ordinary business channels."[210] In 1966, the Johnson administration formalized the first permanent directive for government contracting with the Bureau of the Budget's Circular A-76: "Each agency will compile and maintain an inventory of its commercial or industrial activities having an annual output of products or services costing $50,000 or more or a capital investment of $25,000 or more."[211] Moreover, Circular A-76's policy statement was to ensure that "[i]n the process of governing, the Government should not compete with its citizens."[212] A memo from President Johnson explained that Circular A-76 offered "uniform guidelines and principles to conduct the affairs of the Government on an

---

[205] 48 C.F.R. § 7.503(a).
[206] OMB 1983: Attachment A.
[207] House of Representatives 2016: Palatiello testimony.
[208] Commission on Government Procurement 1972: 58.
[209] Commission on Organization of the Executive Branch of the Government 1955.
[210] Congressional Research Service 2007: 3.
[211] OMB 1966: 6.
[212] OMB 1966: 6.

orderly basis; to limit budgetary costs; and to maintain the Government's policy of reliance upon private enterprise."[213]

The OMB made major revisions to Circular A-76 in 1967, 1979, 1983, 1996, 1999, 2000, and 2003. It published a Supplemental Handbook in 1979, "intended to promote more effective and consistent implementation."[214] The 1979 version of Circular A-76 also revised the 1966 policy statement to add a specific type of political system: "In a democratic free enterprise economic system, the Government should not compete with its citizens."[215] The next major change came in 1996 when the Clinton administration used Circular A-76 "to empower federal managers to make sound and justifiable business decisions."[216] The Federal Activities Inventory Reform (FAIR) Act of 1998 gave statutory force to Circular A-76's requirement for submitting annual inventories of commercial functions. Prior to the FAIR Act, federal agencies had a spotty record of submitting their inventories on time. But the FAIR Act also emphasized that "the Clinton administration had no clear set of political or even functional criteria to determine what tasks should remain with the government and the armed forces. Instead it passed the responsibility of defining its core functions back to the military."[217] In order to entice the Pentagon to use more contracting, Clinton's "government deduced the projected savings from contracting out these positions in advance from the defence budgets."[218]

In 2002, Rumsfeld delivered his new doctrine, arguing that in determining core governmental functions, "'core' has been loosely and imprecisely defined, and too often used as a way of protecting existing arrangements."[219] A year later, Circular A-76 was revised. The OMB now required agencies to submit inventories of their inherently governmental activities in addition to commercial activities.[220] Moreover, the revised policy statement removed the 1979 language of a free enterprise system: "The longstanding policy of the federal government has been to rely on the private sector for needed commercial services."[221] The 2003 revision also eliminated the 1966 policy statement that the government should not compete with its citizens.

Even with the 2003 revisions and the Rumsfeld Doctrine, not everyone in the Pentagon was on board with adopting security contractors. A US Army lawyer recalled that the DoD "did not significantly plan for the use of private security contractors when troops first entered Iraq in March 2003. . . . Contractors were not expected to perform inherently governmental functions, such as security in

---

[213]   White House 1966.
[214]   OMB 1967.
[215]   OMB 1979.
[216]   Stanger 2009: 15.
[217]   Krahmann 2010: 127.
[218]   Krahmann 2010: 128.
[219]   Rumsfeld 2002.
[220]   OMB 2003.
[221]   OMB 2003: 1.

a complex battlefield."²²² There was reluctance to move forward without considering "how the military [can] ensure that the private exercise of power is circumscribed by public values and controls."²²³ RAND cautioned: "Over the long run, once the Army gives up a capability, the start-up costs may simply become too high to justify bringing it back in-house, even if it should never have left in the first place."²²⁴ But as life-support firms like Halliburton were awarded large contracts, diplomatic protection and military training contracts soon followed. According to one official, "we crossed the Rubicon in 2002, when we allowed Northrop Grumman to do training for peacekeeping in Africa. Before then, we had used contractors for training in the class room and for computer simulation exercises, but never before had they been deployed in the field."²²⁵ As the wars in Afghanistan and Iraq intensified, the use of armed contractors like Blackwater was no longer seen as a choice.²²⁶

President Obama had already spoken out when Nisour Square occurred on the campaign trail. Within two months after assuming office, he issued a memo stating that "the line between inherently governmental activities that should not be outsourced and commercial activities that may be subject to private sector competition has been blurred and inadequately defined. As a result, contractors may be performing inherently governmental functions. Agencies and departments must operate under clear rules prescribing when outsourcing is and is not appropriate."²²⁷ In the 2009 budget, the Obama administration placed a moratorium on public–private competition that would convert federal employee positions to contractors. The Pentagon faced a separate moratorium in the 2010 National Defense Authorization Act. Moreover, Obama required all federal agencies except the DoD to "devise and implement guidelines" for insourcing. But "the procurement workforce [argued that] no adequate definition for inherently governmental function exists."²²⁸ How could that be so?

Defining Inherently Governmental

For twenty-five years, American bureaucrats used Circular A-76's sparse definition of "inherently governmental" as "a function which is so intimately related to the public interest as to mandate performance by Government employees."²²⁹ In 1992, the

---

²²² Fitzsimmons 2015: 150.
²²³ Verkuil 2007: 129.
²²⁴ Verkuil 2007: 131.
²²⁵ Stanger 2009: 87
²²⁶ Percy 2009: 62–63.
²²⁷ White House 2009.
²²⁸ Laubacher 2017: 793.
²²⁹ OMB 1983: 6(e).

H. W. Bush administration published the first comprehensive clarification on "inherently governmental" in Policy Letter 92-1:

> "Inherently governmental" functions include those activities that require either the exercise of discretion in applying Government authority or the making of value judgments in making decisions for the Government. Governmental functions normally fall into two categories: (1) The act of governing, i.e., the discretionary exercise of Government authority, and (2) monetary transactions and entitlements.[230]

Policy Letter 92-1 specified discretionary exercise of authority and control over money as the basis of an inherently governmental function. The letter listed 19 illustrative inherently governmental functions, such as conducting criminal investigations, commanding military forces, conducting foreign policy, and hiring federal employees. It also stated that information gathering, recommendations, and other "ministerial and internal" activities, like "building security, mall operations, [and] operation of cafeterias," are not inherently governmental functions.[231] Finally, the letter introduced functions that are "closely associated" with inherently governmental functions "because of the way in which the contractor performs the contract or the manner in which the government administers contractor performance."[232] All subsequent Circulars A-76 insert a version of Policy Letter 92-1's definition of "inherently governmental" functions; the FAIR Act uses it verbatim.

Under Rumsfeld, the definition was changed in the 2003 revision of Circular A-76 with the addition of one word: "[inherently governmental] activities require the exercise of *substantial* discretion in applying government authority and/or in making decisions for the government."[233] In 2009, the Obama administration urged the Office of Federal Procurement Policy (OFPP) to "create a single definition for the term 'inherently governmental function' that addresses any deficiencies in the existing definitions and reasonably applies to all agencies."[234]

In response, the OFPP issued Policy Letter 11-01 in 2011, which made three changes. First, it restored the definition of inherently governmental functions from 1992, ignoring the addition of *substantial* discretion in 2003. It also expanded the illustrative list of inherently governmental functions from nineteen to twenty-four.[235] Second, it clarified "closely associated" functions, where within the same function various tasks could be coded as governmental, closely associated with governmental, or neither,[236] and modified the 1992 list. Of particular interest is the contracting process itself. While awarding and terminating contracts are inherently

[230] OMB 1992: 45100.
[231] OMB 1992: 45101.
[232] OMB 1992: Attachment B.
[233] OMB 2003: Attachment A, §(B)(1)(a); emphasis added.
[234] White House 2009.
[235] OMB 2011: 56236.
[236] OMB 2011: 56234.

governmental functions, governments may contract out "the evaluation of a contractor's performance" (e.g. collecting information, performing analysis, or recommending performance ratings), and "providing support for assessing contract claims and preparing termination settlement documents."[237] However, if the basis of awarding and terminating contracts depends on contractor evaluation, then the distinction between inherently and closely associated governmental functions becomes more complicated. Third, the 2011 letter introduced "critical functions" that agencies must maintain in-house.[238] The OMB would "hold an agency responsible for making sure that, for critical functions, it has an adequate number of positions filled by Federal employees."[239] Crucially, "so long as agencies have the internal capacity needed to maintain control over their operations, they are permitted to allow contractor performance of positions within critical functions."[240] Since critical functions are unique to each agency's mission, determining overreliance on contractors now depended on whether agencies maintain operational control rather than the ratio of contractors.

Policy Letter 11-01 also developed two tests for identifying inherently governmental functions from "closely associated" functions. The first test is functional and "involves the exercise of sovereign powers of the United States. ... Examples are officially representing the United States in an inter-governmental forum or body, arresting a person, and sentencing a person convicted of a crime to prison."[241] In substituting "sovereign powers" for what used to be "governing authority," the test assumes the language of sovereignty offers more clarity than the language of governance. When sovereign status of a function is unclear, the second test asks whether discretion is required in that "two or more alternative courses of action exist" without precedence.[242] The second test then prohibits contractors from performing functions with "the authority to decide on the overall course of action," but allows that contractors can be "asked to develop options or implement a course of action," as long as the agency "has the ability to override the contractor's action."[243] Thus, contractors may perform "closely associated" with inherently governmental functions when they lack decision-making authority.

Per standard practice, the OMB issued a draft of the letter for public comment in 2010. Commenters were concerned about the shift to "sovereign functions" in the new tests: "Some respondents suggested that the term 'sovereign' be explained while others concluded that the manner in which sovereign authority is exercised is so varied that it is better explained by example than further definition."[244] A vast

[237] OMB 2011: 56234.
[238] OMB 2011: 56228.
[239] OMB 2011: 56229.
[240] OMB 2011: 16188–97.
[241] OMB 2011: 56237–8.
[242] OMB 2011: 56237–8.
[243] OMB 2011: 56237–8.
[244] OMB 2011: 56231.

majority of commenters wanted to exclude security contractors from performing governmental functions, including closely associated. They stated that the illustrative list of inherently governmental functions was too narrow and "suggested the addition of functions involving private security contractors, especially when performed in hostile environments or involving intelligence."[245] Of the 110 original (not form) responses, 60 percent mentioned Blackwater. Commenters invoked Nisour Square:

> I can understand, and agree with, the use of private contractors in war zones if they are engaged, as KBR and Halliburton have sometimes been, in civilian activities such as construction and engineering, but I strongly oppose using them in paramilitary activity, including guarding important persons (as in the case in Baghdad in which Blackwater employees slaughtered 17 civilians "in self-defense").[246]

Commenters also highlighted the problems of distributed accountability for sovereign legitimation:

> It is important that we have representatives of the government who have some accountability rather than private corporations like Blackwater and Halliburton who seem accountable to no one and have actually interfered with the work of the soldiers, etc. They are mercenaries and only in it for the money so they have no concern about human rights, morals, etc. Don't waste taxpayers' money on these people who give America a bad name.[247]
>
> The company involved makes ludicrous amounts of money stolen from the American people, they have no accountability, we are absolved from any national or international legal accountability, but the world knows that it does not absolve us from any moral accountability. We have lost face in the eyes of the world, and have created a lifetime of hatred in the countries we have attacked.[248]

The last comment covers many components of a Weberian legitimation crisis from distributed accountability where armed contractors "steal" American money, are absolved of legal liability, and jeopardize American political standing by "losing face" in international politics.

The bureaucrats accommodated public concerns in two ways. First, they "added to the list of inherently governmental functions: (i) All combat and (ii) security operations in certain situations connected with combat or potential combat."[249] The key addition of "potential combat" is especially relevant for excluding security contractors. Second, they referenced Abu Ghraib by acknowledging that "serving as an interpreter during an interrogation of an enemy prisoner of war could potentially constitute a function approaching inherently governmental. It is less clear that

[245] OMB 2011: 56231.
[246] "David Eggenschwiler," Docket ID OFPP–2010–0001.
[247] "Millie Brady," Docket ID OFPP–2010–0001.
[248] "Bianca de Leon," Docket ID OFPP–2010–0001.
[249] OMB 2011: 56231.

transcribing a recording of that interrogation approaches being inherently governmental."[250] For such entanglements, they introduced another test:

> A function is not appropriately performed by a contractor where the contractor's involvement is or would be so extensive, or the contractor's work product so close to a final agency product, as to effectively preempt the Federal officials' decision-making process, discretion or authority. For example, providing security in a volatile, high-risk environment may be inherently governmental if the responsible Federal official cannot anticipate the circumstances and challenges that may arise, and cannot specify the range of acceptable conduct. . . . In such cases, the function should not be contracted out.[251]

Thus, the bureaucrats singled out armed security contractors as a case of not contracting a closely associated function in a "volatile, high-risk environment," or most war zones.

One important aspect of these debates is that security contractors co-opted deliberation on government contracting. While 43 percent of US federal governmental functions are deemed commercial, security contractors represent a small portion of commercial functions. Even in war contracting, security contractors constituted only 15 percent of Iraqi contractors. However, the last major bureaucratic revisions in the 2003 Circular A-76 and the 2011 Policy Letter featured changes primarily affecting overseas security contractors. The new guidelines do not delineate between foreign and domestic security contractors when altering definitions of "inherently governmental." As a result, war contractors "securitize" the American bureaucracy such that *contractual hybridity* abroad spills over at home. Contractor use is becoming increasingly common within the United States through mass surveillance and the militarization of the police.[252] Meanwhile, security contractors take center stage in shaping public grievances. As this chapter argued, security contractors like Blackwater create many accountability problems. However, most of the issues are specific to war contracting and do not apply to all 1.12 million commercial government functions. By monopolizing public outrage on contracting, security contractors also elide a wider discussion on government contracting.

In sum, Circular A-76 and related policy letters are part of the American backdrop for defining inherently governmental functions. Through revising these tools, bureaucrats aim to redraw the line between public and private in *Idealized Sovereignty* given practices of *Lived Sovereignty*. Following the evolution of what counts as "inherently governmental" captures the dual modalities of *Lived* and *Idealized Sovereignty* in *contractual hybridity*. As Chapter 1 highlighted, core functions of sovereign authority are far from evident. Political theorists and philosophers have spilled a lot of ink on determining the bounds of such a foundational question. Yet,

---

[250] Congressional Research Service 2010: 8.
[251] OMB 2011: 56237–8.
[252] Harcourt 2018.

bureaucrats are tasked with determining precisely this when taking inventory of government functions as inherent, critical, closely associated, or commercial. American federal contracting guidelines show the tremendous effort it takes to codify a neat state and nonstate distinction. Bureaucratic definitions and tests retain wagers about public versus private in the debate over inherently governmental functions. Ultimately, one inherently governmental function is to continually demarcate public and private in what remains a fluid relationship.

CONCLUSION

This chapter illustrated the forms and dynamics of *contractual hybridity* in American wars using the case of Blackwater. Blackwater's *contractual hybridity* was visible in its formal contracts with public funding. *Contractual hybridity* created power payoffs by deploying a contractor force for American wars and raised Weberian legitimacy dilemmas due to limited contractor oversight and distributed accountability. Security contractors also disturb civil–military relations by posing as "civilian combatants" or "unlawful combatants," depending on the preferred definition under international law. Bureaucratic debates that permit contracting revealed the effort it takes to balance between *Idealized* and *Lived Sovereignty*. When Iraqis perceived Blackwater as having the same power as Saddam Hussein, it was an acknowledgment of the new actors entitled to sovereign privilege. By being attentive to formalized and publicized hybrid relations, this chapter thus wrestled with unique problems in sovereign governance that challenge the legitimacy of a sovereign authority that contracts itself.

5

Institutionalizing Markets through the International Chamber of Commerce

We did not elect you to set the rules, so stop manipulating our governments![1]

Global markets operate on rules. For instance, almost all goods we consume have been inside a shipping container at some point. Shipping containers feature terms on their outside that indicate the level of insurance carried by sellers, for example, free on board (FOB) or cost, insurance, freight (CIF). The most widely adopted of these terms, International Commercial Terms (INCOTERMS), are made by the International Chamber of Commerce (ICC). Take another example. A Letter of Credit allows a seller to guarantee release of funds from a buyer's bank following evidence that the transaction has proceeded as described in the Letter. Letters of Credit facilitated an estimated $2 trillion in annual trade in 2016.[2] The ICC's rules for regulating Letters of Credit in its Uniform Customs and Practices for Documentary Credits (UCP) are so prolific that "most banks will not issue an international Letter of Credit unless it is explicitly subject to the UCP."[3] Along these lines, global governance scholars have recognized that "those who set standards wield influence."[4] The ICC's rulemaking extends to lobbying governments and international organizations on free trade and providing services to corporations through its International Court of Arbitration, International Maritime Arbitration, and Commercial Crime Services.

This chapter examines *institutional hybridity* in the ICC as it organizes global markets leveraging a membership of more than 8,000 corporations and chambers of commerce in 130 countries. Headquartered in Paris, the ICC was founded in 1919 in the wake of World War I by financiers, industrialists, traders, and ministers from the Allied bloc to manage German reparations. Thus, it was hybrid at birth. Compared to other transnational business networks, such as the World Economic Forum and

---

[1] Activists protesting outside the International Chamber of Commerce, October 19, 1998. Quoted in Balanya et al. 2003: 109.
[2] ICC 2016: 182.
[3] Levit 2008: 1177.
[4] Büthe and Mattli 2011: 41.

the Bilderberg Group, the ICC is regarded as the oldest, largest, and most effective.[5] Its long existence is crucial to "a sense of tradition and associated 'standing' upon which to focus and build a sense of legitimacy in the modern era."[6] The ICC has variously billed itself as "merchants of peace," "an international movement," a "world parliament of business," a "defender of the multilateral trading system," a "private sector policeman for world trade," and a "diplomacy of technics."[7] These claims are self-aggrandizing, but they serve a purpose. I argue that the ICC constructs itself institutionally as "*the* voice of global business" to be accommodated in global politics. The "difficulty with international commercial usage generally is to determine where international standards [are] to be found. ... What is done in London and New York is not necessarily what is done in Sydney or Tokyo."[8] The ICC's role is to invent "international standards" for global trade and present itself as an institution that "harmonizes" what is done across London, New York, Sydney, and Tokyo. In short, the ICC participates in public/private hybridity for regulating markets by embedding itself in global governance institutions as singularly representative of business interests.

Over the past century, the ICC has nestled into multilateral trade and investment regimes. In the 1920s and 1930s, the ICC collaborated extensively with the League of Nations, serving on official League committees, drafting major texts like the Dawes Plan for economic recovery, and even signing final acts of conferences. Some refer to the ICC and the League as "two of the main international organisations of the interwar era."[9] In the postwar period, the ICC was one of the first to acquire Category "A" consultative status with the UN Economic and Social Council (ECOSOC) in 1946.[10] It was the only nonstate entity given access to the International Trade Organization (ITO) negotiations. After the ITO collapsed, the ICC was the only nongovernmental organization (NGO) that sat on working party meetings of General Agreement on Tariffs and Trade (GATT) – a practice that was "not questioned"[11] – seeing through the success of the Kennedy Round. This led to an ICC–GATT–UN Economic Consultative Committee in 1969, which still brings "together the heads of all principal UN agencies in the economic field, plus those of GATT and the Organization for Economic Co-operation and Development (OECD), for two days of high-level discussions each year with leading ICC members."[12] Since 1961, the ICC has worked with the World Customs Organization to administer regulations in the ATA-Carnet scheme. It has partnered with the World Trade Organization (WTO) since 1996 to manage its Pre-shipment

---

[5] Balanya et al. 2003: 144; Beder 2006; Carroll 2013.
[6] Hocking and Kelly 2001: 211.
[7] Hocking and Kelly 2001: 211.
[8] Goode 1995: 741.
[9] Bertilorenzi 2015: 31–32.
[10] Charnovitz 1997: 253.
[11] Charnovitz 2000: 174.
[12] ICC 1979: 20.

Inspection, "a process conducted outside the ambit of ordinary WTO-NGO relations."[13] In 1999, the ICC was a founding member of the UN Global Compact, the largest corporate social responsibility initiative in the world, and was the only transnational actor to appear at the UN press conference that launched the program.[14] In 2009, the ICC reached a cooperation agreement with the UN Procurement Division to educate outside vendors on how to do business with the UN, which the UN called a "major milestone."[15]

When the international community's attention turned to the environment, the ICC represented chemical companies negotiating the Montreal Protocol.[16] It was also involved in the preparatory meetings leading up to the 1992 Rio Earth Summit and the 2002 World Summit on Sustainable Development in Johannesburg, addressing plenary sessions, establishing the Business Action for Sustainable Development (BASD), whose "green charter" has been endorsed by more than 2,300 global firms,[17] and jointly giving business awards with the UN Environmental Programme (UNEP).[18] It again worked with UNEP and the International Labour Organization (ILO) to make proposals for chemical accident management.[19] The ICC held joint meetings with governments during side events at negotiations for the Kyoto Protocol[20] and the Paris Agreement.[21] Beyond environment, the UN High Commissioner for Refugees has worked with the ICC to coordinate business contributions for humanitarian and technical assistance.[22]

By pushing its business know-how as governance credibility, the ICC works to "institutionalize an international business perspective by providing a forum where capitalists and related professionals can assemble to forge a common international policy framework."[23] As a cross-industry organization, the ICC's purpose "can be fairly fluid, as consensus about interests held in common waxes and wanes."[24] But the ICC is most effective when it projects "a social bloc that extends from the global to the local."[25] The ICC aims for such coherence through its organizational structure headed by a Chair, Vice-Chair, and ex-Chair.[26] A World Council of all National Committees elect the Chair and Vice-Chair every two years. A Secretary-General, appointed by an Executive Board, runs the secretariat. The ICC's

---

[13] Tully 2007: 246.
[14] UN 1999.
[15] UN 2009.
[16] *Financial Times* 1989; Hunt 1989.
[17] Vogel 2009: 158.
[18] Tully 2007: 63–65.
[19] Tully 2007: 79.
[20] Tully 2007: 170.
[21] *Financial Times* 2015.
[22] Tully 2007: 75.
[23] Carroll 2013: 41–42.
[24] Haufler 2010: 107.
[25] Carroll 2013: 209.
[26] Kelly 2005: 263–264.

constitution claims it serves "to further the development of an open world economy with the firm conviction that international commercial exchanges are conducive to both greater global prosperity and peace among nations." Biannual Congresses feature high status plenary speakers, including WTO Directors-General, special representatives to the UN Secretary-General, and heads of governments or their senior representatives. Thus, the structure fuses artifacts from business (Chair, Executive Board) and intergovernmental organizations (Secretary-General, Secretariat, Constitution, World Council). The hybridization "enables the ICC consciously to liken itself to an intergovernmental organization."[27]

The ICC's institutional practices resonate with research on transnational private authority[28] where nonstate actors, "operating singly and through novel collaborations,"[29] "make rules or set standards that others in world politics adopt."[30] Examples abound in financial accounting and auditing, product standards, foreign investment, insurance, bankruptcy, bond ratings, Internet commerce, and forest certification.[31] Private transnational regulatory organizations "operate through markets, not through interstate negotiations or hierarchy."[32] Scholars conceptualize such business actors as a distinct nonstate "market authority" that aims "to place limits on the role of the state in the economy."[33] Related research on public–private partnerships[34] recognizes that public governance is regarded as inefficient, lacking in expertise, and prone to capture, whereas private governance "may deadlock, or be dominated by brute market power," or face legitimacy deficits.[35] Thus, public and private actors may work to "combine their advantages while minimizing their disadvantages."[36] Partnerships merge "public mandates with market- and norm-based mechanisms of steering."[37] In the "Governance Triangle," states, firms, and NGOs act as single-actor regulators at the tips and intermingle along the sides and center of the triangle.[38] In these myriad approaches, the inclusion of business in

---

[27]　Kelly 2005: 264–265.
[28]　Strange 1996; Cutler, Haufler, and Porter 1999; Braithwaite and Drahos 2000; Ronit and Schneider 1999; Hall and Biersteker 2002; Cutler 2003; Sassen 2006; Graz and Nölke 2008; Büthe and Mattli 2011; Green 2014.
[29]　Abbott and Snidal 2009b: 505.
[30]　Green 2014: 4; Cutler, Haufler, and Porter 1999; Hall and Biersteker 2002.
[31]　Dezalay and Garth 1994; Ericson, Barry, and Doyle 2000; Bartley 2003; Porter 2005; Sinclair 2005; Mile and Perry 2007; Sisley and Flyverbom 2008; Halliday and Carruthers 2009; Büthe and Mattli 2011.
[32]　Abbott et al. 2015: 248.
[33]　Lucas 1997: 91; Hall and Biersteker 2002.
[34]　Börzel and Risse 2005; Ruggie 2007; Bäckstrand 2008; Tallberg et al. 2013; Johnson 2014; Andonova 2017.
[35]　Abbott and Snidal 2001: 363.
[36]　Abbott and Snidal 2001: 363.
[37]　Andonova 2017: 9.
[38]　Abbott and Snidal 2009a: 48.

"international political governance structures"[39] distinguishes old hierarchy-based multilateralism and new network-based transnationalism.[40]

I extend and bend this literature to argue that the ICC is illustrative of public/ private hybridity regulating global markets. Examining the ICC's century-long existence historicizes the conventional wisdom that twenty-first-century global governance is a uniquely "remarkable period of experimentation aimed at creating collective problem-solving capacity that is beyond and below the contours" of the state.[41] For instance, one periodization of the Governance Triangle lists no firm-only or state–firm transnational regulation before 1985, some firm-only regulation post-1985, while the greatest number of firm-only and firm–state regulation occurs after 1994.[42] Scholarship on the institutional linkages between transnational actors and international organizations claims that both GATT and WTO are "traditionally hesitant to engage directly with transnational actors,"[43] and are counted among "IOs with a historical record of no or limited access."[44] UN Secretary-General Kofi Annan is said to have proposed the Global Compact without an "intergovernmental blueprint" of "engaging business and other actors in the core affairs of the UN."[45] While global governance scholars have acknowledged the ICC's standard-setting,[46] lobbying,[47] and arbitration,[48] they have yet to fully examine the ICC and its hybrid relations. Moreover, I argue that rather than exemplifying nonstate market authority, the ICC's institutional linkages actually enable the sovereign regulation of global markets.

While there are strong contractual elements to the ICC, its novelty for public/ private hybridity is the cultivation of insider rules through institutional linkages. The ICC's *institutional hybridity* is apparent across four phases of global regulation:[49]

1. Issue-definition through prioritizing business opinions over others
2. Agenda-setting through gaining access to important global venues and leaders
3. Rulemaking in "self-regulatory" standards and constructing commercial crime
4. Rule implementation through commercial arbitration and lobbying for its adoption.

---

[39] Brühl and Hofferberth 2013: 354.
[40] Andonova 2017: 4; Abbott and Snidal 2009b.
[41] Grande and Pauly 2005: 285; Andonova 2017: 13. Examples of pre-1990 public-private collaborations include the International Red Cross and Geneva Conventions, the ILO, and NGOs and UNICEF.
[42] Abbott and Snidal 2009a: 54.
[43] Tallberg et al. 2013: 5.
[44] Tallberg et al. 2014: 742. The authors give a score of 0 to GATT bodies between 1950 and 1994 on a composite transnational openness index (with a theoretical maximum of 12).
[45] Andonova 2017: 67.
[46] Abbott and Snidal 2001.
[47] Woll 2013.
[48] Mattli 2001.
[49] Avant, Finnemore, and Sell 2010: 3; Haufler 2010: 108.

I examine each regulatory phase in the ICC using archival records, including minutes from its top executives' meetings from 1919 to 1970 (last available year) and international congresses. I also assemble an original news corpus of all mentions of the ICC in *The Financial Times*, regarded as one of the premier outlets for the global business elite, from 1981 until 2019. Finally, I draw from semi-structured interviews with ICC staff conducted in 2010 and 2016 on background. The research reveals that the ICC helps regulate global markets in *Lived Sovereignty* by maintaining insider rules through institutional relations that are sometimes more formalized and publicized (UN partnerships), while other times less so (lobbying). Yet the ICC avoids claiming sovereign status to circumvent public responsibility.[50] The ICC's role in *institutional hybridity* reveals the exclusionary nature of global commercial networks. For instance, its ECOSOC consultative status led to treaty negotiations with "ICC drafts sponsored by developed states competing with counterproposals (if any) from developing countries."[51] Moreover, the ICC also delegitimizes other civil society participants, especially labor and environmental NGOs. While performing sovereign competence for global commerce in *Lived Sovereignty*, the ICC creates legitimation problems for *Idealized Sovereignty*, as the global trade and investment regime is unaccountable to any public and is unlikely to improve socioeconomic realities for all but a select few.[52]

This chapter proceeds in four examinations mirroring the regulatory phases. First, I overview how the ICC influenced global issue-definition by restricting efforts to assign corporate responsibility for human rights. Second, I trace its multilateral agenda-setting efforts in aggressively liberalizing trade and investment through the ITO/GATT/WTO regime. Third, I focus on the ICC's rulemaking in "self-regulatory" policymaking commissions and constructing particular kinds of commercial crimes. Fourth, I address the sovereign dilemmas of *institutional hybridity* through the lens of ICC's rule implementation in international commercial arbitration, which brings to light the ICC's tremendous influence on regulating market transactions and the elitism delivering benefits of that governance to a select few. This chapter's epigraph quotes activists protesting the ICC's status as unelected global governors making rules for the world. However, unlike the protestors' description of the ICC's tactics as coercive governmental manipulation, I argue that the ICC is only able to succeed in hybridity with governments in elite institutions just as the global economic order is only maintained through public/private hybridity.

LIMITING CORPORATE RESPONSIBILITY[53]

The ICC became more attuned to the interests of transnational corporations (TNCs) as its membership expanded beyond Chambers of Commerce. The ICC's

---

[50] Haufler 2001.
[51] Tully 2007: 66–67.
[52] Cutler 2001; Graz and Nölke 2008; Cutler 2010; Katsikas 2010.
[53] I thank Virginia Haufler for pushing me to develop this section.

1920 constitution made no provision for individual membership for TNCs. Corporations had to go through their National Committees to access the ICC. However, in 1975, the ICC approved the first major revision to the original constitution.[54] The revision allowed the ICC to treat TNCs as independent members, bypassing the National Committee requirement. In this major change, the ICC recognized geographic diversification in supply chains, expanding global markets, and the growing influence of corporations in global governance. A staff member disclosed that ICC services for member TNCs now contribute a higher portion of ICC's revenue than National Committee membership dues.[55] The ICC does not list its corporate members publicly. But corporate signatories to ICC's letters to the media provide a glimpse. A 1992 letter to the *Financial Times* about restarting the Uruguay Round of GATT negotiations was signed by chief executives of IBM, AT&T, General Motors, Toshiba, Proctor and Gamble, Unilever, Nestlé, Exxon, BP, Shell, Volkswagen, Mitsubishi, Sony, Dow Chemical, 3M, Siemens, Birla Group of India, Swiss Bank, Standard Chartered Bank, Bank of Tokyo, Citicorp, Daimler Benz, Fiat, American Express, Deutsche Bank, Lloyds Bank, Price Waterhouse, and many more.[56]

As TNCs became more important to the ICC's revenues, the ICC began defending them from attack by promoting a narrow view of corporate responsibility. The campaign started from the ICC's 1969 Congress in Istanbul with the theme of "International Economic Growth: The Role, Rights and Responsibilities of the International Corporation." The branding of a new "selfless business man" painted TNCs in a positive light in the newly decolonized states. The mid-1970s saw heightened mobilization against TNCs as "the impact of business activities appeared, especially in the industrial states, increasingly to be endangering the health of the biosphere."[57] The ICC wrote letters chastising anti-corporate sentiments:

> If industry suffers from low social esteem, multinational industry has an even greater problem. In spite of the benefits we have as a nation, both through our own investments overseas and as a recipient of investment from other countries, multinational is a dirty word to far too many sincere people who have negative ideas about the power and behaviour of such companies and do not know enough about the positive benefits they bring.[58]

The ICC saw this period where "multinational was a dirty word" as existentially threatening its survival and efforts to promote free trade. The organization thus turned aggressively to control the narrative at intergovernmental forums, primarily the UN, to redirect anger.

[54] ICC 1975 Constitution.
[55] ICC Interview, July 2010.
[56] *Financial Times* 1992.
[57] Hocking and Kelly 2001: 215.
[58] *Financial Times* 1984.

In 1974, the UN established a Commission on Transnational Corporations that led to a Centre on Transnational Corporations (UNCTC). The goal was to create a Code of Conduct on Transnational Corporations. Given the decolonization period, "several governments were concerned that equality of status with states would be recognized if corporations were direct addressees of the Code. Whereas states were 'sovereign entities, full subjects and makers of international law,' corporations were 'qualitatively different participants' within the international legal order and primarily subject to national law."[59] As such, the ICC was given access to participate on behalf of individual corporations in the Commission's sessions and was "permitted to review draft reports, make oral interventions and nominate experts."[60] This recognition elevated the ICC's institutional status and legitimized its exclusive role as the business interlocutor for the UN on corporate responsibility. The ICC raised problems from the outset on how the Commission defined corporations and defended the growing corporate concerns of investment and expropriation (discussed later in the section Politics of Exclusivity in Arbitration). The Code was ultimately shelved when "continuing business support for the Code was jeopardized after the ICC expressed lost confidence."[61]

Meanwhile, the ICC also consulted with the UN on an ad hoc basis on corporate responsibility. For instance, the ICC argued against divestment from the South African apartheid regime, convinced that "disengagement from South Africa of multinational companies would weaken the pressures towards further change and probably lead to the development of a siege economy in which the black community would stand to lose."[62] The ICC also represented this position at a 1985 UN panel on divestment.[63]

The ICC next moved to preempt scrutiny by promoting voluntary principles of corporate responsibility. In 1991, a year before the landmark Earth Summit in Rio, the organization launched a "green charter" and persuaded 200 TNCs, including Ford and GM, to sign the pledge for protecting the environment. The ICC framed the issue as "sustainable development" that "permits economic growth while protecting the global environment." The ICC Chairman called the voluntary charter a "moral commitment involving rigorous self-examination."[64] UNEP and GATT officials endorsed the green charter. Predictably, NGOs like Greenpeace were skeptical: "By proclaiming environmentalism, these companies are trying to avoid responsibility for the fact that their products and practices have wreaked environmental havoc."[65] Still, the success of the green charter for the ICC was that it set the terms of global trade and environment negotiations by prioritizing "better

---

[59]   Tully 2007: 56, citing ECOSOC 1976, para 42.
[60]   Tully 2007: 55.
[61]   Tully 2007: 56.
[62]   Mauthner 1985.
[63]   Simon 1985.
[64]   Hunt 1991a.
[65]   Lamb 1992a.

performance through the workings of the free-market rather than by tougher regulations."[66] The Executive Director of the ICC's Office on Environment emphasized the market logic: "The environment is an asset. Sustainable development is about learning to develop and maintain this asset so we live off the income, not the capital."[67] The ICC Chairman went even further: "The corporate challenge is to take advantage of green consumerism and opportunities such as waste recycling and non-polluting products."[68] Meanwhile, the Secretary-General of the Earth Summit addressed the ICC's pre-conference on sustainable development, agreeing that "future financial profits and attention to the environment would be closely linked."[69] In Rio, two treaties emerged, but the one that had no specific targets for carbon emissions passed. The ICC hailed it as "a realistic and significant step forward."[70]

Delegitimizing NGOs

During the mid-1990s, the ICC relaunched itself under Chairman Helmut Maucher, the chief executive of Nestlé. Maucher brought on Maria Livanos Cattaui from the World Economic Forum as the new ICC Secretary-General. In September 1998, the ICC organized the Geneva Business Dialogue with the UN, featuring 450 business leaders, the WTO Director-General, high-level World Bank officials, UN Under-Secretaries-General, the UNCTAD Secretary-General, and presidents, prime ministers, and other top government officials.[71] Maucher asked the participants to "establish global rules for an ordered liberalism."[72] He signaled *institutional hybridity* when positioning the ICC as "in the front of the discussion, as the voice of business, dialoguing with the WTO and the UN."[73] UN Secretary-General Annan pledged to "build on the close ties between the UN and the ICC."[74] Annan also confirmed the ICC's exclusionary vision of global governance as he "undertook to exclude human rights and environmental conditions from multilateral trade regimes provided corporations made progress in satisfying broader social welfare objectives."[75]

The ICC also used the Geneva Business Dialogue to delegitimize environmental and human rights NGOs. Maucher had already argued in *The Financial Times* that "we have to be careful that [NGOs] do not get too much influence," and that

---

[66] Hunt 1991b.
[67] Lamb 1992a.
[68] Lamb 1992a.
[69] Lamb 1992b.
[70] Lascelles and Lamb 1992.
[71] Balanya et al. 2003: 167, citing Olivier Hoedeman (coauthor), notes made at the Geneva Business Dialogue, September 23–24, 1998.
[72] Balanya et al. 2003: 167.
[73] Balanya et al. 2003: 167.
[74] Balanya et al. 2003: 167–168.
[75] Tully 2007: 62.

"governments have to understand that business is not just another pressure group but a resource that will help them set the right rules."[76] In Geneva, Maucher responded to activists complaining about the UN being "co-opted" by business interests: "We feel that these groups realise that the ICC is now organised more efficiently as the business voice in contact with the UN. ... It is difficult for them to digest that the business voice is also important."[77] In the official concluding statement, Maucher doubled down:

> The emergence of activist pressure groups risks weakening the effectiveness of public rules, legitimate institutions and democratic processes. These organizations should place emphasis on legitimizing themselves, improving their internal democracy, transparency and accountability. They should assume full responsibility for the consequences of their activities. Where this does not take place, rules establishing their rights and responsibilities should be considered.[78]

Under Maucher, the ICC formulated an exclusionary view of the role of business in global regulation arguing that "business has just as much right – more, in [Maucher's] view – to help shape global rules as pressure groups."[79] Maucher argued that the "ICC can speak with a certain moral authority because we're not pushing a particular business interest. We're not going to governments and pushing to sell more Nescafe. If you have good arguments and no hidden agenda you have a chance of being listened to."[80] The idea that business interests for an "ordered liberalism" was *not* an agenda signals how closely the ICC saw the integration of elitist capitalism in global governance institutions.

The ICC kept up its efforts to delegitimize NGOs to redirect attention away from concrete action on corporate responsibility. It suggested a "similar 'weeding out' of certain NGOs" when it met with Prime Minister Tony Blair in May 1998 to present a message for the G8 Summit.[81] Then, in 2002, after the 1999 Seattle protests against the WTO, the ICC called "upon the G8 governments, with the authority they derive from mass democratic elections, to stand firm in the face of groups that are mostly unaccountable and represent small minority views or narrow vested interests. We cannot curb the chances of poor people to profit from participation in a thriving global economy."[82] By the early 2000s, the ICC's changing relationship with the UN afforded a new playbook for dealing with NGOs and other critics. The ICC would assert its institutional status as above other civil society actors through processes of "exclusion from the corridors and hallways of power."[83]

[76] Maucher 1997; Williams 1998b.
[77] Balanya et al. 2003: 173–174.
[78] Maucher 1998.
[79] Williams 1998b.
[80] Williams 1998b.
[81] Balanya et al. 2003: 174.
[82] Beder 2006: 195.
[83] Hocking and Kelly 2001: 220.

The Global Compact

Annan's hope for closer business–UN ties materialized in 1999 as the ICC became the founding partner of the UN Global Compact. The Compact developed voluntary principles on the environment, labor standards, and human rights. Fifty multinational corporations got on board at the outset. The joint ICC–UN press conference (itself conferring institutional legitimacy to the ICC) revealed some of the tensions of bringing together business and human rights at the UN. Annan began optimistically: "Business is calling for a stronger United Nations, especially in the areas of human rights, labour and the environment, because this is seen as the most sensible way forward to safeguard open markets while, at the same time, creating a human face for the global economy."[84] Meanwhile, the ICC Chairman was more cautious: "For the Global Compact to succeed all of us – Governments, the United Nations system and business – must be realistic in our expectations. Companies cannot be expected to take on responsibilities beyond their own sphere of activity that are the proper preserve of Governments."[85] It was a regular ICC strategy to encourage corporate self-governance in global commerce, while also eschewing the responsibility for such governance.

For many, it was surprising that the Compact happened at all. The ICC delegation at the press conference featured a high-ranking executive from Shell, a company still dealing with the fallout from its practices in Nigeria (and was questioned for it at the presser). NGOs argued that the UN was "simply providing legitimacy to companies such as Shell and Nike – which stand accused of major transgressions on the human rights and environmental fronts – and for little more than adherence to loosely monitored principles."[86] Other UN officials anticipated this blowback. Mary Robinson, UN High Commissioner for Human Rights, remarked at the press conference:

> I welcomed this meeting because it was the best opportunity for the Office of the High Commissioner to be in a direct relationship with the ICC, unlike other components of the United Nations Organization. In fact, a paper was prepared for the meeting which showed the considerable contacts that the ICC has had with other agencies or programmes. And the fact that we are now in discussion illustrates that this is, for both sides, a new process.[87]

Even as Robinson called out the ICC's relatively recent interest in human rights, she reified the ICC's institutional linkages as a longtime collaborator of the UN. Predictably, after the Compact launched, the ICC narrowed business obligations for human rights by introducing a new value:

> Business accepts the challenge and is eager to cooperate with the UN and other public sector bodies to enhance all three [human rights, labor standards, and

---

[84] UN 1999.
[85] UN 1999.
[86] Hocking and Kelly 2001: 210.
[87] UN 1999.

environmental practices]. Alongside them however, we must place a fourth value –
the economic responsibility incumbent upon any company to its customers, to its
employees and to its shareholders.[88]

To its members, the ICC pitched the Compact as "a management tool to create
added value in our relationship with employees, customers and society at large."[89]
Thus, the ICC's involvement in the Compact was critical to curtailing a broader
imposition of corporate responsibility.

Meanwhile, the UN asserted that the ICC was important to the UN's global
legitimacy. In October 1998, Annan remarked in a Washington, D.C., address titled
"Why Conservatives Should Support the United Nations":

> The United Nations has developed a stronger appreciation for the private
> sector's expertise, entrepreneurial spirit, and unparalleled ability to create jobs
> and wealth. I have done everything I can to promote close ties since taking
> office. I have met regularly with business groups such as the International
> Chamber of Commerce, and I am heartened by their enthusiasm about
> getting more deeply involved in our work. Put simply, the goals of business
> and the goals of the United Nations can, and should be mutually supportive;
> we need each other.[90]

Annan's comments reflect the scholarly sentiment that "support of the ICC might
help the UN to regain a central position in global policy making, which during the
last years of intense economic globalisation has been predominantly controlled by
the Bretton Woods financial institutions."[91] In 2004, the head of the Compact
argued that its power "comes from getting ideas into the boardroom: which has
more power than all UN operations in all its capacities could ever muster," and
paraphrased Annan's aim to "unite the powers of markets with the authority of
universal principles."[92] The institutional linkages in the Global Compact thus
solidified the status of "the ICC as the preferred dialogue partner for business with
the United Nations and other international institutions," as reported by *The
Financial Times* in the headline: "The Voice of Business Heard around the
World."[93]

Norms and Guiding Principles on Corporate Responsibility for Human Rights

The ICC's issue-definition through *institutional hybridity* is visible in another narrowing of corporate responsibility for human rights. In 1998, the UN Sub-Commission on
the Promotion and Protection of Human Rights took on the task of defining corporate

---

[88]   McCormick 2001.
[89]   Stratte-McClure 2001.
[90]   UN 1998.
[91]   Balanya et al. 2003: 172.
[92]   Turner 2004.
[93]   Williams 1998b.

responsibility for human rights. The ICC publicly contested any impositions of human rights obligations on corporations:

> Business cannot meet demands and expectations for which governments are primarily responsible – ensuring the rule of law, universal access to education, freedom of speech, fair distribution of wealth and an adequate safety net for the old, the sick and the jobless. What companies can do is to be good corporate citizens in their relations with the community in which they operate and in their treatment of employees, suppliers, sub-contractors, customers and business associates.[94]

Undeterred, in 2003, the Sub-Commission produced *The Norms on the Responsibilities of Transnational Corporations and Other Business Enterprises*. The *Norms* asserted that "companies should be subject to the kind of enforcement procedures at the UN Commission for Human Rights previously applied only to nation states."[95] The ICC opposed this approach: "We don't have a problem at all with efforts that seek to encourage companies to do what they can ... to protect human rights. We have a problem with the premise and the principle that the norms are based on."[96]

The ICC lobbied governments by appealing to *Idealized Sovereignty*, just as it did at the Global Compact press conference: "Human rights duties apply to governments not corporations, the Norms impose vague obligations, the Sub-Commission exceeded its authority, transparency and accountability have been subverted and business is a target for vilification."[97] The ICC's American representatives stated: "Laws are made by governments, not by companies."[98] Another business group invoked Marx to argue that the merger of "private power with ruling authority would create 'a rough Marxism where the bourgeoisie acts as the steering committee of the state.'"[99] The ICC continued that the Commission's work should "not weaken or hamper the ability of a state to formulate and implement its own national laws."[100] The UN's Mary Robinson emphasized that the *Norms* were "not aimed at replacing governments' responsibility for human rights. 'What we hope to see is a steady increase in the number of companies that look seriously at international human rights standards when making decisions on their operating methods, personnel policies, procurement and investment decisions.'"[101] Ultimately, the Commission on Human Rights called for "further study" of the 2003 *Norms* in a consensus resolution.[102]

---

[94] *Financial Times* 1999a.
[95] Birchall 2003.
[96] Birchall 2003.
[97] Tully 2007: 132.
[98] Tully 2007: 134.
[99] Tully 2007: 134.
[100] Tully 2007: 134.
[101] Maitland 2003.
[102] Williams 2004.

In 2008, the UN Human Rights Council (UNHRC) developed the *Protect, Respect, and Remedy Framework for Business and Human Rights* under the direction of John Ruggie. The *Framework* thought through the obligations of corporations and their home states (where corporations are domiciled) regarding harmful conduct in human rights. Its three core principles were specifying the state duty to protect against human rights abuses by nonstate actors, including corporations, articulating corporate responsibility to respect human rights, and creating more effective remedy. In 2011, the UNHRC formally adopted the *Guiding Principles on Business and Human Rights*, asking that corporations have "an independent corporate responsibility to respect human rights, which means that business enterprises should act with due diligence to avoid infringing on the rights of others and address adverse impacts with which they are involved."[103]

While the *Guiding Principles* are an important step to formalize corporate responsibility norms, they do not create any new legally binding obligations for TNCs. The UNHRC followed a long-standing ICC talking point that corporations should not be held to the same standards as states. Indeed, the 2008 *Framework* repeated the ICC stance explicitly: "While corporations may be considered 'organs of society,' they are specialized economic organs, not democratic public interest institutions. As such, their responsibilities cannot and should not simply mirror the duties of states."[104] The 2011 *Guiding Principles* again asserted that "the responsibility of business enterprises to respect human rights is distinct from issues of legal liability and enforcement."[105] Scholars have since criticized the *Guiding Principles'* narrow vision of corporate responsibility "as being merely to 'respect' human rights, which [the *Guiding Principles*] defines as avoiding an infringement of such rights. The focus is thus upon a negative responsibility not to infringe rights rather than on any positive responsibility to assist in the realization of human rights."[106] In fact, the *Guiding Principles* focus more on clarifying state duties, such as "judicial, administrative, legislative or other steps to ensure access to an effective remedy," given corporate abuses of human rights.[107]

The ICC's issue-definition related to corporate responsibility at the UN involved consistently framing issues in narrowly neoliberal terms since the 1970s. Key to the ICC's success in *Lived Sovereignty* is to play up its role as an institutional broker that legitimates governmental discussions, while delegitimating other civil society actors, namely, environment and labor NGOs. However, the ICC also challenges any imposition of sovereign accountability that may result from its regulatory roles by mobilizing the discourse of *Idealized Sovereignty* to attribute sovereign responsibility exclusively to states. These framing decisions have ripple effects for the ICC's other

---

[103] Ruggie 2013: 171.
[104] A/HRC/8/5, April 7, 2008 Section 3, para 53.
[105] A/HRC/17/31, March 21, 2011 Section 2A, para 12.
[106] Bilchitz and Deva 2013: 15.
[107] Bilchitz and Deva 2013: 16.

regulatory functions, such as agenda-setting. As I discuss next, key to the ICC's agenda-setting prowess is to present "'free' trade as not about doing away with rules altogether, but rather replacing rules for companies with rules for governments, and replacing rules that protect citizens, consumers and the environment with rules that protect and facilitate traders and investors."[108]

AGENDA-SETTING ON TRADE AND INVESTMENT

I focus this section on the ICC's postwar agenda-setting in international trade and investment regimes.

Early Lessons with the ITO

The International Trade Organization was intended to form a Bretton Woods triad along with the International Monetary Fund and the World Bank after World War II. Unlike the other two, the ITO never got off the ground. The ITO was revolutionary in its attempt to address trade along with labor by specifying a governmental obligation to full employment. The ITO charter left it up to each member country to decide how best to achieve full employment. This created a draft charter with general principles followed by a litany of exceptions. The exceptions were attributed as loopholes "to accommodate countries which have difficulties with their balance of payments, or to permit undeveloped countries to protect their infant industries, or to permit preferential trading arrangements."[109] The loopholes, in turn, were a product of the large number of developing countries present at the final drafting conference in Havana in 1948. Ultimately, the loopholes made the charter untenable for ratification. Others have discussed the details surrounding the death of the ITO;[110] I only highlight the ICC's role in first promoting and then defeating the ITO.

The ICC was supportive of the ITO in the beginning. In 1945, the ICC Chairman said that "the initiative of the U.S. government in drawing up proposals for an international trade organization charter was one for which the ICC had been waiting for many years."[111] The following year, while recognizing the difficult reconciliation of trade and employment, the ICC noted, "it was a remarkable fact that the American Proposals were government proposals and yet [were] imbued with the spirit of free enterprise."[112] The charter drafters reached out to the ICC for early support, as is evident from the presence at the December 1946 ICC Council meeting of Eric Wyndham-White, Executive Secretary of the Preparatory Committee of the

---

[108] Beder 2006: 118.
[109] Bidwell and Diebold 1949: 194.
[110] Bidwell and Diebold 1949; Wilcox 1949; Diebold 1952; Gardner 1956; Krueger 1996; Drache 2000; Toye 2003.
[111] Executive Committee of the ICC, December 6, 1945: 9.
[112] Council of the ICC, June 20–21, 1946: 8.

International Trade and Employment Conference that kicked off the ITO negotiations. Wyndham-White briefed the ICC on the recently concluded draft charter
round in London, acknowledging that it "was a special pleasure and privilege to
address the Council of the ICC in view of his past associations with the Chamber.
He had attended the [ICC] Congress in Berlin in 1937, and at Copenhagen in
1939."[113] In an optimistic tone, Ernest Mercier, chairman of ICC's French National
Committee, emphasized that "employment could not be maximized by governments alone, by business alone, or by labor alone, but demanded that the three work
together in cooperation. Hence, the necessity for the ICC to establish contacts with
governmental organizations on the one hand, and labor organizations on the other,
which was in accordance with the general methods adopted by the Council."[114]
Mercier thus outlined the strategies of the ICC embedding itself in a new international organization.

As the ITO charter negotiations moved to Havana in 1948, the ICC was the only
nongovernmental entity granted access to the plenary sessions and meetings of the
Preparatory Committee. From observing these discussions, the ICC became especially concerned about loopholes: "Great differences of opinion had arisen, mainly
owing to the presence of a large number of countries that had not taken part in the
work of the Preparatory Committee. The most extreme demands had been made by
certain countries."[115] The ICC began to acknowledge the charter's limitations: "The
answer given to these questions by the charter was not the perfect answer."[116] In order
to improve the charter, the ICC sent a report to the drafters offering two suggestions:
establishing a uniform procedure for conciliation and international arbitration, and
recommending the elaboration of a code of fair practice in foreign investments.[117]
The Rapporteur General for the Trade and Employment Conference welcomed the
suggestions: "On a world in which private enterprise was on the defensive, the ICC
had an active part to play. It must help build up an International Trade Organization
that would be a constructive element of world peace."[118]

But the loopholes continued. Once it became clear that the ITO charter was too
restrictive, the ICC faced the tough decision of supporting a compromised charter or
refusing to endorse the first international organization for world trade. There was no
consensus within the ICC membership. The schism was most evident with the
British pushing to support the ITO regardless of its flaws and the Americans refusing
to look beyond "economic nationalism."[119] In the end, there was no formal position
from the ICC. However, the Americans used the ICC's information and prestige to
wage war on the ITO through a domestic coalition with protectionists to block

[113]   Council of the ICC, December 3–4, 1946: 5.
[114]   Council of the ICC, December 3–4, 1946: 9.
[115]   Executive Committee of the ICC, February 25, 1948: 2.
[116]   Executive Committee of the ICC, April 2, 1947: 2.
[117]   Executive Committee of the ICC, April 2, 1947: 3.
[118]   Executive Committee of the ICC, Paris, April 2, 1947: 3.
[119]   ICC Session on the ITO charter, June 3, 1947.

ratification in the US Congress. In 1951, President Truman withdrew the ITO charter for ratification and it was never reintroduced, until a version of it appeared in the WTO forty-four years later. The ICC learned its lessons from the ITO, where it was reacting to the negotiators rather than setting the agenda. In the 1960s, the ICC moved to work more closely with the GATT.

Working with the GATT

After the failure of the ITO, business leaders turned their attention to the GATT to broaden and deepen its scope as "both a set of rules and a negotiating forum."[120] The ICC wrote to GATT officials on January 1951 recommending that "a system of continuous consultation be established between the new organization and international commercial and industrial organizations, particularly the ICC."[121] The GATT Working Party in charge of drawing up a new agreement obliged the ICC's request for official consultation and entertained numerous resolutions from the ICC in the early 1950s.[122] Two ICC resolutions that had the most discussion were about "drawing up a standard definition of value, for worldwide application of customs" and determining the nationality of manufactured goods.[123] The "origin of goods" forms the crux of the most-favored nation principle in trade agreements. The ICC's definition was "based on the principle that the nationality of a manufactured product should be that of the country in which the last manufacturing process has taken place."[124] Further, the ICC said that "transit and manipulation of the goods in a transit country should not affect the nationality of the goods."[125] The GATT Working Party invited the ICC "to send representatives" at their next meeting.[126] From then onward, the Working Party began a frequent consultative relationship with the ICC to collect more information from its members on numerous issues.[127] The ICC continued its consultations via mail and in-person meetings throughout this time.

Once a General Agreement came together in 1955, Eric Wyndham-White, now the Executive Secretary of GATT, spoke at the ICC Congress:

> The proposals that have been made by the Council of the International Chamber of Commerce, both as to the Agreement itself and in the direction of simplifying or abolishing administrative formalities have drawn wide attention in government and business circles and have had most fruitful results. ... The Chamber is now in a position to render further service to the common cause, and I hope that through its

[120] Beder 2006: 110.
[121] GATT/CP/98, February 8, 1951.
[122] GATT/CP.6/7, August 15, 1951.
[123] GATT/CP.6/7, August 15, 1951.
[124] GATT/CP/123, August 29, 1952.
[125] GATT/CP/123, August 29, 1952.
[126] GATT/CP.6/36, October 20, 1951.
[127] GATT/G/28, November 1, 1952.

National Committees it will urge the early approval of the amendments to GATT
and of the agreement establishing the Organization for Trade Cooperation, so that
we may take up the tools and get on with the job.[128]

Wyndham-White regarded the ICC as an institution giving the new GATT body
a platform to make its case to "global business." It thus became a regular
occurrence for high-level GATT executives to speak at ICC Congresses. The
speeches would usually commend "the importance of the support that the
International Chamber of Commerce, because of its influential role, has always
given to the work undertaken in GATT toward the expansion and improvement
of world trade,"[129] while also asking the ICC members to "give all possible
encouragement to your governments so that, when the final decisions are
taken, the most liberal possible solutions are chosen."[130] There was also
a revolving door between GATT officers and the ICC. Jean Royer, former
GATT Deputy Executive Secretary became an ICC technical adviser on trade
policy in the 1960s. GATT Director-General Arthur Dunkel chaired the ICC
policy commission on international trade and investment in the 1990s.
Meanwhile, GATT's Kennedy Round, concluded in 1967, was one of the most
successful in postwar trade with an estimated 50 percent cut in tariff levels. Once
again, the ICC was the only nonstate actor allowed access to the negotiations.[131]

    The ICC also conducted agenda-setting outside formal GATT forums, such as by
organizing informal meetings between business leaders and heads of government to
support the latest trade talks.[132] In 1987, during the early negotiations of the Uruguay
Round, the ICC organized such meetings with "35 heads of delegations to
GATT."[133] The following year, the ICC "held discussions in Geneva between 29
corporate executives and trade negotiators from 37 countries."[134] As the WTO got
ready to launch the Doha talks in 1998, the ICC held "a two-day conference in
Geneva on globalisation attended by business leaders and heads of international
agencies."[135] Even today, the ICC regularly hosts a "B20" of top business people to
coincide with the G20 meetings. The B20 has "sought to become an integral part of
the G20 process and has had two meetings with the 'Sherpas' – the government
officials who prepare the summit agenda – in the run-up."[136] Moreover, the ICC
made frequent media declarations of support to maintain public pressure on the
talks, such as for the Uruguay Round in 1989, 1990, and 1993.[137] The ICC later

---

[128] GATT/233, May 20, 1955.
[129] GATT/1162, June 16, 1975.
[130] GATT/1220, October 3, 1978.
[131] Beder 2006: 111.
[132] Beder 2006: 113.
[133] Dullforce 1987.
[134] *Financial Times* 1988b.
[135] Williams 1998a.
[136] Carnegy 2011.
[137] Montagnon 1989; *Financial Times* 1990, 1991, 1993.

encouraged a "Millennium Round" for the WTO in 1999.[138] After the 1999 meeting featured clashes with anti-WTO activists, the ICC soothed nerves, claiming that "Seattle was a setback, but it did not halt trade liberalization."[139] The ICC pushed for the Doha Round every year starting in 2002 until its conclusion in 2013.[140] It also organized major chief executives to sign open letters, such as in 1992, 1997, 2005, 2007, 2011, and 2013.[141] In fact, these letters have become so routine that their form was satirized in the *Financial Times*: "If you think getting a trade agreement is hard you should try agreeing the wording of a letter with 60 business titans."[142]

Failing Upward with the MAI

Even when ICC proposals do not immediately bear fruit, they still set the agenda for future discussions, as was the case with the Multilateral Agreement on Investment (MAI). Unlike trade, there is no multilateral framework or body to govern global investment. In the 1990s, the OECD hosted MAI deliberations and charged the ICC with "designing the first draft."[143] The ICC "was able to use its ready access to government leaders and its consultative status at major international summits to lobby for the MAI at the highest levels. It argued that governments should have to guarantee the security of investments made in their countries but should not be able to impose performance requirements on foreign investors."[144] The ICC thus foregrounded rules for government rather than corporations.

The MAI was negotiated during the lead-up to the 1999 "Battle in Seattle" featuring anti-WTO environmental and labor activists. The same critics argued that MAI would undermine existing international agreements on the environment like the forthcoming Kyoto Protocol, and asked for some "token environmental and Labour clauses."[145] After Berkeley, California's declaration as a "MAI-Free Zone," other cities in the OECD followed.[146] ICC Chairman Maucher countered that "MAI is not the right place in which to set specific levels of environmental protection" and that "any attempt by OECD governments to use the MAI as a basis for defining and promulgating core labour standards would pre-empt ongoing discussion on these issues at the International Labour Organization."[147] However, France withdrew from the talks in October 1998, bowing to public pressure.

---

[138] *Financial Times* 1999b, 1999c.
[139] *Financial Times* 1999d.
[140] Hill and Mann 2002; *Financial Times* 2003a, 2003b; Fifield 2004; *Financial Times* 2005, 2006; Mitchell 2008; Betts 2009; Donnan 2013.
[141] *Financial Times* 1992, 1997, 2005, 2007, 2011, 2013.
[142] Shrimsley 2005.
[143] Beder 2006: 175.
[144] Beder 2006: 175.
[145] Beder 2006: 182.
[146] Balanya et al. 2003: 117.
[147] Beder 2006: 182.

That same month, more than a hundred activists targeted the ICC directly by occupying its Parisian headquarters, demanding: "We did not elect you to set the rules, so stop manipulating our governments! We call upon our governments to follow the example of France and get the hell out of the OECD's MAI negotiations."[148] The ICC countered in *The Financial Times*:

> The agreement risks being encumbered by excess baggage that would dilute business enthusiasm and discourage non-OECD countries from acceding. ... OECD governments should be careful not to discourage developing countries and emerging economies from joining the agreement. This could happen if they imposed binding requirements governing the environment and labour standards that countries cannot realistically meet. ... Any governments that attempt to use the agreement as a basis for setting core labour standards would pre-empt discussions in the International Labour Organisation, the appropriate forum.[149]

The ICC's American affiliates dismissed the activists as those who "cannot possibly provide the same breadth of advice needed by governments in any sophisticated trade negotiations" as the ICC.[150] Recall how the ICC used the same strategy of delegitimizing NGOs during the Geneva Business Dialogue held in the same year. Yet, the anti-MAI campaigns worked. Canada, Australia, and the United Kingdom followed France in withdrawing. By December 1998, the MAI was shelved.

Despite failing to make progress on the MAI, the ICC succeeded in moving its core ideas to the top of the investment agendas. The MAI would have given TNCs "the right to file complaints about national government policies in non-transparent international dispute settlement panels. In effect, the agreement would have subjected national and local priorities to the needs and wishes of foreign investors."[151] This feature was already present in Bilateral Investment Treaties (BITs), which the ICC promoted through its model BITs and investor–state arbitration. The ICC's institutional embeddedness permits "leap-frogging," or "establishing greater promotion and protection of foreign investment in one forum (for example, a bilateral or regional agreement) and then attempting to match, or exceed, those standards in other fora."[152] As such, once ICC ideas were introduced in the MAI, the organization found "it reasonable to expect that the MAI would serve as a reference, as would other recent investment agreements."[153] As far back as 1949, the ICC had "formulated a code suggesting measures that would create conditions attractive to foreign capital. Many of these have been adopted, including guarantees against expropriation, adoption of favorable tax structures, relaxation of controls and improvements

---

[148]   Balanya et al. 2003: 109. Tony Clarke, as quoted in personal notes made by Olivier Hoedeman (coauthor) during the occupation of ICC headquarters, Paris, October 19, 1998.
[149]   *Financial Times* 1998.
[150]   Beder 2006: 183.
[151]   Balanya et al. 2003: 113.
[152]   Beder 2006: 179.
[153]   Beder 2006: 179.

in administration."[154] Within this context, the MAI was only a temporary setback in institutionalizing rules for global capital.

The ICC generates insider rules through its agenda-setting on global trade and investment. It has been described as "the most completely and extensively organized of all the private business groups, and it has the most direct access to international governmental organizations and agencies. It is indeed the ideal channel for the communication to such bodies of the views of the international business community."[155] This image is central to the ICC's agenda-setting. The ICC does not always get what it wants, but *institutional hybridity* ensures that the organization can play the long game with its governmental interlocutors. The particular content of ICC rules, in turn, originate from its "self-governance" apparatus.

"SELF-GOVERNANCE" IN RULEMAKING

What the ICC promotes as business "self-governance" in fact seeks governmental regulation for narrow commercial interests through *institutional hybridity*. In this section, I study rulemaking in ICC policy commissions and the construction of particular kinds of activities as commercial crimes.

Policy Commissions and Standards

ICC rules typically emerge from one of twelve policy commissions, which consist of business experts drawn from ICC members. The commissions fall under three themes:

(1) *Rules-Writing for Business*: Arbitration and Alternative Dispute Resolution (ADR); Banking; Commercial Law and Practice; Marketing and Advertising
(2) *Trade, Investment and Globalization*: Competition; Customs and Trade Facilitation; Intellectual Property; Taxation; Trade and Investment
(3) *Business in Society Issues*: Corporate Responsibility and Anti-Corruption; Digital Economy; Environment and Energy.[156]

The policy commissions reflect the ICC's mandate to liberalize trade. For instance, the Taxation Commission aims to "promote transparent and non-discriminatory treatment of foreign investments and earnings that eliminates tax obstacles to cross-border trade and investment." The Trade and Investment Policy Commission intends to "promote cross-border trade and investment by business and an open global economy to foster job creation, sustainable development, and improve living standards."

---

[154] Haight 1960: 203.
[155] Haight 1960: 204.
[156] ICC 2022.

The policy commissions are at the center of the ICC's creation of a global self-regulating business society. The spirit of self-regulation is as follows: "Unless we regulate ourselves, governments will do it for us and that could be clumsy, costly and make life very difficult for commerce."[157] The policy commissions work "to harmonize international trade practices through uniform rules and trade terms incorporated into contracts, and through publications of guides devoted to specific fields of activity or specific problem areas."[158] Business self-regulation aims to "reduce risk, enhance reputation, and respond to new ideas within the business community."[159] The ICC refers to the role of the policy commissions as "interpreters of world trade. ... If the law is inefficient you are stuck with it. Voluntary standards, meanwhile, are more flexible and easier to revise."[160] As interpreters, the commissions also monitor the implementation of their rules by issuing opinions on their application.[161] As such, the policy commissions routinely revise rules over time.

Table 5.1 displays sample ICC rules and standards as represented by the organization.[162] The ICC "lobbies for its rules and terms to become the accepted language of trade."[163] Its efforts are often rewarded. I highlighted INCOTERMS in the chapter's introduction. When the 1990 revisions to INCOTERMS came out, the *Financial Times* announced: "Language of Trade Gains a New International Lexicon."[164] When revised in 2000, they were recognized as "the international standards for customs authorities and law courts in most countries."[165]

To take the most recent rulemaking example in Table 5.1, the ICC has been active in cyber governance from 1988 when it drafted the Uniform Rules of Conduct for Interchange of trade Data by electronic transmission (UNCID).[166] By 1995, it worked with governments to create guidelines on encryption. In a prescient move, the ICC debated whether to accommodate "the use of third-party organisations, which would be independent of government, would have the keys and would hand them over to government investigators when demands were justified."[167] The ICC continued working with the OECD to balance government encryption demands and privacy.[168] In 1997, the ICC announced the general usage in international digitally ensured commerce (GUIDEC) as the first guidelines for e-commerce to govern the use of digital signatures to validate documents: "We now offer to world business a set of detailed guidelines that will help to cement the trust in business

[157]   McEwan 1987.
[158]   Goode 1995: 725.
[159]   Haufler 2001: 20.
[160]   Marks 1996.
[161]   Goode 1995: 742.
[162]   ICC 2014.
[163]   ICC 2014.
[164]   Hermann 1990.
[165]   Iskandar 1999.
[166]   *Financial Times* 1988a.
[167]   Jack 1995.
[168]   Marks 1996.

TABLE 5.1 *Sample ICC rules and standards as represented by the organization*

Year	Rule	Purpose
1933	Uniform Customs and Practices for Documentary Credits	Written into virtually every letter of credit, the UCP are accepted throughout the world to transfer billions of dollars yearly from buyers to sellers in payment for goods and services
1936	INCOTERMS	Standard trade definitions used worldwide in international sales contracts to reduce uncertainties arising from differing national interpretations of such terms
1958	ATA Carnet	International customs document that permits duty-free and tax-free temporary import of goods such as commercial samples, professional equipment, goods for presentation for up to one year
1960s	Model Contracts (Various)	Provide a legal basis upon which parties to international contracts can quickly establish an even-handed agreement acceptable to both sides. They are meant to protect the interests of all parties, combining a single framework of rules with flexible provisions
1977	Rules of Conduct to Combat Extortion and Bribery	To provide a basis for corporate self-regulatory action barring extortion and bribery for any purpose, covering judicial proceedings, tax matters, environmental and other regulatory cases, or legislative proceedings
1991	Business Charter for Sustainable Development	For companies to establish their integrated environmental management systems. Referenced at the UN Earth Summit in 1992, the charter was also a foundation for the Global Compact of UN Secretary General Kofi Annan
1992	ICC/UNCTAD Rules for Multimodal Transport Documents	The rules set the only globally accepted standard for multimodal transport documents. They are intended to avoid the problems that would arise for transporters from having to cope with a multiplicity of different regimes when drawing up contracts
1997	General Usage in Digitally Ensured Commerce (GUIDEC)	Establish trust between parties to an online deal and the security of information exchanged. A 2001 update took into account the increases in information-carrying power and flexibility of electronic messages for e-business usage

transactions over open networks that is absolutely essential if the internet is to fulfil its promise as a universal marketplace open to all."[169]

GUIDEC revealed a long-standing tension in self-regulation: wanting to "pre-empt the establishment of regulatory barriers by national governments," while acknowledging that the preemption entails "difficulty in applying them in some jurisdictions, where it is not clear whether or not electronic transmission satisfy writing and signature requirements."[170] To counter this tension, the ICC promoted the self-governing aspect of the internet:

> In cyberspace, the consumer is king, choosing and comparing prices without the constraints of distance and free of the salesman's blandishments. Creating consumer confidence in transactions over the internet is just as important for business as it is for governments. This is a good reason why governments should feel comfortable about relying on business to regulate itself effectively.[171]

The ICC also argued that "once the full power of the internet is unleashed on the world, it will challenge national laws and may eventually elude government control altogether."[172] Meanwhile, in the late-1990s, the ICC hosted conferences on international rules in electronic commerce and the related issues affecting "privacy, security, governance, marketing, and the provision of infrastructure."[173]

In fact, ICC "self-governance" relied on government regulation, only on the ICC's terms. In 1998, the ICC lobbied the European Union (EU) for ICC model privacy clauses to be included in e-contracts for European companies. These clauses were far more progressive than what came later as they made companies outside the EU "undertake to give personal data emanating from within the EU the same level of protection as the EU's new data protection directive which aims to safeguard individual privacy. The clauses also provide[d] for legal remedies if consumers believe[d] their legal rights on privacy have been breached."[174] In 2002, the ICC mobilized against disparate European data retention laws for internet service providers (ISP) by showing that "Finland requires ISPs to store data for two years while Ireland wants a four-year period. The way things are shaping up, it looks as though IT and telecoms companies will have to cope not just with one Big Brother but a whole tribe of them.'"[175] The ICC asked for "streamlining the maze of restrictions on international data transfers under European law."[176] When the EU proposed forcing data retention for three years, the ICC lobbied "each European justice minister asking for the proposal to be dropped and ... urged governments to

---

[169]　Jack 1997.
[170]　Moran 1998.
[171]　*Financial Times* 1998a.
[172]　de Jonquie'res and Kehoe 1998.
[173]　*Financial Times* 1998b.
[174]　Williams 1998c.
[175]　Sherwood and Tait 2002.
[176]　*Financial Times* 2004.

consider 'data preservation' as an alternative to wide-scale mandatory data retention. That would enable law enforcement agencies to freeze specific data on specific subjects with a warrant, rather than requiring wholesale retention of all data."[77] To be clear, the ICC did not become a consumer privacy advocate. Instead, it was concerned about the costs of storing data for ISPs.

The effectiveness of GUIDEC and other ICC standards are part of a debate among international lawyers on the binding nature of the ICC's governance in *Lived Sovereignty*, mimicking the debate about the Law Merchant's existence that I discussed in Chapter 2. ICC standards have legal force when they (a) enter contracts and (b) when those contracts are enforced by national courts. As such, the ICC's "self-governance" is more indicative of public/private hybridity rather than an independent market authority. However, this hybridity also makes the ICC's governance more expansive than statutes or conventions since "they cannot fully control the scope of their own application."[78] The hybrid development of global commercial law lacks clear boundaries for diffusion:

> For example, parties can agree by some entirely independent contract that their rights and duties under a documentary credit should be governed by the UCP, even if the UCP were not incorporated into the text of the credit itself. By the same token, a court can find that the parties had adopted the UCP by implication, for example from a prior and consistent course of dealing incorporating the UCP, or even from the fact that the UCP are of such universal application that their intention to apply them could be assumed.[79]

When evaluating the ICC's capacity for effective regulation, the "crucial question is therefore not an instrument's legal status but whether it effectively influences relevant decisionmakers to apply proscribed standards."[180]

A central engine of the ICC's "self-regulatory" apparatus is lobbying for legislative adoption by constructing a problem and offering "user-friendly stand-alone instruments that are concise, clear, and pragmatic."[181] These regulatory instruments are skewed toward narrow business interests. Legal anthropologist Annelise Riles argues that "the market value of private law resides not so much in its ability to be networked with other forms of expertise as in its propensity to cut itself off, to compartmentalize problems."[182] The ICC has mastered compartmentalization by using its standards for trade as separate from concerns about environment, labor, or consumers. The ICC does not want an unregulated global economy. Instead, it pushes for a narrow interpretation of a

[77]　Sherwood 2004.
[178]　Goode 1995: 728.
[179]　Goode 1995: 728.
[180]　Tully 2007: 142.
[181]　Tully 2007: 142.
[182]　Riles 2008: 628–629.

"balanced" relationship between freedom and rules in the global economy, which appears to encapsulate all of the following: the encouragement of a deepening and widening of the "benefits" of the global knowledge economy (secured in this instance by the "flexible" regulation of the internet where this relates specifically to e-commerce), the encouragement of public acceptance of developments in innovation and technology (such as genetically modified organisms), the deepening and widening of opportunities for trade and investment (calls for a new trade round), and the apportionment of regulatory responsibilities according to a strictly defined set of criteria (excluding "non-trade" issues such as the environment and human rights from the remit of the WTO).[183]

This regulatory mix is promoted by the ICC through elitist networks in *institutional hybridity*, a result of "discussions among a small number of [Policy] Commission members appointed for the purpose, not forged in the fire of the same intensive and prolonged debate, by national committees, trade associations and individual experts around the world."[184] The resulting global regulatory regime is exclusionary at its core, "producing and disseminating knowledge via elite channels and corporate media, lobbying key institutions such as the UN and facilitating consensus formation among global and national elites."[185]

Ultimately, the ICC views self-governance as central to its position of "a 'preferred partner' to governments and international organizations alike – offering, in other words, private solutions to public problems through the generation, extension, and entrenchment of private international trade law."[186] However, the ICC also creates "public" problems out of "private" issues, especially as it constructs particular kinds of commercial activities as crimes.

Constructing Commercial Crime

Since the 1980s, the ICC has been very active in constructing commercial crimes and lobbying for their regulation. This period was especially fruitful for the ICC as it benefited from "the Reagan/Thatcher revolution, which has been associated with a growing dependence of public authority on private money and expertise."[187] In 1982, the ICC established its Commercial Crime Services (CSS) in London. The ICC has claimed that the scope of criminal threats facing businesses grow ever larger as the methods of commercial criminals become increasingly sophisticated. The CSS aims to provide the world business community with a centralized crime-fighting body – one with a global network and reputation as a "private sector policeman for world trade."[188] CSS works closely with law enforcement officials,

[183] Hocking and Kelly 2001: 221.
[184] Goode 1995: 742.
[185] Carroll 2013: 221.
[186] Kelly 2009: 152.
[187] Kelly 2009: 152.
[188] Marks 1996.

including Interpol, and directs its expertise and network of members to supposedly "remain one step ahead of the criminals."[189]

The CSS has four divisions. The International Maritime Bureau (IMB), the oldest, is known for creating and managing the first worldwide database of international pirate attacks. The Financial Investigation Bureau conducts inquiries into money laundering and other forms of financial fraud through document analysis, background checks, and international sanctions checks. The Counterfeiting Intelligence Bureau directs counterfeiting investigations by gathering intelligence, making undercover inquiries, and organizing the seizure of counterfeits. Finally, FraudNet is a specialist network of fraud lawyers who locally investigate fraud in foreign jurisdictions for fraud victims.

One year after the launch of IMB, its head Eric Ellen, former chief constable of the Port of London police, relayed to the press that clients saved $100 million through the ICC's investigation of seventy-eight cases, out of which twenty-one dealt with documentary fraud, nineteen with charter frauds and disputes, four with scuttling, and nine with vessel deviation and cargo theft. Ellen said: "If these were bank robberies, they'd get a lot more publicity."[190] Over the next two decades, Ellen was a regular fixture in manufacturing the threat around counterfeiting and various types of fraud in the media, which the ICC then pointed to when lobbying for regulation. For instance, the ICC claimed in 1987 that its campaigns against counterfeiting in the past five years involved "over 80 investigations in 21 countries, handling everything from bottles of fake champagne traced to a gang in India netting some $ 500,000 a month, to the case of a phantom jigsaw maker in Taiwan."[191]

The ICC had long asked OECD governments to make counterfeiting a criminal offence. It particularly sought to shift the narrative from counterfeiting as "essentially a commercial problem" to a law enforcement problem.[192] In 1985, the ICC said: "By a mixture of better understanding of consumers' desires and more intensive advertising it is possible to convince the British consumer that he will only retain the freedom to choose if he willingly pays the full price of the genuine article and rejects the free ride of a counterfeit purchase. In fact, everyone who buys a counterfeit may be costing someone else a job."[193] The same year it argued that the United Kingdom "was doing less to fight counterfeiting than the Government of Taiwan."[194] Constructing counterfeiting as a crime illustrates further that the ICC's "self-regulatory" efforts entail selective government protection. The organization lobbied for stricter law enforcement of cybercrime in 1999: "As business moves forward into the brave new world of e-commerce, it needs effective law enforcement and judicial

---

[189] ICC 2014.
[190] Fisher 1983.
[191] Guild 1987.
[192] Jack 1996b.
[193] Evans 1985.
[194] *Financial Times* 1985.

networks to ensure that cyberspace does not become a criminal's charter."[195] In a 2004 UN meeting featuring petrochemical, pharmaceutical, software and consumer goods executives, the ICC referred to counterfeiting as "a cancer. It is imperative that business unites and acts at a global level now."[196]

The ICC's construction of commercial crime relies on releasing data. As the deputy director of the World Intellectual Property Organisation elaborated in 2004: "How do you get governments' attention if you don't have good statistics?"[197] In the 1980s, the ICC estimated that "the North American vehicle component industry is estimated to lose $2.7 billion a year to counterfeiters" and that "as many as 250,000 American jobs have been lost as a direct result of counterfeit goods flooding the domestic market."[198] In 1996, the ICC estimated that globally "counterfeiting products costs businesses more than $100 billion a year" and praised France as "one of the few countries in the world where counterfeited goods brought in from abroad can be confiscated by Customs officers even if they are claimed to be for personal use."[199] By 2000, the ICC valued that "counterfeiting and piracy was a $450 billion enterprise, accounting for an estimated 7–9 percent of global trade."[200] In 2002, it claimed that cybercrime cost companies worldwide $25 billion a year.[201] When an OECD report questioned these numbers, the ICC created the Business Action to Stop Counterfeiting and Piracy (BASCAP) to develop "case studies on the damage caused by piracy and counterfeiting before publishing its own indices to measure the problem and persuade governments to act."[202] BASCAP estimated counterfeiting cost global business $316 billion and threatened 200,000 jobs in Europe. By 2007, the ICC upped its estimates to $1,000 billion annual losses.[203] The ICC's efforts bore some fruit when the United States and EU signed an agreement "to establish joint diplomatic and customs teams domestically and abroad, focusing first on Russia and China."[204] Germany also put anti-counterfeiting efforts on the G8 agenda.

Related to counterfeiting, the ICC focused attention on maritime piracy by highlighting the violent nature of attacks. In 1998, it warned that "increasingly violent pirate attacks on merchant seafarers have prompted demands for better policing of the high seas. ... It's the brutality of the attacks and the fact that the pirates are never caught which is causing us concern. Everybody thinks ships are fair game and the psychological damage done to crews is immense."[205] After 9/11, the

---

[195] Burns 1999.
[196] Turner 2004.
[197] Turner 2004.
[198] *Financial Times* 1986.
[199] Jack 1996b.
[200] Levin 2003.
[201] Senhupta 2002.
[202] Beatie and Egdecliffe-Johnson 2005.
[203] Williamson 2007.
[204] Bounds 2006.
[205] Adams 1998.

ICC released figures on crew deaths to underscore the brutality of piracy even when the number of pirate attacks were down.[206] The ICC also integrated terrorist threats and emphasized that "no ship can protect itself against attacks such as the ramming with explosives of the French tanker Limburg in the Gulf of Aden last October. But coastal states should guard approach channels to their ports and step up patrols of coastal waters."[207] Again, the ICC released headline-grabbing statistics by claiming in 2004 that "piracy 'poses greater risk than terrorism' in Malacca Strait with 445 global pirate attacks last year."[208] The ICC has been successful in campaigning for partnership between the navies of various countries and the maritime industry. Based on these efforts, the ICC claimed that in 2021 "maritime piracy and armed robbery attacks reached the lowest recorded level since 1994."[209]

The ICC has also been instrumental in promoting anti-fraud efforts to banks related to Letters of Credit. In the mid-1990s, the ICC estimated that around $1 billion a year was going into fraudulent schemes in London.[210] In a material embodiment of exclusivity, the ICC organized seminars where "delegates, including senior bankers, private investigators and police officers, were given a large restricted-access file compiled by the ICC's Commercial Crime Bureau identifying types of fraudulent banking transaction which appear to be increasing."[211] It warned investors about seemingly obscure frauds, such as an international sugar fraud in developing and eastern European countries costing up to $400 million a year.[212] The ICC also raised alarm that small-island states like Vanuatu, Cook Islands, and Marshall Islands were being targeted for a nonexistent "Sovereign Nation Infrastructure Private Sector (Snips) facility program with guarantees issued on behalf of them representing five times their annual overseas earnings."[213] The ICC sold its FraudNet risk models, claiming they would help identify suspect trade finance transactions.

The ICC's "self-regulation" of global markets through its policy commissions and construction of commercial crime is better seen as seeking protection for insider rules through exclusionary processes. Through *institutional hybridity*, global commercial regulation is produced in elite networks that are indifferent to the state–business divide. The ICC's "self-regulation" furthers elite interests while presenting them as public problems. For instance, its efforts to construct commercial crime ask for law enforcement resources to be directed for the protection of large banks and technology companies. The legitimation challenge of the ICC's *institutional hybridity* is most acutely felt in international commercial arbitration.

---

[206] Williams 2005.
[207] Williams 2003.
[208] Burton and Huband 2004.
[209] IMB 2022.
[210] *Financial Times* 1994.
[211] Burns 1993.
[212] Hargreaves 1995.
[213] Harris 1997.

SOVEREIGN DILEMMAS IN *INSTITUTIONAL HYBRIDITY*

Taking all of the ICC's global regulatory functions discussed so far, it is clear that the ICC is more than a "market authority."[214] The ICC exercises sovereign competence as it works through *institutional hybridity* to develop insider rules for regulating global commerce at the intergovernmental and national levels. The *institutional hybridity* creates power payoffs by directing global capital through shared expertise but raises legitimation challenges due to exclusionary networks that concentrate capital. I now deal with these trade-offs directly by examining the ICC's most controversial function: international commercial arbitration.

Championing "Palm Tree Justice" in International Arbitration

International commercial arbitration is a "tough and powerful institution, and without it, global capitalism would look very different."[215] All big international commercial contracts between buyers and sellers feature a dispute resolution clause. Sometimes the clause specifies "recourse to a national court (that is, litigation) and recourse to private international dispute resolution, namely international commercial arbitration or so-called alternative dispute resolution (ADR) techniques, such as conciliation and mediation."[216] Importantly, parties may select arbitration even if their contract did not specify a dispute-resolution method. They may use an ad hoc arbitration tribunal or go with an institutionalized court in another country. In this way, "if a French company is collaborating with a German company to build a dam in India, they may well end up with a series of agreements governed by English law. There is nothing English about the transaction – except the choice of law."[217]

The ICC created the first international commercial arbitration body in 1923 in its International Court of Arbitration (ICA). Since then, the ICA has seen almost 20,000 cases. The ICA supervises arbitration by selecting arbitrators, monitoring the arbitral process, and approving all arbitral awards, but does not issue any formal judgments itself. Unlike ad hoc arbitration tribunals, "ICC arbitration is characterized not only by a high degree of centralized information gathering but also by the extensive monitoring offered by the Court."[218] International lawyers praise the ICA for its secrecy:

> The proceedings of the ICC's court are out of the light; there is no publicity. The case is often "tried" in a hotel room or by the swimming pool. "Palm tree justice" it has been called. Nevertheless, the parties accept the court's awards. They save a great deal of money in comparison to the costs of formal litigation. The whole affair is carried on in a gentleman-like fashion.[219]

[214]   Cutler, Haufler, and Porter 1999: 13; Hall and Biersteker 2002: 5.
[215]   Sgard 2019: 3.
[216]   Mattli 2001: 920.
[217]   Peel and Croft 2010.
[218]   Mattli 2001: 929.
[219]   Gingold and Blakeway 2000: 32.

Despite the secrecy in the actual proceedings, key to the ICA's institutional status in arbitration is name recognition. The ICC has worked

> hard to get their standard arbitration clause put into people's contracts, so they have a captive market once disputes arise. They do this by publicising their activities and their rules. What they are looking for is "name recognition," so that when someone asks at 3 am – "where shall we arbitrate?" a particular city, arbitration institution and set of rules immediately spring to mind. In Europe, Paris (home of the ICC and its rules) probably has the best name recognition.[220]

The ICA is invoked without the ICC even knowing: "We have no idea how many contracts have an ICC arbitration clause. The request for arbitration is often the first thing we hear about a contract."[221]

The ICC has been on the forefront of championing arbitration over other means of resolving disputes. Particularly, the ICC lobbied to expand the recognition of foreign arbitral awards in national legislation. After arbitration rulings are made, the losing party has to usually pay the winning party or make some other concessions. If the losing party fails to do so, the winning party would move to obtain a court judgment to collect its award. Since arbitration involves parties from various countries going to courts in Paris, London, Hong Kong, or Stockholm for judgment, it is important that national courts have jurisdiction to enforce awards made in these places. Otherwise, the arbitral award in unenforceable. During the ICA's origins in the interwar period, there was no international convention in place that would guarantee arbitral recognition and enforcement. Thus, the ICC proposed and then helped formulate the 1927 Convention on the Recognition and Enforcement of Arbitral Awards with the League of Nations. The 1927 Convention enabled the ICA to become "a self-standing international actor, with a project, a capacity to discuss, adopt and enforce its own rules and, gradually over time, an increasing attraction for businesses with a contractual dispute to resolve."[222] But the Convention was also flawed as "it was limited to awards granted in the territories of contracting states, and to be enforceable the arbitration had to conform to the law of the country where it had taken place."[223] As a result, the early ICA docket concerned "absolutely ridiculous cases: bowler hats, bicycles, fountain pens, etc."[224]

In the postwar period, the ICC wanted to move to bigger cases and knew it had to change the 1927 Convention. It made progress on a new draft in its 1946 and 1951 Congresses. By 1953, the ICC had a working draft ready to circulate to the UN. In 1954, the ICC asked ECOSOC to create a Committee of Experts to discuss the ICC's draft convention, which was approved. The Committee of Experts met the following year to consider the ICC's draft convention, which expanded the

---

[220] Winter 1998.
[221] Marks 1996.
[222] Sgard 2019: 15–6.
[223] Haight 1960: 201.
[224] Sgard 2019: 13.

application of the 1927 Convention to "arbitral awards not considered as domestic awards in the State where their recognition and enforcement are sought." The Committee retained this part of the ICC's proposals but discarded others, such as invoking the ICA as the venue of choice, to "maintain generally recognized principles of justice and respect the sovereign rights of states."[225] Still, the draft convention text was regarded as "a brainchild of the ICC Arbitration Court."[226] At a 1958 conference, the New York Convention was formally adopted and entered into force in 1959. By 1970, it had been ratified by twenty-eight countries, including the United States. Today, 161 states have ratified the New York Convention, including all OECD countries. As a result, "states now execute arbitration awards almost as easily as official judgments: on the back of an award the winning party can access bank accounts, real estate assets or securities."[227]

The decades following the New York Convention saw more domestic openness to international arbitration. In 1974, the US Supreme Court rejected the "'parochial' approach to the interpretation of an arbitration clause in an international agreement[228] and this liberal attitude was strongly reaffirmed in 1985 in which the court held that even an issue on U.S. antitrust law could be validly submitted to arbitration."[229] In 1979, the United Kingdom passed an act that allowed arbitrators to "apply to the High Court and obtain powers to continue with the proceedings 'in like manner as a judge of the High Court may continue with proceedings in that court where a party fails to comply with an order of that court or a requirement of rules of court.'"[230] The British extended judicial immunity to arbitrators, arguing that both "courts and arbitrators are in the same business, namely the administration of justice. The only difference is that the courts are in the public and the arbitrators in the private sector of the industry."[231] In 1981, France followed the United Kingdom.

Meanwhile, the ICA's cases increased in volume and stature. In terms of volume, it took the ICA more than fifty years to reach 3,000 cases between 1923 and 1977. It reached this number in a decade between 1977 and 1987. By 1997, the ICA was receiving 450 new cases a year.[232] By 2003, it was up to 600 new cases a year; by 2005, it was 1,100.[233] In terms of stature, by the 1990s, the ICA was handling two of the biggest cases: a $2.5 billion case of Eurotunnel against British Rail and SNCF, the French railway, and a $14.5 billion case regarding the split of Anderson Consulting, which was the world's biggest accounting and consulting business (and later became

[225]   Haight 1960: 202.
[226]   Sgard 2019: 15.
[227]   Sgard 2019: 3.
[228]   *Scherk* v. *Alberto-Culver Co* (1974).
[229]   *Mitsubishi Motors Corporation* v. *Soler Chrysler-Plymouth Inc* (1985).
[230]   Hermann 1983.
[231]   Schmitthoff 1985.
[232]   Mattli 2001: 930.
[233]   Sherwood and Tait 2003; Moser 2005b.

Accenture).[234] While the success of the New York Convention led to a proliferation of arbitration venues, the ICC claimed the status of being there first as

> the architects of an entirely novel institution, hence as the promoters of a new international public good. . . . The ICC thus remains today, the primus inter pares or the "Old Lady" of the profession, where the difficult cases often end up and around which a large part of the profession congregates. Even Paris has remained the capital of international commercial arbitration, merely because the ICC was established there in 1920, by chance – it could as well have been Brussels, The Hague or Geneva.[235]

Similarly, in 1996, the head of the ICC's Division of International Commercial Practice pitched to lawyers: "After seven decades as the world's pre-eminent arbitral institution, the ICC has acquired an imposing aura of neutrality and respectability, which may be of practical relevance in certain cases."[236] Indeed, the ICA has played a key role in legitimizing the ICC in *institutional hybridity*. Three examples help show this development.

First, by the early 1990s, international lawyers saw the 1979 UK law as allowing too much judicial review of arbitration awards. They invoked the ICA as a worthy institutional competitor:

> While the caseload of the London Court of International Arbitration continues to increase, arbitration under the rules set out by the Paris-based International Chamber of Commerce is the most popular forum for settling disputes. In ICC arbitrations, England is only the third preferred place of arbitration, by a significant margin, after France and Switzerland. [A new draft bill] recognizes the importance of party auton-omy and the decision of the parties to keep their disputes out of the courts. It would therefore greatly reduce the powers of the English courts to intervene in and control arbitrations . . . It would increase the power of arbitrators to control the procedure and to issue orders which were previously in the hands of the courts. Arbitrators have a duty to the parties and the bill would add to their powers and authority.[237]

Ultimately, their lobbying resulted in the 1996 UK Arbitration Act that severely curtailed judicial review of arbitration awards by British judges. I discuss the implications of this move for public/private hybridity in the next section, but want to flag here how the ICA featured into the deliberations.

Second, China used the ICC to make its gradual foray into global trade. In 1995, 162 Chinese companies and associations formed a new ICC China National Committee and "undertook to promote the 'rules, customs and practices' of the ICC, including the Court of Arbitration."[238] The ICC promoted this as "evidence of

[234] Batchelor 1995; Kelly 1997; Peel 2000.
[235] Sgard 2019: 16.
[236] Jimenez 1996: 288.
[237] *Financial Times* 1995b.
[238] *Financial Times* 1995a.

the determination of Chinese business eventually to play a full part in the world trading system."[239] In 1998, China agreed to accept the ICC's ATA-Carnet customs scheme for temporary imports and trade fairs.[240] These institutional linkages eased foreign trade and investment into China before its WTO membership in 2001 offered additional safeguards. By 2005, more than 170 new arbitration bodies sprang up in China.[241] But this growth threatened to lock out the ICC from China as Chinese regulation stated that arbitration bodies had to be *in* China for their awards to be enforced. The ICA claimed that its Hong Kong arbitration center was part of China after 1997. After negotiations, the Chinese reached a resolution that while "the ICC would not be granted official status in China, the awards made by ICC tribunals would be given the same status as 'foreign-related' awards made by Chinese arbitration commissions."[242] Once again, business leaders claimed that the ICC helped China move "towards recognised international practice and help create predictable outcomes in commercial agreements."[243]

Third, the ICA has also been legitimized by overseeing investor–state arbitration. Approximately 10 percent of ICA arbitration involves states.[244] This mirrors the broader landscape of investor–state disputes in the last few decades. For instance, Argentina faced sixty cases in the International Centre for Settlement of Investment Disputes (ICSID) against expropriation of foreign natural gas companies following its 2001 financial crisis. Argentina agreed to pay five arbitration awards. Similarly, one of the earliest ICA cases of investor–state arbitration concerned Venezuela's expropriation of oil companies. In 1995, Venezuela allowed "foreign equity investment in oil exploration and production for the first time since the nationalization of its petroleum industry in 1976."[245] It selected the ICA for arbitration. Then, after Hugo Chavez nationalized oil assets in 2007, Venezuela faced twenty international arbitration cases from ExxonMobil and others. In the ICA arbitration proceedings, Exxon had initially asked for $20 billion for its loss of market capitalization. Venezuela refused: "We are not willing to pay the abusive sum that this transnational is trying to make the sovereign people pay."[246] Venezuela also withdrew from ICSID, claiming: "We do not accept impositions and we are going to rescue our national sovereignty."[247] Exxon then dropped its demands for the ICC case to $12 billion and then again to $6 billion. In 2011, the ICA awarded Exxon $1 billion, still a record amount, of which Venezuela had to pay $747 million. Venezuela did not withdraw from the ICA, where "only the contract was in dispute, but has said it will not respect any decision at the ICSID, where it is the violation of a bilateral

[239]   *Financial Times* 1995a.
[240]   Kynge 1998.
[241]   Moser 2005a.
[242]   Moser 2005b.
[243]   Aglionby 2006.
[244]   ICC 2012: 2.
[245]   Mann 1995.
[246]   Mander 2011.
[247]   Mander and Pfeifer 2012.

investment treaty that is being disputed."[248] The ICA then awarded $2 billion to ConocoPhillips against Venezuela in 2012. This time, Venezuela said it could not pay. ConocoPhillips used foreign arbitration enforcement legislation to seize the assets of Venezuela's nationalized oil company, PDVSA, in the Caribbean, which "left PDVSA without access to facilities that process almost a quarter of Venezuela's oil exports. To avoid the risk of other assets being taken, PDVSA asked its customers to load oil from its anchored vessels acting as floating storage units."[249] The last development signals the legitimation perils of *Lived Sovereignty* operating in exclusionary clubs.

Politics of Exclusivity in Arbitration

Arbitration is often portrayed as an "alternative to state law with all of state law's functional elements – a regime of norms, a set of procedures, a set of problems (disputes)."[250] Yet, at the heart of arbitration is public/private hybridity. From its earliest appearance in the 1889 English Arbitration Act, arbitration "formalized in detail a new rule of interaction between sovereign judicial power and the right given to businesses to opt out of official courts and establish their own private tribunals ... while benefiting from the last-resort support and the legitimacy of public confirmation."[251] In other words, arbitration illustrates the dual use of *Lived Sovereignty* for global commercial regulation through the use of ICA while relying on *Idealized Sovereignty* as a governmental backstop to enforce the court's decisions. Through arbitration, the ICA "progressively imagined, developed and tested its own rules, an experience that led them from the green pastures of a free-wheeling utopia of peace among the markets, to a functioning, private, extra-territorial court ensconced in a tight bundle of agreements and transaction among private actors and with sovereigns."[252] But the exclusive nature of arbitration threatens to expose the hybridity in *Lived Sovereignty* as unequal power relations undermining *Idealized Sovereignty*.

In the twentieth century, champions of international arbitration proclaimed that "nothing bad could come" from it.[253] But the same cases that brought attention to the ICA, making it the 3-am venue of choice for commercial lawyers worldwide, also revealed the problems with *institutional hybridity* through "palm tree justice." In 1992, French lawyer Andrew Armfelt raised the accountability problems with ICC arbitration:

> From the perspective of developing nations and their companies, the fairness and benefits of international arbitration are often questionable. The principal areas in which third-world parties can be disadvantaged are selection of arbitrators, forum, cost, and access to and supervision of legal representatives. Lurking in the background

[248] Mander and Pfeifer 2012.
[249] Long and Rathbone 2018.
[250] Riles 2008: 623.
[251] Sgard 2019: 9–10.
[252] Sgard 2019: 10.
[253] Sgard 2019: 4.

are fundamental issues of national and international policy, under which arbitral awards are increasingly exempted from meaningful judicial review, even when awards violate fundamental norms of domestic public policy. ... There are no authoritative statistics on international arbitration results, owing to the confidential nature of arbitration.[254]

Armfelt points out the unequal access to justice in arbitration forums for developed and developing countries, especially because of secrecy. All ICA proceedings are confidential and reasons for the court's judicial supervisory decisions are not communicated to the arbitrators or parties. Indeed, "as long as two parties agree on the procedure, arbitrators can rule on disputes within the corporate world or between companies and states and even on intergovernmental battles."[255] The confidentiality is paramount to promote arbitration services as "privacy may help firms to hide a number of facts from competitors and the public in general, such as trade secrets and know-how not guaranteed by patents or financial difficulties and other problems."[256]

As investor–state disputes like Venezuela and Argentina become more common, the sovereign dilemmas in *institutional hybridity* heighten for both the ICA and governments. Indeed,

critics claim that international arbitration, once used to challenge injustice, has morphed into a weapon that multinationals wield to threaten governments and influence trade negotiations. ... They point to a surge in cases over the past decade arguing the system has morphed from a legitimate way for foreign investors to challenge extreme injustices such as expropriations, into a way for them to threaten, or influence, government regulations and even policy.[257]

International commercial arbitration undermines the lawmaking authority granted to governments in *Idealized Sovereignty* as "courts, whose duty it is to administer justice pursuant to law and policy, are replaced with private arbitration panels that often see their mission as merely to settle disagreements in accordance with 'general' legal principles and prevailing business practices that favour transnational corporations."[258] Arbitration's secrecy makes it all worse since "if important decisions aren't being made public, the law as a whole suffers as a result of not knowing of those important decisions."[259]

Arbitration thus most clearly shows how the ICC's sovereign competence in *Lived Sovereignty* represents a serious challenge to sovereign authority for regulating markets as expressed in *Idealized Sovereignty*.[260] Scholars of many critical persuasions have argued that "no longer is it the case that national policy-makers possess

[254] Armfelt 1992.
[255] Peel and Croft 2010.
[256] Mattli 2001: 925.
[257] Donnan 2014.
[258] Armfelt 1992.
[259] Peel and Croft 2010.
[260] Hall and Biersteker 2002.

either the sole authority, the expertise, or the material resources to achieve their policy goals in complex negotiating environments."[261] Instead, *institutional hybridity* of the kind described here may lead to "diminishing material resources, the diffusion of policy expertise amongst a growing range of non-state actors, and the erosion of governmental legitimacy."[262] As the ICC claims the mantle of self-regulation through institution-building, "to the extent that these regimes are read as systems of private norms, they appear as self-evidently more real, more legitimate, more innovative, more complex, closer to the ground, than the state itself."[263]

Idealized Sovereignty remains important for global regulation. Cynics argue that "a façade of governmental exclusivity in lawmaking is acceptable if commercial preferences are attained behind the scenes."[264] But for hybridity to actually be effective in producing sovereign competence, the façade of *Idealized Sovereignty* is less ornamental and more integral to the structure of regulation since the ICC's success depends on the legitimacy of governments. In other words, it is not a façade at all. The ICC is cognizant of maintaining this distinction. In 1997, when Maucher took over as ICC Chairman, he wrote an essay for the *Financial Times* titled "Ruling by Consent," arguing:

> Business has no political power and aspires to none, although we clearly are interested in social and political balance and the stability of the countries we work in. However, the many decisions governments have to make collectively on the legal framework for the global economy are of direct and legitimate concern to business. The private sector already plays its part in the area of self-regulation, which in many areas is more effective than government intervention. Striking the right balance between government responsibilities and business self-regulation has never been easy, but it must be done. Since it is business that has the task of investing and trading to create wealth and jobs according to rules set by governments, it is essential that governments draw on the huge reservoir of expertise and experience within companies when they design those rules.[265]

One wonders *who* is ruling by consent in Maucher's editorial. Is the ICC ruling by consent of governments? Or are governments ruling by consent of the ICC? There is no clarity in Maucher's words because in public/private hybridity it is both. The ICC is aware of challenges to its sovereign competence and institutional legitimacy. Its membership "confers the advantages of belonging to a prestigious 'club' whilst simultaneously underlining the fact that the internal workings of such clubs are dominated by their European and North American members."[266] It must then rely on borrowing legitimacy from governments to "continue to act as a 'voice' for business."[267] This relationship props

---

[261] Hocking and Kelly 2001: 206.
[262] Hocking and Kelly 2001: 206.
[263] Riles 2008: 619.
[264] Tully 2007: 306.
[265] Maucher 1997.
[266] Kelly 2005: 269–270.
[267] Kelly 2005: 269–270.

up the sovereign regulation of interconnected markets through insider rules in exclusive clubs.

Ultimately, I echo Riles, who focuses on a different element of commercial hybridity – documentary traders who follow the ICC's Letter of Credit standards in banks – but extracts a complementary interpretation of how we should think about the ICC's sovereign status: "The 'threat,' if any, of global private law inheres instead in the way it replicates and hence supersedes the state in practical, mundane, routine ways."[268] For Riles, "the interface between private authority and state power is itself the very basis for the flurry of activity that is global private law, from an empirical vantage point."[269] Indeed, this chapter has shown that the ICC's various regulating functions of issue-definition, agenda-setting, and rulemaking culminate in "practices of making distinctions, compartmentalizing, cutting off and setting limits," which "is an exercise in creating and manipulating legitimacy that has also long been one of the privileges, and the contributions, the knowledge practices of the state."[270] Thus, the ICC's participation through *institutional hybridity* depends on keeping *Lived* and *Idealized Sovereignty* in suspension to effectively regulate global markets.

CONCLUSION

Institutional hybridity allows the International Chamber of Commerce to be a global regulator for world trade. The ICC's regulatory prowess occurs through constructing itself as "*the* voice of global business" to become the primary interlocutor for inter-governmental bodies when structuring global commerce. I followed various ways in which the ICC embeds itself in global institutions through issue-definition, agenda-setting, and rulemaking. The ICC's "self-regulation" is nothing more than narrowing regulation to fit its aims. I also argued that while the ICC focuses on organizing markets, it should not be seen as an exclusively economic or market power independent from states. Instead, the ICC represents sovereign competence through institutional linkages that boost the privilege of global corporate elites. As such, the study of the ICC in *institutional hybridity* helps us see that "transnational private authority" need not necessitate a retreat of the state, but rather a recomposition of what it means to regulate across borders. The ICC's *Lived Sovereignty* relies fundamentally on the *Idealized Sovereignty* of governments to keep its institutional status. In turn, the governance of global markets through *institutional hybridity* enables all kinds of sovereign elites to reap the benefits of trade and investment at the expense of others. Balancing the legitimacy blowbacks to this elitism is at the core of the politics of institutionalizing rules for global commerce.

[268]   Riles 2008: 607–608.
[269]   Riles 2008: 624.
[270]   Riles 2008: 629.

6

Shadowing for Human Rights through Amnesty International

Amnesty is non-political and yet it is in the heart of politics.[1]

In 1977, the Nobel Prize for Peace was awarded to Amnesty International. The chairman of the prize committee remarked:

> The view is now gaining ground that no state can lay claim to absolute national sovereignty where human rights that are universally recognised are involved. These rights are man's common property, and no power constellation, no dictator, is entitled to deprive us of them. ... In its efforts to implement this programme, Amnesty International has based its work on three irrevocable principles: the organisation must at all times be neutral, impartial, and independent.[2]

The Nobel recognized the then sixteen-year-old organization for challenging *Idealized Sovereignty* by making governments "change their behavior, against their sovereign prerogatives."[3] But the accomplishment of this feat involved Amnesty's own foray into *Lived Sovereignty* as it conjured a global polity and served as its steward. In this endeavor, Amnesty's independence and effectiveness were perpetually in tension managing complex external relations with governments. This chapter focuses on the untold account of *shadow hybridity* in the making of human rights as Amnesty balanced being "non-political" while operating from "the heart of [sovereign] politics."

Amnesty was founded by British lawyer Peter Benenson in 1961 as a campaign for armistice, which became an Appeal for Amnesty that in turn became Amnesty International. Amnesty is now considered the world's leading international nongovernmental organization (INGO) with more than seven million individual members and remarkable longevity to shape the global human rights agenda.[4] Scholars consistently characterize Amnesty as "the NGO that made human rights important."[5] Amnesty began with letter-writing campaigns to release adopted political prisoners it called

---

[1] Andrew Blane interviewing Seán MacBride, AI 987.
[2] Lionæs 1977.
[3] Clark 2001: 20.
[4] Clark 2001; Hopgood 2006; Stroup and Wong 2017: 54–55.
[5] Wong 2012: 84.

"prisoners of conscience." The Nobel felicitation acknowledged that between 1972 and 1975 alone, of the 6,000 prisoners of conscience adopted by Amnesty, at least half were released. Amnesty addressed broader treatment of all prisoners, helping pass the 1984 UN Convention against Torture and mobilizing for an international norm against the death penalty.[6] Amnesty's peers like the International League of Human Rights, Anti-Slavery International, and the International Commission of Jurists did not "really manage to challenge Amnesty's ability to make certain human rights salient."[7] Until 2001, Amnesty's operational mandate remained narrowly focused on this particular segment of human rights.[8] It now also advocates for sexual and reproductive rights, gender nondiscrimination, and refugee and migrants' rights.

Scholars have evaluated Amnesty in terms of the issues it has selected over time, accounting for leadership, group politics, and organizational structure.[9] They have also traced what made Amnesty different as a norm entrepreneur from its peers.[10] This literature generally agrees on two points. First, Amnesty "has provided a basis for our understanding of what human rights are and has consistently supplied a growing global public with information about human rights abuses."[11] Second, Amnesty is "funded entirely by membership support and voluntary donations. . . . The organization accepts no monies from national governments."[12] Historians of human rights and IR scholars are remarkably consistent on the latter point that Amnesty "carved its niche by relying on small donors, many of whom had first been inspired by Benenson's article and responded with cash, time, and in-kind gifts. Because of the success of the Appeal, therefore, Benenson was able to build on the support of volunteers and create an NGO independent of government or foundation funding."[13] Amnesty is said to be "always skeptical about governments and corporate money, seeing its moral mission as the very antithesis of power."[14]

A related literature on INGO strategic action examines facets of the "dirty hands" problem where INGOs' moral purity is compromised by the practical realities of advocacy work.[15] Researchers recognize that "as independent organizations that some-times act as issue advocates and public service providers, some NGOs occupy an uncomfortable space between state forces, the global governance system, and the private sector."[16] Scholars have identified "several NGO scandals related to corruption or the mismanagement and misappropriation of funds."[17] Some treat INGOs like firms to

---

[6]   Larsen 1979; Power 1981; Winner 1991.
[7]   Wong 2012: 86.
[8]   Quelch and Laidler-Kylander 2006; Wong 2012.
[9]   Kaufman 1991; Baehr 1994; Stroup 2010; Wong 2012.
[10]   Clark 2001; Buchanan 2002; Hopgood 2006.
[11]   Wong 2012: 84.
[12]   Clark 2001: 15.
[13]   Buchanan 2009; Wong 2012: 88.
[14]   Hopgood 2013: xii.
[15]   Rubenstein 2015.
[16]   Hortsch 2010: 129.
[17]   Hielscher et al. 2017: 3.

study the balancing of normative concerns and instrumental incentives for organizational survival.[18] For instance, relief INGOs face pressures to secure new contracts, "pushing other concerns – such as ethics, project efficacy, self-criticism – to the margins."[19] For others, principled actors' commitment to mission and their "proper role" make them unwilling to engage in "pragmatic trade-offs."[20] Finally, INGOs also engage in "information politics" by publicizing some causes over others.[21] One study of Amnesty's country reporting between 1986 and 2006 finds that while Amnesty reported on many of the most repressive countries, it did not do so for all.[22]

This chapter uses archival data from Amnesty's first twenty-five years (1961–86), including minutes and reports of all eighty meetings of Amnesty's executive leadership and interview transcripts from the 1983–5 Amnesty Oral History project. The materials show that during this time Amnesty used government and foundation funding for operating expenses and research missions.[23] Amnesty also cultivated a diplomatic network with governments for country access and conducted side bargains with closed countries for private reforms. The records also show that Amnesty was consumed with managing its credibility in light of the growing dependence. The empirical examination complicates the scholarly consensus on Amnesty's financial independence while extending other insights related to INGO strategic action. Amnesty was resistant to some pragmatic trade-offs, such as the "rule of three" – for balancing East, West, and South regions in POC case selection – slowing Amnesty's expansion. But Amnesty was willing to make other pragmatic trade-offs like accepting some government and foundation funding as well as brokering deals with governments for access and reforms. While the literature has referred to Amnesty's "negotiated rather than clandestine entry" for closed countries,[24] specific deals and their implications have not been studied. The side deals presented here situate some of Amnesty's information politics within the organization's survival imperative. More broadly, I interpret the evidence to mean that there is no apolitical moral authority. Instead, Amnesty's public/private relations in *shadow hybridity* help us better appreciate the scope of its sovereign accomplishment of organizing a global polity.

American pragmatist John Dewey helps guide why an organization typically portrayed as antithetical to sovereignty should instead be viewed through the lens of sovereign competence. Amnesty constructs "international human rights standards that govern the relations of states."[25] In order to do so, Amnesty adopts one of Dewey's three traits of "the state": the organization of a public. For Dewey,

---

[18] Prakash and Gugerty 2010: 3.

[19] Cooley and Ron 2002: 16.

[20] Avant 2004.

[21] Keck and Sikkink 1998: 6; Bob 2005; Carpenter 2014.

[22] Ron et al. 2005: 569.

[23] Amnesty archives place a thirty-year moratorium for access due to its sensitive contents. The last available year at the time of data collection was 1986. Srivastava 2022a provides additional context.

[24] Hopgood 2006: 24.

[25] Clark 2001: 19.

those indirectly and seriously affected for good or for evil form a group distinctive enough to require recognition and a name. The name selected is The Public. This public is organized and made effective by means of representatives who as guardians of custom, as legislators, as executives, judges, etc., care for its special interests by methods intended to regulate the conjoint actions of individuals and groups.[26]

However, Dewey recognized that the public is threatened by globalizing forces such "that the resultant public cannot identify and distinguish itself. And this discovery is obviously an antecedent condition of any effective organization on its part. . . . There are too many publics and too much of public concern for our existing resources to cope with."[27] Dewey is also bothered by the lack of territorial attachment that comes with transborder mobility:

> How can a public be organized, when literally it does not stay in place? Only deep issues or those which can be made to appear such can find a common denominator among all the shifting and unstable relationships. . . . Without such communication the public will remain shadowy and formless, seeking spasmodically for itself, but seizing and holding its shadow rather than its substance.[28]

Extracting from Dewey, I argue that a key sovereign function is the identification and organization of a mass of far-flung individuals into a public with collective interests. Amnesty yoked disparate identities into a movement that exceeded one's own immediate interests to form a collective attachment to human rights everywhere. Amnesty did this to solve the fundamental problem of realizing human rights. The problem is that states are both the guarantors and violators of rights: "When the sovereign changes its mind and declares itself and its clients exempt from its own rules, the Global Human Rights Regime is left bereft of moral authority, its claim to universal legitimacy undermined, its compliance with power exposed."[29] Amnesty tackled the problem by forming a transnational coalition of individuals who cared about human rights, did not trust that governments alone could adequately protect human rights, and could collectively pose as an effective public. In a 1973 newsletter, Amnesty announced that "setting up of a continuing international machinery . . . to establish the Campaign for the Abolition of Torture as a world concern, thereby breaking through the popular conception that the treatment of the citizen is the concern of the sovereign state alone."[30] In short, Amnesty helped transnational publics for human rights identify and distinguish themselves.

However, Amnesty had to not only create transnational publics who cared about their own human rights, but also had to form a global *polity* that would "hold these different publics together in an integrated whole."[31] Not all publics form polities.

[26] Dewey 1927: 35.
[27] Dewey 1927: 126.
[28] Dewey 1927: 140–142.
[29] Hopgood 2013: xiii.
[30] AI 1973: 2; cited in Clark 2001: 46.
[31] Dewey 1927: 136.

For instance, Chapter 5 highlighted how the International Chamber of Commerce (ICC) became a global regulator of world markets by projecting itself as "*the* voice of global business," while embedding in prominent international institutions. The ICC manufactures a public on whose behalf it governs, but it does not generate a polity that extends beyond one's own concerns. Amnesty's more expansive mission presents a challenge in categorizing the organization. At Amnesty's founding, the closest model was the International Committee of the Red Cross, which predates Amnesty by almost a century. But the Red Cross did not "normally release to the public the details of what its delegates have witnessed" or shamed governments.[32] Amnesty thus aimed to both preserve its neutrality and stoke the political flames for change. Some argue that Amnesty "most resembles a chapel or a meeting house."[33] Religion certainly played a key role for Benenson who "believed that the world could be changed, and he had seen Amnesty as the vehicle."[34] But the comparison can be stretched further. Just as the Catholic Church shepherds the spiritual education of its transnational flock, Amnesty is the creator and custodian of a global human rights polity. Moreover, the Catholic Church has for centuries advanced sovereign competence while managing complex relations with governments. Amnesty does the same.

Scholars ask whether INGOs like Amnesty are "powerful actors that are able to transform global politics, noisy interest groups whose influence is severely constrained by increasingly complex global structures, or epiphenomenal representations of an increasingly illiberal world order?"[35] I answer: none of the above. Instead, Amnesty engages in sovereign polity-building as a producer and protector of rights around the world. However, it does not succeed as an independent sovereign. Instead, Amnesty relies on *shadow hybridity* configured in nonformalized and nonpublicized public/private relations. Amnesty is thus a "least-likely" case for public/private hybridity as it pursues a human rights agenda whose very success relies on claiming independence from governments. However, Amnesty also needs government support to maintain its global polity in *Lived Sovereignty*. Furthermore, Amnesty exemplifies the legitimation challenges of *shadow hybridity* potentially undermining trust.

In the rest of this chapter, I first analyze how Amnesty built a global polity around human rights in its first two decades. Next, I examine Amnesty's imperatives for moral purity stemming from impartiality and independence. Finally, I showcase Amnesty's multifaceted shadow relations with governments that empowered its polity-building.

---

[32]   Clark 2001: 10.
[33]   Hopgood 2006: 3.
[34]   Buchanan 2002: 595.
[35]   Stroup and Wong 2016: 138.

BUILDING A GLOBAL POLITY

At the end of World War II, a slew of important international activity around human rights took place. Chief among them was the Universal Declaration of Human Rights (UDHR), which governments adopted in 1948. The 1949 Geneva Convention addressed the humanitarian law of armed conflict, including the treatment of prisoners of war and protection of civilians. Despite these agreed-upon principles, by 1960 the world was no closer to implementing human rights. The UN Commission on Human Rights, established in 1946, had an explicit rule prohibiting direct criticism of member states. Over the 1950s, "practical measures to give life to human rights principles began to lag far behind the rhetoric."[36] Seán MacBride, early Amnesty Chairman, former Irish foreign minister and Nobel Peace laureate, recalled:

> There was the realisation that governments would not recognize human rights, and were beginning to gang up with each other to suppress human rights very often, or not protect them as they should. It was then I realised the importance of having a non-governmental organization that would not be tied to governments and that could investigate the situation and that could report on them and draw public attention to them.[37]

Thus, by the time of Amnesty's founding in 1961, "an international 'human rights' regime, or complex of rules, as we now know it did not exist – and there was no good reason to expect one."[38] Instead, Amnesty founders knew they had to "publicize the gap between international human rights principles and practices. No one had framed the task before as such an urgent – and public – undertaking."[39]

On May 28, 1961, *The Observer* published a full-page feature on "The Forgotten Prisoners" by Peter Benenson. Benenson had two aims. The first was to introduce "Prisoners of Conscience," defined as: "Any person who is physically restrained (by imprisonment or otherwise) from expressing (in any form of words or symbols) any opinion which he honestly holds and which does not advocate or condone personal violence." The second purpose was to launch a one-year publicity campaign with an office in London "to collect and publish information about Prisoners of Conscience all over the world." Benenson directly referenced Dewey in the appeal: "How can we discover the state of freedom in the world today? The American philosopher, John Dewey, once said, 'If you want to establish some conception of a society, go find out who is in gaol.'" While this reference is not explicitly to Dewey's work on the public, it does situate a certain pragmatist ethos in the founding of Amnesty.

---

[36] Clark 2001: 3.
[37] MacBride interview, AI 987.
[38] Clark 2001: 4.
[39] Clark 2001: 4. I thank Ann Clark for pushing me to develop this section.

Benenson had been active as a defense counsel for political trials. He was also a founding member of "JUSTICE," an organization of British lawyers.[40] After converting to Catholicism, "he wanted to find something secular that would help others experience that sort of profound change, and he thought political activism was one of the vectors by which to do so."[41] Benenson devised the appeal alongside Louis Blom-Cooper, a renowned attorney and columnist for *The Observer*, and Eric Baker, a Quaker academic and secretary of the National Peace Council.[42] Not everyone was convinced the appeal was going to work, much less lay the foundations for the world's leading INGO. David Astor, the editor of *The Observer*, reflected: "I thought the idea was a bit far-fetched. I didn't see how you could possibly hope to influence foreign governments to let out political prisoners just by making a noise here. It seemed to me an extraordinary notion."[43] Peter Archer, British MP and Solicitor-General, agreed: "My immediate reaction was, 'This is not going to get popular support.' We just had an International Refugee Year, you know, and everybody knows what a refugee is, and if you talk about starving kids everybody knows what a hungry child is. I didn't think we could get over to the public the concept of a political prisoner."[44]

The appeal was published in many foreign newspapers, including *Le Monde*, *The New York Herald Tribune*, and *Die Welt*. The public response was swift and overwhelming. In numerous letters and phone calls, there was an agitation to do something beyond a temporary designation for prisoners of conscience. Benenson placed respondents in groups based on location and asked them to adopt prisoners of conscience and coordinate writing letters of support. Meanwhile, he "engaged in tours of European countries to rile up support for the young movement."[45] His wife, Margaret Benenson, was also involved in the early recruitment efforts by entertaining guests up to "three times a week" at their London home.[46] For Astor, "that Amnesty actually began to collect support, raise money, and employ staff, and finally become a serious organization was very surprising."[47]

A couple of months after the newspaper appeal, Amnesty International was established as a "permanent international movement in defense of freedom of opinion and religion." By 1962, Amnesty "published its first annual report, and tallied seventy prisoner adoption groups meeting in local communities in six

[40] Power 1981: 10.
[41] Wong 2012: 90.
[42] Power 1981: 10; Clark 2001: 5.
[43] Astor interview, AI 979.
[44] Archer interview, AI 978.
[45] Wong 2012: 88.
[46] M. Benenson interview, AI 981. Margaret Benenson also highlights the hidden gendered roles of social movements: "To be honest, Peter could never have done it if I hadn't been very strong. Because if I had collapsed on the job of running the house and the children and so on, he would have had to stop. It's a fact."
[47] Astor interview, AI 979.

countries, with a total of 210 active Prisoner of Conscience cases."[48] Some adoption groups became official national sections who coordinated Amnesty members within their countries and paid dues to the International Secretariat (IS) in return for case sheets about prisoners and other communications. The national sections assembled in biannual International Council Meetings to direct the IS on policy priorities. The International Executive Committee (IEC) interpreted directives from the International Council and served as the executive leadership board of Amnesty with quarterly meetings. Thus, Amnesty had an organizational structure that leveraged centralization in the secretariat and decentralization in the national sections, allowing it "to harness the strength of international mobilization while controlling the fundamental content of what their supporters say about the issue."[49]

Being a British organization, Amnesty received favorable press in the United Kingdom. Its test for reaching a transnational public would come from gaining attention in the international press, especially in the United States. To trace how Amnesty built its reputation to become a household name, I use an original corpus of all 1,419 *New York Times* news stories that mention "Amnesty International" from 1961 until it was awarded the Nobel in 1977. I selected the *Times* for its reputation as the international "paper of record" and unmatched investments in foreign correspondents to cover world affairs. In addition to content, I pay attention to whether Amnesty was the main subject or a passing reference and the placement in the *Times'* pages.[50]

Getting Its Foot in the Door

Amnesty's coverage in *The Times* was sparse in the 1960s. Its first mention came in 1964, when it was reported that Amnesty's commissioner for refugees was refused entry to South Africa. Amnesty was introduced as "a London-based organization ... helping South African refugees to reach the British territory of Bechuanaland" with no additional context on prisoners of conscience or human rights.[51] In 1966, Amnesty was featured in its first front-page story about Indonesia mass slaughtering an estimated half a million communists.[52] Amnesty was referred in passing as "a humanitarian organization of lawyers" making "private soundings" in Jakarta about political prisoners. In 1967, the foreign press had been linking organizations like the International Commission of Jurists with the CIA. The *Times* covered the fallout within Amnesty's secretariat:

> In London, the founder of Amnesty International, which campaigns for the release of political prisoners, demanded that the chairman of the group's executive

---

[48] Clark 2001: 6.
[49] Wong 2012: 85; Stroup 2010.
[50] I cite only a news story at its first mention. All subsequent quotations in that paragraph should assume to refer to the original news story unless specified otherwise.
[51] *New York Times* 1964.
[52] Topping 1966.

committee resign because of a connection with the Central Intelligence Agency. Peter Benenson, a lawyer in London, who founded the organization, said Sean MacBride, an Irish lawyer who is the chairman, should step down. Mr. MacBride is also secretary-general of the International Commission of Jurists, which Mr. Benenson charged, has been a "front for the CIA for the last 15 years." Mr. MacBride denied that. He said all the commission's funds were raised by its members.[53]

The story is important for three reasons. First, it introduced Amnesty as campaigning for the release of political prisoners. Second, Amnesty featured as the main subject. Third, it previewed the discussions about *shadow hybridity* that were roiling within Amnesty during this time, which I explore in greater detail later. But the story did not have any follow-up. Amnesty's next mention came two years later in a story about the UN Commission on Human Rights refusing to accept petitions at its overseas information centers; Amnesty offered to "act as a mailbox."[54]

Amnesty's credibility in the international press only came in the 1970s through establishing publicly hostile relations with governments. In December 1969, Amnesty leaked claims from a completed but unpublished investigation on the torture of Arab prisoners in Israeli prisons.[55] Israel denied the claims and barred future Amnesty visits, alluding to an agreement not to publicize any results from Amnesty investigations. Amnesty responded that its investigation was based on interviews in Jordon and Israel and that it had photographs and medical reports. The *Times* extensively quoted Martin Ennals, Amnesty's Secretary General, in a follow-up story reacting to Israel barring Amnesty.[56] This incident provided more attention to other cases of governments refusing access or retaliating against Amnesty, such as Taiwan.[57]

When Amnesty's official Israel report was published in April 1970, the *Times* referred to Amnesty as "a respected private organization" and quoted the report: "If these allegations are true, then extremely brutal torture is used on a not inconsiderable number of those detained. [The tortures] would also seem to imply that such ill-treatment is continuing up to the present time."[58] This was the first mention of an Amnesty torture report in the *Times*. The story also acknowledged that Amnesty had delayed publication of the report for nearly a year while it "pressed privately to get the Israeli Government to agree to a commission of inquiry." Israel responded with "astonishment" on the publication and accused Amnesty of "permitting itself to be the vehicle for spreading unfounded and unchecked allegations, having their origin in a campaign of atrocity propaganda carried on by the Arab states and their

[53]   Reed 1967.
[54]   Brewer 1969.
[55]   Feron 1969.
[56]   *New York Times* 1969.
[57]   *New York Times* 1970a.
[58]   *New York Times* 1970b.

supporters." Israel also revealed that it made an offer to Amnesty two months prior "to provide facilities for investigating the allegations of torture, provided that 'proper complaints were lodged and that there was an opportunity to take evidence, to conduct cross examination and otherwise observe legal procedures.'" In a follow-up story, the *Times* received the inside scoop that the British and American national sections split in their support for publishing the report.[59] Angry letters to the editor also followed, accusing Amnesty of anti-Israel bias and carelessness.[60]

The attention from the Israel scandal began a period of more sustained coverage of Amnesty in the *Times*. The paper reported on Amnesty's report *The Force of Persecution*, 1970, citing estimates of at least 250,000 prisoners of conscience in 43 countries in the headline.[61] Meanwhile, even when Amnesty was criticized, for instance, for staying silent on Israel's release of fourteen Egyptian sailors in September 1970, the *Times* quoted from sources who equated Amnesty's stature with the UN and the Pope:

> "Where was British Amnesty?" He was referring to a branch of Amnesty International, a London-based organization, which has condemned Israel for jailing Arab suspects on preventive detention. "What happened to those people who investigated conditions in our prisons from afar? Where were the members of the United Nations Commission on Human Rights? What happened to the Pope and the churches?"[62]

Two months later, the *Times* profiled Amnesty for the first time, stating its then membership of 17,000 in 27 countries and annual budget of $103,200 "raised by membership fees, contributions, and fund-raising events."[63] The piece quoted Martin Enthoven, Amnesty's Executive Secretary, promoting group adoption: "It is the responsibility of these people to do what they can to bring about the release of these prisoners by writing to the governments concerned, publicizing the case, and approaching people who may have influence." Six months later, there was another *Times* profile to mark Amnesty's tenth anniversary, this time quoting the head of research, Zybnek Zeman: "Governments use torture now as an instrument of controlling dissent. They've found that if they take 20 students and torture them, then other students will be a little more careful about dissenting."[64]

A pattern emerged of heightened media coverage whenever Amnesty received backlash from governments. For instance, in November 1971 Amnesty's allegation of torture against British troops in Northern Ireland received major coverage.[65] Once again, the *Times* had access to the organizational fracas when Amnesty's Treasurer, Anthony Marreco, resigned over the report and "complained that [the claims] had

[59] Lee 1970.
[60] *New York Times* 1970c, 1970d.
[61] Weinraub 1970a; *New York Times* 1970e.
[62] Grose 1970.
[63] Weinraub 1970b.
[64] Weinraub 1971a.
[65] Lewis 1971; *New York Times* 1971a.

not been independently tested before being issued for publication."[66] The British government acknowledged ill-treatment, but disputed the allegations of widespread brutality: "We consider that brutality is an inhuman or savage form of cruelty. We do not think that happened here."[67] Amnesty followed that up with publicizing its torture report on Brazil, claiming it would share the name of 472 torturers with governments.[68] Brazil retaliated by censoring media coverage of Amnesty.[69]

The early-1970s saw Amnesty frequently peppering the pages of the *Times* with its reports on Spain's treatment of the Basques,[70] American draft dodgers,[71] Indonesian communists in indefinite detention,[72] hunger strikes by Brazilian prisoners,[73] and prisoners in Vietnam.[74] Amnesty also more successfully placed editorial pieces and letters to the editors. In November 1972, Ivan Morris, head of Amnesty's American national section, AIUSA, listed the case histories of nine prisoners of conscience and ended with a plea: "As long as such men continue to be persecuted and imprisoned, the Universal Declaration of Human Rights remains what it has been until now – a mockery. In this crucial field few members of the United Nations have lived up to their obligations. Delinquent countries should constantly be reminded of their commitment to respect human rights."[75] More letters followed to directly communicate Amnesty's stance on Vietnam, Kenya, the United States, USSR, and India, among others.[76]

There also emerged stories about Amnesty inspiring grassroots activism. In 1972, the UN Commission on Human Rights had been "inundated by 27,000 separate human rights complaints."[77] The same year in April, seven months after the Attica prison riots, a Pennsylvania inmate asked for a copy of the 1955 UN standard minimum rules on the protection of prisoners "so I can remind my jailer I am human."[78] Amnesty had just launched a campaign to get "copies of the rules into the hands of everyone who visits prisons." In 1974, the paper profiled Northport High School, which won the fourth High School Human Rights Award from the New York State Division of Human Rights.[79] Students had adopted some Amnesty prisoners of conscience and spoke of the impact: "You feel you're doing something to better the world."

---

[66] *New York Times* 1971b.
[67] Weinraub 1971b.
[68] *New York Times* 1972a.
[69] Howe 1973a.
[70] *New York Times* 1970f.
[71] *New York Times* 1971c.
[72] *New York Times* 1971d.
[73] Notitsji 1972.
[74] Eder 1972.
[75] Morris 1972.
[76] *New York Times* 1972b, 1974a, 1974b, 1974c, 1975a, 1976a.
[77] Clark 2001: 42.
[78] Teltsch 1972a.
[79] *New York Times* 1974d.

By 1972, more regular coverage of Amnesty in the *Times* represented the organization's recognition in the international press as a human rights organization with a worldwide mission to raise awareness. Compared to its work on prisoners of conscience, Amnesty's investigations of torture and resulting fallout with governments found particular salience with the Americans, and by extension the *Times'* global cosmopolitan audience, especially when it concerned allies like Israel and Britain. Once Amnesty broke through to reach this valuable public, it extended polity-building to launch its first transnational campaign.

Campaign for the Abolition of Torture

Amnesty's Campaign for the Abolition of Torture (CAT) originated in Greece. Amnesty sent a mission to Greece in December 1967, where a military coup by George Papadopoulos led to thousands of political prisoners in "the cradle of democracy."[80] Amnesty released its mission report, *Situation in Greece*, in 1968 and circulated it to the Council of Europe. A second mission in March 1968 confirmed the findings, alleging "not only that torture had occurred, but also that it had been official policy."[81] A year later, the European Commission on Human Rights took on the Greek case where Amnesty researchers were the only NGO witnesses. Facing expulsion, Greece withdrew from the Council of Europe in December 1969, in one of the first examples of human rights accountability post-Nuremberg. But the UN Commission on Human Rights failed to even censure Greece. Amnesty found that "human rights principles met with spotty acknowledgment and spottier application because corresponding norms were underdeveloped and not well supported by procedures."[82] Amnesty persisted in supplying hundreds of letters along with the names of 117 prisoners to the UN Commission. Three years later, the UN agreed in a landmark statement that a "consistent pattern of gross violations of human rights" existed in Greece and that it was testing a "'revolutionary concept' in enabling citizens anywhere to write and level charges against their own governments, calling the governments to account before world opinion."[83] This was a marked change from 1969 when the Commission refused to accept letters at its information centers. Within a decade of its founding, Amnesty had a prominent role in expelling a state from one major intergovernmental institution and censuring it from another on the basis of human rights.

Inspired by the Greek case, Amnesty launched CAT in 1973. The campaign was to culminate in the release of a report on the worldwide use of torture "to educate the

---

[80] Clark 2001: 39.
[81] Clark 2001: 41.
[82] Clark 2001: 42.
[83] Teltsch 1972b.

public and to generate a climate of public support for action on torture. At the same time, Amnesty mobilized its members to contact their own governments to ask them to support action against torture in the United Nations."[84] Nigel Rodley, Amnesty's legal adviser and UN Commission on Human Rights representative, articulated how Amnesty used CAT for polity-building:

> By being a grassroots movement, we essentially had embassies in a large number of countries, which could, and did, approach their governments on our concerns. And not only that, it was not just like any other embassy, but it was an embassy which reflected a constituency in their own countries. So they weren't just talking about this foreign body, Amnesty, to their foreign ministers; they were talking about themselves.[85]

Rodley's reflections hint at two crucial aspects of polity-building. First, Amnesty saw itself as having embassies for sovereign representation abroad. Second, the key to organizing a public into a polity is to internalize the issues so that people can have ownership over them – "they were talking about themselves" – even when they refer to prisoners in other countries.

CAT also created a more direct clash with the UN. In December 1973, a week before the conference, Amnesty received word that it could no longer use the UNESCO headquarters in Paris as its venue.[86] UNESCO claimed that Amnesty's *Report on Torture*, expected to be available for sale at the conference, would violate its contractual terms for Amnesty to "refrain from criticizing any of UNESCO's 125 member countries in documentation prepared for and in speeches during the conference." UNESCO's decision brought Amnesty prominent *Times* coverage of the impending torture report (page 2).[87] The *Times* also reported on the conference with the headline "64 Nations Charged in Report as Users of Torture," using graphic details of torture to lead a page-3 story.[88] The piece quoted MacBride that Amnesty aims to "stir up public awareness of this evil where the citizen stands naked and unprotected against the limitless power of the state." It also interviewed Ramsey Clark, the former US Attorney General and an Amnesty supporter, who "called for a world court of criminal justice with strong powers as part of a program to abolish torture: 'If that sounds idealistic we may have to create the unreal and the ideal to get rid of torture.'" Two months later, Shirley Hazzard, a novelist who had worked for the UN, wrote a scathing opinion piece on the UNESCO decision: "Of thousands of documented cases of persecution submitted by Amnesty to the United Nations, not one has ever been forwarded for action to the United Nations Commission on Human Rights."[89] Hazzard echoed MacBride and Clark: "Only direct, unsparing

---

[84] Clark 2001: 44–45.
[85] Clark 2001: 47, citing author's interview with Rodley.
[86] *New York Times* 1973a.
[87] *New York Times* 1973b.
[88] Robertson 1973.
[89] Hazzard 1974.

public pressure, soon to be released by drastic events and expressed by an indignant new generation, can now initiate human systems as global as our emergencies." The CAT conference and UNESCO fiasco generated additional international credibility for Amnesty in the face of powerful governments and an apathetic UN.

If Greece was the spark, then Chile was the catalyst for torture to get on the UN agenda. After the 1973 military coup, Amnesty accused General Augusto Pinochet's military junta of "systematically arresting and executing supporters of the deposed President Salvador Allende Gossens."[90] During the lead-up to the CAT conference, Chile agreed to an "on-the-spot investigation" from Amnesty.[91] After a one-week mission, Amnesty declared: "There is substantial evidence of a persistent and gross violation of the most fundamental human rights."[92] The UN General Assembly referred to Amnesty's reporting when adopting a unanimous resolution in November 1973, expressing "'grave concern' over the continuing practice of torture, reiterated the rejection of torture expressed in Article 5 of the UDHR, and urged all governments to become parties to international instruments outlawing 'torture and other inhuman or degrading treatment or punishment.'"[93] Amnesty released the full Chile report in September 1974, estimating 6,000–10,000 detained political prisoners and countless disappearances.[94]

The Chile report galvanized action at the UN. Amnesty testified before the UN Commission on Human Rights in early 1974, using the attention to implicate a wider variety of countries and participants: "Torture has now become a state institution in more than 30 countries, a rule of pain carried out by technicians, scientists, paramilitary officials, judges and cabinet ministers."[95] The UN General Assembly adopted a second resolution on torture in 1974, sponsored by the Dutch and Swedish governments in close consultation with Amnesty.[96] The following year in December 1975, the General Assembly adopted the Declaration on the Protection of All Persons from Being Subjected to Torture and Other Cruel, Inhuman or Degrading Treatment or Punishment. Sponsors argued "it would impose a moral obligation on governments."[97] Two years later, the General Assembly authorized a resolution for initiating a convention. From March 1979 onward, Amnesty was involved in the drafting sessions as "an informed watchdog role, aware that small turns of phrase could eventually be used to open or close loopholes of state accountability."[98] These efforts eventually resulted in the landmark UN Convention against Torture.

[90] *New York Times* 1973c.
[91] Howe 1973b.
[92] Teltsch 1974a.
[93] Clark 2001: 53.
[94] Teltsch 1974b.
[95] Clavel 1974.
[96] Clark 2001: 56.
[97] Teltsch 1975b.
[98] Clark 2001: 61.

Toward the mid- to late-1970s, the *Times* covered Amnesty's reports of torture and detention regarding Uruguay, Ghana, South Korea, Rhodesia, India, Brazil, Indonesia, Philippines, Yugoslavia, and Chile.[99] Meanwhile, governments began making more elaborate shows of observing human rights norms. Amnesty had accused Spain under Franco of "widespread, regular and virtually unrestricted torture tactics on imprisoned opponents."[100] Spain called the charges "defamation" inspired by the communist party.[101] After Franco's death, in October 1975 Amnesty released a report on the torture of 45 Basque Prisoners and at least 250 Spanish detainees.[102] Responding to growing domestic opposition, the Spanish Premier expressed "pained perplexity with which the Government notes the lack of some support which, at home, it had a right to expect."[103] Spain maintained it was a "victim of universal incomprehension," a succinct summary of what Amnesty was trying to achieve. Yet the government opened an investigation on torture and declared its opposition to it. A leading Spanish weekly published Amnesty's report and a journalist observed the change: "The fact that the press has been able to talk about the subject shows something has changed in Spain. Before, a person could die of mistreatment in a police station and nobody would know about it."[104] Elsewhere, in the Philippines some prisoners mentioned in Amnesty's reports "had been released and at least four of the 88 torturers named have been arrested and charged with crime."[105] The government claimed it did so because it "remains committed to the rule of law ... as a civilized nation."[106] In Ghana, a poet whose case Amnesty had publicized was "found guilty and sentenced to a year's imprisonment, but the sentence was remitted by the ruling Supreme Military Council to the time he had served, and he was freed. It was a face-saving move on the part of the Government."[107]

At the conclusion of CAT, Amnesty's polity-building was in full force. The success of the campaign was seen in a massive growth in Amnesty's membership from 20,000 members in 1969 to 100,000 in 1976, and then 200,000 in 1978.[108] The resulting membership dues also brought Amnesty its first budget surplus in 1975, which I refer to later in this chapter. As Amnesty established itself in the public imagination, it began a more aggressive campaign to not just generate American press, but also impose American responsibility for human rights abuses.

---

[99] Browne 1976; Goodman Jr. 1976; Kandell 1976; *New York Times* 1976c, 1976d, 1976f, 1976g, 1796h; Vecsey 1976.

[100] *New York Times* 1973d.

[101] *New York Times* 1973e.

[102] *New York Times* 1975b.

[103] Giniger 1975.

[104] Giniger 1976.

[105] Laber 1976b.

[106] *New York Times* 1976b.

[107] Darnton 1976.

[108] Eckel 2013: 193.

Imposing American Responsibility

The day the Paris Peace Accords were signed in January 1973 to end the Vietnam War, Amnesty issued a statement arguing that the American-supported South Vietnamese government had well over 100,000 civilian detainees and referred to the killings of an estimated 75,000 in 1955–6.[109] Amnesty's official report on South Vietnam called the situation "one of the most serious cases of political repression in the world today."[110] The South Vietnamese government rejected the report as part of "'a new campaign of intoxication' conducted by international Communism."[111] An editorial promptly rebutted that "rather than helping, the United States should be protesting police inhumanity in South Vietnam."[112] By September, US senators were pushing to eliminate "all support for South Vietnam's police force and prison system from the pending foreign aid bill."[113] Senator James Abourezk spoke colorfully: "Maybe the American people don't have to know about troop movements or the location of nuclear weapons, but by God they sure as hell can decide whether they want to support torture or not." Abourezk offered an amendment that would bar economic aid for policy or prison activity of any foreign government, not just South Vietnam. Public pressure mounted, with editorials identifying "certain threats to humanity which transcend national frontiers, political ideologies, racial differences."[114] Amnesty asked in a letter to the editor: "Why has the United States spent well over $100 billion in the name of protecting 'free choice' in Vietnam, when Saigon arrests anyone who tries to assert basic freedoms?"[115]

South Vietnam set the stage for the eventual passage of the 1974 Foreign Assistance Act, which directed cutbacks for countries that commit human rights violations. Specifically, the Act said that "no security assistance may be provided to any country of which government engages in a consistent pattern of gross violations of internationally recognized human rights, including torture or cruel, inhuman or degrading treatment or punishment; prolonged detention without charges; or other flagrant denials of the right to life, liberty, and the security of the person." The Act essentially eliminated all American security assistance to South Vietnam. While the Act was a victory for human rights accountability, it needed management to be successful. It thus provided a focal point for Amnesty's continued relevance to a growing American constituency. In 1975, the Ford administration told Congress that "it could not specify which nations had committed 'gross violations' of human rights because there was no objective way of distinguishing degrees of guilt."[116] According to the *Times*, Amnesty helped by "providing the most authoritative reports on torture and improper trial and detention practices."

[109] Gordon 1972; *New York Times* 1973h.
[110] *New York Times* 1973i.
[111] *New York Times* 1973j.
[112] Lewis 1973.
[113] Hersh 1973.
[114] Branfman 1973.
[115] *New York Times* 1974e.
[116] Teltsch 1975a.

American policy showed glimmers of a pro-human rights agenda. In June 1976, Secretary of State Henry Kissinger began an eight-day trip to Latin America with a proposal for a stronger role for the Inter-American Human Rights Commission. Kissinger remarked that Chile's human rights violations "had become 'an obstacle' to improved United States-Chilean relations."[117] A resolution asking Chile to allow a monitoring team from the Commission passed with all twenty-three countries voting in favor except Chile and Brazil. Amnesty described Uruguay as the next Chile, calling it an "undisguised military dictatorship" with "the highest per capita concentration of political prisoners in the world."[118] In September 1976, Congress voted to cut $3 million in military aid for Uruguay.[119] By January 1977, in anticipation of the incoming Carter administration, 3,000 political prisoners were freed across Latin America.[120] In addition, in a front-page story, the State Department released its first detailed reports on human rights conditions abroad, often quoting Amnesty as the source.[121]

The arts world was considering its own responsibility. A long feature in the *Times* in August 1976, "Art, Politics, and Torture Chambers," began by asking whether artists should boycott performing in countries with human rights abuses such as Iran and South Africa.[122] It quoted playwright Arthur Miller, "who has denounced the Shah's repressive policies but taken no public boycott: 'I take no more responsibility for who plays my plays than General Motors does for who rides in their Chevrolets.'" The piece wrestled with questions at the heart of art and activism: "In a world beset by violation of human rights, how is a serious artist to pick and choose among competing tyrannies?" It offered three answers. First, "have one's facts straight. Obviously, one can't always do one's own research, but since we live by opinion trusteeship we can choose our authorities carefully and make certain that on an issue as critical as boycott one is acting out of facts and belief rather than propaganda and pressure." Second, "one must decide that the situation lends itself to strategic intervention." Third, prioritize "fundamental human rights" like the "arbitrary taking of life, torture and prolonged detention without charges or trial." While all proposals bore Amnesty's fingerprints, it was dancer Merce Cunningham who picked up on Amnesty's polity-building:

> I think we live in a single world now, masked, to be sure, by a series of national setups that have relinquished all pretense of moral and spiritual leadership, a single world in which people, if possible in spite of governments, can still speak to one another of such things as love, and nature, and life and poetry.

Cunningham's sentiments perfectly encapsulate the kind of universal belonging Amnesty aimed to bring into existence to solve the challenge of human rights.

[117] de Onis 1976.
[118] Laber 1976a.
[119] *New York Times* 1976i.
[120] *New York Times* 1977a.
[121] Gwertzman 1977a.
[122] Navasky 1976.

Other than inspiring artists, Amnesty also resonated with terrorists. In September 1976, six Croatian nationalists hijacked a TWA flight from New York to Chicago with ninety people on board, diverting the plane to Newfoundland and eventually Paris. They asked for the publication of a manifesto, after which they surrendered to French authorities. The manifesto featured statistics from Amnesty, "the most well-known world organization concerned with political prisoners," claiming "there are more political prisoners in Yugoslavia ... than in any other East European land, excluding the Soviet Union."[123] Thus, by the late-1970s, Amnesty's human rights messaging was also being used to legitimate violent movements. During this period, Amnesty took on the Soviet Union, the country with the most political prisoners.

Solidifying the Polity in Cold War Politics

A year before the USSR signed the 1975 Helsinki Agreement that formalized détente, an unofficial Amnesty national section was formed in Moscow. The *Times* remarked on the section's one year anniversary that "perhaps the most significant characteristic of the group is that it still exists."[124] It further reported: "On the one hand, officials have tried to avoid bringing adverse publicity by clashing directly with a respected organization such as Amnesty; on the other, they have taken steps to signal the population that increased contacts and accommodation with the United States do not mean the growing tolerance of political opposition by Soviet citizens." In 1975, four Amnesty members were arrested in Moscow, including Secretary Andrei N. Tverdokhlebov and member Sergei Kovalev. Their cases grabbed international attention.[125] The interest was galvanized by Soviet dissident Andre Sakharov, the 1975 Nobel Peace Prize laureate, who emphasized: "Sometimes, really, there is a feeling that the West isn't very interested in our internal affairs. This is very sad because the future of humanity, depends on what happens in all three worlds. Now, in détente, the whole world must carefully watch what is happening in other countries and especially what goes on in the socialist countries."[126] After Sakharov's Nobel was announced, Amnesty assembled a panel, dubbed the International Sakharov Hearings, on Soviet psychiatric hospitals and prison camps.[127] When Sakharov was denied permission to attend the Nobel ceremony, he maintained that "Western opinion is believed to be one reason for the continued existence of a Moscow chapter of Amnesty International."[128] The

---

[123] *New York Times* 1976j.
[124] Shipler 1975a.
[125] *New York Times* 1975c.
[126] Wren 1975.
[127] *New York Times* 1975d.
[128] Shipler 1975b.

headline was apt: "They Need Listeners: The Dissidents Speak As Much to the West as to the Kremlin."

Amnesty released its first official report on the Soviet Union in November 1975, estimating at least 10,000 political and religious prisoners, which the Kremlin called a "vulgar falsification and defamation of Soviet reality and socialist legitimacy."[129] American businessmen, social workers, and judges responded "by calling attention to the prisoners' cases and, when trials begin, by arranging for foreign lawyers to attend as observers – a practice that, experience suggests, leads to fairer trials and lighter sentences."[130] American computer experts mailed letters on behalf of Valentin F. Turchin, president of Amnesty's Soviet group and author of the Soviet computer language, who was blacklisted.[131] Koralev's trial was followed closely in the United States.[132] He was sentenced to "seven years in a strict-regime labor camp, followed by three years of exile."[133] The injustice retained Western press attention on the remaining Amnesty cases. The Soviets next released Amnesty member Leonid Plyushch from a psychiatric hospital in February 1976.[134] Amnesty used singer Joan Baez in a press conference to celebrate his release and highlight the plight of thirty other Soviet dissidents in psychiatric hospitals. In April, Actor Richard Burton wrote a letter to the editor on Tverdokhlebov's trial, arguing that if he "is convicted for his defense of others, skepticism with respect to Soviet declarations on human rights will be justified."[135] Tverdokhlebov was sentenced relatively leniently to five years of internal exile. Turchin was interviewed by the *Times* in a page-2 story: "Asked why he thought the sentence had not been stiffer, Mr. Turchin said to an American correspondent, 'Thanks to you. There has been a great deal of interest in the West.'"[136] These statements signaled that Amnesty's polity made a difference for human rights progress.

In 1976, the Soviet Union released another prominent dissident, Vladimir Bukovsky, in exchange for a Chilean Communist Party member. *The Times* observed in a front-page story that there "seemed no recent precedent for the Soviet Union to barter political prisoners, though captured spies have been traded in the past."[137] Amnesty had adopted Bukovsky as a prisoner of conscience and organized a press conference in Paris upon his release. He remarked: "I regard this exchange as an extraordinary event, as it is the first time that the Soviet Government officially recognized it has political prisoners. It is a victory for everybody. This exchange brings forward the problem of political prisoners as a universal

[129] Shabad 1975.
[130] Teltsch 1975a.
[131] *New York Times* 1975e.
[132] Shipler 1975c; *New York Times* 1975f.
[133] Shipler 1976a.
[134] Clarity 1976.
[135] *New York Times* 1976k.
[136] Shipler 1976b.
[137] Wren 1976.

problem."[138] Bukovsky's mother was shocked to hear that "people in America shared her grief. ... There were letters and telegrams signed by Arthur Miller, Roger Baldwin, George Meany and many others in the public eye. Senators, Members of Parliament and even Governments petitioned the Soviet leaders. Eloquent appeals came from Harold Pinter, Edward Albee, Vladimir Nabokov."[139] The Soviet pronouncement of Amnesty as "a tiny group of nonentities who represent no one and nothing"[140] assured the organization was anything but.

In 1976, Amnesty was awarded the Erasmus Prize from the Dutch government. Then in early 1977, President Carter, in front-page news, publicly supported Sakharov in an attempt to make the Kremlin "understand that the United States will not remain indifferent to human rights violations."[141] In doing so, Carter upheld the promise in his inaugural address "to restore what he called 'the moral authority' of United States foreign policy to help free the oppressed. 'Because we are free, we can never be indifferent to the fate of freedom elsewhere.'"[142] Carter's presidency made human rights "suddenly chic." But for Amnesty the polity-building was a much longer achievement: "What's happened is that the public at last is learning about the growing use of torture and political imprisonment. People want to find out what they can do about it."[143] When congratulating Amnesty for the 1977 Nobel, the *Times*' editorial board praised it for having "brought hope to thousands, imprisoned and tortured for their political beliefs. The list would be very much longer but for the work of this genuinely international movement."[144] Another featured story quoted a diplomat: "It's a clear signal that human rights is now a dominant issue in the global community."[145]

The Nobel represented a zenith in Amnesty's quest for world recognition for building a human rights polity. I showed the historical development of Amnesty into a household name at length to underscore that success was not inevitable. I also drew attention to cases that were particularly resonant in the international press and which became cornerstones for Amnesty's influence: Israel, the United Kingdom, Greece, Spain, Vietnam, Chile, and the Soviet Union. I next move to examining Amnesty's parallel efforts to maintain its growing global legitimacy.

PROJECTING MORAL PURITY

At the center of Amnesty's polity-building is projecting moral purity. We know that "the degree to which NGOs are linked to principle rather than political interests

[138] *New York Times* 1976l.
[139] Thorne 1977.
[140] Wren 1977.
[141] Gwertzman 1977b.
[142] *New York Times* 1977b.
[143] Teltsch 1977.
[144] *New York Times* 1977c.
[145] Gupte 1977.

enhances the legitimacy and moral force of their arguments."[146] The logic operates on the understanding that "non-governmental organizations are generally perceived by the public as trustworthy and benign actors, particularly in comparison with political institutions and the corporate sector."[147] This trust must be maintained through a continual reproduction of moral purity, which derives "from principled ideas or beliefs about right and wrong."[148] Moreover, in constructing human rights claims, INGOs engage in a "form of communicative counter-hegemony, speaking rights to power."[149] Thus, INGO "authority and influence is based on moral legitimacy and persuasive power."[150]

Amnesty's mission of "bearing witness" had "special, moral authority."[151] Projecting an air of objectivity helped Amnesty "cultivate a position as a disinterested and autonomous 'third party' actor in the international system."[152] Such "moral capital"[153] transfers. For instance, leading INGOs are essential to issue-definition and serve as a legitimating resource for other transnational actors.[154] But in a "dirty hands" problem, INGO moral capital is compromised by the practical realities of advocacy and humanitarian work.[155] On the one hand, INGOs like Amnesty recognize that survival is important so there is someone to defend their causes.[156] On the other hand, "once you have authority, you protect it," which means that Amnesty tries to steer clear of "pollutants such as money, interests, and politics."[157]

Amnesty's sovereign competence relies on "convincing us it is more than merely a veiled attempt to promote the subjective preferences or advantages of some. It must claim a certain objectivity in speaking for the truth."[158] Benenson's appeal in *The Observer* argued that "the force of opinion, to be effective, should be broadly based, international, non-sectarian and all-party." For Amnesty, a nonpolitical stance was about being "even-handed and to be in favour of all political prisoners, not just the ones favoured," rather than being *apolitical*.[159] One symbolic expression of moral purity is Amnesty's logo: a flame in barbed wire. A prominent ethnography of the organization refers to Amnesty staffers as "Keepers of the Flame" and conveys "the weight of moral inferiority just watching staff members go in and out of the security doors that protect the

---

[146]   Clark 2001: 36.
[147]   Hielscher et al. 2017: 3.
[148]   Clark 2001: 21; Hall and Biersteker 2002; Hopgood 2006; Wong 2012.
[149]   Brysk 2013: 16.
[150]   Carpenter 2014: 12–3.
[151]   Hopgood 2006: 26.
[152]   Clark 2001: 11.
[153]   Kane 2001: 10.
[154]   Carpenter 2014: 8–9.
[155]   Slim 2002; Rubenstein 2015.
[156]   Stroup and Wong 2017: 82.
[157]   Hopgood 2006: 14–5.
[158]   Hopgood 2006: 4.
[159]   Astor interview, AI 979.

[International Secretariat's] inner sanctum."[160] Moreover, Amnesty's moral purity was policed by others. In May 1977, the Association against Painful Experiments on Animals accused Amnesty of "horrendous and disgusting" torture experiments on pigs.[161] Amnesty countered that it used "anesthetized hogs to determine whether torture inflicted with cattle prods would leave any marks." Still, the outcry generated prominent page-3 coverage in the *Times*.

The projection of moral purity and being above the political fray was key for Amnesty's most political act: building a global polity. Given the Cold War, the founders had "a quasi-obsessional identification with neutrality."[162] When debating a strategy for Eastern Europe in 1975, Amnesty agreed that "the impartiality of the organization must be stressed as one of the few international NGOs interested in presenting correct information, which if allowed to observe trials, visit prisons, etc. would be able to say with authority whether or not trials were fair and prison conditions good."[163] Similarly, when determining the contents of a report to the ECOSOC Committee on NGOs in 1977, Amnesty stressed "it was essential that we should have our publications readily available at the meeting to justify our impartiality."[164] In these instances, Amnesty explicitly linked its authority and sovereign access with perceived impartiality reflecting a higher moral purity.

Amnesty relied on two main sources of impartiality when projecting moral purity: impartial research expertise and government independence.

Impartial Research Expertise

Amnesty's first source of projecting moral purity was impartial research expertise derived from its policies for case selection and a professionalized research staff. Amnesty chose not to rank countries in human rights reports, separated prisoners "from the reasons for his or her imprisonment," and banned the adoption of violent POCs.[165] More importantly, Amnesty's "rule of threes" for prisoner adoption stated that "each group of Amnesty supporters would adopt three prisoners and work for their release. One would be from a communist-bloc country, one from the West, and one from the Third World."[166] This case selection process appealed to many volunteers and members, who "felt attracted by what they regarded as Amnesty's nonideological or even apolitical character. ... The problem of political prisoners and of torture crosses political boundaries. The issue here is not one of ideology; it is one of human dignity."[167] In addition, Amnesty did

[160] Hopgood 2006: 17.
[161] *New York Times* 1977d.
[162] Dezalay and Garth 2006: 235.
[163] AI 416: 166–167.
[164] AI 418: 109.
[165] Hopgood 2006: 60–62; 100.
[166] Power 1981: 10.
[167] Eckel 2013: 199.

not allow national sections to work on their own countries (WOOC). In a self-study in 1975, Amnesty worried about "'paper' Committee and Committees which were 'fronts' or acting as protection for groups of people whose first loyalty, was to a national political party rather, than to Amnesty International."[168]

Amnesty recognized that the WOOC policy added challenges for polity-building with "the paradox of asking people to work for prisoners in other countries, rather than for their own prisoners."[169] AIUSA especially had issues with adoption groups and the WOOC policy, arguing in 1968 that "groups were not suitable to the American society, [and] was proceeding on the basis on individual members only."[170] But the International Secretariat repeatedly rebuffed these efforts, arguing in 1977 that "the United States would follow the same line of impartiality as for any country in the world."[171] Finally, in the early 1980s, Amnesty made a WOOC policy exception to AIUSA for the campaign to abolish the death penalty. AIUSA's membership took off and it became a formidable national section, eventually eclipsing the traditionally strong Dutch and Scandinavian groups.[172] Amnesty's persistence in keeping the rule of three and WOOC policies despite its organizational consequences reflects the commitment to signaling impartiality via case selection.

In addition, the Research Department was Amnesty's "hidden center – directly or indirectly, Amnesty's international influence depended on the Department's work."[173] A senior Amnesty staffer reflected:

> What was special about it was what it purported to try and deliver. Which was objective information about individuals in particular parlous situations vis-à-vis their governments. That it was accurate, it was careful, it was not grinding political axes. It was providing the information that others could grind political axes with if they wanted to. That's fine. But that it was just simply a voice of cool, calm documentation to prevent history being written by the victors.[174]

Experts who worked with researchers bought into this vision: "'I liked it because it was non-political. It was strictly a matter of human rights,' a psychotherapist explained."[175] The Research Department professionalized by instituting a central filing system in 1968.[176] It next established a responsible handling of information policy and a classification system for "confidential" material in 1977.[177] Even the archival records became more organized. In June 1976, the IEC meeting minutes had an index for the

---

[168] AI 416: 127.
[169] AI 416: 128.
[170] AI 412: 71.
[171] AI 418: 78.
[172] Hopgood 2006: 105–145; Wong 2012: 110.
[173] Eckel 2013: 195.
[174] Hopgood 2006: 14.
[175] Eckel 2013: 199.
[176] AI 412: 64.
[177] AI 425: 22–23.

first time.[178] Through the appearance of a professional Research Department performing "cool documentation" on sensitive issues, Amnesty's "information and interpretation capacity helped … elicit expectations of governmental accountability."[179]

But Amnesty's Research Department realized that "information is never
objective."[180] In 1976, the Department organized an internal focus group and issued
a report. Its most prominent complaint to the Secretariat was about conflicting
mandates in applying the principles of impartiality and balance: "These are two
words which are frequently used in the context of AI research work, but their
meanings and their implications for our work have never been defined."[181] Pointing
out that the "rule of threes" forces researchers to underrepresent countries with
serious human rights abuses, they concluded that Amnesty's "attempts to adhere to
the concept of balance may have, ironically, damaged [its] impartiality."[182]
Researchers also identified a selection bias based on country access because they
"often devote[d] too much attention to relatively open countries at the expense of
more closed and more repressive countries."[183] In regard to Vietnam in the late-
1960s, Amnesty leaders acknowledged that "very little has been done with regard to
this country, only a few isolated cases are under adoption as it is virtually impossible
to obtain accurate information."[184] The researchers also called out dominant
national sections in setting research priorities:

> Once case sheets and publicity material are produced on such countries,
> a 'clientele' of groups, co-groups, and interested members develops within the
> organisation. This 'clientele' then pushes harder for more work on the country of
> their particular interest with the result that the researcher comes under even more
> pressure to work on the country, and research priorities become even further
> distorted.[185]

It was thus not easy to maintain research impartiality. Yet, Amnesty gave an opportunity for researchers to register their complaints officially, which speaks to the
organization's commitment to keep striving for moral purity.

Finally, Amnesty's construction of impartial research expertise included cali-
brating what reports would be released when. In 1966, the IEC "stressed the fact
that Amnesty must not get involved in the Cold War, and in a case such as the
Siniavsky/Daniel affair Amnesty should wait until the general interest had died
down before bringing the case up again."[186] In 1968, it "agreed to continue to

---

[178]   AI 417: 90–91.
[179]   Clark 2001: 17.
[180]   Wong 2012: 94.
[181]   AI 424: 58.
[182]   AI 424: 58.
[183]   AI 424: 51.
[184]   AI 412: 32–33.
[185]   AI 424: 58.
[186]   AI 412: 32.

elect a 'prisoner of the year,' although there was some feeling that this was no more than a publicity gimmick."[187] In 1970, Amnesty considered its recent mission to Brazil noting that

> although Amnesty was late in the field on Brazil, it should nevertheless publish a short report confirming statements, made by other organisations and putting forward recommendations to the Brazilian Government relating to an International Tribunal. It was pointed out that to publish now might detract from the impact of the Israeli report and also earn Amnesty the reputation of being an organisation solely interested in torture.[188]

Government Independence

Amnesty's second source of projecting moral purity was independence from governments. I have already mentioned in this chapter's introduction that it was crucial that Amnesty was seen as member-driven and independent of government support. Neville Vincent, Amnesty's first treasurer, reflected on receiving government funds:

> As I remember it there was the odd occasion, it wouldn't actually be said to be from the government, but we had reason to think it would and we felt that would have swayed our judgement, anyway made us . . . and it would have been wrong in every way to accept it. I don't know of any occasion when I was there that we knowingly received any government funds of any kind.[189]

Within the first five years of its founding, Amnesty is claimed to have "cemented an unambiguous policy of refusal either to conduct private negotiations with governments or to take government funds."[190] In fact, even when Amnesty worked diligently on UN resolutions on torture, it "rarely publicized its participation in norm-drafting activities and never claimed authorship of specific drafting language."[191] Amnesty did so because it believed "it is not credible to name and shame a government with which you consistently align."[192] Amnesty also publicly proclaimed a distrust of governments. MacBride reflected on the European Convention on Human Rights as "the first international body for receiving complaints of any individual, even against his own government," which was important "because you can't depend on governments; you can't rely on governments."[193] As the previous section showed, Amnesty's publicly hostile relations with governments generated sustained international media coverage of its activities and reports.

---

[187] AI 412: 60.
[188] AI 413: 3.
[189] Vincent interview, AI 993.
[190] Clark 2001: 14–15.
[191] Clark 2001: 8.
[192] Hopgood 2013: xiii.
[193] MacBride interview, AI 987.

In the beginning, Amnesty had not committed to a clear position against govern-ment involvement. When discussing the original appeal, the *Observer's* editor could "not even imagine anybody asking" the British government's support.[194] However, Benenson did ask. He already had "friendly" relations with the British government, having worked for British Intelligence during World War II.[195] He was educated at elite institutions like Summer Fields, Eton, and Balliol College (Oxford University), all training grounds for future British leaders.[196] In a 1961 letter to Prime Minister Harold Macmillan, Benenson mentioned that they shared a past as a "Colleger and Balliolman," when asking for Macmillan's support for the appeal.[197] However, MacMillan cautioned Benenson from a public alliance of Amnesty with govern-ments, "pointing out that the value of movements such as Amnesty lay precisely in their not having any direct links with governments. Benenson replied that this should not prevent the campaign 'from having private understandings, or for its ultimate objectives from being those of Her Majesty's Governments.'"[198]

However, the stakes of government independence became clear in twin crises of 1966–7 that threatened to end the young organization. First, Benenson agreed to take £30,000 (£563,000 today) for humanitarian funds in Rhodesia from the British government, which claimed it to be from a secret millionaire.[199] A report commis-sioned by the IEC "not only noted that government money for Rhodesia had been handled by Benenson, but also that Amnesty appeared to have received such assistance for salaries and possibly also for investigative missions abroad."[200] Benenson seemed to believe the money came from a millionaire, but admitted it was wrong to not disclose his negotiations with the government to the IEC. Second, Amnesty had written a report documenting the British government's torture of prisoners in British-occupied Aden (now part of Yemen). Robert Swann, who managed daily affairs as Benenson's health deteriorated, embargoed the report. Based on the Rhodesia affair and a break-in at Amnesty offices, Benenson "suspected government infiltration of Amnesty and had the report published outside of Britain without AI's official approval."[201] Peter Archer, MP and founding member of Amnesty, disclosed: "In those early years we'd got on quite well with the Foreign Office, but this was predominantly a British organiza-tion criticizing foreigners, and the British Foreign Office thought that was fine. And we really fouled up our relationship when we criticized the British govern-ment over Aden."[202]

[194] Astor interview, AI 979.
[195] Letter, Benenson to Hoare & Co., January 9, 1967, Amnesty Oral History Archives, B6.
[196] Buchanan 2002: 577–578.
[197] Letter, Benenson to Philip Woodfield, June 4, 1961, Amnesty Oral History Archives, B6.
[198] Buchanan 2002: 588.
[199] Buchanan 2004: 272–273.
[200] Buchanan 2004: 274.
[201] Clark 2001: 15.
[202] Archer interview, AI 978.

The scandals led to Benenson's resignation and established Amnesty's need to be wary of formal government links. It also created a new Amnesty policy requiring members of the Secretariat and observers "to state in writing that they are not in the employment of any secret service, nor have been for the previous five years."[203] In the future, Amnesty was careful not to publicize its network of governmental contacts. In a 1975 discussion on a government relations strategy with Eastern Europe, the IEC decided:

> In discussing the tension between publicity and discussions with governments, it was AGREED that although at no time would there be any diminution of a campaign, any increase in activity and the level of publicity would have to be considered in the light of AI's existing relations with that particular government and any intended negotiations and contacts with such governments, and indeed all governments in the Eastern European block as they were interlinked in a way unknown to Western countries.[204]

Amnesty managed its image carefully by being attuned to the consequences of government interdependence for polity-building.

Thus, Amnesty's sovereign competence to build a global polity for human rights relied on projecting moral purity. In its first twenty-five years, Amnesty projected moral purity through symbols, policies for research impartiality and government independence, and response to crises. Amnesty Chairman Seán MacBride underscored that "one of Amnesty's challenges all along has been whom it allies with and whom it doesn't ally with; what issues it allies with and which it doesn't, because the organization is constantly being pulled."[205] As the events of 1966–7 illustrate, "Amnesty's political autonomy was not always maintained in practice."[206] However, the appearance of independence "became vital to protect Amnesty as a symbolic moral authority."[207] Yet, "only in a prolonged process of trial and error did the Secretariat manage to build up the institutional strength necessary for Amnesty to wage forceful public 'campaigns.'"[208] I next examine the shadow relations necessary for Amnesty's institutional strength that contradicted its ideals but allowed the organization to do its job.

SOVEREIGN DILEMMAS IN *SHADOW HYBRIDITY*

Amnesty's polity-building clearly helped make human rights a reality. However, the global human rights polity could only be sustained through relations of *shadow hybridity* as seen through nonformalized and nonpublicized governmental back channels and side bargains. Amnesty's Research Department noted in 1976 that "there is need to recognise and define the role of 'hidden front' work, whereby

[203] AI 412: 55.
[204] AI 416: 167–168.
[205] MacBride interview, AI 987.
[206] Dezalay and Garth 2006: 237.
[207] Hopgood 2006: 72.
[208] Eckel 2013: 196.

AI works without publicity through other people and institutions."[209] Even the Nobel Peace Prize was a product of intense behind-the-scenes campaigning. Amnesty was first nominated in 1967.[210] Four years later, the IEC asked member Kari Poppe to back channel with her contact on the Norwegian prize committee to discuss Amnesty's prospects.[211] In February 1972, Poppe returned with the insight that Amnesty needed a more centralized international campaign.[212] Amnesty's Campaign for the Abolition of Torture was launched the same year. After Amnesty Chairman MacBride was awarded the Nobel in 1974 but Amnesty itself was snubbed, the IEC hired a Promotions Department to better coordinate its brand.[213] Upon the announcement of the 1977 prize, an IEC member wrote to the head of the Promotions Department:

> to acknowledge and thank with warm appreciation for the decisive part which the Promotion Department and yourself have played in my opinion in successfully obtaining this prize for Amnesty International. . . . There is no question that to receive the prize it needs promotion and lobby, applied intelligently, systematically and with proper strategy. It was one of your aims for the Promotion Campaign from the very beginning to culminate Prisoner of Conscience Year by the award of the Nobel Peace Prize.[214]

Amnesty's lobbying for the Nobel was thus "applied intelligently, systematically and with proper strategy." To be clear, Amnesty is no less deserving of the prize because it lobbied for it. However, uncovering such relations of *shadow hybridity* helps us appreciate the work required to uphold human rights in a state-based international regime as well as consider its trade-offs for legitimating hybrid governance.

In this section, I draw on all IEC meeting minutes between 1961 and 1986 to argue that the successful cases for Amnesty's polity-building were made possible by relations of *shadow hybridity*.[215] I focus on three areas where *shadow hybridity* was most pronounced for Amnesty: securing early financing, gaining country access, and negotiating reforms.

Financing Help to Exit a Crisis

In order to build a polity, Amnesty first had to survive. Benenson urges researchers: "If you really want the crux of the history of early Amnesty, I just say: 'look at the accounts.'"[216] Amnesty did not begin as a membership-based subscription scheme it is today. Instead, it relied on ad hoc donations from an eclectic bunch of donors that

[209] AI 424: 53.
[210] AI 412: 49.
[211] AI 413: 61.
[212] AI 413: 67.
[213] AI 417: 18.
[214] AI 426: 27.
[215] I have retracted personally identifying information for Amnesty's field agents and contacts.
[216] Benenson interview, AI 983.

included church groups, lawyers, and art smugglers. Benenson recalls one particularly amusing benefactor: "Now this fellow not only gave us $500, but kept on getting letters from me because I thought he was a rich American, and he gave us more dollars in the course of the year, turned out to be a sculpture smuggler."[217] Internal conflicts in the early years between Benenson, MacBride, and Eric Baker, an Amnesty co-director, often revolved around Benenson's dubious-sounding contacts.

Benenson also sought government funding from the very beginning. He admitted getting "help from the Information Research Department (IRD), the anti-Communist propaganda section of the British Foreign Office, while setting up Amnesty, and this relationship continued after 1961."[218] Publicly, however, Amnesty denied taking money from governments. Benenson qualified his more easy-going attitude in contrast to a stricter Amnesty policy on government funding:

> INTERVIEWER: But did you feel that funding coming from a government source was of itself negative? Or potentially so?
> BENENSON: No ... not open funding from a government source, I think that's perfectly acceptable. I know Amnesty's always set against it, but...[219]

Even Amnesty's treasurer characterized the policy of refusing governmental funding as having exceptions: "One major [exception] is we can accept direct subsidies from government for the specific purpose of relief. The other is that we accept indirect subsidies in the form of conscientious objectors allowed by the governments to work in the Amnesty office during their time of conscientious objection service, or in the form of charity status, or sometimes lower rent on property."[220] Thus, the oral histories show more nuance in Amnesty's relationship to government funding than it otherwise acknowledged.

As Amnesty expanded in the early 1960s, its expenses ballooned for salaries, conferences, printing, mailing, and research trips. Staffers bought their own office supplies.[221] Fundraising was a challenge: "Nothing was more difficult than to raise money for Amnesty. Not like the [National Society for the Prevention of Cruelty to Children] for children, or seeing pictures of a starving child as Oxfam show. We couldn't do that too easily. We did eventually, we had people behind bars and so on."[222] Benenson was acutely aware of the challenge. Following reports of the CIA financing the International Commission of Jurists in 1967, Benenson believed the charges as "you can't get that sort of money out of the ordinary giving public."[223]

---

[217] Benenson interview, AI 983.
[218] Buchanan 2004: 270.
[219] Benenson interview, AI 982.
[220] Vincent interview, AI 993.
[221] Hopgood 2006: 23.
[222] Vincent interview, AI 993.
[223] Benenson interview, AI 982.

By 1965, Amnesty was in a serious financial crisis, "making it necessary to think carefully whether it was now possible to expand, or remain static."[224] It projected an annual income of £12,600 to stay afloat, of which approximately £3,500 came from the Prynce Hopkins Fund, an American foundation that had funded Amnesty from the beginning.[225] By September, the Rowntree Foundation in Britain agreed to give £2,500 annually.[226] In March 1966, the Prynce Hopkins Fund increased its donation to £5,000.[227] Thus, more than half of Amnesty's budget in the mid-1960s came from two large foundations rather than from small donors. Moreover, Amnesty engaged in "creative" accounting by using Prisoner of Conscience relief monies to "pay administrative expenses."[228] Amnesty stopped misusing the funds after a warning from the British tax authorities.

The financial gap remained, however. The crisis forced the IEC to issue its first formal policy decision on accepting money from governments in March 1966: "The Swedish Section applied for a million kroner from the Swedish Government and a discussion followed as to whether Amnesty could accept money from governments. It was decided that in this case the initiative should be left to National Sections and each case should be considered individually on its merits."[229] The IEC thus refused to create a blanket prohibition on accepting money from governments. In fact, Chairman MacBride would then "meet the Swedish Foreign Minister to discuss this application by the Swedish Section of Amnesty International."[230] The Swedish government bankrolled many important Amnesty research missions over the next few years, including Algeria (1967), Iran (1968), Malawi (1968), Brazil (1968, 1969), Greece (1969, 1970), Indonesia (1969, 1970), Tunisia (1970), Spain (1970), and Vietnam (1973).[231]

Despite this funding source, by November 1968 Amnesty had a budget deficit in the region of £10,000 (£150,000 today).[232] This became a problem for Amnesty's participation in the Kyoto Congress the following year, in an event which was "an excellent opportunity for Amnesty to assert a leadership role with regard to the treatment of political prisoners and prisoners of conscience throughout the world. It was agreed that efforts should be made to raise £5,000 [£75,000 today] to cover a special project in this field."[233] The Swedes pledged £400.[234] In March 1969, the IEC issued its second official policy on government funding. The discussion first "noted that the UN had

[224] AI 412: 23–24.
[225] AI 412: 23–24.
[226] AI 412: 29.
[227] AI 412: 31–32.
[228] Hopgood 2006: 70.
[229] AI 421: 18.
[230] AI 412: 31–32.
[231] Algeria: AI 412: 43; Iran: AI 412: 66–67; Malawi: AI 412: 57; Brazil: AI 412: 66–67; AI 412: 91; Greece: AI 412: 86; AI 413: 13; Indonesia: AI 412: 76; AI 413: 4; Tunisia: AI 413: 9; Spain: AI 413: 4–5; Vietnam: AI 414: 64.
[232] AI 412: 62.
[233] AI 412: 69–70.
[234] AI 413: 3.

expressed no objection to NGOs receiving donations from governments and that the new Human Rights Institute to be established in Strasbourg was inviting donations from governments."[235] Then, the IEC agreed that Amnesty

> may receive donations towards the budget of the organisation from governments, provided the donation is disclosed to all enquirers and to the IEC and National Sections. ... Any National Section is entitled to write to the Secretary General inquiring about sources of funds for each mission but it was recognised that it would not always be possible to make such information available.[236]

In December 1969, Amnesty also pursued funding from large American foundations, such as Ford and Carnegie.[237] In the postwar context, Ford had "strategically timed" funding to those "who were building the foundations of the human rights field."[238] Examples include seed money for the Natural Resources Defense Council (NRDC) in 1970 and Helsinki Watch in 1979, which became Human Rights Watch.[239] It is thus puzzling why Ford did not fund Amnesty. The NRDC attracted Ford funding as a first mover in a sparse field and reputation as an entrepreneur.[240] These characteristics would apply equally to Amnesty. The literature provides some explanations for Ford overlooking Amnesty. Funders preferred local NGOs over INGOs.[241] Moreover, Ford became interested in political prisoners only in 1974–5, years after Amnesty's dire funding requests.[242] Also, Ford staffers claimed their colleagues thought of Amnesty as "a communist front organization" as of 1976.[243] Other interviews reveal that Ford believed that Amnesty would not accept foundation money for operating expenses and would only do so for special programs.[244] But when Ford became interested in funding South African litigation through a special grant to Amnesty, Amnesty's nonviolent policy prohibited consideration.[245] Instead, Ford funded the Lawyers Committee and the ICRC.

In any case, over the early 1970s, Amnesty slowly took charge of its finances. In 1972, it hired McKinsey and Anderson consultants (under greatly reduced fees) that recommended strict austerity and more targeted fundraising.[246] The success of CAT in 1973 led to an explosion in membership dues, allowing Amnesty to record its first budget surplus in 1975.[247] In 1969, Amnesty's budget was £20,000.[248] By 1979, it

---

[235] AI 412: 79.
[236] AI 412: 79.
[237] AI 412: 91.
[238] Wong et al. 2017: 91–92.
[239] Dezalay and Garth 2006, 241–242; Korey 2007.
[240] Young 2010: 32.
[241] Wong et al. 2017: 82.
[242] Korey 2007: 36.
[243] Dezalay and Garth 2006: 241–242.
[244] Korey 2007: 44.
[245] Korey 2007: 152.
[246] AI 413: 84.
[247] AI 416: 13–15.
[248] Eckel 2013: 193.

was £1.3 million.[249] The early financial struggles provided an impetus for conducting government and foundation relations. As Amnesty's financial outlook improved, these connections transformed into a network for tackling a different problem: getting access to countries for conducting research and government talks.

Leveraging Access and Advocacy through a Diplomatic Network

As Amnesty's human rights reports gained international attention, it saw a serious curtailment in its country access. In 1971, the IEC "expressed concern at the number of countries that were refusing missions by Amnesty."[250] Amnesty's treasurer remembered being sent back by Portugal after a damning report was made public:

> I went again to do a follow-up on what their people had said. Well, then I got to Portugal and I got through the customs and I was just about to hail a taxi when two men came up to me and asked me my name, or they knew my name, and I was rather flattered, and said that I wasn't welcome in their country. And they shoved me back on the same plane that I'd just landed on.[251]

Gaining access to "closed countries" was vital so it did not appear Amnesty only selected prisoners from more open countries.[252] Access was such a problem that in 1979 "only six countries accounted for three quarters of all Amnesty Prisoner of Conscience adoption groups."[253]

Amnesty sent agents covertly, but it did not always go well. In 1966, Amnesty member Niels Groth went unofficially to Guinea to inquire about the status of Amnesty's 1965 Prisoner of Conscience of the Year. Groth was arrested within 48 hours of arrival. The IEC debated whether they should claim Groth as an official delegate or declare "he was simply a member of Amnesty travelling in that part of the world and making incidental enquiries."[254] Amnesty decided to support Groth as an official delegate while negotiating with the Danish Ambassador to Ghana and Guinea for his release behind the scenes. Amnesty was also "in contact with various aluminum companies with great influence in Guinea and that some pressure could perhaps be brought to bear along these lines."[255] Amnesty would continue sending unofficial delegates or observers when it could not obtain official access, such as in Malawi in 1968.[256]

For a more sustainable solution, Amnesty built extensive networks with both "friendly" and "unfriendly" governments. Friendly governments were largely Western European countries that were early backers of Amnesty, such as the Scandinavians.

[249]   Hopgood 2006: 84.
[250]   AI 413: 36.
[251]   Vincent interview, AI 993.
[252]   Hopgood 2006: 100.
[253]   Eckel 2013: 205.
[254]   AI 412: 37.
[255]   AI 412: 44.
[256]   AI 412: 57.

Unfriendly governments were those whom Amnesty was investigating at the time, which of course changed frequently. Often the prior relationship did not predetermine the role a government would play in Amnesty's diplomatic network. Amnesty's UN representative recalled that in the mid-1970s the Libyan Ambassador to the UN "took us around [the General Assembly] and introduced us to a number of the Arab diplomats and said 'I advise you to know these people – you may need them some day!'"[257] Similarly, Benenson referenced being snubbed by the United States for diplomatic assistance early on: "The U.S. State Department was extremely suspicious. It was only when they learned that I was a Catholic that they would pursue the conversation at all."[258]

Amnesty used the diplomatic network in four ways. First, diplomatic relations were useful for obtaining visas and accessing government officials. For its report on Israel in 1969, Amnesty worked with the Arab League to secure access to Jordan.[259] The Swedish Ambassador to the Soviet Union helped obtain access to Indonesia in 1969.[260] For a mission to Mexico in 1970, Amnesty secured assistance from the Mexican Ambassador to the United States.[261] The Polish Ambassador to Norway was used for securing a mission to Poland in 1970.[262] Amnesty used the Soviet Ambassador to Switzerland to help arrange a Scandinavian parliamentary delegation in early 1970.[263] Amnesty met repeatedly with the Soviet Ambassador to Britain for setting up government talks in Moscow throughout summer 1971.[264] At the same time, Amnesty negotiated access to South Vietnam with their Ambassador in Germany.[265] The British Ambassador to Turkey helped fast-track visas in 1971.[266]

Second, ambassadors also acted as intermediaries for passing information. At the height of the crisis resulting from the Israel report in 1970, Amnesty negotiated with the Israeli Ambassador to the UN at side events.[267] The British Ambassador to Brazil would discuss allegations of genocide with Amnesty.[268] The Mexican Ambassador in the United States indicated a favorable time to approach the newly elected government for releasing prisoners.[269] The Brazilian Ambassador to Britain suggested that June would be better than March for applying for a mission in 1971.[270] The same ambassador warned that some uncoordinated national section activity in Brazil interfered with Amnesty's

---

[257]　MacBride interview, AI 987.
[258]　Benenson interview, AI 983.
[259]　AI 412: 66–67.
[260]　AI 412: 88.
[261]　AI 413: 3.
[262]　AI 413: 5.
[263]　AI 412: 93.
[264]　AI 413: 30.
[265]　AI 413: 35.
[266]　AI 413: 74.
[267]　AI 412: 93.
[268]　AI 413: 4.
[269]　AI 413: 12.
[270]　AI 413: 29–30.

official mission.[271] The Turkish Ambassador to Britain said Amnesty's mission report was outdated and gave an additional list of ten nonviolent torture cases in early 1973.[272] MacBride discussed his visit to North Vietnam with the South Vietnamese Ambassador to Britain in 1972.[273]

MacBride's stature made him especially useful as an Amnesty go-between in his unofficial capacity. When attending a UN seminar on Human Rights in Developing Africa at Dakar in February 1966, MacBride agreed that "although he could not be an official delegate of AI he could have informal discussions with Ministers."[274] Later that year, MacBride visited Malawi to discuss the situation of political prisoners with the Attorney-General, who admitted there were at least 500. MacBride "felt that most effective action could be taken in London and said that he would see the Head of the Malawi Department at the Commonwealth Relations Office to see what could be done."[275] MacBride was also the key to Amnesty's relationship with the Soviet Union, as I detail later in the chapter.

Third, Amnesty's diplomatic network helped with research missions on the ground. Amnesty's diplomatic back channels were instrumental for the success of the Greek case. The mission was important as it came right after Amnesty's scandals and Benenson's resignation. In 1967, as Amnesty lobbied against Greece in the Council of Europe, it sent a high-level Italian delegate who described "the extremely unco-operative attitude he had met with in Athens, both from Ministers and from contacts given to him by the International Secretariat."[276] Amnesty then turned to friendly governments as emissaries. It sent a group of eleven Scandinavian parliamentarians from Denmark, Sweden, Norway, and Finland to Greece. Unlike Amnesty's delegate, the parliamentarians "were granted interviews with all the chief Ministers in Athens. They were also allowed to visit Andreas Papandreou and a prison in Athens where 12 men were held, six of them former Centre Union deputies. They were allowed to talk to these prisoners for more than two hours."[277] In January 1968, Amnesty released a torture report, "Situation in Greece." Following the parliamentarians, Amnesty was able to send Anthony Marreco on an official mission to Greece, after which the IEC perceived Amnesty "had reaffirmed its position and regained public confidence."[278] A second report followed in March, alleging "not only that torture had occurred, but also that it had been official policy."[279] In November, Amnesty met with the Human Rights Commission at the Council of Europe to provide additional reporting from Marreco's missions. Amnesty considered "what could happen in the event that despite

[271]   AI 413: 36.
[272]   AI 414: 15.
[273]   AI 413: 97.
[274]   AI 412: 30.
[275]   AI 412: 32–33.
[276]   AI 412: 47–48.
[277]   AI 412: 47–48.
[278]   AI 412: 52.
[279]   Clark 2001: 41.

the overwhelming evidence of torture in Greece, the Council of Ministers decided to take no action."[280] It agreed to "have discussions with prominent parliamentarians likely to participate in the debates in January 1969." As the lobbying intensified, Greece denied Amnesty access in summer 1969.[281] However, by the end of the year, Greece withdrew from the Council of Europe under massive pressure, marking a momentous victory for Amnesty and its diplomatic network.

Finally, the diplomatic networks also aided Amnesty's lobbying in intergovernmental forums. Regarding the 1984 UN Convention against Torture, Ann Clark details how Amnesty worked with governments as an "active participant in the norm-drafting process."[282] Amnesty provided information to friendly governments at the UN Commission on Human Rights.[283] New data show Amnesty also pumped government contacts for information. At the Commission, Amnesty's representative Nigel Rodley had access to confidential working groups where NGOs were officially excluded. In a report on the 1976 meeting of the UN Sub-Commission on Prevention of Discrimination and Protection of Minorities, Rodley knew that the Sub-Commission had forwarded the cases of Bolivia, Equatorial Guinea, Malawi, Uganda, South Korea, and Sri Lanka to the Commission. He elaborated:

> The communications relating to South Korea and Sri Lanka were from AI reports on these countries. The failure of the working group to take up Brazil while at the same time taking up the situation in Sri Lanka can only be described as extraordinary. In the end the full sub-commission decided to hold Sri Lanka back for a year while forwarding the other cases.[284]

Knowing that Brazil was not recommended, Rodley drew special attention to it at the general meeting. Crucially, Rodley "was able to break precedent by naming specific countries since [he] was able to associate that had already been made by individual members of the sub-commission. This opened the way for other NGOs to do the same thing."[285] Moreover, with the help of the Swedish Ambassador, Rodley succeeded in pushing for a new working group of five members to examine the inadequate documentation received by the Sub-Commission from the Commission.[286]

As Amnesty established itself as a government watchdog, its diplomatic network simultaneously required nurturing governmental relations through *shadow hybridity*. Amnesty did not shy away from exerting pressure against its diplomatic network. For instance, the IEC asked all national sections to contact their Brazilian ambassadors after the publication of the Brazil Torture Report in late 1972[287] and to approach American

[280] AI 412: 66.
[281] AI 412: 86.
[282] Clark 2001: 35.
[283] Martens 2006: 381.
[284] AI 424: 3.
[285] AI 424: 3.
[286] AI 424: 4.
[287] AI 413: 137.

ambassadors to discuss prisoners before the Paris Peace Accord on Vietnam.[288] Thus, in using governments for access while also shaming them, Amnesty was practicing the art of foreign relations. In 1977, Amnesty would describe these functions as "External Affairs."[289]

Bargaining for Access and Reforms in Closed Countries

Amnesty's external affairs strategy with closed countries consisted of making private bargains for access or reforms. After Amnesty had concluded a mission in a country, it presented the government with an opportunity to make reforms before Amnesty went public with its findings. Amnesty would refer to these as "high-level" governmental missions as opposed to "low-level" research or trial observation missions.[290] Scholars have noted that Amnesty "worked rather silently, if persistently, prodding repressive governments with letter writing, diplomatic contacts, and occasional publications."[291] This section makes explicit that the "silent" work was conducted quite frequently in high-level talks. Such talks were part of Amnesty's strategy from the beginning, as is evident from how Amnesty secured the release of its first Prisoner of Conscience:

> Perhaps with an eye to publicity we selected Archbishop Beran, later Cardinal, who had for eight years been imprisoned away from his archdiocese at Prague. An Irish Catholic seemed as a good a choice as we could find for the mission, and who else was available and willing but Sean MacBride himself. Although he came back with a reasonably favourable published report on the situation of Catholics in Czecho-Slovakia, this was presumably the price he had to pay for securing a loosening of the Archbishop's bonds.[292]

MacBride returned with "a reasonably favorable published report" as "a price he had to pay" for the release. Over the years, the IEC would regularly debate what and how much to publicize from its missions with an eye toward its progress in government relations.

Amnesty had four strategic uses of publicity in closed countries. First, Amnesty wielded international publicity as a weapon for continued country access. In 1965, a Spain and Portugal mission report noted that

> although the Spanish Government appeared to be on unusually good terms with the AMNESTY movement, they were responsible for a very irate letter being recently sent to Sean MacBride in his capacity as Secretary-General of the International Commission of Jurists; on the other hand, the Portuguese are on good terms with the International Commission, but are Anti-AMNESTY to the extent of not allowing our last two delegates to leave the airport at Lisbon. However, since then AMNESTY sent an investigator "incognito."

[288]   AI 414: 13.
[289]   AI 418: 146.
[290]   AI 412: 75–78.
[291]   Eckel 2013: 196.
[292]   Benenson interview, AI 982.

It was generally thought that Spain was improving; and that things there were nothing like so bad as had been so in recent years. . . . It was decided that the report on Portugal should be sent to Sir Ronald Russell of the Council of Europe. It was decided that every effort should be made to publicise and criticize recent arrests in Portugal. It was decided that Spain should not be commented upon, until after an effort had been made to influence the Portuguese government.[293]

The contrast between Amnesty's strategy toward Spain and Portugal in publicizing its human rights findings is directly related to its differing governmental relations. As already mentioned, Portugal denied access to Amnesty and was being uncooperative, whereas Spain had been more open in accepting Amnesty field agents and was on "unusually good terms." Amnesty decided to send the Portugal report to the Council of Europe and did not publicly comment on Spain at the time or refer it to the Council.

Amnesty's relation with Libya is another instance of trading publicity for access in closed countries. Amnesty tried getting access to President Gaddafi in a high-level mission in 1976 to discuss recent amendments to the Penal Code. Amnesty had no trouble securing a visa through the Libyan Ambassador in London. But once Amnesty's field agents landed in Tripoli, the Legal Department said only Gaddafi could approve prison visits and that a meeting would not happen. Over the next several days, Amnesty's agents worked with contacts in the Libyan Ministry of Foreign Affairs to lobby different government officials.[294] They finally succeeded. The agents remarked that although it took them "five days to get a meeting with the President, we should consider ourselves lucky: the Dutch Ambassador to Egypt, accredited to Libya, spent two weeks in a hotel in Tripoli waiting to present his credentials, before leaving in disgust."[295] In the meeting it became clear that "Gaddafi appeared to have very little real understanding of what AI is all about."[296] Still, he allowed Amnesty to visit prisons. The IEC agreed with the agents' recommendation to not publish the mission report.[297]

Second, Amnesty also used publicity to make side bargains with closed countries for private reforms. Amnesty had maintained ongoing relations with Iran since the late-1960s. In a March 1969 mission, the IEC

agreed that the report should be treated confidentially until the end of April by which time, it was felt that the Iranian authorities would have had an adequate opportunity for carrying out the reforms and gestures of leniency which [Amnesty's field agent] had requested. If there were no response by the end of April, a public statement would be made by the International Secretariat and National Sections would be encouraged to campaign on the basis of the report.[298]

---

[293] AI 412: 25–26.
[294] AI 425: 80.
[295] AI 425: 80.
[296] AI 425: 80.
[297] AI 425: 82.
[298] AI 412: 76.

The Shah promised amendments to the Penal Code to limit the power of military courts in political trials and of SAVAK (secret police) during pre-trial interrogations. In November, the IEC considered these reforms and

> agreed that there was need for clarification and substantiation of the intentions of the Shah on these two points. The IEC noted that an amnesty had been announced for Human Rights Day, and it was agreed to await the 10th December before publishing the Iran report in a revised form. If there were a substantial number of Amnesty adopted prisoners released a further decision would be taken regarding publication.[299]

These side bargains would often delay reports by one or two years as negotiations continued.

Amnesty's external relations with the Soviet Union for private reforms took many years to establish. Amnesty's first low-level mission to seek out research contacts was in 1969.[300] Then, it organized a Scandinavian parliamentary delegation in 1970 "to try to obtain some form of recognition by the USSR of the function and value of Amnesty International and to recognise in general the role of non-governmental organisations."[301] The next phase occurred when MacBride led a delegation to Moscow during the World Congress of Peace Forces in October 1973 for "opening a regular dialogue between Amnesty and the USSR."[302] The visit received international attention because of the mention of human rights at the conference.[303] However, the press did not report that MacBride met the Soviet Minister of Justice and the Procurator General.[304] The Amnesty delegation concluded that "the Soviet authorities are prepared to continue discussions with Amnesty. The Chairman stressed that any accusations against the Soviet authorities should always be well-founded and backed by concrete evidence, although it was clear that Amnesty work in the Soviet Union must continue as before."[305] The IEC also agreed that maintaining a Soviet connection would positively "influence the attitude of other Eastern European countries and could form the basis for new approaches to Czechoslovakia and East Germany in particular." Moreover, Amnesty decided its report on Soviet psychiatric hospitals should not "be for immediate release."[306] The report would not be published until two years later when the Soviet authorities detained Amnesty's Soviet group members in 1975.

Third, Amnesty's bargains for reforms invoked different levels of international publicity, ranging from publishing a report publicly to sharing findings privately. In March 1969, Amnesty was ready to release the previously mentioned report on Israeli torture. After high-level talks, Amnesty "agreed that the Israeli Government should be

[299] AI 412: 92.
[300] AI 412: 75–78.
[301] AI 412: 93.
[302] AI 414: 62.
[303] Smith 1973.
[304] AI 414: 113.
[305] AI 414: 122.
[306] AI 414: 124; AI 415: 73–74.

asked to set up a commission to investigate allegations of ill-treatment of Arabs during the period of interrogation and immediately after arrest. If no favourable response were received by the end of April, from the Israeli authorities, the reports on Israel and the Middle East would be published."[307] The report remained unpublished. In the September 1969 IEC meeting, Amnesty discussed the Israeli government's request for Amnesty not to "give evidence to the special UN Committee making a study of the treatment of Arab prisoners by the Israeli authorities."[308] Amnesty decided it would give evidence to the UN but also agreed "not to publish the report at the present stage."[309] This compromise set the stage for Israel banning Amnesty in December 1969, when word of Amnesty's UN meeting leaked. Again, Amnesty withheld release of the Israel report for a full year as it pursued back channel talks with the Israeli government.

Finally, Amnesty's high-level missions led to pragmatic trade-offs[310] for building the human rights movement. In 1975, Amnesty had identified expanding National Sections in right-wing dictatorships as a high priority. In 1976, a year after General Franco's death, Amnesty's Spanish mission considered the dangers of creating a National Committee that was not accepted by the new government:

> A lot of the effectiveness of AI's work in Spain depends on the prestige of the organization within the legal and governmental bodies. If for example our application was turned down the consequences would be grave for our work. It would mean that in some eyes we were not a powerful enough body to obtain acceptance and in others that there were positive valid reasons for returning our application, i.e. political views of members. It is most important that we retain such goodwill as exists within the government as without it we could easily have certain privileges withdrawn.[311]

When given the opportunity to expand its official presence in a post-Franco Spain that still carried out brutal tactics of the previous regime, Amnesty decided against authorizing establishing a group that would compromise its governmental relations.

By the mid-1970s, more Amnesty missions were approved for high-level government talks than for research or the observation of trials. In April 1975, half of the four proposed missions and 60 percent of the seventeen pending missions were for government talks.[312] In July 1975, all three proposed missions were for high-level talks.[313] By the end of the year, 83 percent of the twelve proposed missions were for high-level talks.[314] The Research Department drew attention to this trend, pointing out in August 1976 that "very few IEC-approved missions in the past year had been designated specifically and solely as research missions. ... They were in strong agreement that research missions are

[307]   AI 412: 77.
[308]   AI 412: 84–85.
[309]   AI 412: 84–85.
[310]   Avant 2004.
[311]   AI 425: 51.
[312]   AI 416: 60.
[313]   AI 416: 117.
[314]   AI 416: 188.

important to the quality of AI research."[315] As a result, at the following IEC meeting, none of the four proposed missions were for government talks, but 55 percent of the twenty pending missions still were.[316] A year later, 56 percent of the pending eighteen missions were for government talks.[317]

By fielding so many high-level missions, a large majority of the IEC's time was spent on external relations. In recognition of this, the IEC officially created a subcommittee on "government relations" in 1975, which was renamed "strategy" in 1976. The aim of the subcommittee was to write strategy papers on Amnesty's dealings with governments to streamline IEC discussions. For instance, an Iraq strategy paper in April 1976 recommended:

> Indirect pressure should be asserted on Iraq through other Arab governments (such as Egypt, Saudi Arabia), European governments (such as France and Germany), non-governmental bodies, both Arab Muslim and European.
>
> It was AGREED that Amnesty International's approaches to governments etc., on behalf of Iraq should not be publicized.
>
> It was AGREED to increase the input of information on AI into the Middle East press; it was proposed that the South Yemeni Briefing Paper should be translated into Arabic and widely distributed throughout the Middle East.
>
> The need for preserving the confidentiality of the Iraq strategy paper was NOTED, and it was AGREED that a separate paper be prepared for circulating to national sections.[318]

The Iraq strategy encapsulates many of Amnesty's *shadow hybridity* covered so far: using an informal governmental network of friendly and unfriendly governments, not publicizing its relations with governments, feeding information to the press, and keeping the National Sections at bay by circulating a less confidential version of the strategy paper. In April 1977, the IEC requested the secretariat "to prepare guidelines on the problem of AI having a uniform policy in relation with all governments including national sections' relations with their own and other governments."[319] The guidelines never materialized as the 1970s came to an end.

Politics of Mistrust in Realizing Human Rights

In 1975, Amnesty reflected on its beginnings and future directions, articulating some basic principles for the coming decades. The first principle claimed Amnesty as the "sum total of its members," while the second principle asserted its polity-building: "Amnesty International functions in defence of fundamental human rights which have been declared to be universal values and which ultimately can be guaranteed only if

---

[315] AI 424: 50–51.
[316] AI 424: 105–106.
[317] AI 425: 13.
[318] AI 417: 63.
[319] AI 418: 68.

they are defended by the world community."[320] I have argued that we should interpret Amnesty's mandate as organizing many transnational publics into a global polity for the protection of universal human rights. Following Dewey, I regard this as a sovereign function much like waging war or regulating commerce. As such, Amnesty fits one narrative of *Idealized Sovereignty* by articulating and promoting an absolutist universal ideology that is fundamental to the strength of a worldwide polity. Many governments share and support Amnesty's vision of globalizing human rights. Others have begrudgingly accepted the legitimacy costs to their sovereign authority from these developments. In fact, Amnesty's innovation is in helping states achieve their own ideals of international politics as enshrined in the post-World War II institutions.

Where others view Amnesty's movement as a challenge to *Idealized Sovereignty*, the theoretical framework presented here pivots to viewing Amnesty's accomplishment as part of the overall arc of sovereign competence. In fact, Amnesty did not deliberate the consequences of its actions for *Idealized Sovereignty*. The only mention of sovereignty in the entirety of the IEC meeting minutes during its first twenty-five years comes from a 1975 discussion on the strategy of government relations in Eastern Europe where Amnesty acknowledges national variations in sovereignty: "Efforts must be made to make an approach in a way acceptable to the government concerned, and the best method of doing this would be to seek advice from the officials involved, thus vitiating any accusation of meddling in the internal affairs of the country and offending their concept of national sovereignty."[321] Clearly, governments around the world perceived international human rights as interfering in domestic affairs, thus using the shield of *Idealized Sovereignty* for rejection or noncompliance with emerging norms. But Amnesty's polity-building helped create an additional expectation to guarantee universal rights as part of the sovereign compact, five decades before the *Responsibility to Protect* doctrine made the same argument. In short, Amnesty expanded the contents of *Idealized Sovereignty*. Authority claims in *Idealized Sovereignty* aim to settle not just who is responsible for protecting citizens but also for what. Amnesty's polity-building introduced the expectation of realizing universal rights as part of the sovereign compact.

Moreover, just as the previous cases of sovereign competence occurred through diverse performances in *Lived Sovereignty*, Amnesty too succeeded only because of its hybridity. IR scholarship on transnational policy networks and communities has noted the informal linkages between state and nonstate actors "based on shared or pooled authority and repeated, enduring, and reciprocal relationships among likeminded actors in different national jurisdictions."[322] Since the end of the Cold War, "technological change, economic openness, and demands for transnational political collaboration have created conditions for network proliferation in recent decades," leading to "new forms of governance in international relations, distinct

---

[320] AI 416: 132.
[321] AI 416: 166–167.
[322] Keck and Sikkink 1998; Slaughter 2004; Mattli and Woods 2009: 19–20; Avant and Westerwinter 2016.

from more familiar types of intergovernmental collaboration."[323] Amnesty's *shadow hybridity* fits this understanding of informal governance. However, transnational policy networks do not require denying or hiding government collaborations, a feature that is central to *shadow hybridity*. From its accidental founding as an organization to its establishment as a household name and Nobel laureate, Amnesty relied on shadow deals with friendly and unfriendly governments to do its most basic operations. These were dangerous liaisons because Amnesty, more than any other case covered in this book, based its sovereign competence on moral purity. As such, the consequences of *shadow hybridity* for engendering mistrust and creating backlash toward the human rights polity were high.

Amnesty did not typically reflect on its growing sovereign competence. A rare exception was in an exchange of internal memos in the 1976 government relations subcommittee. Researcher Margo Picken asked about the appropriateness of Amnesty inviting Cuba to take part in discussions related to torture at the UN:

> Is it our place to "invite" Cuba to take part in CAT at the UN?
> I think it should always be borne in mind that the UN in an intergovernmental body and that AI is not a government. We have achieved what we wanted at the UN i.e. torture has been taken up and over by certain governments. We can continue to lobby governments to ensure that momentum on torture is maintained and to press more governments to be active and make speeches condemning torture but I cannot see how AI as an NGO can cooperate, coordinate, or collaborate. We have nothing to give nor anything to bargain with. We are definite outsiders in the UN game at intergovernmental level.
> Governments belong to the same family; they coordinate their activities and cooperate on the question of torture. They 'trust' each other to a certain extent. . . . They cooperate with us. We do not cooperate with them.
> I don't think it is our place either to sit in judgement, or to intervene in this highly complex and highly political game. . . . We are very vulnerable and risk getting badly burnt by involving ourselves in intergovernmental processes which are too complex for us to handle.[324]

When Picken downplays Amnesty's leverage – "we have nothing to give nor anything to bargain with" – she is referring to intergovernmental forums like the UN. Picken perceived these as the appropriate venues for governments that "belong to the same family," in a classic use of *Idealized Sovereignty* to preserve sovereign privileges for states. But just earlier in the year, Nigel Rodley had reported on Amnesty's success at the UN Commission on Human Rights by breaking a critical procedural rule that prohibited calling out specific countries in addition to creating a new working group. Picken's statement is actually more reflective of the anxiety of offending governments since Amnesty has complicated governmental relations and "risk[s] getting badly burnt." In short, Picken's

[323] Kahler 2009: 1, 3.
[324] AI 424: 18–19.

underlying concern was about losing moral purity seen as necessary for Amnesty's sovereign competence in *Lived Sovereignty*.

Amnesty Chairman Thomas Hammarberg affirms this interpretation when responding to Picken:

> We sometimes have a tendency to look up ourselves as a government. We certainly do not have that role, neither in UN nor anywhere else.
>
> More generally, I think we have to be careful in our UN lobby work not to be seen as annex to some governments, or they to us.
>
> We should act as – and be seen to act as – an international pressure group that wants as much as possible to be done against torture, etc. It is not up to us to make the tactical decisions, when and how to propose things. I think we have to keep ourselves at some distance on that point. Otherwise we risk being drawn into situations where it would be difficult to stay "clean."[325]

Hammarberg's response touches on the two central facets of Amnesty's participation in *shadow hybridity*. First, Amnesty has a "tendency to look up [itself] as a government." As it developed external relations with governments to organize a global polity, Amnesty's sovereign competence was not completely lost on its executives. Second, Amnesty must be careful to not be seen this way to maintain its image as "an international pressure group" in order to "stay clean." Amnesty must then carefully erase traces of governmental ties and support, conducting some of its most important dealings in the shadows.

The balancing act between competence and purity for realizing human rights and humanitarian governance has only become more acute since the end of the Cold War.[326] One recent way to maintain moral purity in human rights and humanitarian polities is through imposing standards of INGO accountability where "an NGO holds itself openly responsible for what it believes, what it does and what it does not do in a way which shows it involving all concerned parties and actively responding to what it learns."[327] In 2006, Amnesty along with Greenpeace, Oxfam, and Save the Children announced the INGO Accountability Charter, since known as "Accountable Now." Amnesty Secretary-General Irene Khan argued:

> The legitimacy of international NGOs to act is based on universally-recognised freedoms of speech, assembly and association on the trust people place upon us, and on the values we seek to promote. NGOs are playing an increasingly prominent role in setting the agenda in today's globalised world. This places a clear responsibility on us to act with transparency and accountability. The Accountability Charter clearly shows that NGOs are willing to adhere to a code of conduct, lead by example, and encourage others to follow.[328]

[325] AI 424: 17.
[326] Hielscher et al. 2017.
[327] Slim 2002: 10.
[328] *Scoop Independent News* 2006.

Retaining legitimacy through public trust thus remains important to Amnesty's success. Two sections of the Charter deal with government relations. First, on independence: "We aim to be both politically and financially independent. Our governance, programmes and policies will be non-partisan, independent of specific governments, political parties and the business sector." Second, on advocacy: "We will ensure that our advocacy is consistent with our mission, grounded in our work and advances defined public interests. We will have clear processes for adopting public policy positions (including for partners where appropriate), explicit ethical policies that guide choices of advocacy strategy, and ways of identifying and managing potential conflicts of interest among various stakeholders."

CONCLUSION

Amnesty International's chief sovereign accomplishment should be seen as organizing a global human rights polity from disparate transnational publics in *Lived Sovereignty*. However, shadow relations with governments in its first two decades threatened to derail the moral purity that undergirds the protection of human rights in *Idealized Sovereignty*. Successfully navigating *shadow hybridity* has thus been a central yet understudied feature of Amnesty. To some readers it may be jarring to present a human rights organization to illustrate *shadow hybridity* in a book that also includes Blackwater where we might expect it more. But in showing that shadow relations persist even where we least expect them, namely, in a government watchdog that depends on government independence for claiming its authority, the chapter underscores that the framework of public/private hybridity applies more generally than the obvious candidates. As such, I do not take a normative stance on whether Amnesty's *shadow hybridity* is inappropriate. My aim is to contextualize the difficult choices Amnesty has made to become the world's leading INGO. Even high-profile crises early in the organization's history did not deter Amnesty from continuing with its shadow relations. Amnesty thus helps us see that hybrid relations endure even when the stakes are very high, exemplifying the pervasiveness of hybrid sovereignty in global politics.

7

Conclusions on Power and Responsibility in Hybrid Sovereignty

To engage with the public and private in contemporary global affairs is to open up some of the most vexing and yet urgent questions of modern politics.[1]

This book's central claim is that global sovereign power is constituted by public/private hybridity in *Lived Sovereignty*, while sovereign authority is recognized as indivisibly public in *Idealized Sovereignty*. In relations of hybrid sovereignty, the lived realities of public/private hybridity are in tension with the idealized imperatives of determining what is public versus private. Public/private hybridity makes an appearance in some of the most profound world historical moments: the spread of the British empire, the founding of America, the establishment of free trade, the realization of global human rights, and the wars of the twenty-first century. In these contexts, public/private hybridity takes on different characteristics of *contractual*, *institutional*, and *shadow* forms based on the formalization and publicization of public/private relations. Thus, the book presents sovereignty as hybrid in two related arguments: sovereignty is both *Idealized* and *Lived*; and public/private hybridity appears in different incarnations within *Lived Sovereignty*.

As I write this, the COVID-19 pandemic has transformed the world. I cannot help but view some of the changes through this book's dynamics. For instance, in April 2020, Donald Trump invoked *Idealized Sovereignty* when insisting that he has ultimate control over when American states may end their lockdowns: "When somebody is the president of the United States, the authority is total."[2] Constitutional lawyers quickly disabused him of this notion. The Governor of Washington State, Jay Inslee, retorted: "No one with even the most basic understanding in our middle schools thinks that we have a royalty situation." Then, governors accused the Trump administration of not distributing stockpiles of personal protective equipment, like masks and ventilators, leading states to compete for limited supplies and create regional coalitions.[3] We may see Trump's statement and

---

[1] Abrahamsen and Williams 2014: 250–251.
[2] Baker and Haberman 2020.
[3] Linton 2020.

the retaliatory response as the continued relevance of *Idealized Sovereignty* for sovereign grandstanding.

Meanwhile, in *Lived Sovereignty*, Apple and Google announced a new software tool for public health departments for contact tracing via cell phones.[4] In response to previous backlash, the technology giants proposed a "privacy preserving" model that does not store location data. These terms, however, have made it more difficult for governments to adopt the tool. A North Dakota official asked: "'Do we try to do this on our own? Or do we just bow to the demands of Apple and Google?'" If North Dakota follows the companies' rules, it would have to build a new app. If the state opts out of the tech giants' system, it won't be able to reach as many smartphone users who may be at risk of the virus."[5] Ninety-seven percent of the world's smartphones run on Apple and Google's systems, which makes their governance initiatives crucial for effective mobile contact tracing. However, even seemingly inclusive rulemaking, in this case privacy-preserving, may be seen as exclusionary based on who is making the rules and their structural power in hybrid arrangements.

In this book's Introduction, I quoted from philosopher John Dewey that "the moment we utter the words 'The State' a score of intellectual ghosts rise to obscure our vision."[6] *Hybrid Sovereignty in World Politics* vanquishes some ghosts to clarify how sovereign power operates in hybrid relations that conflict with indivisible sovereign authority. In these concluding thoughts, I address how the book's analysis reconsiders sovereign power in IR and speculate on a structural model of responsibility that takes hybrid sovereignty seriously.

RECONSIDERING SOVEREIGN POWER

The study reconsiders sovereign power in world politics in four ways. First, it broadens IR's understanding of sovereign authority and sovereign power to clarify their relational nature. Sovereign authority is particularly important for international politics, especially in debates on whether certain actions bear favorably on a state's sovereignty. Sovereign power is featured in some guise in all facets of politics – theorizing what it is and its history, comparing its features across different national contexts, highlighting its different manifestations in American politics, or exploring the international dimension of projecting sovereign power abroad. Yet, the relationship between sovereign authority and power is far from self-evident. Tracing hybrid relations allows a rare glimpse into the relationship as the indivisible political fiction underlying sovereign authority in *Idealized Sovereignty* comes up against the divisible and diverse process of producing sovereign power in *Lived Sovereignty*, and vice versa.

---

[4]   Nicas and Wakabayashi 2020.
[5]   Bond 2020.
[6]   Dewey 1927: 8–9.

Second, the book foregrounds public/private hybridity as a vital source for exercising sovereign power. I take on a foundational myth in IR, which associates public with sovereign and private with nonsovereign. In the foundational myth, the "tidy public/private distinction splits up the hybrid obscuring its enmeshment, elusiveness, and power."[7] This book introduced a new framework of sovereign politics that focused on the hybridity between public and private. I did so rhetorically by placing "public/private" together rather than apart; I did so theoretically by arguing we can only know about public/private by adjudicating their entanglements; and I did so empirically by tracing differing public/private hybrid relations in *contractual, institutional,* and *shadow* configurations. The ideal-types of public/private hybridity underscore that most sovereign contests happen in relational hybridity, where it becomes difficult to imagine where one begins and the other ends. Hybridity thus zooms in on the production of sovereign statehood to show multitudes within what appears to be a unity. The multitudes are not simply "sub-state" groups or pre-social individuals, traditionally conceived as the origins of state preferences, but rather reflect hybrids across space and time. These multitudes have a strong bearing on what sovereign power is and does in the world.

Third, public/private hybridity also reflects different kinds of power relations. In global governance, Michael Barnett and Bud Duvall outline four kinds of power: compulsory power, which "exists in the direct control of one actor over the conditions of existence and/or the actions of another"; institutional power, or "actors' indirect control over the conditions of action of socially distant others"; structural power, which "operates as the constitutive relations of a direct and specific – hence, mutually constituting – kind"; and productive power, that "works through diffuse constitutive relations to produce the situated social capacities of actors."[8] The ideal-types of public/private hybridity cut across these power conceptions. *Contractual hybridity* in Blackwater may produce institutional power through an indirect influence on how the American bureaucracy defines its inherent governing functions. *Institutional hybridity* in the International Chamber of Commerce may work through compulsory power in its arbitration directly exerting control over the economic policies of governments. *Shadow hybridity* in Amnesty International may reflect productive power by empowering the social capacities of various transnational publics through diffuse relations. But we may rearrange these linkages just as easily. In the English East India Company, *contractual hybridity* revealed structural power as its charter directly conferred monopoly status; *institutional hybridity* displayed compulsory power as its MP-Directors directly stewarded favorable parliamentary bills; *shadow hybridity* exposed institutional power in indirectly controlling European proxy wars in Asia. Hence, configurations of public/private hybridity accommodate a wide variety of power relations.

---

[7] Leander 2014: 198.
[8] Barnett and Duvall 2005: 13–21.

Finally, public/private hybridity has implications for other powerful hierarchies. As this chapter's epigraph argues, foregrounding the study of public/private reckons with one of the most enduring problems in modern politics. In IR, the distinction is "intrinsic to how we conceive of other highlighted distinctions in the discipline, between the national and the international, citizen and noncitizen, the particular and the universal. By studying the public/private distinction we are embarking on an intellectual journey into the very heart of the 'dividing discipline.'"[9] Distinctions ultimately reinforce hierarchy, such as by allocating "prestige to the first category – man, public, international – over the second – woman, private, domestic."[10] Hybridity has the potential to dismantle dualisms that rely on the "master distinction" of public/private, such as international/domestic, internal/external, and citizen/noncitizen. There is an anti-foundationalist ethos that runs through the book, which resonates with such destabilization. But there is also a parallel foundationalist strand that contextualizes why it is difficult to tear everything down, namely: what happens when there are limited alternatives to address sovereign irresponsibility outside the state/nonstate binary?

NEW CHALLENGES TO SOVEREIGN IRRESPONSIBILITY

The legitimation challenges of public/private hybridity in global governance has prompted "increasing concerns about the scope of this new type of influence and the opacity of the means involved."[11] For some, "the delegation of sovereign citizens' rights to non-elected bodies corresponds to a reinvention of corporatism: private interest groups and other private organisations are gaining public status and direct access to the political system in order to supposedly secure a stronger consensus."[12] Others are interested in *what* public/private hybridity privileges, such as "the reproduction of transnational capitalism by generating legal forms that both create and legitimate capitalist productive relations on a transnational scale."[13] Following the US Supreme Court *Citizens United* ruling, "while feminists rallied around the notion that the private is the public, large corporate interests were quietly insisting that the public is the private."[14]

The underlying concern is about assigning sovereign responsibility, typically conceived within state-centric discourses of *Idealized Sovereignty*: "The concept of state responsibility rests upon distinguishing acts and omissions that can be attributed to the state from those that cannot for it is axiomatic that 'private conduct is not in principle attributable to the state.'"[15] Changing notions of sovereign responsibility

[9] Lu 2006: 5.
[10] Edkins and Pin-Fat 1997: 291–293.
[11] Graz and Nölke 2008: 7.
[12] Graz and Nölke 2008: 22.
[13] Cutler 2010: 108.
[14] Cohen and O'Byrne 2013: 40.
[15] Chinkin 1999: 387–388.

in world politics, for instance the Responsibility to Protect,[16] are indexed to developments in *Idealized Sovereignty* that are themselves tuned to *Lived Sovereignty*. Indeed, different conceptions of what it means to be a "well regarded" sovereign state have informed changing practices of intervention.[17] While this book focuses only on the public indivisibility aspect of sovereignty, one may expand its insights to include other idealized features of sovereignty such as the nonintervention norm.[18] With regard to the Responsibility to Protect, it was not established a century ago that sovereign states have a dual obligation to (1) protect their citizens and (2) other citizens if their states fail to uphold the first obligation. The development of Responsibility to Protect reflects the underlying practices of state intervention in *Lived Sovereignty* in the post-Cold War period. But the status of the doctrine still remains controversial precisely because it unsettles a core feature of *Idealized Sovereignty*. Thus, sovereign responsibility is informed by *Idealized Sovereignty*, which itself is in dialogue with *Lived Sovereignty*.

However, changes between *Lived Sovereignty* and *Idealized Sovereignty* are not guaranteed to keep pace with each other. Not every change in how sovereign power lives also results in a change in the idealized representation of sovereign authority. *Idealized Sovereignty* is indeed variable; but its stickiness is also what makes international relations possible. The idealized treatments of assigning sovereign responsibility in law and politics lag behind actual practices of sovereign power. In this way, public/private hybridity opens the door for unchecked sovereign irresponsibility.

Thus, the lines drawn between state and nonstate in *Idealized Sovereignty* matter for managing any sovereign irresponsibility that may emerge from public/private hybridity in *Lived Sovereignty*. This book began with the harrowing account of a Blackwater civilian massacre in Iraq; harrowing because the firm seemed to get away with impunity on the new battlefield. Chapter 4 depicted more examples of sovereign irresponsibility through gaps in distributed accountability, which Blackwater and the United States exploited for advantage. Chapter 5 showed sovereign irresponsibility in the International Chamber of Commerce's insider rules to protect free capital at the expense of labor and the environment. Chapter 6 portrayed how even those with a stated mandate to promote sovereign responsibility, like Amnesty International, can fall prey to the shadow dynamics of producing sovereign power. While the book's empirics have showcased the different problems of public/ private hybridity for responsibility, none of the cases offers a clear blueprint for how to deal with irresponsibility in hybrid sovereignty.

Consider the latest instance of public/private hybridity in *Lived Sovereignty*: Facebook, the social platform whose 2.8 billion users amount to a *third* of the global population. Seventy percent of Americans use Facebook. On average, users spend forty-five minutes a day on it, which is the most on any activity outside sleep, work,

---

[16] Bellamy 2009.
[17] Finnemore 2004: 107.
[18] Krasner 1999: 20.

and family. Of the sixty-eight percent of Americans who report getting news from social media, their primary source is Facebook. In some countries, Facebook *is* the internet as it comes preinstalled on phones with free data and cannot be deleted. Facebook algorithms sort News Feed content visibility for cat memes and COVID-19 vaccines; they nudge users into joining groups to share knitting patterns and organize violent mobs to attack the US Capitol.[19] In 2020, Facebook launched a content oversight board, informally referred to as "Facebook Supreme Court." Facebook sets global parameters for information, speech, and privacy, among other governance issues. Journalists cover Facebook's Founder and Chief Executive Officer, Mark Zuckerberg, as they would state leaders: "Facebook is so colossal that [top executive changes] have the effect of creating powerful new characters on the global policy stage. Mr. Zuckerberg has elevated lieutenants to win over hostile territories – the Republican operative Joel Kaplan in Washington, and the former deputy prime minister of Britain, Sir Nicholas Clegg, in the eurozone."[20] The statement captures the dynamics of public/private hybridity as Facebook makes "global policy" through "lieutenants to win over hostile territories" by hiring former high-ranking politicians. (It should come as no surprise that analyzing the unique corporate politics of Facebook and Big Tech is next on my research agenda.)

When reports of fake news on Facebook influencing the 2016 US election first came out, Zuckerberg called it a "pretty crazy idea."[21] However, in 2017, it was revealed that the profiles of at least eighty-seven million Americans were compromised from a third-party application made by a voter profiling firm, Cambridge Analytica, which was employed by the Trump campaign. After the scandal broke, Zuckerberg went on a public apology tour around the American states, "sitting on tractors, attending church, bottle-feeding calves."[22] He also appeared in multiple Congressional testimonies in 2018, arguing in his opening statement at the US Senate:

> We didn't take a broad enough view of our responsibility, and that was a big mistake. And it was my mistake. And I'm sorry. I started Facebook, I run it, and I'm responsible for what happens here. So, now, we have to go through our – all of our relationship with people and make sure that we're taking a broad enough view of our responsibility. Across the board, we have a responsibility to not just build tools, but to make sure that they're used for good.[23]

Other than acknowledging that he did not "take a broad enough view of [Facebook's] responsibility," Zuckerberg's testimony was remarkable for two other reasons. First, at least forty-four senators were present, when by contrast only nine were in attendance when the CIA head George Tenet testified before the 9/11 Joint

[19] Srivastava 2021.
[20] Isaac, Frankel, and Kang 2020.
[21] Solon 2016.
[22] Isaac, Frankel, and Kang 2020.
[23] Zuckerberg 2018.

Intelligence Investigation. Second, while this was Zuckerberg's first public appearance, he made references to prior sustained communications between Facebook and American legislators on a vast array of issues, including tax reform, immigration, counterterrorism, and surveillance.

A week before appearing in front of Congress, Zuckerberg acknowledged in a rare interview: "In a lot of ways Facebook is more like a government than a traditional company."[24] When challenged on Facebook's lax content moderation, Zuckerberg countered, "it's just not clear to me that us sitting in an office here in California are best placed to always determine what the policies should be for people all around the world." And yet, Facebook does precisely that by algorithmically determining what information people have access to and how they engage with each other, "more like a government than a traditional company," without assuming any adjoining sovereign responsibility. As Shoshana Zuboff puts succinctly: "One man at Facebook who does not enjoy the legitimacy of the vote, democratic oversight, or the demands of shareholder governance exercises control over an increasingly universal means of social connection along with the information concealed in its networks."[25]

At stake in Facebook and the other cases in this book is this: How should we deal with sovereign irresponsibility in public/private hybridity? Hybridity like Facebook's fits uneasily into existing legal frameworks. The landmark 2011 United Nations *Guiding Principles on Business and Human Rights* assert that companies have obligations to conduct human rights due diligence and enact relevant remedies.[26] But the extent of due diligence and remedies remain underspecified. As referenced in Chapter 5, the *Guiding Principles* assume that "while corporations may be considered 'organs of society,' they are specialized economic organs, not democratic public interest institutions. As such, their responsibilities cannot and should not simply mirror the duties of states." However, there are new promising legal avenues to confront public/private hybridity, especially in national contexts. American legal scholars have challenged the state/nonstate distinction to articulate accountability modeled on "public utility regulation" that considers Big Tech companies vital public infrastructures providing "foundational goods and services on which the rest of society depend[s]" to impose special obligations for access and nondiscrimination.[27] Another "state action" approach proposes that companies that contract with the state could be deemed accountable for constitutional violations, as has been acknowledged for private physicians in prisons.[28] The European Union passed the General Data Protection Regulation (GDPR) in 2016 and started implementation in 2018, which has led to more disclosure in privacy policies and foregrounded opt-out messaging for tracking cookies across the web. In

---

[24] Klein 2018.
[25] Zuboff 2019: 127.
[26] Srivastava 2020b.
[27] Rahman 2018: 1639.
[28] Crawford and Schultz 2019: 1962.

2366

December 2020, the European Commission proposed a Digital Services Act, which would impose additional obligations on "digital gatekeepers," including liability for content moderation and forcing disclosures of how their algorithms work.

While the recent heightened scrutiny of Facebook and others in Big Tech have led to welcome advances in existing frameworks of legal responsibility, hybridity inevitably exceeds legal demarcations. Thus, we must turn to embedding sovereign responsibility into deeper structures beyond law.

STRUCTURAL RESPONSIBILITY AND HYBRID SUBJECTIVITY

The concept of "responsibilization" addresses what kinds of responsibility one is fit for. For instance, "by treating children as if they were fit to be held responsible, parents may help to induce in them the self-awareness and self-regulation such fitness requires."[29] Typically, theories of responsibilization rely on an "interactional model" which locates responsibility in the interactions between peoples or states and often adopts a liability logic (i.e. A caused B harm and is therefore liable). The interactional approach is largely associated with legal accountability meant to correct backward-looking violations.[30] While interactional accountability may be appropriate to address harms perpetrated between clearly identifiable agents equal under the law within a shared political system, such conditions are not always met in politics. Thus, political theorists have developed a "structural model" of responsibility that better addresses the diffuse and complex connections of injustice.[31]

The structural model foregrounds responsibilization on a different basis of politics.[32] In *Eichmann in Jerusalem*, Hannah Arendt wrestles with how an individual, Adolf Eichmann, whose job it was to oversee the transportation of many thousands of people to extermination camps during the Holocaust, did not view himself as morally responsible. Arendt controversially calls Eichmann an "unthinking person" whose banality (sniffling from a cold, speaking in trite aphorisms, disinterested in his own case, etc.) was a far cry from matching the depravity of his actions. Arendt claims that Eichmann lost the capacity to think critically, which removed him from moral calculations of good and bad. Arendt did not doubt that Eichmann was *guilty* in the individual sense. But she found it problematic to assign Eichmann self-conscious individual responsibility separate from his association with the German state. It was this distinction between guilt and responsibility that led Arendt to develop a collective form of responsibility where individuals like Eichmann are politically responsible for what governments do in their name or on their behalf.[33]

[29] List and Pettit 2011: 157.
[30] Vetterlein and Hansen-Magnusson 2020: 10.
[31] Arendt 1963, 1987; Erskine 2003, 2008; Young 2004, 2010; Lu 2017; Ackerly 2018.
[32] Srivastava and Muscott 2021 offer a recent overview for IR.
[33] Arendt 1987: 44.

Iris Marion Young builds on Arendt's notion of collective responsibility to extend the theorization beyond the state. Young begins with the observation of a global basic structure where "workers, owners and even the nation-states that have jurisdiction over them are embedded in transnational economic structures which connect individuals and institutions in faraway corporate boardrooms and retail outlets to them."[34] Young then conceptualizes a distinct political responsibility based on the global supply chain that applies to "relations between strangers in the same country or city as much as transnationally."[35] For Young, "the global structure provides the umbrella, and the supply chain provides the path" to discharge structural responsibility.[36] Extrapolating from Arendt and Young, the interactional model "assigns responsibility according to what particular agents have done," whereas in the structural model "individuals are responsible precisely for things they themselves have *not* done."[37] The structural approach "brings into question precisely the background conditions that ascriptions of blame or fault assume as normal."[38]

Two recent scholars have used the structural model for reconceptualizing responsibility in IR. Catherine Lu's *Justice and Reconciliation in World Politics* builds on Young to define social structures as "the normative, institutional, and material resources that together compose the background institutional rules and conditions that enable and constrain agency."[39] Lu specifies that "structural injustices place individuals and groups in social positions or socially produced categories that entail vulnerability to unjust treatment, structural indignity, or objectionable social conditions."[40] Importantly, Lu argues that no one "benefits" from structural injustice. Instead, "it is not because contemporary agents have benefited but because they have inherited burdens of historic injustice – in the form of contemporary structural injustices – that they have responsibilities."[41] In *Just Responsibility*, Brooke Ackerly also produces a structural theory of responsibility that is grounded in human rights activism. Ackerly theorizes "a theory of injustice that is attentive to the ways in which complex causality, exploitable power inequalities, and our shared social understandings (through shared epistemologies, normalization, and individual-level cognitive biases) create and conceal unjust power."[42] Ackerly terms this "injustice itself" as opposed to misfortune or tragedy, arguing that injustice is "a power relation, not merely the consequence of a power relation."[43] For Ackerly, structural "responsibility is the responsibility we have to look behind and beyond the visible crises and

---

[34] Young 2004: 374–375.
[35] Young 2004: 366.
[36] Ackerly 2018: 47.
[37] Young 2004: 375, emphasis original.
[38] Young 2004: 378.
[39] Lu 2017: 148.
[40] Lu 2017: 35.
[41] Lu 2017: 170.
[42] Ackerly 2018: 7.
[43] Ackerly 2018: 72.

consequences of injustice and to transform our political communities, bases of political accountability, and practices of political leadership so as to take on injustice itself together."[44]

The structural approaches to responsibilization offer two insights for sovereign irresponsibility in hybridity. First, public/private hybridity is emergent in social structures where public/private interactions are hard to disentangle for clear attributions of liability. We saw these entanglements play out in high-profile instances in the empirics, such as the 1684 *Sandys* case challenging the English East India Company's authority and the four trials following Blackwater's 2007 Nisour Square shootings. But the social structures of hybridity are also enmeshed within and make possible other irresponsible sovereign structures. There could be no British empire without the English East India Company. The apathetic brutality of the US occupation of Iraq is symbolized by its use of Blackwater. The UN Global Compact derives legitimacy through the International Chamber of Commerce's capitalist "know-how." Amnesty International's advocacy for human rights relies on a Eurocentric prioritization of some as more deserving of protection over others. Empire, Occupation, Capitalism, and Eurocentrism live on through hybridity. The book has catalogued these structural linkages so that future scholars may take public/private hybridity more seriously to explain and understand international politics.

Second, the structural model helps see how we are all implicated in injustice and therefore have a shared responsibility to stay engaged in sovereign politics. This book reveals some moments of backlash to hybrid sovereignty: the scrutiny of the Bengal famine and the reining in of English East India Company's wealth in the mid-1700s, the bureaucratic response to new American policy guidelines to define "inherently governmental functions," the activists occupying the International Chamber of Commerce's headquarters in 1998, and the fallout from Amnesty's cozy relations with the British government in the 1967 Aden scandal. In these instances, "the public" took on the challenges of distributed accountability, elitist networks, and undermined trust that accompanies the accomplishment of sovereign power through hybrid relations. In doing so, "the public" exercised its leverage for sovereign legitimation to drag allegedly "private" power into the sovereign sphere. Discussions of hybrid relations often centers around privatization framed as public functions being removed from politics.[45] We should instead think of hybrid relations as taking on political character. If we start from public/private hybridity, it is easier to create awareness and dialogues surrounding sovereign irresponsibility. Diversifying the terms beyond privatization expands political accountability and brings hybrid relations under more scrutiny.

Thus, assigning structural responsibility begins when we adopt a more extensive role as constituents rather than passive users or observers in public/private hybridity.

---

[44] Ackerly 2018: 30.
[45] Dickinson 2011.

In other words, it means challenging Zuckerberg to acknowledge that he is responsible for not just setting company policies, but also for sovereign governance. Moreover, it requires internalizing that Zuckerberg does not govern alone; instead he is part of sovereign politics that includes us, too. Hybrid sovereignty thus demands an accompanying "hybrid subjectivity." Sovereigns rely on consent from their subjects to be seen as legitimate. As sovereign governance takes on hybrid characteristics, sovereign subjects should adjust their expectations of who governs them. Developing a hybrid subjectivity requires being attuned to the public/private enmeshment propping up our sovereign structures. As the meaning of what is sovereign changes, subjects must reorient their sights on whom to legitimate and how to deal with illegitimate sovereigns. Better responsibilization of public/private is only possible when more of us are primed to identify hybridity undergirding how we organize violence, conduct commerce, and secure rights. This book's study of hybrid sovereignty ultimately serves to train the sovereign subject – that is, all of us – to make better sense of hybridity in our politics.

References

MAIN ARCHIVAL COLLECTION

From the International Institute of Social History, Amsterdam

Amnesty International. International Executive Committee Internal Documents, 1963–1977. AI 33 – AI 40; AI 408 – AI 410; AI 972 – AI 975.

Amnesty International. Meeting Minutes of the International Executive Committee, 1961–1986. AI 412 – AI 426.

Amnesty International. Minutes of the International Council Meetings, 1961–1986. AI 1 – AI 25.

Amnesty International. Oral History Project, 22 interviews, 1983–1984. AI 976 – AI 994.

Amnesty International. Oral History Project Documents and Correspondence, 1961–1967. AI 1000 – AI 1033.

Amnesty International. Reports and Decisions of the International Council Meetings, 1969–1983. AI 26 – AI 32.

From the British Library, London

English East India Company, Court of Directors Meeting Minutes, 1678–1795. IOR/B/35 – IOR/B/120.

English East India Company, Publications, 1670–1780. 102.k, 115.k, 279.a., 288.a., 522.I., 533.d., 1029.h., 1139.g., 2075, 8022.a., 8218.a.-b., 8223.d., c.40., c.112., c.161., c.192., cup.645, Rb.23., T 48416, T 39900, T 39915, T 39920–1, T48408, T 48410, V 7690, W 7019.

English East India Company, Tracts, 1621–1780. Tr.50, Tr.61, Tr.63–64, Tr.83–84, Tr.117, Tr.128–129, Tr.133, Tr.135, Tr.167, Tr.174, Tr.182, Tr.202, Tr.215, Tr.235, Tr.376, Tr.378, Tr.381, Tr.384, Tr.404, Tr.417, Tr.419–420, Tr.424, Tr.454, Tr.487, Tr.669, Tr.688, Tr.818, Tr.1151, Tr.1157.

From the International Chamber of Commerce Documentation Centre, Paris

International Chamber of Commerce, Meeting Minutes of the Council, 1920–1968. ICC 1923 – ICC 1966.

International Chamber of Commerce, Proceedings of the Organization Meetings in *Comptes Rendus Des Congres Vol. 1–6, 1920–1959*.

International Chamber of Commerce, Publications, 1919–1977. All volumes in Hf294, Hf5011, Hd59, Hd2755, xxk1082, xxk5216.

GOVERNMENT RECORDS

Commission on Government Procurement. 1972. "Report, Vol. 1."

Commission on Organization of the Executive Branch of the Government. 1955. "Business Enterprises."

Commission on Wartime Contracting. 2011. "Transforming Wartime Contracting: Controlling Costs, Reducing Risks," August 31.

Congressional Budget Office. 2008. "Contractors' Support of U.S. Operations in Iraq," August.

Congressional Research Service. 2007. "The Federal Activities Inventory Reform Act and Circular A-76," April.

Congressional Research Service. 2010. "Inherently Governmental Functions and Other Work Reserved for Performance by Federal Government Employees: The Obama Administration's Proposed Policy Letter," October.

Congressional Research Service. 2017. "Department of Defense Contractor and Troop Levels in Iraq and Afghanistan: 2007–2017," April.

Congressional Research Service. 2021. "Federal Workforce Statistics Sources: OPM and OMB," June 24.

Department of Defense. 2004. "Coalition Provisional Authority Order Number 17," June 27.

Department of Defense. 2006a. Memorandum: "Request to Contract for Private Security Companies in Iraq," January 10.

Department of Defense. 2006b. "Quadrennial Defense Review Report," February 6.

Department of Defense. 2009a. Instruction: "Private Security Contractors Operating in Contingency Operations," July 22.

Department of Defense. 2009b. "Report of the Office of the Special Inspector General for Iraq Reconstruction," October.

Department of Defense. 2016. Under Secretary of Defense for Acquisition, Tech, and Logistics: "Contractor Support of U.S. Operations in the USCENTCOM Area of Responsibility," April.

Department of Justice. 2019. "Report on the Investigation into Russian Interference in the 2016 Presidential Election," March.

Department of State. 2021. "Articles of Confederation, 1777–1781," Milestones in the History of U.S. Foreign Relations.

Fay, George. 2004. "AR 15–6 Investigation of the Abu Ghraib Detention Facility and 205th Military Intelligence Brigade," August.

House of Representatives Committee on Oversight and Government Reform. 2007a. "Hearing: Blackwater USA," October 2.

House of Representatives Committee on Oversight and Government Reform. 2007b. "More Dollars, Less Sense: Worsening Contracting Trends under the Bush Administration," June.

House of Representatives Subcommittee on Government Operations. 2016. "Hearing: Contracting Fairness," July 8.

International Committee for the Red Cross [ICRC]. 2008. "The Montreux Document: On Pertinent International Legal Obligations and Good Practices for States Related to Operations of Private Military and Security Companies during Armed Conflict."

Library of Congress. 2021. "Creating the United States," Road to the Constitution.

Office of Management and Budget [OMB]. 1966. "Circular A-76," March 3.

OMB. 1967. "Circular No. A-76, Revised."

OMB. 1979. "Acquiring of Commercial Industrial Products and Services Needed by the Government; Policy Revision."

OMB. 1983. "Circular A-76 (Revised)," August 4.

OMB. 1992. "Policy Letter on Inherently Governmental Functions," September 30.

OMB. 2003. "Circular A-76 (Revised)."

OMB. 2011. "Performance of Inherently Governmental and Critical Functions," September 12.

Richter, Jean. 2007. U.S. Department of State Memo: "Blackwater Performance in Iraq," August 31.

Rumsfeld, Donald. 2002. "Annual Report to the President and Congress."

Schakowsky, Jan. 2007. "Press Release: Schakowsky Condemns State Department for Covering Up Blackwater Shootings," October 2007.

Senate Armed Services Committee Hearing. 2004. "Treatment of Iraqi Prisoners," May 7.

United Nations [UN]. 1998a. Department of Public Information: "Business and the UN: An Overview," June.

UN. 1998. Press Release: "Secretary-General Confident That United States and United Nations Can Find Way to Mutually Supportive Relationship," October 16.

UN. 1999. Press Release: "Transcript of Press Conference by Secretary-General Kofi Annan and Leadership of International Chamber of Commerce at Geneva," July 5.

UN. 2009. Press Release: "UN to Sign Key Agreement with ICC World Chambers Federation," June 4.

United Nations Economic and Social Council [ECOSOC]. 1976. "TNCs: Issues Involved in the Formulation of a Code of Conduct," UN Document E/C.10/17.

White House. 1966. "Memorandum Announcing Revised Guidelines Governing Development by the Government of Products or Services for Its Own Use," March 3.

White House. 2009. "Memorandum for the Heads of Executive Departments and Agencies Subject to Government," March 4.

White House. 2019. "President Donald Trump is Defending Our Sovereignty and Constitutional Rights from the United Nations Arms Trade Treaty," April 26.

Zuckerberg, Mark. 2018. "U.S. Senate Commerce and Judiciary Committees Joint Hearings," April 10.

NEWS REPORTS

Abdul-Zahra, Qassim and Tarek El-Tablawy. 2007. "Iraq's al-Maliki Stresses Commitment to National Reconciliation, Boosting Political Process." *Associated Press*, September 25.

Adams, Christopher. 1998. "Action to Curb Rise in Piracy Urged." *Financial Times*, January 20.

Aglionby, Andrew. 2006. "An Arbitration Clause Safety Net." *Financial Times*, April 12.

Amnesty International [AI]. 1973. "Continuing Action against Torture." Amnesty International Newsletter 3(10), October.

Apuzzo, Matt. 2015. "Blackwater Crew Given Long Terms for Killing Iraqis." *New York Times*, April 14.

Armfelt, Andrew. 1992. "Avoiding the Arbitration Trap." *Financial Times*, October 27.

Baker, Peter and Maggie Haberman. 2020. "Trump Leaps to Call Shots on Reopening Nation, Setting up Standoff with Governors." *New York Times*, April 13.

Barstow, David, James Glanz, Richard A. Oppel, Jr., and Kate Zernike. 2004. "Security Companies: Shadow Soldiers in Iraq." *New York Times*, April 19.

Bartlett, Donald and James Steele. 2007. "Washington's $8 Billion Shadow." *Vanity Fair*, March.

Batchelor, Charles. 1995. "Tribunal Rejects 2.5bn Eurotunnel Claim." *Financial Times*, November 1.

BBC. 2011. "Geithner on 'Terrible Judgement' of Standard and Poor," August 8.

Beatie, Alan and Andrew Egdecliffe-Johnson. 2005. "CEOs in Drive to Combat Piracy." *Financial Times*, October 5.

Benenson, Peter. 1961. "The Forgotten Prisoners." *The Observer*, May 28.

Bergner, Daniel. 2005. "The Other Army." *New York Times*, August 14.

Betts, Paul. 2009. "Piracy Around Horn of Africa on Private Sector Radar." *Financial Times*, June 16.

Birchall, Jonathan. 2003. "UN Plans to Scrutinise Multinationals." *Financial Times*, August 13.

Blackwater USA. 2005. Press Release: "Joseph E. Schmitz Becomes Chief Operating Officer and General Counsel for The Prince Group," September 13.

Bloomberg Government. 2019. "BGOV200" Database.

Blumenthaul, Sidney. 2004. "This is the New Gulag." *The Guardian*, May 6.

Bond, Shannon. 2020. "Apple, Google Coronavirus Tool Won't Track Your Location. That Worries Some States." *National Public Radio*, May 13.

Bounds, Andrew. 2006. "US and EU to Take Joint Action over Fake Goods." *Financial Times*, June 19.

Branfman, Fred. 1973. "Caged by Saigon." *New York Times*, September 27.

Brewer, Sam Pope. 1969. "Protest by Dissidents in Soviet Brings U.N. Curb on Petitions." *New York Times*, October 4.

Browne, Malcolm. 1976. "Hand of the Police Seen in Yugoslav Political Trials." *New York Times*, October 25.

Burns, Jimmy. 1993. "Loss from Fraud 'Likely to Rise'." *Financial Times*, March 16.

Burns, Jimmy. 1999. "Efforts to Combat Cybercrime 'Hit By Poor Co-Operation'." *Financial Times*, December 8.

Burns, Jimmy and John Mason. 1995. "Hard-To-Prove Crime Ruins Many Investors." *Financial Times*, September 7.

Burton, John and Mark Huband. 2004. "Piracy 'Poses Greater Risk Than Terrorism' in Malacca Strait." *Financial Times*, July 1.

Carnegy, Hugh. 2011. "Business in G20 Push for Growth." *Financial Times*, October 31.

Chon, Gina. 2008. "Talks on U.S.-Iraq Security Pact Hit 'Dead End'; Deal to Set Terms for Troop Presence as Mandate Lapses." *Wall Street Journal*, June 14.

Clarity, James. 1973. "Saigon Aide Says Graft is Limited." *New York Times*, September 24.

Clarity, James. 1976. "A Freed Dissident Says Soviet Doctors Sought to Break His Political Beliefs." *New York Times*, February 4.

Clavel, Jean-Pierre. 1974. "Torture, an Official Way of Life in 30 Countries." *New York Times*, August 4,

Cole, August. 2008. "Contractors Face Loss of Immunity in Iraq." *Wall Street Journal*, August 23.

Crittenden, Ann. 1976. "Loans from Abroad Flow to Chile's Rightist Junta." *New York Times*, February 20.

Darnton, John. 1976. "Ghanaian Poet Who Taught in U.S. is Out of Jail and Back in African University Post." *New York Times*, November 18.

Dayen, David. 2018. "Below the Surface of ICE: The Corporations Profiting from Immigrant Detention." *In These Times*, October.

de Jonquie'res, Guy and Louise Kehoe. 1998. "Should Governments or Markets Regulate Cyberspace?" *Financial Times*, October 8.

de Onis, Juan. 1976. "OAS Appealing to Chile on Rights." *New York Times*, June 17.

Debusmann, Bernd. 2007. "Editorial: The U.S. Addiction to Privatising Wars." *Reuters*, October 24.

Debusmann, Bernd. 2008. "Editorial: Two faces of Blackwater." *Reuters*, April 9.

DeYoung, Karen. 2007. "State Department Struggles to Oversee Private Army." *Washington Post*, October 21.

DeYoung, Karen and Ann Scott Tyson. 2007. "Blackwater Faces New Monitoring from State Dept." *Washington Post*, October 6.

DeYoung, Karen and Pamela Constable. 2009. "Anti-U.S. Wave Imperiling Efforts in Pakistan, Officials Say." *Washington Post*, September 25.

Digby, Marie Claire. 2021. "Indian Food That's Better than the Takeaway? Here's How to Do It at Home." *The Irish Times*, February 12.

Donnan, Shawn. 2013. "Up in the Air." *Financial Times*, December 3.

Donnan, Shawn. 2014. "Toxic Talks." *Financial Times*, October 7.

Dullforce, William. 1987. "Early Result Sought from Uruguay Trade Talks." *Financial Times*, April 30.

Eder, Richard. 1972. "Private Group Seeks to Protect Political Prisoners in Vietnam." *New York Times*, November 3.

Evans, Richard. 1985. "Minister Doubtful on Law to Protect Trademarks." *Financial Times*, November 7.

Feron, James. 1969. "Israelis Dispute Study on Prisons; They Say Panel 'Prejudged' Treatment of Arabs." *New York Times*, December 8.

Fifield, Anna. 2004. "Business Urges Priority for Doha Round." *Financial Times*, June 7.

Fifield, Anna. 2013. "Contractors Reap $138bn from Iraq War." *Financial Times*, March 18.

Financial Times. 1984. Letters to the Editor, April 17.

Financial Times. 1985. Letters to the Editor, November 13.

Financial Times. 1986. "It is Estimated that an Industry Worth $60 Billion a Year in Counterfeit Goods Currently Exists on the World's Markets," September 1.

Financial Times. 1988a. "Minimum Standards of Professional Behaviour for Organisations Engaged in Trade Deals Involving Electronic Data Have Been Drafted by the International Chamber of Commerce," February 4.

Financial Times. 1988b. "Failure to Show Progress at the Mid-Term Review of Gatt's Uruguay Round of Negotiations in December Could Trigger a Repeat of Last October's Stock Market Collapse," May 4.

Financial Times. 1989. "ICI Chief Calls on All Governments to Back the Montreal Protocol on the Ozone Layer," March 6.

Financial Times. 1990. Letters to the Editor, April 25.

Financial Times. 1991. Letters to the Editor, December 20.

Financial Times. 1992. Letters to the Editor, April 15.

Financial Times. 1993. "G7 Meeting's Success Will Hinge on Tariff Talks," July 3.
Financial Times. 1994. "Move on Letters of Credit," May 21.
Financial Times. 1995a. Letters to the Editor, January 6.
Financial Times. 1995b. "Dust Settles over Disputes; New Proposals on Arbitration," August 15.
Financial Times. 1997. Letters to the Editor, September 22.
Financial Times. 1998a. Letters to the Editor, January 15.
Financial Times. 1998b. "Guide to the Week," October 26.
Financial Times. 1999a. Letters to the Editor, March 24.
Financial Times. 1999b. Letters to the Editor, August 31.
Financial Times. 1999c. Letters to the Editor, November 26.
Financial Times. 1999d. Letters to the Editor, December 17.
Financial Times. 2003a. Letters to the Editor, April 2.
Financial Times. 2003b. Letters to the Editor, July 9.
Financial Times. 2004. Letters to the Editor, April 26.
Financial Times. 2005. Letters to the Editor, November 8.
Financial Times. 2006. Letters to the Editor, February 22.
Financial Times. 2007. Letters to the Editor, March 1.
Financial Times. 2011. Letters to the Editor, April 14.
Financial Times. 2013. Letters to the Editor, December 3.
Financial Times. 2015. Letters to the Editor, June 3.
Fisher, Andrew. 1983. "Crime Wave on the High Seas; Fraud, Scuttling and Piracy Flourish." *Financial Times*, February 21.
Freifeld, Karen. 2017. "Moody's Pays $864 Million to U.S., States, over Pre-Crisis Ratings." *Reuters*, January 13.
Gearan, Anne. 2008. "US Ambassador Says No Permanent Bases in Iraq." *Associated Press*, June 5.
Gerstenzang, James and Alexandra Zavis. 2007. "Bush, Iraqi Prime Minister Discuss Security, Sovereignty." *The Los Angeles Times*, September 26.
Giniger, Henry. 1975. "Madrid Rejects Foreign Protests." *New York Times*, October 1.
Giniger, Henry. 1976. "Madrid Investigating Torture Reports but Orders Press to be Silent." *New York Times*, June 18.
Goodman, Jr., George. 1976. "Uruguay Charged with Repression." *New York Times*, February 20.
Gordon, Max. 1972. "An Earlier Bloodbath." *New York Times*, December 1.
Gotsch, Kara and Vinay Basti. 2019. "Capitalizing on Mass Incarceration: U.S. Growth in Private Prisons." *The Sentencing Project*, August 2.
Grose, Peter. 1970. "Israel Frees Fourteen Egyptian Sailors Despite Anger over Guerrillas' Hostages." *New York Times*, September 13.
Guild, Alastair. 1987. "Race to Run against Crime – Advances in Technology Offer Some Consolation to Those Fighting Crime against Companies." *Financial Times*, September 21.
Gupte, Pranay. 1977. "Amnesty Chief For U.S. Sees Long Struggle." *New York Times*, October 11.
Gwertzman, Bernard. 1977a. "U.S. Says 6 Nations Curb Human Rights." *New York Times*, January 2.
Gwertzman, Bernard. 1977b. "U.S. Again Comments on Soviet Dissident." *New York Times*, February 8.
Hancock, Jay. 2020. "They Pledged to Donate Rights to Their COVID Vaccine, Then Sold Them to Pharma." *KHN*, August 25.

Hargreaves, Deborah. 1995. "International Sugar Fraud Leaves Buyers Feeling Sour." *Financial Times*, November 16.

Harris, Clay. 1997. "Cheating Poor Nations is a SNIPS." *Financial Times*, February 12.

Hasan, Mehdi. 2019. "'Interview with Erik Prince', Head to Head with Mehdi Hasan." *Al Jazeera*, March 8.

Hastings, Deborah. 2007. "Contractors in Iraq Accused of Opening Fire on Civilians and Soldiers." *Associated Press*, August 9.

Hazzard, Shirley. 1974. "The Patron Saint of the UN is Pontius Pilate." *New York Times*, February 23.

Hermann, A. H. 1983. "An Arbitration Tale of Two Cities." *Financial Times*, October 20.

Hermann, A. H. 1990. "Language of Trade Gains a New International Lexicon." *Financial Times*, August 6.

Hersh, Seymour M. 1973. "Senate Liberals Will Oppose Aid to Saigon Police." *New York Times*, September 16.

Hider, James. 2004. "Soldiers of Fortune Rush to Cash in on Unrest in Baghdad." *The Times of London*, March 31.

Hill, Andrew and Michael Mann. 2002. "EU Takes Further Step Towards Retaliation on Steel." *Financial Times*, May 8.

Howe, Marvine. 1973a. "Brazil Imposes Sweeping Press Curbs and Installs Censors in Newsrooms of the Few Papers That Resist." *New York Times*, February 17.

Howe, Marvine. 1973b. "Chilean Military Will Keep Curbs." *New York Times*, October 9.

Hunt, John. 1989. "London Conference on the Ozone Layer: Seeking Recruits in Fight to Save Atmosphere." *Financial Times*, March 4.

Hunt, John. 1991a. "Leading Companies in 'Green' Pledge." *Financial Times*, April 11.

Hunt, John. 1991b. "Business and the Environment: Industry on the Warpath to Fight Greenhouse Battle." *Financial Times*, April 17.

Hurst, Steven R. 2007. "U.S. Ambassador Calls Blackwater Shooting Horrific, But Still Feels High Regard for Guards." *Associated Press*, October 25.

International Chamber of Commerce [ICC]. 1979. *World Peace through World Trade: ICC 1919–1979*.

International Chamber of Commerce [ICC]. 1998. "Business and the Global Economy." Statement to the G-8 Summit, May 15–17.

ICC. 2011. "Program of Action."

ICC. 2012. Commission Report: "States, State Entities, and ICC Arbitration."

ICC. 2014. "Making Rules for Business."

ICC. 2016. "Rethinking Trade and Finance: An ICC Private Sector Development Perspective." ICC Publication No. 878E.

ICC. 2022. "Policy Commissions" Accessed Online: https://iccwbo.org/leadership/

International Maritime Bureau [IMB]. 2022. "Piracy and Armed Robbery Against Ships: Report for the period 1 January–31 December 2021," January.

Isaac, Mike, Sheera Frankel, and Cecelia Kang. 2020. "Now More Than Ever, Facebook is a 'Mark Zuckerberg Production'." *New York Times*, May 16.

Iskandar, Samer. 1999. "Updated Trade Terms Please Exporters." *Financial Times*, September 15.

Jack, Andrew. 1995. "Encryption Rules to be Prepared." *Financial Times*, December 21.

Jack, Andrew. 1996a. "Big Rise in Use of Fake Bank Documents." *Financial Times*, March 1.

Jack, Andrew. 1996b. "Groups Will Have to Fund Own Fight on Fraudsters." *Financial Times*, March 14.

Jack, Andrew. 1997. "Rules for Trade on Internet Planned." *Financial Times*, November 6.

Jackson, Gary. 2004. *Blackwater Tactical Weekly*, May 17.

Jordan, Lara Jakes. 2007. "FBI Finds 14 of the 17 Blackwater Shootings Unjustified." *Associated Press*, November 14.

Kandell, Jonathan. 1976. "'Death Squad' Arousing New Concern in Rio, with 21 Murdered in 10 Days." *New York Times*, June 7.

Kelly, Jim. 1997. "Andersen Split to Go to Arbitration." *Financial Times*, December 18.

Kessler, Glenn and Karen DeYoung. 2007. "Blackwater Focused on Cost, Not Safety, Report Says." *Washington Post*, September 28.

Klein, Ezra. 2018. "Mark Zuckerberg on Facebook's Hardest Year, and What Comes Next." *Vox*, April 2.

Kratovac, Katarina. 2007. "U.N. Looks Whether War Crimes Were Committed in Contractor Shootings of Iraqis." *Associated Press*, October 11.

Kynge, James. 1998. "China in $4.5bn Deal with Shell." *Financial Times*, February 11.

Laber, Jeri. 1976a. "Torture and Death in Uruguay." *New York Times*, March 10.

Laber, Jeri. 1976b. "Philippines Torture." *New York Times*, October 30.

Lamb, Christina. 1992a. "Green Shoots of Good Intention from Business: The Boardroom View of the Earth Summit." *Financial Times*, June 1.

Lamb, Christina. 1992b. "Businesses 'Crucial to Success of Summit'." *Financial Times*, May 28.

Lascelles, David and Christina Lamb. 1992. "Collor Signs Treaty on Greenhouse Gases." *Financial Times*, June 9.

Lee, John. 1970. "Charge of Israeli Torture Splits Amnesty's British, U.S. Units." *New York Times*, April 4.

Lee, Matthew and Mike Baker. 2009. "Denied License, Blackwater to Keep Guarding US Diplomats in Iraq through Summer." *Associated Press*, April 20.

Levin, Myron. 2003. "Big Tobacco's Real Problem with Fakes." *Financial Times*, November 25.

Lewis, Anthony. 1971. "Torture Alleged in North Ireland." *New York Times*, November 9.

Lewis, Anthony. 1973. "Peace with Honor." *New York Times*, July 16.

Lewis, Anthony. 1974. "The Meaning of Torture." *New York Times*, May 30.

Lewis, Anthony. 1975. "For Which We Stand: III." *New York Times*, October 6.

Linton, Caroline. 2020. "Cuomo Announces 7-State Coalition for Purchasing Medical Equipment." *CBS News*, May 4.

Lionæs, Aase. 1977. "Nobel Peace Prize Award Ceremony Speech." *The Nobel Prize*, December 10.

Long, Gideon and John Paul Rathbone. 2018. "Creditors Eye Venezuela Oil Assets in Battle over Unpaid Debt." *Financial Times*, August 16.

Maitland, Alison. 2003. "Companies Set to Work with UN Ethics Code." *Financial Times*, December 9.

Maitland, Leslie. 1976. "Four-Master from Chile is Called 'Torture' Ship." *New York Times*, June 20.

Mander, Benedict. 2011. "Caracas Ready to Pay Exxon $1bn." *Financial Times*, September 23.

Mander, Benedict and Slyvia Pfeifer. 2012. "Venezuela to Settle Its Own Oil Disputes." *Financial Times*, January 17.

Mann, Joseph. 1995. "Venezuela Opens up Oil Industry." *Financial Times*, July 6.

Marks, Jon. 1996. "Trade's Global Police Force." *Financial Times*, May 8.

Maucher, Helmut. 1997. "Ruling by Consent." *Financial Times*, December 6.

Maucher, Helmut. 1998. "The Geneva Business Declaration," statement at the Geneva Business Dialogue, September 24.

Mauthner, Robert. 1985. "ICC Opposes Imposition of Sanctions." *Financial Times*, September 3.

Mazzetti, Mark and James Risen. 2009. "Blackwater Said to Pursue Bribes to Iraq after 17 Died." *New York Times*, November 11.

McCormick, Richard. D. 2001. "Good Business Practices Make Sound Commercial Sense." *International Herald Tribune*, January 25.

McEwan, Feona. 1987. "The Fight for Self-Control – Advertising Codes." *Financial Times*, September 24.

McMaster, H. R. and Gary Cohn. 2017. "America First Doesn't Mean America Alone." *The Wall Street Journal*, May 31.

Mercury. 2001. "It's Not Going to Be Pretty, CIA Says." October 20.

Meyer, Josh and Julian E. Barnes. 2007. "Congress Moves to Rein in Private Contractors." *Los Angeles Times*, October 4.

Miller, T. Christian. 2007. "Contractors Outnumber Troops in Iraq." *Los Angeles Times*, July 4.

Mitchell, Tom. 2008. "Top Business Lobby Warns over Doha." *Financial Times*, June 24.

Montagnon, Peter. 1989. "International Chamber of Commerce Urges Industrial Powers to Put Uruguay Trade Talks Back on Track." *Financial Times*, March 31.

Moran, Nuala. 1998. "Internet and the Law – Tensions Rise between Governments and the World of Business." *Financial Times*, April 2.

Morris, Ivan. 1972. "Prisoners of Conscience." *New York Times*, November 11.

Moser, Michael. 2005a. "New Rules for an Old Game: A Revamp of Arbitration Procedures is Good News for Everyone." *Financial Times*, January 12.

Moser, Michael. 2005b. "No Good Tidings yet for ICC – The International Chamber of Commerce Wants Access to the Mainland for Its Court." *Financial Times*, December 21.

Navasky, Victor S. 1976. "Art, Politics, and Torture Chambers." *New York Times*, August 15.

New York Times. 1964. "South Africa Bars Official of Group Helping Refugees," August 23.

New York Times. 1969. "Ennals Expresses Surprise," December 8.

New York Times. 1970a. "Taiwan is Reported to Bar Aid of Prisoners Group," February 4.

New York Times. 1970b. "Torture Inquiry in Israel Sought," April 2.

New York Times. 1970c. Letters to the Editor, April 4.

New York Times. 1970d. Letters to the Editor, April 14.

New York Times. 1970e. "World's Political Prisoners Believed to Exceed 250,000," June 22.

New York Times. 1970f. "European Protests Mount," December 30.

New York Times. 1971a. "Soldier is Killed in Ulster; Belfast Bombing Reported," November 8.

New York Times. 1971b. "Ex-Aide Criticizes Amnesty Unit Study," November 11.

New York Times. 1971c. "U.S. Draft Laws Criticized by Amnesty International," January 16.

New York Times. 1971d. "Indonesia Gets Appeal on Behalf of Prisoners," August 12.

New York Times. 1972a. "Amnesty Group Accuses Brazil of Torturing Political Prisoners," September 7.

New York Times. 1972b. Letters to the Editor, November 18.

New York Times. 1973a. "UN Unit Drops Support of Conference on Torture," December 4.

New York Times. 1973b. "Amnesty Group Prepares Charges of Chilean Torture," December 12.

New York Times. 1973c. "Junta in Chile Reported Killing Many of Allende's Supporters," September 16.

New York Times. 1973d. "Spain Accused of Torturing Jailed Opponents Regularly," August 27.

New York Times. 1973e. "Spanish Police Call Charge of Torture 'a Defamation'," August 28.

New York Times. 1973f. "2 More are Seized as Security Arrests Continue in Athens," March 29.

New York Times. 1973g. "Warning to the Colonels," April 18.

New York Times. 1973h. "Safety of Prisoners in Saigon Doubted," January 27.

New York Times. 1973i. "Aid for Prisoners in Vietnam Urged," July 2.

New York Times. 1973j. "Report on Prisons Assailed by Saigon," July 3.

New York Times. 1974a. Letters to the Editor, March 19.

New York Times. 1974b. Letters to the Editor, January 16.

New York Times. 1974c. Letters to the Editor, March 20.

New York Times. 1974d. "School is Given Human Rights Award," May 5.

New York Times. 1974e. Letters to the Editor, March 19.

New York Times. 1975a. Letters to the Editor, October 31.

New York Times. 1975b. "Much Torturing of Basques Cited," October 1.

New York Times. 1975c. Letters to the Editor, October 7.

New York Times. 1975d. "Panel on Rights Dubious on Soviet," October 20.

New York Times. 1975e. "Computer Experts Appeal for Russian," November 6.

New York Times. 1975f. "Soviet Opens Trial of Kovalev, Dissident Biologist," December 10.

New York Times. 1976a. Letters to the Editor, May 2.

New York Times. 1976b. Letters to the Editor, November 23.

New York Times. 1976c. "17 Seoul Critics Said to be Held," March 5.

New York Times. 1976d. "Rhodesian Torture is Called Routine," March 31.

New York Times. 1976e. Letters to the Editor, May 2.

New York Times. 1976f. "Report on Chilean Arrests," June 7.

New York Times. 1976g. "Amnesty International Declares Jakarta Holds 100,000 Prisoners," September 22.

New York Times. 1976h. "Manila Investigated Torture Charge," September 29.

New York Times. 1976i. "Congress Conferees Cut $3 Million Uruguay Aid," September 16.

New York Times. 1976j. "Text of 'Declaration' Issued by 'Headquarters of Croatian National Liberation Forces'," September 12.

New York Times. 1976k. Letters to the Editor, April 9.

New York Times. 1976l. "Bukovsky Tells of Harsh Soviet Prison Conditions," December 20.

New York Times. 1977a. "3,000 are Released from Latin Prisons," January 2.

New York Times. 1977b. "Human Rights at Different Weights," February 27.

New York Times. 1977c. "Two Nobel Awards," October 11.

New York Times. 1977d. "Amnesty International Denies Torturing Hogs," May 31.

New York Times. 2004. Editorial: "Privatizing Warfare," April 21.

New York Times. 2021. "Tracking Coronavirus Vaccinations Around the World," August 9.

Nicas, Jack and Daisuke Wakabayashi. 2020. "Apple and Google Team Up to 'Contact Trace' the Coronavirus." *The New York Times,* April 10.

Noguchi, Yuki. 2019. "No Meaningful Oversight: ICE Contractor Overlooked Problems at Detention Centers." *National Public Radio,* July 17.

Notitsji, Joseph. 1972. "Brazil Prisoners Apparently Fail." *New York Times,* July 16.

O'Harrow, Jr., Robert and Ellen McCarthy. 2004. "Private Sector Has Firm Role at the Pentagon." *Washington Post,* June 9.

Parker, Jennifer. 2007. "Iraq Disputes Blackwater's Account of Baghdad Killings." *ABC News,* September 19.

Parker, Ned. 2007. "U.S. Restricts Movement of its Diplomats in Iraq." *Los Angeles Times,* September 19.

Parker, Ned and Salman Raheem. 2007. "'Wall of Silence' Protects Security Contractor in Iraq." *Los Angeles Times,* September 21.

Patrick, Stewart. 2017. "Trump's Sovereignty Doctrine." *U.S. News and World Report*, September 23.

Peel, Michael. 2000. "Andersen Break-Up Approved." *Financial Times*, August 8.

Peel, Michael and Jane Croft. 2010. "Case Closed." *Financial Times*, April 16.

Pleming, Sue. 2007. "Rice Puts Cameras on Blackwater Convoys." *Reuters*, October 5.

Priest, Dana and Mary Pat Flaherty. 2004. "Under Fire, Security Firms Form an Alliance." *Washington Post*, April 8.

Priest, Dana and William Arkin. 2010a. "A Hidden World, Growing beyond Control." *The Washington Post*, July 19.

Priest, Dana and William Arkin. 2010b. "National Security, Inc." *The Washington Post*, July 20.

Priest, Dana and William Arkin. 2010c. "The Secrets Next Door." *The Washington Post*, July 21.

Priest, Dana and William Arkin. 2010d. "Monitoring America." *The Washington Post*, December 20.

Prince, Erik. 2017. "The MacArthur Model for Afghanistan." *The Wall Street Journal*, May 31.

Pritchard, Ambrose Evans. 2016. "Brexit Vote is about the Supremacy of Parliament and Nothing Else." *The Telegraph*, June 13.

Project for Excellence in Journalism. 2007. "A Media Mystery: Private Security Companies in Iraq," June 21.

Reed, Roy. 1967. "Goldwater Says C.I.A. is Financing Socialism in U.S." *New York Times*, February 27.

Reid, Robert. 2007. "Iraq Orders U.S. Government's Security Firm out of the Country in Wake of Killings." *Associated Press*, September 17.

Reuters. 2020. "Trump Pardon of Blackwater Iraq Contractors Violates International Law – UN," December 30.

Riechmann, Deb. 2010. "Karzai Pushes Back Ban on Private Security Guards after Donor Nations Say They're Still Needed." *Associated Press*, October 27.

Risen, James. 2008. "Use of Iraq Contractors Costs Billions, Report Says." *The New York Times*, August 11.

Risen, James. 2010. "3 Blackwater Guards Called Baghdad Shootings Unjustified." *New York Times*, January 16.

Risen, James. 2014. "Before Shooting in Iraq, a Warning on Blackwater." *New York Times*, June 29.

Robertson, Nan. 1973. "64 Nations Charged in Report as Users of Torture." *New York Times*, December 16.

Ruane, Alyssa. 2018. "Tikka Masala and Curry are Not Indian Cuisine." *Charlotte Magazine*, May 18.

Rubin, Alissa. 2007. "Iraqi Cabinet Votes to End Security Firms' Immunity." *New York Times*, October 31.

Rubin, Alissa. 2008. "Talks with U.S. on Security Pact are at an Impasse, the Iraqi Prime Minister Says." *New York Times*, June 14.

Rubin, Alissa and Andrew Kramer. 2007. "Iraqi Premier Says Blackwater Shootings Challenge His Nation's Sovereignty." *New York Times*, September 24.

Scahill, Jeremy. 2007. "All Cowboys Out Now." *The Nation*, November 26.

Schmidt, Michael S. and Eric Schmitt. 2012. "Flexing Muscle, Baghdad Detains U.S. Contractors." *New York Times*, January 16.

Schmitthoff, Clive M. 1985. "Why Arbitration is the Favoured Method of Dispute Settlement." *Financial Times*, October 4.

Scoop Independent News. 2006. "NGOs Lead by Example with Accountability Charter," June 9.

Senhupta, Reena. 2002. "Crackdown on Cybersquatters." *Financial Times*, February 25.

Shabad, Theodore. 1975. "Report Criticizes Soviet on its Political Prisoners." *New York Times*, November 18.

Sherwood, Bob. 2004. "Data Call Gets a Poor Reception." *Financial Times*, May 17.

Sherwood, Bob and Nikki Tait. 2002. "Data Retention Backlash." *Financial Times*, December 9.

Sherwood, Bob and Nikki Tait. 2003. "More Turn to Arbitration." *Financial Times*, February 24.

Shipler, David. 1975a. "A Small Chapter of Amnesty International, Begun in a Moscow Apartment, Survives Its First Anxious Year." *New York Times*, September 7.

Shipler, David. 1975b. "They Need Listeners: The Dissidents Speak as Much to the West as to the Kremlin." *New York Times*, November 16.

Shipler, David. 1975c. "Sakharov in Vigil at Friend's Trial." *New York Times*, December 11.

Shipler, David. 1976a. "Soviet is Expected to Try Three in Separate Cases of Dissidence." *New York Times*, April 7.

Shipler, David. 1976b. "Soviet Jails a Tatar and Exiles an Amnesty Official for 'Slander.'" *New York Times*, April 16.

Shishkin, Philip. 2007. "Blackwater Shooting Crisis Rallies Baghdad." *Wall Street Journal*, September 24.

Shrimsley, Robert. 2005. "A WTO Wake-Up Call to the World." *Financial Times*, November 9.

Simon, Bernard. 1985. "UN Panel Meets on Investment in South Africa." *Financial Times*, September 16.

Sizemore, Bill. 2006. "On the Front Lines." *The Virginian-Pilot*, July 25.

Smith, Hedrick. 1973. "Moscow Congress." *New York Times*, November 4.

Solon, Olivia. 2016. "Facebook's Fake News: Mark Zuckerberg Rejects 'Crazy Idea' that it Swayed Voters." *The Guardian*, November 11.

Spiegel, Peter. 2007. "Blackwater Told to Clear Disclosures." *Los Angeles Times*, September 26.

Stockman, Farah. 2004. "Civilians ID'd in Abuse May Face No Charges." *Boston Globe*, May 4.

Stratte-McClure, J. 2001. "The Business of Building a Better World." *International Herald Tribune*, January 25.

Styron, Rose. 1974. "Terror in Chile II: The Amnesty Report." *New York Review of Books*, May 30.

Taylor, Alan. 2011. "Occupy Wall Street." *The Atlantic*, September 30.

Teltsch, Kathleen. 1972a. "UN Prison Code Being Promoted." *New York Times*, April 9.

Teltsch, Kathleen. 1972b. "UN Unit Said to Report Greeks Violate Human Rights." *New York Times*, September 21.

Teltsch, Kathleen. 1974a. "Chile is Accused in Report to UN." *New York Times*, January 20.

Teltsch, Kathleen. 1974b. "Torture in Chile Said to Continue." *New York Times*, September 11.

Teltsch, Kathleen. 1975a. "World Network Helps Political Prisoners." *New York Times*, November 22.

Teltsch, Kathleen. 1975b. "UN Panel Votes Text on Torture." *New York Times*, November 25.

Teltsch, Kathleen. 1977. "Human Rights Groups are Riding a Wave of Popularity." *New York Times*, February 28.

Thorne, Ludmilla. 1977. "Mother Courage: How Vladimir Bukovsky was Saved." *New York Times*, February 27.

Topping, Seymour. 1966. "Slaughter of Reds Gives Indonesia a Grim Legacy." *New York Times*, August 24.

Trofimov, Yaroslav. 2010. "Afghans Begin to Disarm Private Security Firms." *Wall Street Journal*, October 4.

Turner, Mark. 2004a. "Effort to Bury Mistrust." *Financial Times*, June 24.

Turner, Mark. 2004b. "Vivendi Boss to Lead War on Piracy." *Financial Times*, October 13.

Vecsey, George. 1976. "Arrest of a Poet in Ghana Stirs Stony Brook Campus." *New York Times*, February 22.

Virginian-Pilot. 2007. Editorial: "No One's Ever to Blame for Bad News in Iraq," September 26.

Washington Post. 2010. "Top Secret America: Methodology and Credits," July 18.

Weinraub, Bernard. 1970a. "Political Prisons Holds Many Types." *New York Times*, June 28.

Weinraub, Bernard. 1970b. "Appeal is Made by Amnesty Unit." *New York Times*, November 22.

Weinraub, Bernard. 1971a. "Amnesty Group Marks 10th Year." *New York Times*, May 9.

Weinraub, Bernard. 1971b. "British Commission Denies Brutality in Ulster Prisons." *New York Times*, November 17.

Williams, Frances. 1998a. "Brussels Outlines its Agenda for Global Trade Talks." *Financial Times*, September 24.

Williams, Frances. 1998b. "The Voice of Business Heard Around the World." *Financial Times*, December 29.

Williams, Frances. 1998c. "Data Protection Plan for Electronic Commerce." *Financial Times*, September 25.

Williams, Frances. 2003. "Call to Cut Risk of Ship Piracy." *Financial Times*, January 30.

Williams, Frances. 2004. "Human Rights Stay on UN Agenda." *Financial Times*, April 21.

Williams, Frances. 2005. "Fall in Global Sea Piracy Incidents." *Financial Times*, February 8.

Williams, Timothy. 2010. "Iraqis Angered at Dropping of Blackwater Charges." *New York Times*, January 2.

Williamson, Hugh. 2007. "OECD Slashes Estimate of Piracy Losses." *Financial Times*, May 8.

Winter, Jeremy. 1998. "Resolution in a Neutral Forum." *Financial Times*, April 21.

Wolman, Clive. 1986. "The Crime That Can Span a Host of Countries: International Fraud in the City." *Financial Times*, April 14.

Wren, Christopher. 1975. "For Sakharov, New Hope." *New York Times*, October 11.

Wren, Christopher. 1976. "Soviet to Free Leading Dissident in Trade for Chilean Communist." *New York Times*, December 18.

Wren, Christopher. 1977. "For Dissenters at Home or Abroad, Human Rights is a Very Human Issue." *New York Times*, July 10.

Zakaria, Tabassum. 2007. "Bush Presses Maliki on Iraq Reconciliation Laws." *Reuters*, September 25.

Zavis, Alexandra. 2006. "Iraq Struggles with Rise of Guns-for-Hire." *Associated Press*, May 7.

SCHOLARLY REFERENCES

Abbott, Kenneth and Duncan Snidal. 2001. International "Standards" and International Governance. *Journal of European Public Policy* 8(3): 345–370.

Abbott, Kenneth and Duncan Snidal. 2009a. The Governance Triangle: Regulatory Standards Institutions and the Shadow of the State. In *The Politics of Global Regulation*, Walter Mattli and Ngaire Woods, eds. Princeton: Princeton University Press, 44–88.

Abbott, Kenneth and Duncan Snidal. 2009b. Strengthening International Regulation through Transnational New Governance: Overcoming the Orchestration Deficit. *Vanderbilt Journal of Transnational Law* 42(2): 501–578.

Abbott, Kenneth, Philipp Genschel, Duncan Snidal, and Bernhard Zangl, eds. 2015. *International Organizations as Orchestrators*. Cambridge: Cambridge University Press.

Abrahamsen, Rita and Michael C. Williams. 2011. *Security beyond the State: Private Security in International Politics*. Cambridge: Cambridge University Press.

Abrahamsen, Rita and Michael C. Williams. 2014. Publics, Practices, and Power. In *The Return of the Public in Global Governance*, Jacqueline Best and Alexandra Gheciu, eds. Cambridge: Cambridge University Press, 243–256.

Ackerly, Brooke. 2018. *Just Responsibility: A Human Rights Theory of Justice*. New York: Oxford University Press.

Adams, Randolph Greenfield. 1922. *Political Ideas of the American Revolution: Britannic-American Contributions to the Problem of Imperial Organization, 1765–1775*. Durham: Trinity College.

Adler, Emanuel and Vincent Pouliot, eds. 2011. *International Practices*. Cambridge: Cambridge University Press.

Agamben, Giorgio. 1995. *Homo Sacer: Sovereign Power and Bare Life*. Palo Alto: Stanford University Press.

Agensky, Jonathan. 2019. Evangelical Globalism and the Internationalization of Sudan's Second Civil War. *Cambridge Review of International Affairs* 33(2): 274–293.

Agnew, John. 2005. Sovereignty Regimes: Territoriality and State Authority in Contemporary World Politics. *Annals of the Association of American Geographers* 95(2): 437–461.

Agnew, John. 2009. *Globalization and Sovereignty*. Lanham: Rowman & Littlefield.

Aleinikoff, Alexander T. 2002. *Semblances of Sovereignty: The Constitution, the State, and American Citizenship*. Cambridge, MA: Harvard University Press.

Allan, Bentley B. 2018. *Scientific Cosmology and International Orders*. Cambridge: Cambridge University Press.

Almond, Gabriel A. and Stephen J. Genco. 1977. Clocks and Clouds and the Study of World Politics. *World Politics* 29(4): 489–522.

Aman, Alfred C. 1998. The Globalizing State: A Future-Oriented Perspective on the Public/Private Distinction, Federalism, and Democracy. *Vanderbilt Journal of Transnational Law* 31(3): 769–870.

Amoore, Louise. 2006. Biometric Borders: Governing Mobilities in the War on Terror. *Political Geography* 25(3): 336–351.

Amsden, Alice H. 1989. *Asia's Next Giant: South Korea and Late Industrialization*. New York: Oxford University Press.

Anderson, Benedict. 1983. *Imagined Communities: Reflections on the Origin and Spread of Nationalism*. London: Verso.

Andonova, Liliana. 2017. *Governance Entrepreneurs: International Organizations and the Rise of Global Public-Private Partnerships*. Cambridge: Cambridge University Press.

Aradau, Claudia. 2018. Articulations of Sovereignty. *Oxford Research Encyclopedia of International Studies*. http://doi.org/10.1093/acrefore/9780190846626.013.375

Arendt, Hannah. 1958. *The Human Condition*. Chicago: University of Chicago Press.

Arendt, Hannah. 1963. *Eichmann in Jerusalem: A Report on the Banality of Evil*. New York: Viking Press.

Arendt, Hannah. 1987. Collective Responsibility. In *Amor Mundi: Explorations in the Faith and Thought of Hannah Arendt*, James W. Bernauer, ed. Dordrecht: Martinus Nijhoff, 43–50.

Aronovitch, Hilliard. 2012. Interpreting Weber's Ideal-Types. *Philosophy of the Social Sciences* 42(3): 356–369.

Arrighi, Giovanni. 1999. Globalization, State Sovereignty, and the "Endless" Accumulation of Capital. In *States and Sovereignty in the Global Economy*, David Smith, Dorothy Solinger, and Steven Topik, eds. London: Routledge, 53–72.

Ashley, Richard K. 1984. The Poverty of Neorealism. *International Organization* 38(2): 225–286.

Ashley, Richard K. and Robert B. J. Walker. 1990. Reading Dissidence/Writing the Discipline: Crisis and the Question of Sovereignty in International Studies. *International Studies Quarterly* 34(3): 367–416.

Auld, Graeme, Steven Bernstein, and Benjamin Cashore. 2008. The New Corporate Social Responsibility. *Annual Review of Environment and Resources* 33(1): 413–435.

Austin, John. 2009 [1832]. *The Province of Jurisprudence Determined*. Cambridge: Cambridge University Press.

Avant, Deborah. 2004. Conserving Nature in the State of Nature: The Politics of INGO Policy. *Review of International Studies* 7(1): 361–382.

Avant, Deborah. 2005. *Market for Force: The Consequences of Privatizing Security*. Cambridge: Cambridge University Press.

Avant, Deborah. 2006. The Privatization of Security: Lessons from Iraq. *Orbis* 50(2): 327–340.

Avant, Deborah. 2016. Pragmatic Networks and Transnational Governance of Private Military and Security Services. *International Studies Quarterly* 60(2): 330–342.

Avant, Deborah and Kara Kingma Neu. 2019. The Private Security Events Database. *Journal of Conflict Resolution* 63(8): 1986–2006.

Avant, Deborah and Lee Sigelman. 2010. Private Security and Democracy: Lessons from the US in Iraq. *Security Studies* 19(2): 230–265.

Avant, Deborah, Martha Finnemore, and Susan K. Sell, eds. 2010. *Who Governs the Globe?* Cambridge: Cambridge University Press.

Avant, Deborah and Oliver Westerwinter, eds. 2016. *The New Power Politics: Networks and Transnational Security Governance*. Oxford: Oxford University Press.

Avant, Deborah and Renee de Nevers. 2011. Military Contractors and the American Way of War. *Daedalus* 140(3): 88–99.

Avant, Deborah and Virginia Haufler. 2014. The Dynamics of "Private" Security Strategies and their Public Consequences: Transnational Organizations in Historical Perspective. In *The Return of the Public in Global Governance*, Jacqueline Best and Alexandra Gheciu, eds. Cambridge: Cambridge University Press, 47–69.

Bäckstrand, Karin. 2008. Accountability of Networked Climate Governance: The Rise of Transnational Climate Partnerships. *Global Environmental Politics* 8(3): 74–102.

Baehr, Peter R. 1994. Amnesty International and Its Self-Imposed Limited Mandate. *Netherlands Quarterly of Human Rights* 12(1): 5–21.

Baker, John H. 1979. The Law Merchant and the Common Law before 1700. *Cambridge Law Journal* 38(2): 295–322.

Balanya, Bélen, Ann Doherty, Olivier Hoedeman, Adam Ma'anit, and Erik Wesselius. 2003. *Europe Inc: Regional and Global Restructuring and the Rise of Corporate Power*. London: Pluto Press.

Barkin, J. Samuel. 2021. *Sovereignty Cartel*. Cambridge: Cambridge University Press.

Barkin, J. Samuel and Bruce Cronin. 1994. The State and the Nation: Changing Norms and the Rules of Sovereignty in International Relations. *International Organization* 48(1): 107–130.

Barkin, J. Samuel and Laura Sjoberg, eds. 2017. *Interpretive Quantification: Methodological Explorations for Critical and Constructivist IR.* Ann Arbor: University of Michigan Press.

Barnett, Michael and Raymond Duvall, eds. 2005. *Power in Global Governance.* Cambridge: Cambridge University Press.

Bartelson, Jens. 1995. *A Genealogy of Sovereignty.* Cambridge: Cambridge University Press.

Bartelson, Jens. 2006. The Concept of Sovereignty Revisited. *European Journal of International Law* 17(2): 463–474.

Bartelson, Jens. 2011. On the Indivisibility of Sovereignty. *Republics of Letters* 2(2): 85–94.

Bartley, Tim. 2003. Certifying Forests and Factories: States, Social Movements, and the Rise of Private Regulation in the Apparel and Forest Products Fields. *Politics & Society* 31(3): 433–464.

Basile, Mary Elizabeth, Jane Fiar Bestor, Daniel R. Coquillette, and Charles Donahue, Jr., eds. 1998. *Lex Mercatoria and Legal Pluralism: A Late Thirteenth Century Treatise and Its Afterlife.* Cambridge: Ames Foundation.

Beder, Sharon. 2006. *Suiting Themselves: How Corporations Drive the Global Agenda.* London: Earthscan.

Bell, Stephen. 2008. Rethinking the Role of the State: Explaining Business Collective Action at the Business Council of Australia. *Polity* 40(4): 464–487.

Bellamy, Alex. 2009. *Responsibility to Protect: The Global Effort to End Mass Atrocities.* Cambridge: Polity Press.

Bennett, Andrew and Colin Elman. 2007. Case Study Methods in the International Relations Subfield. *Comparative Political Studies* 40(2): 170–195.

Benson, Bruce L. 1989. The Spontaneous Evolution of Commercial Law. *Southern Economic Journal* 55(3): 644–661.

Benton, Lauren. 2009. *A Search for Sovereignty: Law and Geography in European Empires, 1400–1900.* Cambridge: Cambridge University Press.

Berger, Klaus-Peter. 1999. *The Creeping Codification of the Lex Mercatoria.* The Hague: Kluwer.

Berman, Harold J. 1983. *Law and Revolution: The Formation of Western Legal Tradition.* Cambridge, MA: Harvard University Press.

Berman, Paul Schiff. 2005. From International Law to Law and Globalization. *Columbia Journal of Transnational Law* 43(2): 485–556.

Berman, Paul Schiff. 2009. The New Legal Pluralism. *Annual Review of Law and Social Science* 5(1): 225–242.

Berman, Paul Schiff. 2012. *Global Legal Pluralism: A Jurisprudence of Law beyond Borders.* New York: Cambridge University Press.

Berndtsson, Joakim and Maria Stern. 2011. Private Security and the Public–Private Divide: Contested Lines of Distinction and Modes of Governance in the Stockholm-Arlanda Security Assemblage. *International Political Sociology* 5(4): 408–425.

Bernstein, Lisa. 1996. Merchant Law in a Merchant Court: Rethinking the Code's Search for Immanent Business Norms. *University of Pennsylvania Law Review* 144(5): 1765–1821.

Bernstein, Steven. 2014. The Publicness of Non-state Global Environmental and Social Governance. In *The Return of the Public in Global Governance*, Jacqueline Best and Alexandra Gheciu, eds. Cambridge: Cambridge University Press, 120–148.

Bertilorenzi, Marco. 2015. Legitimising Cartels: The Joint Roles of the League of Nations and of the International Chamber of Commerce. In *Regulating Competition: Cartel Registers in the Twentieth-Century World*, Susanna Fellman and Martin Shanahan, eds. London: Routledge, 30–47.

Best, Jacqueline and Alexandra Gheciu, eds. 2014. *The Return of the Public in Global Governance*. Cambridge: Cambridge University Press.

Betts, Richard K. 2000. Is Strategy an Illusion? *International Security* 25(2): 5–50.

Bhabha, Homi. 1994. *The Location of Culture*. London: Routledge.

Bickerton, Christopher, Philip Cunliffe, and Alexander Gourevitch, eds. 2007. *Politics without Sovereignty: A Critique of Contemporary International Relations*. London: University College London Press.

Bidwell, Percy W. and William Diebold, Jr. 1949. The United States and the International Trade Organization. *International Conciliation* 449(March): 187–237.

Biersteker, Thomas and Cynthia Weber, eds. 1996. *State Sovereignty as Social Construct*. Cambridge: Cambridge University Press.

Bilchitz, David and Surya Deva. 2013. The Human Rights Obligations of Business: A Critical Framework for the Future. In *Human Rights Obligations of Business: Beyond the Corporate Responsibility to Respect?* Surya Deva and David Bilchitz, eds. Cambridge: Cambridge University Press, 1–26.

Blachford, Kevin. 2020. Revisiting the Expansion Thesis: International Society and the Role of the Dutch East India Company as a Merchant Empire. *European Journal of International Relations* 26(4): 1230–1248.

Blackstone, William. 1765. *Commentaries on the Laws of England*. Oxford: Clarendon Press.

Blaney, David and Naeem Inayatullah. 2000. The Westphalian Deferral. *International Studies Review* 2(2): 29–64.

Bob, Clifford. 2005. *The Marketing of Rebellion: Insurgents, Media, and International Activism*. Cambridge: Cambridge University Press.

Bodin, Jean. 1992 [1576]. *On Sovereignty: Four Chapters from the Six Books of the Commonwealth*, Julian H. Franklin, ed. and trans. Cambridge: Cambridge University Press.

Bogart, Dan. 2017a. Policy Risk, Uncertainty, and Investment: Evidence from the English East India Company. Paper presented at the Society for Institutional and Organizational Economics annual meeting. http://papers.sioe.org/paper/1906.html

Bogart, Dan. 2017b. The East Indian Monopoly and the Transition from Limited Access in England, 1600–1813. In *Organizations, Civil Society, and the Roots of Development*, Naomi R. Lamoreaux and John Joseph Wallis, eds. Chicago: University of Chicago Press, 23–49.

Bolts, William. 1772. *Considerations on India Affairs; Particularly Respecting the Present State of Bengal Dependencies, etc.* London: Almon, Elmsley, Richardson and Urquhart.

Börzel, Tanja A. and Thomas Risse. 2005. Public-Private Partnerships: Effective and Legitimate Tools of International Governance? In *Complex Sovereignty: On the Reconstitution of Political Authority in the 21st Century*, Edgar Grande and Louis W. Pauly, eds. Toronto: University of Toronto Press: 195–216.

Börzel, Tanja A. and Thomas Risse. 2010. Governance without a State: Can It Work? *Regulation & Governance* 4(2): 113–134.

Bowen, H. V. 1991. *Revenue and Reform: The Indian Problem in British Politics, 1757–1773*. Cambridge: Cambridge University Press.

Bowen, H. V. 2005. *The Business of Empire: The East India Company and Imperial Britain, 1756–1833*. Cambridge: Cambridge University Press.

Braithwaite, John and Peter Drahos. 2000. *Global Business Regulation*. Cambridge: Cambridge University Press.

Bräutigam, Deborah, Lise Rakner, and Scott Taylor. 2002. Business Associations and Growth Coalitions in Sub-Saharan Africa. *The Journal of Modern African Studies* 40(4): 519–547.

Brenner, Neil. 2004. *New State Spaces: Urban Governance and the Rescaling of Statehood.* Oxford: Oxford University Press.

Briody, Dan. 2004. *The Halliburton Agenda: The Politics of Oil and Money.* New Jersey: John Wiley.

Brooks, Doug. 2000. Messiahs or Mercenaries? The Future of International Private Military Services. *International Peacekeeping* 7(4): 129–144.

Brown, W. Jethro. 1906. Sovereignty. *The Juridical Review* 18(1): 1–17.

Brown, Wendy. 2010. *Walled States, Waning Sovereignty.* New York: Zone Books.

Brühl, Tanja and Matthias Hofferberth. 2013. Global Companies as Social Actors: Constructing Private Business in Global Governance. In *The Handbook of Global Companies,* John Mikler, ed. New York: Wiley, 351–370.

Brysk, Alison. 2013. *Speaking Rights to Power: Constructing Political Will.* Oxford: Oxford University Press.

Buchanan, Tom. 2002. "The Truth Will Set You Free": The Making of Amnesty International. *Journal of Contemporary History* 37(4): 575–597.

Buchanan, Tom. 2004. Amnesty International in Crisis, 1966–7. *Twentieth-Century British History* 15(3): 267–289.

Buchanan, Tom. 2009. Human Rights Campaigns in Modern Britain. In *NGOs in Contemporary Britain: Non-state Actors in Society and Politics since 1945,* Nick Crowson, Matthew Hilton, and James McKay, eds. New York: Palgrave Macmillan, 113–128.

Burdick, Francis M. 1902. What Is the Law Merchant? *Columbia Law Review* 2(7): 470–485.

Burke, Edmund. 1909. *Speeches on the Impeachment of Warren Hastings,* 2nd ed. Calcutta: Bangabasi Press.

Büthe, Tim. 2004. Governance through Private Authority: Non-State Actors in World Politics. *Journal of International Affairs* 59(1): 281–290.

Büthe, Tim and Walter Mattli. 2011. *The New Global Rulers: The Privatization of Regulation in the World Economy.* Princeton: Princeton University Press.

Butterfield, L. H., ed. 1961. *Diary and Autobiography of John Adams.* Harvard: Harvard University Press.

Buzan, Barry and George Lawson. 2015. *The Global Transformation: History, Modernity and the Making of International Relations.* Cambridge: Cambridge University Press.

Callahan, David. 2017. *The Givers: Wealth, Power, and Philanthropy in a New Gilded Age.* New York: Vintage.

Canclini, Nestor Garcia. 1995. *Hybrid Cultures: Strategies for Entering and Leaving Modernity.* St. Paul: University of Minnesota Press.

Carpenter, Charli. 2014. *"Lost" Causes: Agenda Vetting in Global Issue Networks and the Shaping of Human Security.* Ithaca: Cornell University Press.

Carr, E. H. 1981 [1939]. *The Twenty Years' Crisis 1919–1939.* London: Palgrave.

Carroll, William K. 2013. *The Making of a Transnational Capitalist Class: Corporate Power in the 21st Century.* New York: Zed Books.

Carruthers, Bruce G. 1996. *City of Capital: Politics and Markets in the English Financial Revolution.* Princeton: Princeton University Press.

Caruso, Daniela. 2006. Private Law and State-Making in the Age of Globalization. *International Law and Politics* 39(1): 1–74.

Cashore, Benjamin, Graeme Auld, and Deanna Newsom. 2004. *Governing through Markets: Forest Certification and the Emergence of Non-state Authority.* New Haven: Yale University Press.

Casini, Lorenzo. 2014. "Down the Rabbit-Hole": The Projection of the Public/Private Distinction beyond the State. *International Journal of Constitutional Law* 12(2): 402–428.

Cederman, Lars-Erik. 1997. *Emergent Actors in World Politics: How States and Nations Develop and Dissolve.* Princeton: Princeton University Press.

Cha, Taesuh. 2016. The Return of Jacksonianism: The International Implications of the Trump Phenomenon. *The Washington Quarterly* 39(4): 83–97.

Charlesworth, Hilary. 1995. Worlds Apart: Public/Private Distinctions in International Law. In *Public and Private: Feminist Legal Debates*, Margaret Thornton, ed. Australia: Oxford University Press, 243–260.

Charnovitz, Steve. 1997. Two Centuries of Participation: NGOs and International Governance. *Michigan Journal of International Law* 18(2): 183–286.

Charnovitz, Steve. 2000. Opening the WTO to Nongovernmental Interests. *Fordham International Law Journal* 24(1–2): 173–216.

Charnovitz, Steve. 2004. Transparency and Participation in the World Trade Organization. *Rutgers Law Review* 56(4): 927-960.

Chaudhuri, K. N. 1978. *The Trading World of Asia and the English East India Company, 1600–1760.* Cambridge: Cambridge University Press.

Chinkin, Christine. 1999. A Critique of the Public/Private Dimension. *European Journal of International Law* 10(2): 387–395.

Chowdhury, Arjun and Raymond Duvall. 2014. Sovereignty and Sovereign Power. *International Theory* 6(2): 191–223.

Ciepley, David. 2013. Beyond Public and Private: Toward a Political Theory of the Corporation. *American Political Science Review* 107(1): 139–158.

Clark, Ann Marie. 2001. *Diplomacy of Conscience: Amnesty International and Changing Human Rights Norms.* Princeton: Princeton University Press.

Cocks, Joan. 2014. *On Sovereignty and Other Political Delusions.* London: Bloomsbury.

Cohen, Ronnie and Shannon O'Byrne. 2013. "Can You Hear Me Now ... Good!" Feminism(s), the Public/Private Divide, and Citizens United v. FEC. *UCLA Women's Law Journal* 20(1): 39–70.

Cohen, Samy. 2006. *The Resilience of the State.* London: Hurst.

Colas, Alejandro and Bryan Mabee, eds. 2010. *Mercenaries, Pirates, Bandits and Empires: Private Violence in Historical Context.* London: Hurst & EIC.

Collingwood, R. G. 1989. *Essays in Political Philosophy.* Oxford: Oxford University Press.

Connolly, William E. 2005. *Pluralism.* Durham: Duke University Press.

Cook, Helena. 1996. Amnesty International at the United Nations. In *The Conscience of the World: The Influence of Non-Governmental Organizations in the UN System*, Peter Willets, ed. Washington, DC: Brookings Institution, 181–213.

Cooley, Alexander and Hendrik Spruyt. 2009. *Contracting States: Sovereign Transfers in International Relations.* Princeton: Princeton University Press.

Cooley, Alexander and James Ron. 2002. The NGO Scramble: Organizational Insecurity and the Political Economy of Transnational Action. *International Security* 27(1): 5–39.

Costa Lopez, Julia, Benjamin de Carvalho, Andrew Latham et al. 2018. Forum: In the Beginning There was No Word (for it): Terms, Concepts, and Early Sovereignty. *International Studies Review* 20(3): 489–519.

Cox, Robert. 1986. Social Forces, States and World Orders: Beyond International Relations Theory. In *Neorealism and Its Critics*, Robert Keohane, ed. New York: Columbia University Press, 204–254.

Crawford, Kate and Jason Schultz. 2019. AI Systems as State Actors. *Columbia Law Review* 119 (7): 1941–1972.

Cutler, A. Claire. 1997. Artifice, Ideology and Paradox: The Public/Private Distinction in International Law. *Review of International Political Economy* 4(2): 261–285.

Cutler, A. Claire. 2001. Critical Reflections on the Westphalian Assumptions of International Law and Organization: A Crisis of Legitimacy. *Review of International Studies* 27(2): 133–150.

Cutler, A. Claire. 2003. *Private Power and Global Authority: Transnational Merchant Law in the Global Political Economy*. Cambridge: Cambridge University Press.

Cutler, A. Claire. 2010. Constituting Capitalism: Corporations, Law, and Private Transnational Governance. *St Antony's International Review* 5(1): 99–115.

Cutler, A. Claire, Virginia Haufler, and Tony Porter, eds. 1999. *Private Authority and International Affairs*. Albany: State University of New York Press.

Dahl, Robert. 1999. Can International Organizations Be Democratic? A Skeptic's view. In *Democracy's Edges*, Ian Shapiro and Casiano Hacker-Gordon, eds. Cambridge: Cambridge University Press, 19–36.

Dalrymple, William. 2019. *The Anarchy: The East India Company, Corporate Violence, and the Pillage of an Empire*. London: Bloomsbury.

de Nevers, Renée. 2009. (Self) Regulating War? Voluntary Regulation and the Private Security Industry. *Security Studies* 18(3): 479–516.

de Witte, Bruno. 2006. Sovereignty and European Integration: The Weight of a Legal Tradition. In *Relocating Sovereignty*, Neil Walker, ed. Aldershot: Ashgate, 491–520.

Denis, Jean-Louis, Ewan Ferlie, and Nicolette Van Gestel. 2015. Understanding Hybridity in Public Organizations. *Public Administration* 93(2): 273–289.

Denning, Lord. 1990. *Introduction to the European Court of Justice: Judges or Policy Makers?* London: Bruges Group.

Deutsch, Karl W. 1957. *Political Community and the North Atlantic Area*. Princeton: Princeton University Press.

Dewey, John. 1927. *The Public and Its Problems*. Chicago: Sage.

Dezalay, Yves and Bryant Garth. 1994. *Dealing in Virtue: International Commercial Arbitration and the Construction of a Transnational Legal Order*. Chicago: University of Chicago Press.

Dezalay, Yves and Bryant Garth. 1995. Merchants of Law as Moral Entrepreneurs: Constructing International Justice from the Competition for Transnational Business Disputes. *Law & Society Review* 29(1): 27–64.

Dezalay, Yves and Bryant Garth. 2006. From the Cold War to Kosovo: The Rise and Renewal of the Field of International Human Rights. *Annual Review of Law and Social Science* 2(1): 231–255.

Dicey, A. V. 1885. *The Law of the Constitution*. London: Liberty Fund.

Dickinson, Laura A. 2011. *Outsourcing War and Peace: Preserving Public Values in a World of Privatized Foreign Affairs*. New Haven: Yale University Press.

Diebold, Jr., William. 1952. The End of the ITO. In *Essays in International Finance* (16). Princeton: Princeton University.

Dietz, Mary G., ed. 1990. *Thomas Hobbes and Political Theory*. Lawrence: University Press of Kansas.

Dirks, Nicholas. 2008. *The Scandal of Empire: India and the Creation of Imperial Britain*. Cambridge, MA: Harvard University Press.

Donahue, Jr., Charles. 2004. Medieval and Early Modern Lex Mercatoria: An Attempt at the Probatio Diabolica. *Chicago Journal of International Law* 5(1): 21–37.

Doner, Richard F. and Ben Ross Schneider. 2000. Business Associations and Economic Development: Why Some Associations Contribute More than Others. *Business and Politics* 2(3): 261–288.

Doty, D. Harold and William H. Glick. 1994. Typologies as a Unique Form of Theory Building: Toward Improved Understanding and Modeling. *The Academy of Management Review* 19(2): 230–251.

Doty, Roxanne L. 1996. Sovereignty and the Nation: Constructing the Boundaries of National Identity. In *State Sovereignty as Social Construct*, Thomas Biersteker and Cynthia Weber, eds. Cambridge: Cambridge University Press, 121–143.

Doty, Roxanne L. 2007. States of Exception on the Mexico–U.S. Border: Security, "Decisions," and Civilian Border Patrols. *International Political Sociology* 1(2): 113–137.

Drache, Daniel. 2000. The Short but Significant Life of the International Trade Organization: Lessons for Our Time. CSGE Working Paper No. 62/00.

Duffield, Mark. 2007. *Development, Security and Unending War: Governing the World of Peoples*. Cambridge: Polity.

Dunigan, Molly. 2011. *Victory for Hire: Private Security Companies' Impact on Military Effectiveness*. Stanford: Stanford University Press.

Dunigan, Molly and Ulrich Petersohn, eds. 2015. *The Markets for Force: Privatization of Security across World Regions*. Philadelphia: University of Pennsylvania Press.

Eckel, Jan. 2013. The International League for the Rights of Man, Amnesty International, and the Changing Fate of Human Rights Activism from the 1940s through the 1970s. *Humanity* 4(2): 183–214.

Eckert, Amy. 2016. *Outsourcing War: The Just War Tradition in the Age of Military Privatization*. Ithaca: Cornell University Press.

Eckstein, Harry. 1975. Case Studies and Theory in Political Science. In *Handbook of Political Science*, Fred Greenstein and Nelson Polsby, eds. Reading: Addison-Wesley, 79–138.

Edkins, Jenny and Véronique Pin-Fat. 1997. Jean Bethke Elshtain: Traversing the Terrain between. In *The Future of International Relations: Masters in the Making?* Iver B. Neumann and Ole Wæver, eds. London: Taylor & Francis, 312–338.

Edkins, Jenny and Veronique Pin-Fat. 1999. The Subject of the Political. In *Sovereignty and Subjectivity*, Jenny Edkins, Nalini Persram, and Veronique Pin-Fat, eds. Boulder: Lynne Rienner, 1–19.

Edkins, Jenny, Veronique Pin-Fat, and Michael Shapiro, eds. 2004. *Sovereign Lives: Power in Global Politics*. London: Routledge.

Elliot, Jonathan. 1836–59. *The Debates in the Several State Conventions on the Adoption of the Federal Constitution, etc*. Philadelphia: J. B. Lippincott.

Elshtain, Jean Bethke. 1981. *Public Man, Private Woman: Women in Social and Political Thought*. Princeton: Princeton University Press.

Epstein, Richard A. 2004. Reflections on the Historical Origins and Economic Structure of the Law Merchant. *Chicago Journal of International Law* 5(1): 1–20.

Ericson, Richard, Dean Barry, and Aaron Doyle. 2000. The Moral Hazards of Neo-liberalism: Lessons from the Private Insurance Industry. *Economy and Society* 29(4): 532–558.

Erikson, Emily. 2014. *Between Monopoly and Free Trade: The English East India Company, 1600 – 1757*. Princeton: Princeton University Press.

Erskine, Toni, ed. 2003. *Can Institutions Have Responsibilities? Collective Moral Agency and International Relations*. New York: Palgrave Macmillan.

Erskine, Toni. 2008. Locating Responsibility: The Problem of Moral Agency in International Relations. In *The Oxford Handbook on International Relations*, Christian Reus-Smit and Duncan Snidal, eds. Oxford: Oxford University Press, 699–707.

Evans, Peter. 1995. *Embedded Autonomy: States and Industrial Transformation*. Princeton: Princeton University Press.

Fainaru, Steve. 2008. *Big Boy Rules: America's Mercenaries Fighting in Iraq*. Philadelphia: Da Capo Press.

Falk, Richard. 1999. *Predatory Globalization: A Critique*. Cambridge: Cambridge University Press.

Farrell, Henry and Abraham L. Newman. 2014. Domestic Institutions beyond the Nation-State: Charting the New Interdependence Approach. *World Politics* 66(2): 331–363.

Fassberg, Celia Wasserstein. 2004. Lex Mercatoria – Hoist with Its Own Petard? *Chicago Journal of International Law* 5(1): 67–82.

Feaver, Peter D. 1996. The Civil-Military Problematique: Huntington, Janowitz and the Question of Civilian Control. *Armed Forces and Society* 23(2): 149–179.

Feigenbaum, Harvey and Jeffrey Henig. 1994. The Political Underpinnings of Privatization: A Typology. *World Politics* 46(2): 185–208.

Finnemore, Martha. 2004. *The Purpose of Intervention: Changing Beliefs about the Use of Force*. Ithaca: Cornell University Press.

Fitzsimmons, Scott. 2013. Wheeled Warriors: Explaining Variations in the Use of Violence by Private Security Companies in Iraq. *Security Studies* 22(4): 707–739.

Fitzsimmons, Scott. 2015. *Private Security Companies during the Iraq War: Military Performance and the Use of Deadly Force*. London: Routledge.

Flanigan, Shawn Teresa. 2012. Terrorists Next Door? A Comparison of Mexican Drug Cartels and Middle Eastern Terrorist Organizations. *Terrorism and Political Violence* 24(2): 279–294.

Flathman, Richard E. 1980. *The Practice of Political Authority: Authority and the Authoritative*. Chicago: University of Chicago Press.

Foucault, Michel. 1980. *Power/Knowledge: Selected Interviews and Other Writings 1972–1977*. New York: Vintage.

Foucault, Michel. 2007. *Security, Territory, Population: Lectures at the Collège De France 1977–1978*. New York: Picador.

Fowler, Michael Ross and Julie Marie Bunck. 1995. *Law, Power, and the Sovereign State: The Evolution and Application of the Concept of Sovereignty*. College Station: Penn State University Press.

Friedrich, Carl J., ed. 1958. *NOMOS I: Authority*. Cambridge, MA: Harvard University Press.

Fuchs, Doris. 2007. *Business Power in Global Governance*. Boulder: Lynne Rienner.

Gardner, Richard R. 1956. *Sterling Dollar Diplomacy: Anglo-American Collaboration in the Reconstruction of Multilateral Trade*. New York: Oxford University Press.

Gaudet, Michel. 1982. The International Chamber of Commerce Court of Arbitration. *Proceedings of the Annual Meeting of American Society of International Law* 76: 172–175.

George, Alexander and Andrew Bennett. 2005. *Case Studies and Theory Development in the Social Sciences*. Cambridge: MIT Press.

Gibbon, Edward. 1996. *The History of the Decline and Fall of the Roman Empire*. London: Penguin Classics.

Giddens, Anthony. 1985. *The Nation-State and Violence*. Berkeley: University of California Press.

Gill, Stephen. 1998. European Governance and New Constitutionalism: Economic and Monetary Union and Alternatives. *New Political Economy* 3(1): 5–26.

Gillette, Clayton P. 2004. The Law Merchant in the Modern Age: Institutional Design and International Usages under the CISG. *Chicago Journal of International Law* 5(1): 157–179.

Gilpin, Robert. 1981. *War and Change in World Politics*. Cambridge: Cambridge University Press.

Gilroy, Paul. 1993. *The Black Atlantic: Modernity and Double Consciousness*. London: Verso.

Gingold, Edward and Darrell Blakeway. 2000. A Visit to the International Chamber of Commerce: A Salute to Unsung Heroes. *Chitty's Law Journal and Family Law Review* 48 (1): 31–36.

Glanville, Luke. 2013a. The Myth of "Traditional" Sovereignty. *International Studies Quarterly* 57(1): 79–90.

Glanville, Luke. 2013b. *Sovereignty and the Responsibility to Protect: A New History*. Chicago: University of Chicago Press.

Goddard, Stacie E. and Ronald R. Krebs. 2015. Rhetoric, Legitimation, and Grand Strategy. *Security Studies* 24(1): 5–36.

Goertz, Gary and James Mahoney. 2012. *A Tale of Two Cultures: Qualitative and Quantitative Research in the Social Sciences*. Princeton: Princeton University Press.

Goffman, Erving. 1956. *The Presentation of the Self in Everyday Life*. New York: Random House.

Goldsmith, Jack and Tim Wu. 2006. *Who Controls the Internet? Illusions of a Borderless World*. New York: Oxford University Press.

Goldsworthy, Jeffrey. 1999. *The Sovereignty of Parliament: History and Philosophy*. Oxford: Oxford University Press.

Goode, Roy. 1995. Abstract Payment Undertakings and the Rules of the International Chamber of Commerce. *Saint Louis University Law Journal* 39(3): 725–744.

Grande, Edgar and Louis W. Pauly, eds. 2005. *Complex Sovereignty: Reconstituting Political Authority in the Twenty-First Century*. Toronto: University of Toronto Press.

Granovetter, Mark. 1995. Coase Revisited: Business Groups in the Modern Economy. *Industrial and Corporate Change* 4(1): 93–130.

Graz, Jean-Christophe. 2006. Hybrids and Regulation in the Global Political Economy. *Competition and Change* 10(2): 230–245.

Graz, Jean-Christophe and Andreas Nölke, eds. 2008. *Transnational Private Governance and Its Limits*. London: Routledge.

Green, Jessica. 2014. *Rethinking Private Authority: Agents and Entrepreneurs in Global Environmental Governance*. Princeton: Princeton University Press.

Green, Jessica and Graeme Auld. 2017. Unbundling the Regime Complex: The Effects of Private Authority. *Transnational Environmental Law* 6(2): 259–284.

Grimm, Dieter and Belinda Cooper. 2015. *Sovereignty: The Origin and Future of a Political and Legal Concept*. New York: Columbia University Press.

Grovogui, Siba. 2002. Regimes of Sovereignty: International Morality and the African Condition. *European Journal of International Relations* 8(3): 315–338.

Hafner-Burton, Emilie. 2013. *Making Human Rights a Reality*. Princeton: Princeton University Press.

Haggard, Stephan. 1990. *Pathways from the Periphery: The Politics of Growth in the Newly Industrializing Countries*. Ithaca: Cornell University Press.

Haight, George W. 1960. Activities of the International Chamber of Commerce and Other Business Groups. *Proceedings of the American Society of International Law at Its Annual Meeting* 54: 200–205.

Hall, Peter and David Soskice, eds. 2001. *Varieties of Capitalism: The Institutional Foundations of Comparative Advantage*. Oxford: Oxford University Press.

Hall, Rodney Bruce and Thomas Biersteker, eds. 2002. *The Emergence of Private Authority in Global Governance*. Cambridge: Cambridge University Press.

Halliday, Terence C. and Bruce G. Carruthers. 2009. *Bankrupt: Global Lawmaking and Systemic Financial Crisis*. Palo Alto: Stanford University Press.

Halliday, Terence C. and Gregory Shaffer, eds. 2014. *Transnational Legal Orders*. Cambridge: Cambridge University Press.

Harcourt, Bernard E. 2011. *The Illusion of Free Markets: Punishment and the Myth of Natural Order*. Cambridge, MA: Harvard University Press.

Harcourt, Bernard E. 2018. *The Counterrevolution: How Our Government Went to War against Its Own Citizens*. New York: Basic Books.

Hardt, Michael and Antonio Negri. 2000. *Empire*. Cambridge, MA: Harvard University Press.

Hathaway, James C. 2005. *The Rights of Refugees under International Law*. Cambridge: Cambridge University Press.

Haufler, Virginia. 2001. *A Public Role for the Private Sector: Industry Self-Regulation in the Global Economy*. Washington, DC: Carnegie Endowment for International Peace.

Haufler, Virginia. 2010. Corporations in Zones of Conflict: Issues, Actors, and Institutions. In *Who Governs the Globe?* Deborah Avant, Martha Finnemore, and Susan Sell, eds. Cambridge: Cambridge University Press, 102–130.

Hausmann, Ricardo and Dani Rodrik. 2003. Economic Development as Self-Discovery. *Journal of Development Economics* 72(2): 603–633.

Hegel, Georg Wilhelm Friedrich. 1991 [1820]. *Philosophy of Right*. Cambridge: Cambridge University Press.

Held, David. 2004. Democratic Accountability and Political Effectiveness from a Cosmopolitan Perspective. *Government and Opposition* 39(2): 364–391.

Heller, Hermann. 2019. *Sovereignty: A Contribution to the Theory of Public and International Law*, David Dyzenhaus, ed. Oxford: Oxford University Press.

Herzog, Don. 2013. *Household Politics*. New Haven: Yale University Press.

Herzog, Don. 2020. *Sovereignty, R.I.P.* New Haven: Yale University Press.

Hielscher, Stefan, Jan Winkin, Angela Crack, and Ingo Pies. 2017. Saving the Moral Capital of NGOs: Identifying One-Sided and Many-Sided Social Dilemmas in NGO Accountability. *Voluntas* 28(4): 1–33.

Hinsley, F. H. 1986. *Sovereignty*. Cambridge: Cambridge University Press.

Hobbes, Thomas. 1996 [1651]. *The Leviathan*. Cambridge: Cambridge University Press.

Hocking, Brian and Dominic Kelly. 2001. Doing the Business? The International Chamber of Commerce, the United Nations, and the Global Compact. In *Enhancing Global Governance: Towards a New Diplomacy?* Andrew Cooper, John English, and Ramesh Thakur, eds. New York: United Nations University Press, 203–228.

Holdsworth, William Searle. 1928. *Some Lessons from Our Legal History*. New York: Columbia University Press.

Hopgood, Stephen. 2006. *Keepers of the Flame: Understanding Amnesty International*. Ithaca: Cornell University Press.

Hopgood, Stephen. 2009. Moral Authority, Modernity and the Politics of the Sacred. *European Journal of International Relations* 15(2): 229–255.

Hopgood, Stephen. 2010. Amnesty International: The Politics of Morality. *openDemocracy*. www.opendemocracy.net/en/amnesty_morality_3625jsp/

Hopgood, Stephen. 2013. *The Endtimes of Human Rights*. Ithaca: Cornell University Press.

Hortsch, Diana. 2010. The Paradox of Partnership: Amnesty International, Responsible Advocacy, and NGO Accountability. *Columbia Human Rights Law Review* 42(1): 119–155.

Horwitz, Morton J. 1982. The History of the Public/Private Distinction. *University of Pennsylvania Law Review* 130(6): 1423–1428.

Howell, Thomas Bayly and Thomas Jones Howell. 1816. *A Complete Collection of State Trials and Proceedings for High Treason and Other Crimes and Misdemeanors from the Earliest Period to the Year 1820*, Volume 10. London: T. C. Hansard.

Huckerby, Jayne and Sir Nigel Rodley. 2009. Outlawing Torture: The Story of Amnesty International's Efforts to Shape the UN Convention against Torture. In *Human Rights Advocacy Stories*, Deena Hurwitz and Margaret Satterthwaite, eds. New York: New York Foundation Press/Thomson West, 15–41.

Hunt, Isaac. 1775. *The Political Family*. Philadelphia: James Humphrey.

Huntington, Samuel. 1957. *The Soldier and the State: The Theory and Politics of Civil-Military Relations*. Cambridge, MA: Harvard University Press.

Hurd, Ian. 1999. Legitimacy and Authority in International Politics. *International Organization* 53(2): 379–408.

Hurd, Ian. 2007. *After Anarchy: Legitimacy and Power in the United Nations Security Council*. Princeton: Princeton University Press.

Hurd, Ian. 2017. *How to Do Things with International Law*. Princeton: Princeton University Press.

Hurt, Shelley and Ronnie Lipshutz, eds. 2016. *Hybrid Rule and State Formation: Public-Private Power in the 21st Century*. New York: Routledge.

Hutnyk, John. 2005. Hybridity. *Ethnic and Racial Studies* 28(1): 79–102.

Inayatullah, Naeem and David L. Blaney. 1995. Realizing Sovereignty. *Review of International Studies* 21(1): 3–20.

Isenberg, David. 2004. *A Fistful of Contractors: The Case for a Pragmatic Assessment of Private Military Companies in Iraq*. London: British-American Security Information Council.

Isenberg, David. 2008. *Shadow Force: Private Security Contractors in Iraq*. Westport: Praeger Security International.

Isenberg, David. 2009. *Private Military Contractors and U.S. Grand Strategy*. International Peace Research Institute Report 1/2009.

Ishay, Micheline R. 2004. *The History of Human Rights: From Ancient Times to the Globalization Era*. Berkeley: University of California Press.

Jackson, John H. 2003. Sovereignty-Modern: A New Approach to an Outdated Concept. *The American Journal of International Law* 97(4): 782–802.

Jackson, Patrick Thaddeus. 2017. The Production of Facts: Ideal-Typification and the Preservation of Politics. In *Max Weber and International Relations*, Richard Ned Lebow, ed. Cambridge: Cambridge University Press, 79–96.

Jackson, Robert. 1990. *Quasi-States: Sovereignty, International Relations and the Third World*. Cambridge: Cambridge University Press.

Jackson, Robert. 1999. Sovereignty in World Politics: A Glance at the Conceptual and Historical Landscape. *Political Studies* 47(3): 431–456.

Jackson, Robert. 2007. *Sovereignty: The Evolution of an Idea*. Cambridge: Polity.

Jayasuriya, Kanishka. 2001. Globalization, Sovereignty, and the Rule of Law: From Political to Economic Constitutionalism? *Constellations* 8(4): 442–460.

Jervis, Robert. 1978. Cooperation under the Security Dilemma. *World Politics* 30(2): 167–214.

Jervis, Robert. 1997. *System Effects: Complexity in Political and Social Life*. Princeton: Princeton University Press.

Jimenez, Guillermo. 1996. The International Chamber of Commerce: Supplier of Standards and Instruments for International Trade. *Uniform Law Review* 1(2): 284–299.

Joerges, Christian, Inger-Johanne Sand, and Gunther Teubner, eds. 2004. *Transnational Governance and Constitutionalism*. Portland: Hart.

Johnson, Tana. 2014. *Organizational Progeny: Why Governments are Losing Control over Proliferating Structures of Global Governance*. Oxford: Oxford University Press.

Josselin, Daphne and William Wallace, eds. 2001. *Non-State Actors in World Politics*. New York: Palgrave.

Kadens, Emily. 2004. Order within Law, Variety within Custom: The Character of the Medieval Merchant Law. *Chicago Journal of International Law* 5(1): 39–65.

Kadens, Emily. 2012. The Myth of the Customary Law Merchant. *Texas Law Review* 90(5): 1153–1206.

Kaeuper, Richard W. 1988. *War, Justice and the Public Order*. Oxford: Clarendon Press.

Kahler, Miles, ed. 2009. *Networked Politics: Agency, Power and Governance*. Ithaca: Cornell University Press.

Kalmo, Hent and Quentin Skinner, eds. 2010. *Sovereignty in Fragments: The Past, Present and Future of a Contested Concept*. Cambridge: Cambridge University Press.

Kane, John. 2001. *The Politics of Moral Capital*. Cambridge: Cambridge University Press.

Kantorowicz, Ernst. 1957. *The King's Two Bodies*. Princeton: Princeton University Press.

Kaplan, Morton A. 1957. *System and Process in International Politics*. New York: John Wiley.

Katsikas, Dimitrios. 2010. Non-State Authority and Global Governance. *Review of International Studies* 36(S1): 113–135.

Kaufman, Edy. 1991. Prisoners of Conscience: The Shaping of a New Human Rights Concept. *Human Rights Quarterly* 13(3): 339–367.

Keck, Margaret E. and Kathryn Sikkink. 1998. *Activists beyond Borders: Advocacy Networks in International Politics*. Ithaca: Cornell University Press.

Keene, Edward. 2002. *Beyond the Anarchical Society: Grotius, Colonialism, and Order in World Politics*. Cambridge: Cambridge University Press.

Kelly, Claire R. 2008. Institutional Alliances and Derivative Legitimacy. *Michigan Journal of International Law* 29(4): 605–664.

Kelly, Dominic. 2005. The International Chamber of Commerce. *New Political Economy* 10 (2): 259–271.

Kelly, Dominic. 2009. The International Chamber of Commerce. In *Handbook of Transnational Economic Governance Regimes*, Christian Tietje and Alan Brouder, eds. Leiden: Martinus Nijhoff, 143–154.

Keohane, Robert O. 1984. *After Hegemony: Cooperation and Discord in the World Political Economy*. Princeton: Princeton University Press.

Kinsey, Christopher. 2006. *Corporate Soldiers and International Security: The Rise of Private Military Companies*. London: Routledge.

Klare, Karl. 1982. The Public/Private Distinction in Labour Law. *University of Pennsylvania Law Review* 130(6): 1358–1422.

Kobrin, Stephen J. 2009. Private Political Authority and Public Responsibility: Transnational Politics, Transnational Firms, and Human Rights. *Business Ethics Quarterly* 19(3): 349–374.

Koh, Harold Hongju. 1996. Transnational Legal Process. *Nebraska Law Review* 75(1): 181–207.

Korey, William. 1968. *The Key to Human Rights Implementation*. New York: Carnegie Endowment for International Press.

Korey, William. 1998. *NGOs and the Universal Declaration of Human Rights: "A Curious Grapevine."* New York: St. Martin's Press.

Korey, William. 2007. *Taking on the World's Repressive Regimes: The Ford Foundation's International Human Rights Policies and Practices*. New York: Palgrave Macmillan.

Korff, S. A. 1923. The Problem of Sovereignty. *The American Political Science Review* 17(3): 404–414.

Koskenniemi, Martti. 2010. Conclusion: Vocabularies of Sovereignty – Powers of a Paradox. In *Sovereignty in Fragments: The Past, Present and Future of a Contested Concept*, Hent Kalmo and Quentin Skinner, eds. Cambridge: Cambridge University Press, 222–242.

Krahmann, Elke. 2010. *States, Citizens, and the Privatization of Security*. Cambridge: Cambridge University Press.

Kraidy, Marwan. 2005. *Hybridity, or the Cultural Logic of Globalization*. Philadelphia: Temple University Press.

Krasner, Stephen. 1993. Westphalia and All That. In *Ideas and Foreign Policy: Beliefs, Institutions, and Political Change*, Judith Goldstein and Robert Keohane, eds. Ithaca: Cornell University Press, 235–264.

Krasner, Stephen. 1995. Compromising Westphalia. *International Security* 20(3): 115–151.

Krasner, Stephen. 1999. *Sovereignty: Organized Hypocrisy*. Princeton: Princeton University Press.

Krasner, Stephen, ed. 2001a. *Problematic Sovereignty: Contested Rules and Political Possibilities*. New York: Columbia University Press.

Krasner, Stephen. 2001b. Abiding Sovereignty. *International Political Science Review* 22(3): 229–251.

Krasner, Stephen. 2001c. Review: Sovereignty Redux. *International Studies Review* 3(1): 134–138.

Kratochwil, Friedrich. 1986. Of Systems, Boundaries, and Territoriality: An Inquiry into the Formation of the State System. *World Politics* 39(1): 27–52.

Kratochwil, Friedrich and John Ruggie. 1986. International Organization: A State of the Art or an Art of the State? *International Organization* 40(4): 753–775.

Krueger, Anne O., ed. 1996. *The WTO as an International Organization*. Chicago: University of Chicago Press.

Lake, David. 2003. The New Sovereignty in International Relations. *International Studies Review* 5(3): 303–323.

Landes, Joan B., ed. 1998. *Feminism, the Public and the Private*. Oxford: Oxford University Press.

Landes, Joan B. 2003. Further Thoughts on the Public/Private Distinction. *Journal of Women's History* 15(2): 28–39.

Larsen, Egon. 1979. *A Flame in Barbed Wire: The Story of Amnesty International*. New York: W. W. Norton.

Laski, Harold. 1916a. The Personality of Associations. *Harvard Law Review* 29(4): 407–425.

Laski, Harold. 1916b. The Sovereignty of the State. *The Journal of Philosophy, Psychology and Scientific Methods* 13(4): 85–97.

Latour, Bruno. 2007. How to Think like a State. In *The Thinking State*, Wim van de Donk, ed. The Hague: Scientific Council for Government Policy, 19–32.

Laubacher, Thomas. 2017. Simplifying Inherently Governmental Functions: Creating a Principled Approach from Its Ad Hoc Beginnings. *Public Contract Law Journal* 46(4): 791–832.

Lawson, George. 2006. The Promise of Historical Sociology in International Relations. *International Studies Review* 8(3): 397–423.

Lawson, Philip. 1993. *The East India Company: A History*. London: Longman.

Leander, Anna. 2005. The Power to Construct International Security: On the Significance of Private Military Companies. *Millennium* 33(3): 803–826.

Leander, Anna. 2014. Understanding US National Intelligence: Analyzing Practices to Capture the Chimera. In *The Return of the Public in Global Governance*, Jacqueline Best and Alexandra Gheciu, eds. Cambridge: Cambridge University Press, 197–220.

Lemay-Hebert, Nicolas and Rosa Freedman, eds. 2017. *Hybridity: Law, Culture, and Development*. New York: Routledge.

Levit, Janet Koven. 2008. Bottom-up Lawmaking through a Pluralist Lens: The ICC Banking Commission and the Transnational Regulation of Letters of Credit. *Emory Law Journal* 57 (5): 1147–1225.

Levitsky, Steven and Lucan Way. 2010. *Competitive Authoritarianism: Hybrid Regimes after the Cold War*. Cambridge: Cambridge University Press.

Lindblom, Charles E. 1977. *Politics and Markets: The World's Political Economic System*. New York: Basic Books.

Lippert, Randy. 2004. Sanctuary Practices, Rationalities and Sovereignties. *Alternatives* 29(5): 535–555.

List, Christian and Philip Pettit. 2011. *Group Agency: The Possibility, Design, and Status of Corporate Agents*. Oxford: Oxford University Press.

Locke, John. 1988 [1689]. *Two Treatises of Government*. Cambridge: Cambridge University Press.

Lockwood, Erin. 2020. From Bombs to Boons: Changing Views of Risk and Regulation in the Pre-Crisis OTC Derivatives Market. *Theory & Society* 49(2): 215–244.

Lottholz, Philipp. 2017. Nothing More Than a Conceptual Lens? Situating Hybridity in Social Inquiry. In *Hybridity: Law, Culture, and Development*, Nicolas Lemay-Hebert and Rosa Freedman, eds. New York: Routledge, 17–36.

Lu, Catherine. 2006. *Just and Unjust Interventions in World Politics: Public and Private*. New York: Palgrave MacMillan.

Lu, Catherine. 2017. *Justice and Reconciliation in World Politics*. Cambridge: Cambridge University Press.

Lucas, John. 1997. The Politics of Business Associations in the Developing World. *The Journal of Developing Areas* 32(1): 71–96.

Lynch, Cecelia. 2014. *Interpreting International Politics*. London: Routledge.

Lyons, Gene and Michael Mastanduno, eds. 1995. *Beyond Westphalia? State Sovereignty and International Intervention*. Baltimore: Johns Hopkins University Press.

Machiavelli, Niccolò. 1977 [1513]. *The Prince*. New York: Norton.

MacKinnon, Catharine A. 1989. *Toward a Feminist Theory of the State*. Cambridge, MA: Harvard University Press.

Madison, James, Alexander Hamilton, and John Jay. 2003 [1788]. *The Federalist Papers*. Cambridge: Cambridge University Press.

Mahoney, Charles W. 2017. Buyer Beware: How Market Structure Affects Contracting and Company Performance in the Private Military Industry. *Security Studies* 26(1): 30–59.

Mallard, Grégoire and Pierre Pénet. 2013. Seeing Like a Credit Rating Agency: The Constitution of Financial Uncertainties during the Greek Sovereign Debt Crisis. In *Financial Crises: Identification, Forecasting and Effects on Transition Economies*, Cooper Hawthorn, ed. New York: Nova, 164–174.

Martens, Kerstin. 2006. Institutionalizing Societal Activism within Global Governance Structures: Amnesty International and the United Nations System. *Journal of International Relations and Development* 9(4): 371–395.

Mattli, Walter. 2001. Private Justice in a Global Economy: From Litigation to Arbitration. *International Organization* 55(4): 919–947.

Mattli, Walter and Ngaire Woods. 2009. *The Politics of Global Regulation*. Princeton: Princeton University Press.

McFate, Sean. 2014. *The Modern Mercenary: Private Armies and What They Mean for World Order*. Oxford: Oxford University Press.

McKinney, John C. 1966. *Constructive Typology and Social Theory*. New York: Meredith.

Merry, Sally Engle. 1988. Legal Pluralism. *Law and Society Review* 22(5): 869–896.

Merry, Sally Engle. 1991. Law and Colonialism. *Law and Society Review* 25(4): 889–892.

Michaels, Ralf. 2005. The Re-State-Ment of Non-State Law: The State, Choice of Law, and the Challenge from Global Legal Pluralism. *The Wayne Law Review* 51(3): 1209–1259.

Michaels, Ralf. 2009. Global Legal Pluralism. *Annual Review of Law and Social Science* 5(1): 243–262.

Michaels, Ralf and Nils Jansen. 2006. Private Law beyond the State? Europeanization, Globalization, Privatization. *The American Journal of Comparative Law* 54(4): 843–890.

Mikler, John. 2018. *The Political Power of Global Corporations*. Cambridge: Polity.

Milanovic, Branko. 2016. *Global Inequality: A New Approach for the Age of Globalization*. Cambridge, MA: Harvard University Press.

Mile, Andreas and James Perry. 2007. The Power of Transnational Private Governance: Financialization and the IASB. *Business and Politics* 9(3): 1–25.

Milgrom, Paul R., Douglass C. North, and Barry R. Weingast. 1990. The Role of Institutions in the Revival of Trade: The Law Merchant, Private Judges, and the Champagne Fairs. *Economics and Politics* 2(1): 1–23.

Millar, Gearoid. 2014. Disaggregating Hybridity: Why Hybrid Institutions Do Not Produce Predictable Experiences of Peace. *Journal of Peace Research* 51(4): 501–514.

Miller, David. 2007. *National Responsibility and Global Justice*. Oxford: Oxford University Press.

Mills, Alex. 2011. Antinomies of Public and Private at the Foundations of International Investment Law and Arbitration. *Journal of International Economic Law* 14(2): 469–503.

Milner, Helen and Andrew Moravcsik. 2009. *Power, Interdependence, and Nonstate Actors in World Politics*. Princeton: Princeton University Press.

Mitchell, Timothy. 1991. The Limits of the State: Beyond Statist Approaches and Their Critics. *American Political Science Review* 85(1): 77–96.

Mitzen, Jennifer. 2015. Illusion or Intention? Talking Grand Strategy into Existence. *Security Studies* 24(1): 61–94.

Morgenthau, Hans J. 1948. The Problem of Sovereignty Reconsidered. *Columbia Law Review* 48(3): 341–365.

Morgenthau, Hans J. 1966. *Politics Among Nations*. New York: Knopf.

Mueller, Milton. 2009. *Ruling the Root: Internet Governance and the Taming of Cyberspace*. Cambridge, MA: MIT Press.

Murphy, Alexander. 1996. The Sovereign State System as Political-Territorial Ideal: Historical and Contemporary Considerations. In *State Sovereignty as Social Construct*, Thomas Biersteker and Cynthia Weber, eds. Cambridge: Cambridge University Press, 81–120.

Namier, Lewis and John Brooke, eds. 1964. *The History of Parliament: The House of Commons 1754–1790*. London: Boydell and Brewer.

Neumann, Iver B. and Ole Jacob Sending. 2010. *Governing the World Polity: Practice, Mentality, Rationality*. Ann Arbor: University of Michigan Press.

Nye, Jr., Joseph. 2004. *Soft Power: The Means to Succeed in World Politics*. New York: Public Affairs.

O'Flaherty, Michael. 1996. *Human Rights and the UN: Practice before the Treaty Bodies*. London: Sweet and Maxwell.

Okin, Susan Moller. 1992. *Women in Western Political Thought*. Princeton: Princeton University Press.

Olson, Mancur. 1965. *The Logic of Collective Action*. Cambridge, MA: Harvard University Press.

Onuf, Nicholas. 1991. Sovereignty: Outline of a Conceptual History. *Alternatives* 16(4): 425–446.

O'Reagan, Douglas. 2017. Know-How in Postwar Business and Law. *Technology and Culture* 58(1): 121–153.

Osiander, Andreas. 2001. Sovereignty, International Relations, and the Westphalian Myth. *International Organization* 55(2): 251–287.

Owens, Patricia. 2010. Distinctions, Distinctions: "Public" and "Private" Force? In *Mercenaries, Pirates, Bandits and Empires: Private Violence in Historical Context*, Alejandro Colas and Bryan Mabee, eds. London: Hurst, 15–32,

Paolini, Albert, Christian Reus-Smit, and Anthony Jarvis, eds. 1998. *Between Sovereignty and Global Governance: The United Nations and World Politics*. London: Macmillan.

Park, Sub. 2009. Cooperation between Business Associations and the Government in the Korean Cotton Industry, 1950–70. *Business History* 51(6): 835–853.

Parsons, Talcott. 1949. *The Structure of Social Action*. Glencoe: The Free Press.

Pateman, Carole. 1989. *The Disorder of Women: Democracy, Feminism and Political Theory*. Stanford: Stanford University Press.

Patrick, Stewart M. 2018. *The Sovereignty Wars: Reconciling America with the World*. Washington, DC: Brookings Institution Press.

Paul, Joel R. 1988. The Isolation of Private International Law. *Wisconsin International Law Journal* 7(1): 149–178.

Pelton, Robert. 2007. *Licensed to Kill: Hired Guns in the War on Terror*. New York: Three Rivers Press.

Percy, Sarah. 2007. *Mercenaries: The History of a Norm in International Relations*. Oxford: Oxford University Press.

Percy, Sarah. 2009. Private Security Companies and Civil Wars. *Civil Wars* 11(1): 57–74.

Perez-Aleman, Paola. 2003. A Learning-Centered View of Business Associations: Building Business–Government Relations for Development. *Business and Politics* 5(2): 193–213.

Phillips, Andrew. 2007. Constructivism. In *International Relations Theory for the Twenty-First Century: An Introduction*, Martin Griffiths, ed. New York: Routledge, 60–74.

Phillips, Andrew. 2016. Company Sovereigns, Private Violence and Colonialism. In *Routledge Handbook of Private Security Studies*, Anna Leander and Rita Abrahamsen, eds. London: Routledge, 39–48.

Phillips, Andrew and Jason Sharman. 2015. *International Order in Diversity: War, Trade, and Rule in the Indian Ocean*. Cambridge: Cambridge University Press.

Phillips, Andrew and Jason Sharman. 2020. *Outsourcing Empire: How Company-States Made the Modern World*. Princeton: Princeton University Press.

Philpott, Daniel. 1995. Sovereignty: An Introduction and Brief History. *Journal of International Affairs* 48(2): 353–368.

Philpott, Daniel. 1996. On the Cusp of Sovereignty: Lessons from the Sixteenth Century. In *Sovereignty at the Crossroads? Morality and International Politics in the Post-Cold War Era*, Lugo LE, ed. London: Rowman and Littlefield, 37–62.

Philpott, Daniel. 2001. *Revolutions in Sovereignty: How Ideas Shaped Modern International Relations*. Princeton: Princeton University Press.

Porter, Tony. 2005. *Globalization and Finance*. Cambridge: Polity.

Power, Jonathan. 1981. *Amnesty International: The Human Rights Story*. New York: McGraw-Hill.

Power, Jonathan. 2001. *Like Water on Stone: The Story of Amnesty International*. Boston: Northeastern University Press.

Prakash, Aseem and Mary Kay Gugerty. 2010. Introduction. In *Advocacy Organizations and Collective Action*, Aseem Prakash and Mary Kay Gugerty, eds. Cambridge: Cambridge University Press, 1–28.

Prokhovnik, Raia. 1998. Public and Private Citizenship: From Gender Invisibility to Feminist Inclusiveness. *Feminist Review* 60(1): 84–104.

Quelch, John A. and Nathalie Laidler-Kylander. 2006. *The New Global Brands: Managing Non-Government Organizations in the 21st Century*. Mason: Thomson-South Western.

Rahman, Sabeel. 2018. The New Utilities: Private Power, Social Infrastructure, and the Revival of the Public Utility Concept. *Cardozo Law Review* 39(5): 1621–1689.

Raymond, Mark and Laura DeNardis. 2015. Multistakeholderism: Anatomy of an Inchoate Global Institution. *International Theory* 7(3): 572–616.

Raz, Joseph, ed. 1979. *The Authority of Law: Essays on Law and Morality*. Oxford: Clarendon Press.

Raz, Joseph. 1990. *Authority*. Oxford: Basil Blackwell.

Reus-Smit, Christian. 1999. *The Moral Purpose of the State: Culture, Social Identity and Institutional Rationality in International Relations*. Princeton: Princeton University Press.

Reus-Smit, Christian. 2001. Human Rights and the Social Construction of Sovereignty. *Review of International Studies* 27(4): 519–538.

Reus-Smit, Christian. 2002. Imagining Society: Constructivism and the English School. *British Journal of Politics and International Relations* 4(3): 487–509.

Reus-Smit, Christian. 2005. Constructivism. In *Theories of International Relations*, 3rd ed., Scott Burchill, Andrew Linklater, Richard Devetak et al., eds. London: Palgrave Macmillan, 188–212.

Rhee, Jong-Chan. 1994. *The State and Industry in South Korea: The Limits of the Authoritarian State*. New York: Routledge.

Riles, Annelise. 2008. The Anti-Network: Private Global Governance, Legal Knowledge, and the Legitimacy of the State. *American Journal of Comparative Law* 56(3): 605–630.

Ringeisen-Biardeaud, Juliette. 2017. "Let's Take Back Control": Brexit and the Debate on Sovereignty. *Revue Française de Civilisation Britannique* XXII-2. http://doi.org/10.4000/rfcb.1319

Risse-Kappen, Thomas. 1995. *Bringing Transnational Relations Back In: Non State Actors, Domestic Structures and International Institutions*. Cambridge: Cambridge University Press.

Roberts, Simon. 2005. After Government? On Representing Law without the State. *Modern Law Review* 68(1): 1–24.

Robins, Nick. 2006. *The Corporation that Changed the World: How the East India Company Shaped the Modern Multinational*. London: Pluto Press.

Rogers, James Steven. 1995. *The Early History of the Law of Bills and Notes: A Study of the Origins of Anglo-American Commercial Law*. Cambridge: Cambridge University Press.

Romany, Celina. 1993. Women as Aliens: A Feminist Critique of the Public/Private Distinction in International Human Rights Law. *Harvard Human Rights Journal* 6: 87–125.

Ron, James, Howard Ramos, and Kathleen Rodgers. 2005. Transnational Information Politics: NGO Human Rights Reporting, 1986–2000. *International Studies Quarterly* 49(3): 557–587.

Ronit, Karsten and Volker Schneider. 1999. Global Governance through Private Organizations. *Governance: An International Journal of Policy and Administration* 12(3): 243–266.

Rosen, Mark D. 2004. Do Codification and Private International Law Leave Room for a New Law Merchant? *Chicago Journal of International Law* 5(1): 83–90.

Rousseau, Jean Jacques. 1997 [1762]. *The Social Contract*. Cambridge: Cambridge University Press.

Rowan, Herbert. 1984. *The King's State*. New Brunswick: Rutgers University Press.

Rubenstein, Jennifer. 2015. *Between Samaritans and States: The Political Ethics of Humanitarian INGOs*. New York: Oxford University Press.

Ruggie, John G. 1983. Continuity and Transformation in the World Polity: Toward a Neorealist Synthesis. *World Politics* 35(2): 261–285.

Ruggie, John G. 1993. Territoriality and beyond: Problematizing Modernity in International Relations. *International Organization* 47(1): 139–174.

Ruggie, John G. 1998. *Constructing the World Polity: Essays on International Institutionalization*. New York: Routledge.

Ruggie, John G. 2007. Business and Human Rights: Mapping International Standards of Responsibility and Accountability for Corporate Acts. Human Rights Council (A/HRC/4/35). New York: United Nations.

Ruggie, John G. 2013. *Just Business: Multinational Corporations and Human Rights*. New York: W. W. Norton.

Ryall, David. 2001. The Catholic Church as a Transnational Actor. In *Non-state Actors in World Politics*, Daphne Josselin and William Wallace, eds. London: Palgrave Macmillan, 41–58.

Sabel, Charles F. 1994. Learning by Monitoring: The Institutions of Economic Development. In *Rethinking the Development Experience: Essays Provoked by the Work of Albert O. Hirschman*, Lloyd Rodwin and Donald A. Schon, eds. Washington, D.C.: The Brookings Institution, 231–276.

Sachs, Stephen E. 2006. From St. Ives to Cyberspace: The Modern Distortion of the Medieval "Law Merchant." *American University International Law Review* 21(5): 685–812.

Santos, Boaventura de Sousa. 2002. *Toward a New Legal Common Sense: Law, Globalization, and Emancipation*, 2nd ed. London: Butterworths.

Santos, Boaventura de Sousa. 2006. Globalizations. *Theory, Culture & Society* 23(2-3): 393–399.

Sassen, Saskia. 1996. *Losing Control? Sovereignty in an Age of Globalization*. New York: Columbia University Press.

Sassen, Saskia. 1998. *Globalization and Its Discontents*. New York: New Press.

Sassen, Saskia. 2006. *Territory, Authority, Rights: From Medieval to Global Assemblages*. Princeton: Princeton University Press.

Scahill, Jeremy. 2008. *Blackwater: The Rise of the World's Most Powerful Mercenary Army*. New York: Nation Books.

Schäferhoff, Marco, Sabine Campe, and Christopher Kaan. 2007. Transnational Public-Private Partnerships in International Relations: Making Sense of Concepts, Research Frameworks and Results. SFB-Governance Working Paper No. 6, DFG Research Center (SFB) 700.

Schmitter, Philippe and Wolfgang Streeck. 1981. The Organization of Business Interests: Studying the Associative Action of Business in Advanced Industrial Societies. Koln: Max-Planck-Institut fur Gesselschaftsforschung, Discussion Paper 99/1.

Schneider, Ben Ross. 1998. Elusive Synergy: Business-Government Relations and Development. *Comparative Politics* 31(1): 101–122.

Schneider, Ben Ross. 2002. Why is Mexican Business so Organized? *Latin American Research Review* 37(1): 77–118.

Scott, James C. 1998. *Seeing Like a State: How Certain Schemes to Improve the Human Condition Have Failed*. New Haven: Yale University Press.

Seitz, Karolin and Jens Martens. 2017. Philanthrolateralism: Private Funding and Corporate Influence in the United Nations. *Global Policy* 8(5): 46–50.

Sending, Ole Jacob, Vincent Pouliot, and Iver B. Neumann, eds. 2015. *Diplomacy and the Making of World Politics*. Cambridge: Cambridge University Press.

Sewell, William H. 1992. A Theory of Structure: Duality, Agency, and Transformation. *American Journal of Sociology* 98(1): 1–29.

Sgard, Jerome. 2019. The International Chamber of Commerce, Multilateralism, and the Invention of International Commercial Arbitration. Draft Paper presented at the 1919 Paris Peace Conference, June 5–8.

Shaffer, Gregory C. 2009. How Business Shapes Law: A Socio-Legal Framework. *Connecticut Law Review* 42(1): 147–183.

Shaffer, Gregory C., ed. 2013. *Transnational Legal Ordering and State Change*. Cambridge: Cambridge University Press.

Sharman, J. C. 2017. Sovereignty at the Extremes: Micro-States in World Politics. *Political Studies* 65(3): 559–575.

Sharman, J. C. 2019. Power and Profit at Sea: The Rise of the West in the Making of the International System. *International Security* 43(4): 163–196.

Shilliam, Robbie. 2015. *The Black Pacific: Anti-Colonial Struggles and Oceanic Connections*. London: Bloomsbury.

Shinko, Rosemary E. 2017. Sovereignty as a Problematic Conceptual Core. *Oxford Research Encyclopedia of International Studies*. http://doi.org/10.1093/acrefore/9780190846626.013.300

Shinoda, Hideaki. 2000. *Re-Examining Sovereignty from Classical Theory to the Global Age*. London: Macmillan.

Shklar, Judith. 1984. The Liberalism of Fear. In *Liberalism and the Moral Life*, Nancy Rosenblum, ed. Cambridge, MA: Harvard University Press, 21–38.

Simmons, Beth A. 2009. *Mobilizing for Human Rights: International Law in Domestic Politics*. New York: Cambridge University Press.

Sinclair, Timothy. 2005. *The New Masters of Capital: American Bond Rating Agencies and the Global Economy*. Ithaca: Cornell University Press.

Singer, Peter W. 2001. Corporate Warriors: The Rise of the Privatized Military Industry and Its Ramifications for International Security. *International Security* 26(3): 186–220.

Singer, Peter W. 2003. *Corporate Warriors: The Rise of the Privatized Military Industry*. Ithaca: Cornell University Press.

Singer, Peter W. 2005. Outsourcing War. *Foreign Affairs* 82(2): 119–132.

Singer, Peter W. 2007. Can't Win with 'Em, Can't Go to War without 'Em: Private Military Contractors and Counterinsurgency. Brookings Policy Paper No. 4.

Sisley, Sven and Mikkel Flyverbom. 2008. Transnational Private Governance of the Internet: The Roles of Business. In *Transnational Private Governance and Its Limits*, Jean-Christophe Graz and Andreas Nölke, eds. London: Routledge, 129–141.

Skinner, Quentin. 2010. The Sovereign State: A Genealogy. In *Sovereignty in Fragments: The Past, Present, and Future of a Contested Concept*, Hent Kalmo and Quentin Sikkiner, eds. Cambridge: Cambridge University Press, 26–46.

Slaughter, Anne Marie. 2004. Disaggregated Sovereignty: Towards the Public Accountability of Global Government Networks. *Government and Opposition* 39(2): 159–190.

Slaughter, Anne Marie. 2005. *A New World Order*. Princeton: Princeton University Press.

Slim, Hugo. 2002. By What Authority? The Legitimacy and Accountability of Non-Governmental Organizations. *Journal of Humanitarian Aid* www.jha.ac/a082/

Smyth, Albert Henry. 1905. *The Writings of Benjamin Franklin*. New York: Macmillan.

Snyder, David V. 2003. Private Lawmaking. *Ohio State Law Journal* 64(2): 371–449.

Spanogle, John. 1991. The Arrival of Private Law. *George Washington Journal of International Law and Economics* 25(2): 477–522.

Spath, Konrad. 2005. Inside Global Governance: New Borders of a Concept. In *Criticizing Global Governance*, Markus Lederer and Philipp S. Muller, eds. New York: Palgrave Macmillan, 21–44.

Spruyt, Hendrik. 1994. *The Sovereign State and its Competitors: An Analysis of Systems Change*. Princeton: Princeton University Press.

Spruyt, Hendrik. 2002. The Origins, Development, and Possible Decline of the Modern State. *Annual Review of Political Science* 5(1): 127–149.

Srivastava, Swati. 2013. Assembling International Organizations. *Journal of International Organization Studies* 4(3): 73–85.

Srivastava, Swati. 2020a. Varieties of Social Construction. *International Studies Review* 22(3): 325–346.

Srivastava, Swati. 2020b. Corporate Responsibility. *Oxford Research Encyclopedia of International Studies*. http://doi.org/10.1093/acrefore/9780190846626.013.582

Srivastava, Swati. 2021. Algorithmic Governance and the International Politics of Big Tech. *Perspectives on Politics*. http://doi.org/10.1017/S1537592721003145

Srivastava, Swati. 2022a. Navigating NGO-Government Relations in Human Rights: New Archival Evidence from Amnesty International, 1961–1986. *International Studies Quarterly* 66(1). http://doi.org/10.1093/isq/sqab009

Srivastava, Swati. 2022b. Corporate Sovereign Awakening and the Making of Modern State Sovereignty: New Archival Evidence from the English East India Company. *International Organization*. http://doi.org/10.1017/S002081832200008X

Srivastava, Swati and Lauren Muscott. 2021. How to Hold Unjust Structures Responsible in International Relations. *International Studies Quarterly* 65(3): 573–581.

Stanger, Allison. 2009. *One Nation under Contract: The Outsourcing of American Power and the Future of Foreign Policy*. New Haven: Yale University Press.

Steinhardt, Ralph. 1991. The Privatization of Public International Law. *George Washington Journal of International Law and Economics* 25(2): 523–553.

Stern, Philip. 2008. "A Politie of Civil and Military Power": Political Thought and the Late Seventeenth-Century Foundations of the East India Company-State. *Journal of British Studies* 47(2): 253–283.

Stern, Philip. 2011. *The Company-State: Corporate Sovereignty and the Early Modern Foundations of the British Empire in India*. Oxford: Oxford University Press.

Strange, Susan. 1995. The Defective State. *Daedalus* 124(2): 55–74.

Strange, Susan. 1996. *The Retreat of the State: The Diffusion of Power in the World Economy*. Cambridge: Cambridge University Press.

Strayer, Joseph. 1970. *On the Medieval Origins of the Modern State*. Princeton: Princeton University Press.

Stroup, Sarah. 2010. *Borders Among Activists: International NGOs in the United States, Britain, and France*. Ithaca: Cornell University Press.

Stroup, Sarah and Wendy Wong. 2016. The Agency and Authority of International NGOs. *Perspectives on Politics* 14(1): 138–144.

Stroup, Sarah and Wendy Wong. 2017. *The Authority Trap: Strategic Choices of International NGOs*. Ithaca: Cornell University Press.

Subotic, Jelena. 2009. *Hijacked Justice: Dealing with the Past in the Balkans*. Ithaca: Cornell University Press.

Sullivan, Donna. 1995. The Public/Private Distinction in International Human Rights Law. In *Women's Rights Human Rights: International Feminist Perspectives*, Julie Peters and Andrea Wolper, eds. New York: Routledge, 126–134.

Sutherland, L. Stuart. 1934. The Law Merchant in England in the Seventeenth and Eighteenth Centuries. *Transactions of the Royal Historical Society* 17 : 149–176.

Syrett, Harold and Jacob Cooke, eds. 1961. *The Papers of Alexander Hamilton*, Vol. 1., 1768–1778. New York: Columbia University Press.

Tallberg, Jonas, Thomas Sommerer, Theresa Swuatrito, and Christer Jönsson. 2013. *The Opening Up of International Organizations: Transnational Access in Global Governance.* Cambridge: Cambridge University Press.

Tallberg, Jonas, Thomas Sommerer, Theresa Swuatrito, and Christer Jönsson. 2014. Explaining the Transnational Design of International Organizations. *International Organization* 68(3): 741–774.

Tamanaha, Brian. 2001. *A General Jurisprudence of Law and Society.* Oxford: Oxford University Press.

Tamanaha, Brian. 2008. Understanding Legal Pluralism: Past to Present, Local to Global. *Sydney Law Review* 30(3): 375–411.

Taylor, Charles. 2007. *A Secular Age.* Cambridge, MA: Harvard University Press.

Teschke, Benno. 2003. *The Myth of 1648: Class, Geopolitics, and the Making of Modern International Relations.* New York: Verso.

Teubner, Gunther. 1997. "Global Bukowina": Legal Pluralism in the World Society. In *Global Law without a State*, Gunther Teubner, ed. Aldershot: Dartmouth, 3–30.

Teubner, Gunther. 2002. Hybrid Laws: Constitutionalizing Private Governance Networks. In *Legality and Community*, Robert Kagan and Kenneth Winston, eds. Berkeley: Berkeley Public Policy Press, 311–331.

Thompson, Andrew. 2008. Beyond Expression: Amnesty International's Decision to Oppose Capital Punishment, 1973. *Journal of Human Rights* 7(4): 327–340.

Thomson, Janice E. 1989. Sovereignty in Historical Perspective: The Evolution of State Control over Extraterritorial Violence. In *The Elusive State*, James Caporaso, ed. Newbury Park: Sage, 227–254.

Thomson, Janice E. 1994. *Mercenaries, Pirates, and Sovereigns: State-Building and Extraterritorial Violence in Early Modern Europe.* Princeton: Princeton University Press.

Thomson, Janice E. 1995. State Sovereignty in International Relations: Bridging the Gap Between Theory and Empirical Research. *International Studies Quarterly* 39(2): 213–233.

Tilly, Charles. 1985. War Making and State Making as Organized Crime. In *Bringing the State Back In*, Peter Evans, Dietrich Rueschemeyer, and Theda Skocpol, eds. Cambridge: Cambridge University Press, 169–191.

Tilly, Charles. 1990. *Coercion, Capital, and European States, AD 990–1992.* Cambridge: Blackwell.

Toye, Richard. 2003. Developing Multilateralism: The Havana Charter and the Fight for International Trade Organization, 1947–1948. *The International History Review* 25(2): 282–305.

Trakman, Leon E. 1983. *The Law Merchant: The Evolution of Commercial Law.* Littleton: Fred B. Rotham.

Trakman, Leon E. 2003. From the Medieval Law Merchant to E-Merchant Law. *University of Toronto Law Journal* 53(3): 265–304.

Trubek, David M., Yves Dezaley, Ruth Buchanan, and John R. Davis. 1994. Global Restructuring and the Law: Studies in the Internationalisation of the Legal Fields and Transnational Arenas. *Case Western Law Review* 44(2): 407–498.

Trubowitz, Peter. 2011. *Politics and Strategy: Partisan Ambition and American Statecraft.* Princeton: Princeton University Press.

Tully, Stephen. 2007. *Corporations and International Lawmaking.* Leiden: Martinus Nijhoff.

Van Harten, Gus. 2007. The Public-Private Distinction in the International Arbitration of Individual Claims against the State. *The International and Comparative Law Quarterly* 56 (2): 371–394.

Varese, Federico. 2018. *Mafia Life: Love, Death and Money at the Heart of Organised Crime.* London: Profile Books.

Vaughn, James. 2019. *The Politics of Empire at the Accession of George III: The East India Company and the Crisis and Transformation of Britain's Imperial State.* New Haven: Yale University Press.

Verkuil, Paul. 2007. *Outsourcing Sovereignty: Why Privatization of Government Functions Threatens Democracy and What We Can Do about It.* New York: Cambridge University Press.

Vernon, Raymond. 1971. *Sovereignty at Bay.* New York: Basic Books.

Vetterlein, Antje and Hannes Hansen-Magnusson. 2020. The Rise of Responsibility in World Politics. In *The Rise of Responsibility in World Politics*, Hannes Hansen-Magnusson and Antje Vetterlein, eds. Cambridge: Cambridge University Press, 1–31.

Vincent, R. J. 1986. *Human Rights and International Relations.* Cambridge: Cambridge University Press.

Vincke, Francois. 2014. Emerging Control of and Sanctions against Corruption: The International Chamber of Commerce. In *Preventing Corporate Corruption*, Stefano Manacorda, Francesco Centonze, and Gabrio Forti, eds. London: Springer International, 295–308.

Vogel, David. 2009. The Private Regulation of Global Corporate Conduct. In *The Politics of Global Regulation*, Walter Mattli and Ngaire Woods, eds. Princeton: Princeton University Press, 151–188.

Volckart, Oliver and Antje Mangels. 1999. Are the Roots of the Modern Lex Mercatoria Really Medieval? *Southern Economic Journal* 65(3): 427–450.

von Benda-Beckmann, Franz. 2002. Who's Afraid of Legal Pluralism? *Journal of Legal Pluralism* 34(47): 37–82.

Walker, Kristen. 1994. An Exploration of Article 2 (7) of the United Nations Charter as an Embodiment of the Public/Private Distinction in International Law. *International Law and Politics* 26(2): 173–199.

Walker, Neil, ed. 2006. *Relocating Sovereignty.* Aldershot: Ashgate.

Walker, Robert B. J. 1990. Sovereignty, Security, and the Challenge of World Politics. *Alternatives* 15(1): 3–28.

Walker, Robert B. J. 2004. Conclusion: Sovereignties, Exceptions, Worlds. In *Sovereign Lives: Power in Global Politics*, Jenny Edkins, Veronique Pin-Fat, and Michael J. Shapiro, eds. London: Routledge, 239–249.

Walker, Robert B. J. 2010. *After the Globe, before the World.* London: Routledge.

Walker, Robert B. J. and Saul Mendlovitz, eds. 1990. *Contending Sovereignties: Rethinking Political Community.* Boulder: Lynne Rienner.

Waltz, Kenneth. 1959. *Man, the State, and War: A Theoretical Analysis.* New York: Columbia University Press.

Waltz, Kenneth N. 1979. *Theory of International Politics.* New York: McGraw-Hill.

Weber, Cynthia. 1995. *Simulating Sovereignty: Intervention, the State and Symbolic Exchange.* Cambridge: Cambridge University Press.

Weber, Eugen. 1976. *Peasants into Frenchmen: The Modernization of Rural France, 1870–1914*. Palo Alto: Stanford University Press.

Weber, Max. 1930. *The Protestant Ethic and the Spirit of Capitalism*. London: Routledge.

Weber, Max. 1946. Science as a Vocation. In *From Max Weber*, H. H. Gerth and C. W. Mills, trans. and eds. New York: Oxford University Press, 129–156.

Weber, Max. 1947. *The Theory of Social and Economic Organization*. New York: Oxford University Press.

Weber, Max. 1949. *The Methodology of the Social Sciences*, Edward Shils and Henry Finch, trans. Glencoe: Free Press.

Weber, Max. 1978. *Economy and Society: An Outline of Interpretive Sociology*, 2 Volumes, Guenther Roth and Claus Wittich, eds. Berkeley: University of California Press.

Weber, Max. 2004. Politics as a Vocation. In *The Vocation Lectures: Science as a Vocation; Politics as a Vocation*, David Owen and Tracy Strong, eds. Indianapolis: Hackett, 32-94.

Weintraub, Jeff A. 1997. The Theory and Politics of the Public/Private Distinction. In *Public and Private in Thought and Practice: Perspectives on a Grand Dichotomy*, Jeff Weintraub and Krishan Kumar, eds. Chicago: University of Chicago Press, 1–42.

Weiss, Paul. 1954. The International Protection of Refugees. *The American Journal of International Law* 48(2): 193–221.

Wendt, Alexander. 1992. Anarchy Is What States Make of It: The Social Construction of Power Politics. *International Organization* 46(2): 391–425.

Wendt, Alexander. 1999. *Social Theory of International Politics*. Cambridge: Cambridge University Press.

Wendt, Alexander and Daniel Friedheim. 1996. Hierarchy under Anarchy: Informal Empire and the East German State. In *State Sovereignty as Social Construct*, Thomas Biersteker and Cynthia Weber, eds. Cambridge: Cambridge University Press, 81–120.

Wendt, Alexander and Raymond Duvall. 2008. Sovereignty and the UFO. *Political Theory* 36 (4): 607–633.

Werner, Wouter G. and Jaap H. de Wilde. 2001. The Endurance of Sovereignty. *European Journal of International Relations* 7(3): 283–313.

Wilcox, Clair. 1949. *A Charter for World Trade*. New York: MacMillan.

Williams, Bernard. 2005. *In the Beginning Was the Deed: Realism and Moralism in Political Argument*. Princeton: Princeton University Press.

Willis, Hugh. 1929. The Doctrine of Sovereignty under the United States Constitution. Articles by Maurer Faculty, Paper 1256.

Willoughby, W. W. 1918. The Juristic Conception of the State. *American Political Science Review* 12(2): 192–208.

Wilson, Richard. 1997. *Human Rights, Culture, and Context: Anthropological Perspectives*. London: Pluto Press.

Winner, David. 1991. *Peter Benenson*. Milwaukee: Gareth Stevens.

Winston, Morton. 2001. Assessing the Effectiveness of International Human Rights NGOs: Amnesty International. In *NGOs and Human Rights: Promise and Performance*, Claudia Welch, ed. Philadelphia: University of Pennsylvania Press, 25–54.

Wittgenstein, Ludwig. 2009 [1953]. *Philosophical Investigations*, 4th ed., G.E.M. Anscombe, P. M. S. Hacker and Joachim Schulte, trans. Oxford: Wiley-Blackwell.

Woll, Cornelia. 2013. Global Companies as Agenda Setters in the World Trade Organization. In *The Handbook of Global Companies*, John Mikler, ed. Hoboken: Wiley, 257–271.

Wong, Wendy. 2012. *Internal Affairs: How the Structure of NGOs Transforms Human Rights*. Ithaca: Cornell University Press.

Wong, Wendy, Ron Levi, and Julia Deutsch. 2017. The Ford Foundation. In *Professional Networks in Transnational Governance*, Leonard Seabrooke and Lasse Folke Henriksen, eds. Cambridge: Cambridge University Press, 82–100.

Wood, Gordon. 1998 [1969]. *The Creation of the American Republic, 1776–1787*. Durham: University of North Carolina Press.

Worster, William Thomas. 2012. The Evolving Definition of the Refugee in Contemporary International Law. *Berkeley Journal of International Law* 30(1): 94–160.

Yanow, Dvora and Peregrine Schwartz-Shea, eds. 2006. *Interpretation and Method: Empirical Research Methods and the Interpretive Turn*. New York: M. E. Sharpe.

Young, Iris Marion. 2004. Responsibility and Global Labor Justice. *Journal of Political Philosophy* 12(4): 365–388.

Young, Iris Marion. 2010. *Responsibility for Justice*. New York: Oxford University Press.

Young, McGee. 2010. The Price of Advocacy: Mobilization and Maintenance in Advocacy Organizations. In *Advocacy Organizations and Collective Action*, Aseem Prakash and Mary Kay Gugerty, eds. Cambridge: Cambridge University Press, 31–57.

Zamparelli, Stephen J. 1999. Contractors on the Battlefield: What Have We Signed Up For? *Air Force Journal of Logistics* 23(3): 11–19.

Zuboff, Shoshana. 2019. *The Age of Surveillance Capitalism: The Fight for a Human Future at the New Frontier of Power*. New York: Public Affairs.

Index

CAMBRIDGE STUDIES IN INTERNATIONAL RELATIONS

For EU product safety concerns, contact us at Calle de José Abascal, 56–1°,
28003 Madrid, Spain or eugpsr@cambridge.org.

www.ingramcontent.com/pod-product-compliance
Ingram Content Group UK Ltd.
Pitfield, Milton Keynes, MK11 3LW, UK
UKHW020357140625
459647UK00020B/2531